Franz Kafka: A Writer's Life

Studies in Austrian Literature, Culture, and Thought

Joachim Unseld

Franz Kafka

A Writer's Life

Translated by

Paul F. Dvorak

ARIADNE PRESS

Translated from the German *Franz Kafka. Ein Schriftstellerleben.*
*Die Geschichte seiner Veröffentlichungen. Mit einer Bibliographie
sämtlicher Drucke und Ausgaben der Dichtungen Kafkas 1908-1924.*
©1982 Carl Hanser Verlag, München, Wien

Library of Congress Cataloging-in-Publication Data

Unseld, Joachim.
    [Franz Kafka, ein Schriftstellerleben. English]
    Franz Kafka, a writer's life / Joachim Unseld ; translated by
Paul F. Dvorak.
          p.   cm. -- (Studies in Austrian literature, culture, and
thought)
          Includes bibliographical references and index.
          ISBN 0-929497-78-3.--ISBN 1-57241-007-8 (pbk).
          1. Kafka, Franz, 1883-1924. 2. Kafka, Franz, 1883-1924--
Publishers. 3. Authors, Austrian--20th century--Biography.
I. Title. II. Series
PT2621.A26Z939713   1994
833'.912--dc20
[B]   94-635
                                 CIP

Cover design:
Art Director and Designer: George McGinnis
Photo ©Archiv Klaus Wagenbach, Berlin

Copyright ©1994
by Ariadne Press
270 Goins Court
Riverside, CA 92507

To my parents

Franz Kafka, Berlin 1923/24
Photo courtesy Dr. Klaus Wagenbach

Contents

Translator's Note

I have made every attempt to balance the need for providing a readable text aimed at an English-speaking audience with that of preserving the scholarly references and materials of the original German version. The extensive endnotes have been included in their entirety and do not interfere with the body of the text. German titles and phrases have been retained for accuracy but have been supplemented for the most part with translations to assist the English reader. For actual quotations, the published English translations of Kafka's works have been cited in the text and notes whenever available, even though some wording may occasionally appear a little awkward. Several parenthetical expressions or alternate translations appear in those instances where an important discrepancy exists between the German wording and the published English version. For other sources I have supplied my own translation and cited the original German edition.

Several minor corrections, amendments, and additions have been made to the original German text for the sake of clarity and accuracy, but none of these alter or misrepresent the author's thesis.

I would like to thank my colleagues at Virginia Commonwealth University who have encouraged me during this project and also acknowledge the University's faculty grant-in-aid program, which supported me during the final stages of my work.   P.F.D.

Preface

> The case of the writer Kafka is unusual in that his minor works were published during his lifetime and the major ones, in so far as the author did not destroy them before his death, posthumously.   Franz Blei

The few books that Kafka himself released for publication aroused little public interest and met with little success. The extraordinary significance of his work was only recognized after his death and after the publication of the posthumous edition. As the publisher Kurt Wolff commented, "Every good book must be published at the appropriate time, with the appropriate publisher, and with the appropriate enthusiasm, otherwise it is hopelessly lost."[1] Did Franz Kafka's books appear at the wrong time? Or did the writer fail to meet that appropriate publisher or encounter that appropriate enthusiasm during his lifetime? According to the poet Paul Valéry, achieving literary fame requires the "interaction of two factors that can always be viewed independently of one another: the first is necessarily the creation of the work itself, the second is the determination of the specific value of the work by those who treasure it, have helped it gain acceptance, and have insured its distribution, preservation, and lasting future."[2]

The current universal impact of Franz Kafka is based precisely on those works that were not fully edited during his lifetime and that he himself had directed to be destroyed in his will (though of course not without a disavowal). As is well-known, the seven books he published between 1912 and 1924 represent only a portion of his entire opus. Less known, however, is the fact that Kafka, despite all his reservations about the publication of his works, made each of his completed texts available to the public and that most of these prose works appeared several times, some as many as four. Thus the most central question to raise is why other works were not completed, and subsequently published, and especially why the three major novels, *America*, *The Trial*, and *The Castle*, remained fragments, even though Kafka quite clearly undertook them with the intention of eventual publication. The answer to this question has great significance for Kafka's work as well as for his life. For upon the foundation that the publication of a major work would have provided, living a writer's life would no longer have remained illusory for him. Kafka himself was well aware of this fact. His inability to publish a major work developed into a complex and confirmed his perception of the impossibility of being or of becoming a writer.

The fourfold interrelationship of writing, publication and reception, professional life, and private life produced a never-ending vicious circle for Kafka. This matrix forms the subject matter of this work. Although Kafka derived creative energy from the painful confrontation between the life he gladly imagined for himself as a writer and the unpleasant reality of life as an insurance official, he became increasingly uncertain of that which gave meaning to his life, namely, literature. Whenever his writing failed commercially in the public realm, he was forced to rely even more on the career that supported him financially but that simultaneously made writing more impossible. To be able to write something of genuine value would have required giving up this everyday job. But conversely he would only be prepared to take such a step after he had been successful at producing something tangible and concrete. Thus writing, life, and publication became entwined in an irresolvable contradiction.

For Kafka literature was "something holy, absolute, incorruptible, something majestic and pure,"[3] an ideal. He always measured writing against the standard of prayer ("[w]riting as a form of prayer" [DF312]).[4] This was his conception of what his parents from early on had reproachfully labeled a harmful "pastime" (F46). Kafka viewed literature first of all as the most suitable activity, and finally as having an unconditional claim on him; it represented the only possible, authentic form of life for him. Yet the literary scene of his day proved little more than a negative, distorted image of this ideal. Not only did Kafka view contemporary modern literature skeptically, but he was also alienated by the active industriousness of his literary colleagues in attempting to ensure their success at any cost. Nevertheless, he relied on the literary judgment of the well-known publishing houses, as they, increasingly supported by the critics, endorsed the literary trends of the times. Unable to gain a foothold in the literary world on his own, Kafka sought to encourage interest and support from that side. He waited respectfully for a publisher who would mediate between Franz Kafka the writer and the public.

Within a stormy literary epoch subject to rapid change brought about by external events, Franz Kafka's life as a writer unfolded uneventfully. He waited in the wings of a lively stage and consciously rejected the enervating, normal path of making a name for himself with the public as a young writer. He lacked the "ability to assume responsibility" (L380) to follow the customary mechanisms, which were the only ones the literary world could offer him for fulfilling the pure literary existence he so desired. And when he occasionally availed himself of such offers and even summoned up the courage to embark energetically on his own campaign for the publication of a work, he encountered neither the understanding he anticipated nor the recognition he had hoped for in the environment around him.

But why did Kafka not develop a positive relationship with the literary industry of the day? Why did he fail to permanently establish a genuine existence as a writer? And why did his major works remain incomplete and therefore unpublished during his lifetime? The present study attempts to answer some of these questions by chronologically describing the clearly delineated developments of the pragmatic considerations that determined the publication of Kafka's work. A systematic investigation of the totality of conditions relating to the author's publications, i.e., of his relationships to publishers as well as all of his other relationships relevant to the history of his publications during his lifetime, provides the background for this manageable undertaking. The key author-publisher relationship demonstrates that there were other impediments as well to Kafka's possible success during his life. It was not simply a matter of writing at the wrong time. (This includes especially the completion of the novel fragments.) The fragmentary nature of Kafka's work is seen in a new light as also resulting from the negative interaction between writer and literary industry, between the author and his publisher. Therefore, intrinsic extensions of the limited pragmatic question are identified both methodologically and factually; they are also the points where the history of publishing overlaps with literary history[5] and where the sociology of literary agencies, instead of remaining outside the work, project themselves into the understanding of its inner realization and reality.

An empirical-historical pragmatic study of Franz Kafka's publications leads to a revision of the dominant view still held today about him. The myth of a difficult author who would rather see his books burned than made public is shattered by the author's decisive and frequently demonstrated will to have his works published. The myth about Kafka as an avant-garde expressionist is exposed, and the problematic nature of the multifaceted role that Max Brod played as his friend's literary mentor revealed. Those individuals whose influence promoted Kafka and his works are drawn into the foreground: Franz Blei, Paul Wiegler, Otto Pick, Franz Werfel, Robert Musil, Martin Buber, Rudolf Kayser, Kurt Tucholsky, and Ludwig Hardt. The commonly held view that Kafka was bound to a single publisher, Kurt Wolff, in a lifelong, harmonious, and mutually productive relationship bears special critique. Kafka's relationships with other publishers, including those with Ernst Rowohlt and Georg Heinrich Meyer as well as with the Berlin publishing house *Die Schmiede*, have consistently been relegated to the background in comparison to that with Kurt Wolff.

Since this study investigates the conditions and practical considerations related to Kafka's writing, it is not the finished product that stands in the foreground but rather the evolutionary process, not the publication date of a particular work but Kafka's desire to publish. This history of Kafka's publications is therefore not organized according to the actual publication dates (they appear in this format only once in the appended bibliography of primary works published during his lifetime), but first and foremost according to how the author planned his publication projects, whether they actually materialized or not.

Such an arrangement corresponds strikingly to clearly demarcated biographical and creative phases in the writer's life. The primary focus of Kafka's biographers up to the present day has been directed almost exclusively to the years 1883-1912; Kafka's childhood and youth have been treated exhaustively in the literature. By contrast, studies about the author's life after 1912, the year in which his first book, *Meditation*, appeared, are clearly underrepresented, even on a purely quantitative basis.[6]

Since analyses of Kafka's attempts at marriage dominate in these
biographies, his actual life as a writer and his desperate struggle
to establish his ideal (literary) existence are scarcely noted, at
least not in the proportion necessary to understand the totality of
his life. Therefore, a necessary and indispensable precondition
for any history of Kafka's works must include extensive biographical material from the years 1912-1924. In this context the
present study of the life of Franz Kafka the writer is a contribution to his biography.

I

Purposeful Hesitation: Franz Kafka's Attitude toward the Publication of his Writings before 1912

> The moment I were set free from the office I would yield at once to my desire to write an autobiography. I would have to have some such decisive change before me as a preliminary goal when I began to write in order to be able to give direction to the mass of events. But I cannot imagine any other inspiriting change than this, which is itself so terribly improbable. Then, however, the writing of the autobiography would be a great joy because it would move along as easily as the writing down of dreams, yet it would have an entirely different effect, a great one, which would always influence me and would be accessible as well to the understanding and feeling of everyone else. (Kafka's diary entry, December 16, 1911)

*T*he history of Franz Kafka's publications begins with the appearance of minor works in journals during the years 1908-1912. The writer's relationship to his literary work and to its publication and his attitude toward literary publication and its various agencies all bore a characteristic mark right from the start. The predispositions of his personality at this time and the decisions in the intellectual and more mundane spheres of his life remained prescriptive for Kafka's future development. This is true of friendships and personal relationships as well as of literary contacts that resulted from his initial publications.

The climate for the publication of minor literary works at this time was generally quite favorable; studies of the literary periodicals of this era point to the strong reading interest of an intellectual class and to the large offering of literary periodicals as well as of literary holiday supplements in daily newspapers.[1] From the turn of the century until the outbreak of World War I, new literary periodicals were announced almost weekly. Many German critics bemoaned not only the impenetrable flood of books but especially the unfathomable state of the contemporary periodical market.[2] Nevertheless, it was this flood of periodicals that supported and promoted writers and facilitated their access to the public.

1. The Unsuccessful Start: Participation in a Literary Competition (1906)

It is well known that the fifteen-year-old Rainer Maria Rilke published his first work after participating in a literary competition that helped shape his literary future.[3] It is much less known that Franz Kafka also attempted to achieve his first publication through a literary competition. As a twenty-three-year-old student he participated in a competition sponsored by the Viennese newspaper *Die Zeit*, which in all likelihood took place in 1906. Presumably the competition was organized for a Christmas issue; this manner of introducing contemporary literature was quite popular at the time. The story Kafka submitted, *Heaven in Narrow Streets*, was apparently not received favorably by the Viennese judges: "The entry did not gain a mention in the competition, and has disappeared" (FK60).

It was from a comment Kafka made about his unsuccessful

participation in the competition that Max Brod first learned of his friend's literary ambitions. Three decades later Brod noted how taken aback he had been: "I went about with Kafka for several years without knowing that he wrote" (FK60). Kafka mentioned his writing (already begun in 1897-1898) in his letters to his friend for the first time in the spring of 1907; Brod probably found out about it initially between the winter of 1906 and the spring of 1907.

The extensive literary activity of Brod, whom he had known since the winter of 1902, was of course no secret to Kafka. Many of Brod's works had already appeared in newspapers and magazines, and his first book was published in 1906. Moreover, from 1904 on Brod regularly brought Kafka along to literary meetings at the home of the young writer, Oskar Baum, where a small circle of writers read weekly from their works in progress.[4] In light of this fact, it is even more astonishing that Kafka kept his own literary activity a secret.

2. The "Discovery" of the Writer Franz Kafka by Max Brod (1907)

In his extensive memoirs about Franz Kafka, Max Brod emphasizes again and again the close and intimate friendship that joined the two together for more than two decades up until Kafka's death in 1924. As late as 1966 Brod wrote: "I met Kafka (1902) in the 'German Student Reading and Lecture Hall' when he was nineteen and I was eighteen years old. Our friendship remained at a peak without interruption until his death in 1924."[5] Obviously Max Brod stands to be corrected on this point. Not only the particular nature, but also the sobriety of this friendship must be emphasized, something that led Kafka to say as late as 1913 that between him and Brod there had never been "a long coherent conversation involving my entire being, as should inevitably follow when two people with a great fund of independent and lively ideas and experiences are thrown together" (F271). Brod's chronology is also inexact; the friendship that became so central for Kafka first evolved from their interactions during the years 1907-1908. In his memoirs Brod projects later developments upon an earlier time. Although it is true that their friendship between 1902 and 1907 included many common activities, each of them had his own, narrower circle of friends. The first letter Max Brod received from Franz Kafka, the "Wolf's Gorge Letter," reveals a dual problem: the difficulty of a reserved, almost shy Kafka fitting into Brod's circle of friends and his embarrassment at bringing Brod into his own group.[6] Only when both began their bureaucratic careers did their friendship deepen. Toward the end of his studies, Kafka's adolescent friendships with Oskar Pollak and Ewald Příbram, both of whom left Prague, dissolved. Brod turned entirely toward his friendship with Kafka, when his closest friend of many years, Max Bäuml, died suddenly in April 1908.[7]

Details of the relationship between Kafka and Brod before 1907-1908 indicate that Brod at first misconstrued Kafka's special human qualities as well as his reserve. In his story *Insel Carina* ("Carina Island," 1908), Brod depicted Kafka as a pure "aesthete," a "miscategorization" he was later to correct (SL184). During this period Kafka withheld certain things from Brod, and it was impossible for him to talk to his friend at that time about matters of deepest importance, one of which was his writing.

However, in the letter Kafka sent to his adolescent friend Oskar Pollak, one gains a sense of these important matters. Pollak knew about Kafka's writing; Kafka engaged him early on in his reflections about the problematic divide between writing and life. In 1903 Kafka even sent Pollak a "bundle," which, as Kafka writes, "will contain everything I have written up to now, original or derivative. Nothing will be missing except the childhood things . . . then the stuff I no longer have, then the stuff I regard as worthless in this context . . ." (L8). Similarly a letter of 1903 from Kafka to Pollak reads: "By the way, no writing's been done for some time. It's this way with me: God doesn't want me to write, but I—I must. So there's an everlasting up and down; after all, God is the stronger, and there's more anguish in it than you can imagine." At the end of the letter Kafka added "some verses" with the directive to his friend: "Read them when you are in the proper mood" (L10). A similar openness to communicate with Brod developed only after 1907-1908, when he and Kafka began to see each other daily. Kafka admired the vitality and occasional stormy impulsiveness of Brod, who had suffered from severe curvature of the spine from the age of four and had overcome this handicap through exceptional will-power. Brod's presence was for Kafka, as became clear from a diary entry, at all times a "consolation" (DI123). He felt magnetized by the productivity (something that was becoming almost proverbial in Prague) that Brod displayed in his double life as an employee of the Post Office Divisional Administration and as a writer.

For his part, Brod admired the calm that emanated from Kafka's person. He praised Kafka's unconditional nature, his uncompromising, honest rigor with regard to himself and others, his striving for perfection. The openness with which Brod sketched his best friend's character in a review of Kafka's *Meditation* in 1913 is characteristic of the close relationship they shared later on:

Everyone who knows Franz Kafka personally, the reserved

person working down to the last minute detail, will confirm
what I write here: His main characteristic is that he would
rather accomplish nothing at all than something which is
incomplete or faulty. This extremely refreshing, unintentional
rigorousness influences all of his activities in life. Whenever
he cannot achieve perfection or the most ecstatic happiness, he
withdraws entirely.[8]

If Kafka represented for Brod the "moral advisor" to whom
he poured out his troubles and who was always appropriately on
hand to deal with vital questions, then Kafka, forced to the
periphery, perceived in his friend the mediator of the active
world and of the reality that he himself could only partially
control. Walter Benjamin described this symbiosis as early as
1929 with great empathy: "So sober was . . . his friendship with
Max Brod. Nothing less than a fraternal order or a secret
society, but an intimate and trusting friendship among writers
based entirely upon their individual work and its public recognition."[9]

Kafka's personal circle of friends became one of the most
important factors influencing the realization of his first minor
publications. The group of young writers referred to in literary
history as the "inner Prague circle" became Kafka's source of
orientation for his own position as a writer, though admittedly in
an ambivalent manner.[10] To be sure, Max Brod provided Kafka
a visible model of a successful young writer; but as much as
Kafka admired his friend's self-assurance and perseverance, he
was equally alienated by the apparent facility with which Brod
established important contacts for himself as a writer beyond
Prague and skillfully exploited them to his advantage. Through
their daily encounters a negative picture of what it meant to be
an independent writer emerged in Kafka's eyes. Brod's relentless
public efforts to establish himself as a young literary talent who

despite considerable success was forced to earn a living, as well as the spontaneous determination with which he initiated literary contacts and worked tirelessly at them, almost overburdened editors with his manuscripts, and inundated his publishers with projects—all of these aspects of the artistic life were incompatible with Kafka's conception of an uncompromising, independent, authentic life. Moreover, the compulsive rapidity with which Brod wrote—the prerequisite for making a purely literary existence possible—was totally alien to Kafka's nature. When Brod discovered his friend's literary ambitions and immediately proceeded to promote him in public with the same means he himself used, Kafka emphatically rejected the techniques of the literary trade Brod had mastered so well.

Brod experienced Kafka's obstinacy early on. When it came to writing, Kafka did not fit Brod's image of a writer: "The friendly dealings with Kafka proceeded according to different laws than with the overwhelming majority of writers and poets life has brought me into contact with" (ÜFK325). Brod needed to overcome Kafka's defensiveness and shyness before he could speak with his friend about his writing. While the other authors Brod knew spent their entire time with him discussing their own works, it was "exactly opposite" with Kafka: he spoke with the "most genuine interest" about the progress of the work of others and "only by way of exception did he of his own accord come to speak of his own 'work in progress'" (ÜFK326).

Yet upon reading the first samples of Franz Kafka's early prose, Brod was convinced "that here was no ordinary talent speaking, but a genius" (FK61). "I see," Brod wrote in his diary, "the greatest writer of our day in Kafka" (SL189). At the same time Brod knew that Kafka had absolutely no suitable literary ties, which in his experience laid the necessary foundation for a writer's initial publications. His hasty diagnosis of

Kafka's lack of drive and his conviction that his defensive manner was rooted in feelings of inferiority led Brod to intervene persistently for his friend. During 1907-1908 he began his efforts to publicize Kafka's works. Moreover, his concern for his friend's work became his life's duty ("a striving, that became overpowering in me and against which I did not struggle, since I considered it correct and natural").[11]

In February 1907, only a few months after learning of his friend's literary activities, Brod used the opportunity of reviewing a recently published book by Franz Blei to draw public attention to the "poet" Franz Kafka for the first time. Even before Kafka had published a single line, Brod listed him among "a hallowed group" of writers that included Franz Blei, Heinrich Mann, Frank Wedekind, and Gustav Meyrink.[12] In a letter Kafka responded with brilliant irony to being included in this group portrait of such well-known authors. He attempted to explain that his name was mentioned merely for its phonetic value; his friend could not simply break off this chain of names with a mute "Meyrink," "obviously a curled-up hedgehog." In order to salvage the sentence, an open vowel was needed at the end. Surely he derived a certain sense of joy, for "this winter I have taken a dance step after all." His "merit," nevertheless, was "minimal," and it seemed to him like a "Carnival, pure Carnival, but of the most amiable sort." The letter continues: "A pity, though—I know you did not mean it that way—that it will now become an indecent act for me to publish something later, for that would blast the delicacy of this first public appearance. And I would never achieve an effect equal to the one assigned me in your sentence." Kafka closed his letter with the remark that he felt Brod omitted: "This name will have to be forgotten."[13]

3. Franz Kafka as a Graphic Artist (1907)

Brod's initial, well-intentioned promotion of Kafka failed to produce the desired effect. Moreover, Kafka felt himself less a writer during 1907 than in the years preceding or following. After a one-year law internship Kafka made a decisive career choice during this year. The position he accepted so abruptly with the Assecurazioni Generali in October 1907 (he had previously sought a position with the post office, among other jobs, to no avail) conveyed to him a sense of the pervasive mercilessness of a privately organized insurance company within the Danube Monarchy of the day with its long, exhausting work day and minimal time off. For Kafka, especially, the "work is dreary" (L35). Kafka's entry into this despised occupation must be viewed as the main reason that he almost completely abandoned his writing in the two years that followed. Several sources support the conclusion that Kafka felt more inclined toward graphic art at this time than toward writing. Looking back some time later, he wrote a letter accompanied by an illustration to Felice Bauer in February 1913: "How do you like my drawing? I was once a great draftsman, you know, but then I started to take academic drawing lessons with a bad woman painter and ruined my talent. Think of that!" (F189).

The reference continues: "Those sketches pleased me more than anything else at that time, but that is years ago." One scarcely has a feel for Kafka's graphic art today. Only a few sketches and illustrations, for the most part long unpublished, have been preserved. There are still about fifty odd sketches and illustrations by Kafka preserved in Max Brod's posthumous materials.[14] The woodcut-type sketches with their strongly contoured thrusts of movement clearly bear definite expressionistic traits and indicate above-average talent, which is confirmed by judgments of contemporaries. According to Brod's notebooks, Kafka was almost more indifferent, or to put it more accurately, more antagonistically inclined toward his sketches than toward his literary work. In fact Kafka later destroyed all remnants of his graphic work and directed in his will that his remaining sketches, as well as his manuscripts, be destroyed. Everything that Brod was unable to salvage is lost forever.[15]

Brod subsequently began to promote Kafka's graphic works in artists' circles. The memoirs of the painter Fritz Feigl, one of Kafka's early schoolmates, contain the statement: "I can name for you the name of a great artist—Franz Kafka." Brod made this statement in a discussion during a meeting of the modern painters *Die Acht* ("The Eight"), a group of young artists including the painters Max Horb, Willy Nowak, and Fritz Feigl. The omnipresent Brod, who even in this domain sought to become a mentor for his friend, then brought along several sketches by Kafka, which, as Feigl continues, "were reminiscent of the first ones by Paul Klee or [Alfred] Kubin. They were expressionistic."[16]

Kafka personally ascribed no further significance to his drawing after beginning his occupation. Yet the reference to his drawings is important because it casts new light on his intent to be active artistically, an unconditional inner intention, which at this time was not limited solely to literature. Thus it is impossible to speak of purely literary intent prior to the end of 1907. Only after abandoning his graphic art and after the change to the comparatively moderate working environment at the Worker's Accident Insurance Institute in the summer of 1908, did Kafka concentrate exclusively on his writing.

4. The Early Publications

Hyperion

Franz Kafka's first publication appeared in March 1908 in the first number of the newly established Munich bi-monthly journal *Hyperion* under the title *Meditation*. Kafka's publications in *Hyperion* are closely linked to its editor, Franz Blei. A major literary figure from before the turn of the century up until the beginning of the expressionist movement, Blei was a typical representative of literary *Jugendstil*, the new literary trend at the turn of the century, and of those stylistic tendencies associated with neoromanticism. The literature of this period bridged the gap that formed after the naturalistic movement had run its course. The wealth of literary styles which Blei supported during this period as well as the range of his own literary activities (the literary efforts of Franz Blei, who was recognized in literary circles as a major writer, represent only a minor part, even if the part most heatedly commented upon) can be demonstrated by the number of discriminating literary-artistic journals he brought to life.

Blei, who began as a philosophical writer, was not merely an author, editor, and his own translator; he was also a renowned essayist and critic. He distinguished himself especially in the discovery and promotion of young literary talent and demonstrated a great sensitivity and feeling for quality. He discovered Robert Musil and was the first person before the turn of the century to champion the almost totally unknown Swiss writer Robert Walser, whom he thereafter strove to promote.[17] Blei also played an important role as a mediator and promoter of modern French literature in Germany.

The journals Blei established—there were probably over a

dozen—had a literary appeal for the most part; they contained the best of illustrations and, in accordance with the preference of the times, were produced in luxurious bibliophile format. However, they did not survive their infancy. *Amethyst* and *Opal*, which were almost exclusively private publications and actually only circulated among a very select group of subscribers, preceded the start of *Hyperion*. *Amethyst* and *Opal* characterized the artistic-literary development that flowed into a heightened sensuality and new decadence during the period of radical ideological change after the turn of the century and the positivist maxims of the naturalists. Blei presented high-quality modern literature alongside quite dubious and erotically extreme contributions in his earlier journals.

Along with Brod, Kafka was a subscriber to both of these journals. Brod himself had already published in *Amethyst* and became one of the most active collaborators on *Opal*. In 1907 Brod's short novel *Das czechische Dienstmädchen* ("The Czech Servant Girl") appeared there and bore the telling dedication: "Written for Franz Blei because he enjoyed himself so much in Prague."[18] Even before he became acquainted with Brod, Blei had written a favorable review of his first book in which he, as Brod recounts, "blared a trumpet fanfare" about him.[19] As was a common practice of the day among literary colleagues, Brod then returned the favor with the aforementioned review of Blei's book in *Die Gegenwart* ("Present Day"). In this manner a personal relationship developed between Brod and Blei, as well as a friendship based on mutual literary interests. As Brod writes in his memoirs, Blei thereafter came repeatedly as his guest from Munich to Prague and "felt at home with us."[20]

During one of his visits to Prague, Brod introduced Blei to Kafka, whose name Blei surely already knew through the review in *Die Gegenwart*. The intellectual affiliation and openness he so often affirmed had made Blei a central intellectual figure in what at that time was still a very provincial Prague. Kafka was immediately drawn to the man whom he viewed as "an oriental teller of anecdotes who had wandered into Germany"[21] and whom he described in 1911 as "that admirable man who was driven into the thick of literature by the impetuosity and, even more, the variety of his talents; being unable, however, to liberate or maintain himself there, he escaped with transformed energies into the founding of literary magazines" (PC315). It was these very journals of Blei that Kafka enjoyed reading so much.

At the time of their first encounter in early 1907, Blei was toying again with the idea of founding a major new journal. What he conceived was more discriminating and above all more literary than either *Amethyst* or *Opal*, whose erotic components were to be totally discarded. In Carl Sternheim he had already found a financial backer for the journal he christened *Hyperion*. (This detail is also an essential element in the further publishing history of Kafka's work.) Interested in the plan, Sternheim, whom Blei happened to meet at an antique shop, put up ten thousand marks, and the Munich ("Onionfish") publisher Hans von Weber agreed to have his house edit the journal under this arrangement.[22] "Just as *Pan* and *Insel* for their times," this new journal was supposed to present "the literary and intellectual forces of the day in their strongest formulations" and be "a document of our will and ability for the future."[23]

Probably at Blei's request, Kafka assembled eight small prose pieces under the title *Meditation* during the summer of 1907 for the first number of *Hyperion*; these pieces were taken in part from the first manuscript of his novella *Description of a Struggle* and partially from works written in the preceding months. Apparently Kafka did not rely upon Brod's assistance for this first publication. The January-February edition containing Kafka's first publication was delivered after some delay in March 1908 in an edition of 950 copies; he was the only unknown alongside such noteworthy authors as Hugo von Hofmannsthal and Rainer Maria Rilke.[24]

General reaction to the first volume of *Hyperion* was sparse; in the public eye this expensive, limited edition journal was essentially a pretentious collector's item. However, its appearance was carefully noted in the literary trade itself. Alfred Walter Heymel, cofounder of *Insel* and director of Insel Publishing until 1904, inquired immediately of Blei whether Franz Kafka was not a pseudonym for Robert Walser, Blei's passionately promoted protégé.[25] The bibliophile *Zeitschrift für Bücherfreunde* ("Journal for Book-Lovers") wrote about the recent publication of *Hyperion* in laudatory fashion: "a real joy for us bibliophiles because of its marvelous physical appearance, its content is destined for circles of literary connoisseurs." Kafka's contribution is mentioned there as well.[26] A later volume of the journal characterizes *Hyperion* as the most distinguished artistic-literary journal in Germany.[27] Ernst Rowohlt, even before Rowohlt Publishing but in a thoroughly publisher-like frame of mind, expressed the opinion to Insel's publisher, Anton Kippenberg, in a letter of January 1909 that "*Hyperion* had little chance, for its whole design was not especially favorable and above all Blei has too many enemies."[28]

That same year Brod sent Blei two additional prose texts from Kafka's fragment *Description of a Struggle*. Brod must have pressed Kafka extremely hard to agree to this step, because Kafka distanced himself completely from the publication of these two grotesque episodes, *Conversation with the Supplicant* and *Conversation with the Drunken Man*, which came entirely from the totally unrevised version of his novella. He later criticized

Brod for the fact that the works were published.[29] Fascinated by them, Blei wrote back to Brod: "I like Kafka's [works] and I am going to print them."[30] Both *Conversations* appeared in the March-April number of the second volume of *Hyperion*; the journal was printed in an edition of 1050 copies first released in May 1909.[31]

Hyperion, which the publisher proclaimed as a "monumental work providing an encompassing view of the best that poetry and art of our day has produced,"[32] was attractive because of the high level of its literary contributions in all genres. Among the contributors to the journal were Rudolf Borchardt, Brod, Hans Carossa, Richard Dehmel, Hofmannsthal, Heinrich Mann, Musil, Rilke, Sternheim, and R. A. Schröder. "The journal had merit, but no influence," it was noted too prematurely elsewhere, for judgments of contemporaries proclaimed *Hyperion*'s standing as the last bastion of the literary avant-garde prior to the dawning of the expressionistic movement. With *Hyperion* Blei himself hoped to fill the gap in the literary marketplace left by *Insel* and *Pan*. Max Krell recollects that in its two-year existence "all the poets with any sort of reputation [were] represented there," and that *Hyperion* became the "calling card" with which one "gained attention in bibliophile circles."[33]

The importance Kafka placed upon *Hyperion* and how much he subsequently felt bound, or even obligated, to the place of his debut—a characteristic also marking Kafka's later relationship to his publishers—is revealed in his actions following his first two publications. In the two years that followed Kafka published one literary memorial address and two literary reviews, texts that must be viewed as the direct result of his association with Franz Blei and *Hyperion*. By early 1909 his review of Blei's most recent volume of tales *Die Puderquaste. Ein Damenbrevier* ("The Powder Puff. A Lady's Breviary") appeared.[34] A year later Kafka reviewed Felix Sternheim's *Roman der Jugend* ("A Novel about Youth") for the Prague daily *Bohemia*.[35] (This book by Carl Sternheim's brother, the former coeditor of *Hyperion*, appeared in the Hyperion Verlag, which was overseen by Blei and affiliated with *Hyperion*.) These are the only reviews Kafka ever published.[36]

Because of its financially bleak condition and also because of differences of opinion between editor and publisher, *Hyperion* was forced to cease operations after only two volumes.[37] Kafka published the memorial address *A Departed Journal* in 1911, in which he for the first time clearly expressed his affection, even though aloofly. *Hyperion*'s role and value as well as its short-comings and weaknesses were discussed. Along with the reference to the preciosity of the bibliophile venture, which could only be supported by "self-sacrificial coverage" and "enthusiastic self-delusion," and to the heroic literary collection, with which Blei hoped to "fill that gap in the literary magazine field,"[38] Kafka spoke of the "error" of the journal. "It wanted to grant a representation, a great and vital one, to those who dwelled on the peripheries of literature"; however, "[t]hose whose natures keep them at a distance from the community cannot appear regularly without damage in a magazine where they feel placed in a kind of limelight next to the rest of the contents and look stranger than they are." In accord with Kafka's own experience it could not be the responsibility of *Hyperion* to represent, show, defend, and strengthen these persons and writers living on the periphery; in a manner typical of his own position within *Hyperion*, a literary journal had hardly ever erred *more nobly*, and therefore "in ten or twenty years it will be nothing less than a *bibliographical* treasure" (PC315). Kafka was correct in this prediction.[39]

Bohemia and the *Herder-Blätter*

As a direct result of the collaboration on *Hyperion*, Kafka's attitude toward the matter of publication now turned more positive. Within a few months after the appearance of both *Conversations* in *Hyperion*, Brod was able to persuade his friend to publish another piece. On the trip they took together to Riva in the summer of 1909, Kafka wrote the article *The Aeroplanes at Brescia* as the result of a literary wager instigated by Brod. As Brod reports, Kafka at that time had not written anything for months and complained that "his talent was obviously seeping away" (FK104). Brod knew that it was not a question of despair but rather that Kafka needed a definite motivation and concentration on his writing "to bring his gift into working order again" (FK104). Therefore, he urged his friend to keep a travel diary. Brod intended to keep a parallel one for himself[40] so that Kafka and he could compare notes at the end of the trip and analyze whose text had more accurately captured what they had seen and experienced. Kafka, who was always more relaxed, more energized, and less problematic on his trips than in his home city of Prague because of the distance from parental and job contacts, took up the suggestion without hesitation. Brod's "plan" succeeded, and what Franz wrote "with joy" (FK104) resulted in a report of precise episodes about the aviation week in Brescia that was framed as a simulated competition. The article was also the first description of modern flying machines in all of German literature.[41]

This report was certainly not Brod's ultimate goal, but he had become cautious in his appeals to Kafka. His overriding intention was "to bring Franz's pleasure in creation into flow again" (FK105) and simultaneously to make publishing palatable to him. In investigating possibilities for future publications, Brod came upon another literary contact, the writer, essayist, and translator Paul Wiegler, who had come to Prague from Berlin in November 1908 to edit the art and literary section of Prague's German newspaper *Bohemia*. Shortly before, Brod and Wiegler had corresponded because of their mutual admiration of Jules Laforgue. Both translated and promoted Laforgue, who was unknown in the German-speaking world and who had been harshly judged by the surrealists in his native land.[42] Having arrived in Prague, Wiegler turned to Brod, and the two developed a cordial friendship.

At the same time this opened up another literary contact that Brod subsequently used to his advantage. Immediately after their return from Brescia in September 1909, Brod—himself of course an active contributor to *Bohemia*—convinced Wiegler to print Kafka's *Aeroplanes at Brescia* in the newspaper. In his diary entry for September 15 he noted: "with Wiegler because of Kafka's essay Aeroplane."[43] Wiegler expressed his readiness, probably with the stipulation that the article be shortened for printing. This was possible because the text was more a report and therefore clearly distinguishable from Kafka's literary work. Had it been otherwise, Kafka would have certainly rejected such a compromise. *The Aeroplanes at Brescia* appeared on September 29, 1909, in considerably abbreviated form in the morning edition of *Bohemia*.[44]

However, Kafka's motivation to continue his creative writing was only temporary. Although he later characterized this publication as "fairly tolerable" (F392) and accordingly had found a new place for publication following the collapse of *Hyperion*, he retreated into that depression which made writing impossible for him after his return to Prague. Wiegler readily accepted the reviews for *Bohemia* that had been inspired by Kafka's experience with *Hyperion*; but, much to Brod's dismay,

Kafka did not follow up on Wiegler's requests to submit a manuscript. In a resigned tone Brod wrote in his diary: "He can't decide to do the simple things in life, for example, to submit a manuscript (even though Wiegler requested him to.)"[45] On only one occasion, on the evening of March 19, 1910, did Kafka (exhorted by Brod and apparently with great reservation) release five prose pieces to Wiegler, "unhappily" as Brod noted in his diary.[46]

These pieces, which Wiegler collected to Kafka's dismay under the title *Betrachtungen* ("Meditations"), represented his contribution to the Easter literary supplement of *Bohemia*, a compilation offering a kind of panorama of Prague writers. (Further contributors included among others Oskar Baum, Max Brod, Otto Pick, Ernst Feigl, Paul Leppin).[47] Those expecting something new from Kafka must have been disappointed; of the five small prose pieces printed in *Bohemia* four had already appeared in *Hyperion*. The only new text was *Reflections for Gentlemen-Jockeys*, which Kafka had presumably just recently written or completed. Kafka did change the titles of two pieces, but he reversed this decision later when he published his first book.

Brod insisted again that they write down their travel impressions in parallel fashion on the vacation they took together in 1911. Kafka's surprising suggestion that they undertake writing a novel together about their trip, was of course something Brod reacted to favorably.[48] By doing so, Brod could continue to hold his friend's "nose to the grindstone" and get him accustomed to concentrated and above all to "regular work" (FK126). Initially the cooperation between two very close friends went well as expected; both worked with great zeal and "tossed ideas back and forth to each other like shining balls."[49] But soon, however, the inherent differences in their personalities and the polar opposites of their literary temperaments became evident. Work on the common novel bogged down shortly after they returned to Prague. Increasingly they worked in isolation, and more and more frequent differences of opinion arose. In contrast to Brod, who had already had experience with this type of collaborative effort, Kafka reacted to every sentence Brod introduced for the novel (to be called "Richard and Samuel") "bound up with a reluctant concession on my part which I feel painfully to my very depths" (DI156).

Brod's role in the joint novel became increasingly unbearable for Kafka. But Brod too now began to criticize more and more openly what Kafka wrote. Kafka was satisfied with how he completed the first chapter by himself; he viewed it as a success with the conclusion as he had written it. About the success of this piece he added the well-known sentence: "Even more, I think that something is happening within me that is very close to Schiller's transformation of emotion into character" (DI169). On this point too he had to contend with Brod's rejection: "The last section I wrote hasn't pleased Max, probably because he regards it as unsuitable for the whole, but possibly also because he considers it bad in itself" (DI170).[50] Just prior to this, only two months after their collaboration began (and suspecting this serious dissent), Kafka explained with regret to his friend that the novel was going nowhere.[51] Experiencing with great anger the worthlessness of our travel notes (KI92), Brod was nevertheless able to see to it that "at least a respectable segment of the book had been written" (FK126).

This first and only collaborative effort with Brod led Kafka to recognize the differences in their temperaments (DI156); in this failed collaboration he also perceived his own personal incapacity for friendship (DI204). By the spring of 1912 only the first, self-contained chapter of this joint novel had been completed. Nevertheless, though he already feared the worthlessness [!] of their travel notes, Brod had met with at least partial success. His choice of terms already discloses the basic problematical relationship between the two writers. The fact that Brod also read from Kafka's travel notes during their literary sessions with Oskar Baum, much to Kafka's displeasure (KI92), points to the motivation behind Brod's actions. Without a doubt Brod wanted to facilitate Kafka's first major publication. He hoped he would be able to support his friend with this joint novel and promote him on the path to independent publication.

In spite of, or precisely because of, such an interest, Brod sought to have the first chapter published. An invitation by the young Prague editor Willy Haas to contribute to the third number of his Prague *Herder-Blätter* proved opportune. Since its inception Brod had published in this newspaper, which was the first to lend expression to what generally became known later on as the "Prague School" or the "Prague Circle"; Kafka had not contributed to it.

The J. G. Herder Organization, at whose commission the *Herder-Blätter* appeared since 1911 in loose succession for a select circle of subscribers, was comprised of young members of the Prague lodge of the Jewish Order of B'nai B'rith. Its editor, Haas, characterized it as a student journal like thousands of others past and present. As fate would have it at this particular point in time, the young Franz Werfel, Brod, Kafka, Max Mell, Musil, Carl Ehrenstein, Ernst Blass, Kurt Hiller, Blei and others were alive, and the *Herder-Blätter* developed into something more than the other student publications around 1910.[52] The most obvious characteristic of the *Herder-Blätter* today is that in contrast to the other journals of the early expressionistic period and in contrast to the then extremely popular and famous weekly and monthly journals, almost all of the contributors to this

student paper are still known today. After the splendid first
edition supported by the Order, the paper stood on the brink of
financial extinction. No honoraria could be paid; it was a purely
idealistic, private undertaking of the young Haas, who placed his
friend Werfel (for whom he had initiated the paper) on center
stage. After Werfel left Prague for Leipzig, the newspaper
stopped production in October 1912 with the double number 4/5.
The list of contributors demonstrates the zenith and period of
closest unity and most intensive collaboration among the Prague
circle of authors. The *Herder-Blätter* was their first independent
journal.

Kafka and Brod treasured the journal because it was able to
give such clear expression to modern German Prague literature
in such modest framework and because, in sharp contradiction
to the increasingly nationalistic-chauvinistic tendencies of
Germans in Prague, it supported the newer Czech literature. On
April 8, 1912, they met with Haas, who apparently commented
favorably on Brod and Kafka's joint effort. After introducing the
first chapter of "Richard and Samuel," Kafka noted with amazement his unintentional acquiescence to the publication and to the
praise expressed by Haas by speaking so "affectedly" about the
travel report in order to "continue by fraud the fraudulent or
lying effect of the travel report" and to make "Haas' amiable lie
. . . easier for him" (DI259-60).

Bearing the title "First Chapter of the Book 'Richard and
Samuel'—the First Long Train Trip (Prague-Zurich)," Brod and
Kafka's joint effort appeared in the third number of the *Herder-
Blätter* in June 1912.[53] The text was preceded by an outline of
the entire novel and concluded with the remark: "Continuation
to follow." But Kafka, who described this publication as "quite
intolerable" (F392) in a letter to Felice Bauer in 1914, no longer
put any stock in a sequel. "In our joint story," Kafka wrote a

month later in July 1912 to Max Brod, "aside from details I enjoyed only the sitting beside you on Sundays . . ." (L82). In the following and final edition of the *Herder-Blätter*, the double number 4/5 of October 1912, Brod and Kafka published separately: three poems by Brod in large print in the main section and Kafka's small prose piece *Great Noise* in the appendix and in tiny print under the rubric "Notes."[54]

5. 1906-1912: Publication as Problem

Over this span of five years only six literary publications by Franz Kafka actually materialized. These published prose pieces and fragments probably represent only a portion of what Kafka had actually written up to 1912. From one of the earliest extant diary entries of December 1910 it is clear that almost everything Kafka wrote in that year was "put aside and crossed out" (DI34); a veritable "mountain" hindered him from continuing his writing because it revealed to him what was bad and therefore the impossibility of his writing. According to Kafka, what he destroyed represented "five times as much as I have in general ever written, and by its mass alone it draws everything that I write away from under my pen to itself" (DI34-35). Then in March 1912 the laconically despairing note so characteristic of Kafka's later life followed: "Today burned many old, disgusting papers" (DI250).

In 1907, when his entry into the bureaucratic world forced him to reorient his life, it must have been clear to Kafka simultaneously that his special type of writing, his faulty intuition at that time, and his sporadic and impetuously drafted inspirations, set narrow limits on his literary possibilities. The languor and even sluggishness with which his writing progressed could not provide him with the firm foundation of a secure literary life. His dogmatic, ideal conception of poetic existence (at this point in his life Goethe, Kleist, and Flaubert were models, and the impressions from reading Franz Grillparzer's autobiographical notes and above all Hofmannsthal's "Letter of Lord Chandos" dominated) contrasted sharply with the mundane example of Max Brod's literary existence. Nevertheless, concentrated training as a writer began in tandem with the progressing routine of everyday work. The schedule by which Kafka spent every day between eight and eleven o'clock in the evening writing was a direct expression of his intention. The main place for writing was the diary, which he began to keep regularly from December 1910 on.

The question Brod raised about the value of this writing must have unsettled Kafka. Basically he had not written anything up to 1912 that measured up to his own stringent standards. The question about the purpose of publishing his writings must have depressed him at that time. But he was firmly convinced he could write "better things" and actually desired to present them to the public (F7).[55]

Nevertheless, despite all the reservations and painful concessions, the publications resulting from everything he had written between 1907 and 1912 were not totally due to Brod's direct intervention. Kafka himself apparently sensed the necessity of making a debut. Dependency on his occupation was compounded further because he was compelled to participate in a family business. Kafka faced tremendous pressure to succeed, for his father measured his activities against those of Bruno Kafka's rapidly rising career. But the pressure to succeed from his circle of friends, who were totally involved with literature, was considerably stronger. Since 1907 Kafka had seen many other younger writers from similar backgrounds foisting their works upon the public and gaining recognition. Prague's reputation as the cradle of a vibrant new literature had already reached Berlin, the Mecca of literary life. Writers from Prague had opportunities as never before; "literature from Prague" became an actual slogan in Berlin. Not only had Brod, Blei, and Wiegler published several books already, but Baum had appeared in print in Axel Juncker's highly regarded house, and the sensational successes of the young Franz Werfel were just beginning.

Certainly these other writers from Kafka's circle of friends had different backgrounds from his and received support for their literary ambitions from their families. Kafka admired his friends, just as he envied the apparent ease with which they met with success. In a note from 1911 that was not published in the German edition of the diaries, this ambivalence comes clearly to light in the example of Werfel: Werfel had "written a lot of good things with musical sense early on and easily; he has the most happy life behind him and before him. I, however, work with weights which I cannot cast off" (Wa90). About Baum, Kafka noted similarly in 1911: "Envy at the nominal success of Baum whom I really like so much. With this, the feeling of having in the middle of my body a ball of wool that quickly winds itself up, its innumerable threads pulling from the surface of my body to itself" (DI131).

Even within his circle of friends Kafka felt pressured. He had to think about publishing something if he wanted to continue to keep the possibility of a writer's life alive. Early on Brod had made reference to him publicly in his review in *Die Gegenwart*. But how could he present an unsuccessful piece of writing to the public, a piece that was criticized by his friends and which Werfel disregarded as regionally restricted literature?[56] Publications that Kafka had doubts about he decidedly refused to pursue. He was conscious of the fact at this time that he had by no means reached the limits of his abilities and was capable of greater things. In November 1911 he wrote in his diary:

> I explain it to myself by saying that I have too little time and
> quiet to draw out of me all the possibilities of my talent. For
> that reason it is only disconnected starts that always make an
> appearance, disconnected starts . . . If I were ever able to
> write something large and whole, well shaped from beginning
> to end, then in the end the story would never be able to detach
> itself from me and it would be possible for me calmly and
> with open eyes, as a blood relation of a healthy story, to hear
> it read, but as it is, every little piece of the story runs around
> homeless and drives me away from it in the opposite direction.
> (DI134)

II

The First Book: *Meditation* (1912)

> The sample page which you so kindly sent me is altogether beautiful. Let me speedily and by registered mail express my approval of the typeface and thank you from the bottom of my heart for your solicitude toward my little book. (Franz Kafka to Rowohlt Publishing, October 18, 1912)

*I*nsofar as it is mentioned at all, the literature on Franz Kafka is for the most part rather consistent in its assessment of the publishing industry's guardianship of Kafka's work in general and of his relationship to it specifically. Reference is made repeatedly to a successful meshing of publisher's initiative and writer's wishes and to a kind of ideal author-publisher relationship which bound Kafka solely to Kurt Wolff from the publication of his first small book throughout the remainder of his life.[1]

What the ideal author-publisher relationship should be is not within the scope of this study. Any abstract description would in the end only lead to banal reduction. Presenting factual relationships, by example if possible, is preferable. For what one author considers a decisive factor for his success in his relationship with a publisher—above all the fact of being published—is to others perhaps secondary or self-evident. The most important point of reference for determining such a relationship may therefore be something else, a phenomenon taking place in the sphere between author and publisher, which distinguishes the ideal relationship from an otherwise average one. This can be observed as a gradually differentiated, mutual interaction between the author and his publisher; a mutual personal and intellectual exchange is critical. All significant author-publisher relationships share such an observable positive interaction.

The first contact between an author and a publisher often determines the author's future relationship to the world of literary intermediaries and can even exert a decisive influence on his future works.[2] In the initiation of contact between author and publisher, a manuscript undergoes its first critical examination from the outside, i.e., an examination of the author through his text. By accepting a first manuscript, a literary publisher signals his hope for future works from an author. For Franz Kafka, communication between author and publisher is cast in terms of failure; there is the inability of initiating a dialogue with the publisher and of arriving at a mutually influential relationship.

1. June 29, 1912—First Contact with a Publisher

In a radio talk entitled "On Publishing in General and on the Question of How Authors and Publishers Meet," the publisher Kurt Wolff looked back fifty years later at the circumstances that brought Franz Kafka to his publishing house:

> Because I had accepted a manuscript by Max Brod and he anticipated publishing his entire *oeuvre* there, he sent me a young countryman and friend, Franz Werfel, and one day personally brought me another friend and countryman, Franz Kafka . . . It was more by accident than merit that they came to the publishing house. Naturally one could sense that each in his own way, and to his own degree, was deserving of careful consideration by a publisher.[3]

Kurt Wolff's depiction requires some basic further clarification. From the publisher's point of view, the discovery of Franz Kafka was certainly more accidental than deserved. But Max Brod, who had brought Kafka to Wolff's attention and put him on his trail, had in many ways forced the accident. At least as important as these factors, if not more so, were the "[p]ublishers' personal obligations" (DII289) in deciding and determining the nature of Franz Kafka's first encounter with the publishing world.

From another perspective it appeared to be "quite by chance" (F132) to Kafka as well. Certainly it was a significant accident, for although Kafka had scarcely any hope of publishing a book because of the very esoteric nature of what he had written up to the time of this first encounter, he was suddenly confronted with the prospect of a major, individual publication. This prospect may simultaneously have nourished the hope that he could end the "horrible double life from which there is probably no escape but insanity" (DI44) and begin the "real life in which, with the progress of my work, my face will finally be able to age in a natural way" (DI211).

Kurt Wolff's recollections about accepting Franz Kafka into his publishing house must be modified in yet another regard: at that time Kafka did not come to Kurt Wolff Publishing but rather to Ernst Rowohlt Publishing. The publisher who took notice of Kafka at the time was not Kurt Wolff but Ernst Rowohlt. Furthermore, Kafka's first book did not appear with Kurt Wolff but with Ernst Rowohlt Publishing. The pithy comment in a monograph about Ernst Rowohlt that "[w]hen Kafka considered a publisher for his first stories, he immediately thought of Rowohlt"[4] is equally false. As the history of Kafka's early publications clearly shows, Max Brod was the intermediary for all of his friend's literary dealings up until 1912. In long evening conversations in Brod's apartment and on their lengthy walks and weekend excursions around Prague, the prominent writer Max Brod informed his friend about present-day literary life, about his experiences with his publishers, and about the nature of publishing. These talks with Brod were, as Kafka once referred to them, his "literary news."[5]

Max Brod continually attempted to intercede with editors and publishers he knew on behalf of manuscripts by young Prague authors. Even his first publisher, Axel Juncker in Berlin, to whom the young but "mature" literary talent entrusted his first dozen books between 1906 and 1912, experienced Brod's desire to intercede. Brod's letters to Juncker reveal that the ever-active promoter recommended Max Mell, Hedda Sauer, Kurt Hiller, Otto Pick, and Paul Leppin to him.[6] Following an urgent suggestion by Brod, Juncker had already published a book by Oskar Baum. Brod was subsequently successful in 1909 in interesting his publisher in Franz Kafka.[7] Brod's attempt to have a book by Kafka published failed at that time for unknown reasons. With great personal attention Brod then attempted to establish his newest discovery, his countryman and poet friend Franz Werfel, with Juncker Publishing. Apparently Brod was only able to advance Werfel's first work, the collection of poems *Der Weltfreund* ("The Friend of the World"), in the face of the greatest resistance from the publisher and finally only with the threat of "himself not publishing again in a house which would reject and fail to recognize such a masterpiece."[8]

The example of *Der Weltfreund* clearly shows to what unconditional and energetic extremes Brod was prepared to go. After the disagreement over Werfel, Brod never reestablished a productive working relationship with Juncker. The delicate balance of trust had been disturbed. Just as with Brod's first publication, it was Gustav Meyrink who filled the void and advised the publisher Ernst Rowohlt to extend an invitation to this promising Prague author in spring 1912.

Rowohlt's goal as a publisher was to develop a strong program of modern literature. Desiring to turn his company into a publishing house for the young authors waiting in the wings at the time of its establishment, he exhibited an interest in modern literature from 1912 on. Over a long period of time he had observed Brod, who in spite of his youth was considered one of the most promising of modern writers and was at the same time the leader of the already familiar Prague Circle. "I have followed your work closely over the last few years with great interest," Rowohlt wrote to Brod in April 1912, "but didn't want to approach you directly, since I thought that you had quite exclusive contracts with Axel Juncker."[9] Encouraged by Meyrink to take this step, Rowohlt now showed an enthusiastic interest in accepting all future works by Brod and made an offer to him.

Thus Brod was closely tied to Rowohlt Publishing when he and Kafka planned their vacation trip together for the summer of 1912. The trips they regularly undertook together after 1909 offered Brod and Kafka a particular contrast to their day-to-day bureaucratic lives. After the trips to Riva in 1909 and to Paris in 1910, they embarked on an ambitious train trip through central Europe. The last of their stops was to be Germany, and specifically Weimar, the residence of their esteemed Goethe. This visit was the fulfillment of a long-awaited wish for Kafka, whose admiration for Goethe had remained constant since his days at the *Gymnasium*. Through their "love of Goethe" and "the study we had been making of Goethe's works for years," they were "especially well prepared" for this trip (FK122). Brod, however, had another purpose in mind with the choice of Weimar, for it gave him the opportunity to meet personally with Rowohlt. It was agreed that they would stop in Leipzig for a day. Brod would then have enough time there to speak with the publisher, while

Kafka took a walk through the city.

Several detailed descriptions about the meeting in Leipzig by the parties involved still exist. With the exception of Kafka's diary notes and several of Brod's notes, however, the details of these events were only recorded years later and with the hindsight of knowing how Kafka's life subsequently developed. These accounts are therefore not fully reliable.

Having arrived in Leipzig the previous evening, Brod and Kafka went their separate ways on the morning of June 29, 1912, as planned. Kafka went to the city, Brod to Rowohlt at Königsstraße 10, the company headquarters at the time. It was Brod's wish—and Kafka supported him enthusiastically—to abandon Axel Juncker Publishing and to join a more active and financially secure publisher. At the same time Brod was pondering several other projects and wanted to discuss their feasibility personally with Rowohlt. Brod's place in the world had already been established by virtue of the eleven books [!] he had published up to that time;[10] he had also made a name for himself through a number of smaller publications in newspapers and magazines (up to July 1912 he had published almost 500 such prose pieces, poems, essays, and reviews).[11] Yet living a writer's life remained only a dream, for Brod was still forced to rely on an unwanted profession to earn a living. On this day in Leipzig he explored the possibility of closer collaboration with Rowohlt Publishing; he wanted to propose working as a reader or editor for Rowohlt and request some type of literary position which would secure his financial base.

Thus Brod came to Rowohlt not only as an author, but also and especially as an advocate and a prolifically active literary advisor. According to his diary, Brod suggested a whole panoply of ideas to Rowohlt and to his partner Kurt Wolff, including a selection of Franz Grillparzer's memoirs for which he himself wanted to write an introduction and editions of Flaubert and Laforgue that he would develop. They also discussed a large-scale project, a periodical to be edited by him for the poets mentioned in his *Smetana Essay*.[12] The conversations transpired to the satisfaction of both parties. Brod's suggestions were seen as provocative, and his relationship to Juncker was of special interest. He was assured a contract from the publisher.[13]

While discussing the publication of a collection of Brod's essays, the conversation turned for the first time to Franz Kafka; Brod suggested that Kafka's *Brescia* be placed alongside his own article on the same topic.[14] In addition, Brod had brought along samples of Kafka's early prose to present to Rowohlt in Leipzig because, as he said, "I had long cherished the burning desire to see a book of my friend's in print" (FK124-25). Kafka was not an unknown entity to Ernst Rowohlt. As a young literary publisher searching for new talent, he attentively followed literary magazines and was already familiar with several of the small prose pieces from *Hyperion*. Since Rowohlt—as he later jokingly formulated it with hindsight—preferred knowing a potential author personally to reading a manuscript, a lunch was arranged for the two. Kafka must have been surprised by Rowohlt's invitation, for he had already eaten his noon meal before his return from his walk. Brod brought his friend to "Wilhelms Weinstube" anyway, a winehouse where Rowohlt and several of his colleagues were already waiting. Prior to that, Brod had noted with obvious satisfaction in his travel journal: "I'm to bring Kafka, about whom they are all very curious, they know of him through *Hyperion*."[15]

Thus this noon meal at Wilhelm's winehouse entered the annals of literary history. What Kafka labeled a "dimly lit tavern in a courtyard" with a "[q]ueer daily lunch" (DI288) had become a traditional meeting spot of the day. A circle of young people enthusiastically devoted to literature and art met almost daily in a back room of the locale under the leadership of a commanding "colossus," Ernst Rowohlt.[16] Kurt Pinthus, a long-time lector for Ernst Rowohlt and Kurt Wolff, places this establishment on equal footing for the expressionistic movement with the groups tied to the Berlin journals *Aktion* and *Sturm* (two journals that were the focal point of the literary and artistic scene of Berlin, which spawned expressionism). In his memoirs Pinthus speaks of the "winehouse circle" as the seedbed of contemporary literature; later it became its center, and finally a pilgrimage site for writers from German-speaking countries. Pinthus continues: "Anyone of the younger generation or of those who were slightly older from Berlin, Prague, Munich, Vienna, or the west of Germany knew that he would meet the publisher and Werfel and Hasenclever and myself and others of the kind in this tavern."[17] Kafka was now introduced by Brod to Rowohlt and the other members of the circle present, Walter Hasenclever and Kurt Pinthus, both of whom were still part-time literary advisors for Ernst Rowohlt at the time. Also present was the author Gerd von Bassewitz, whose plays Rowohlt had been publishing since 1911. Kurt Wolff, Rowohlt's companion, did not normally participate in these meetings.

Franz Kafka was inept in social situations; he suffered physically and mentally all the more during such encounters. Even on this day he was especially reserved and reacted to the unexpected meeting with shy skepticism. He observed with precision the circle around him; he took note of the obviously animated conversation of the group and of Rowohlt, who surpassed all the others by far with his verve and energy. In his travel diary Kafka captured the liveliness of the conversation at the table: "All three flourished sticks and arms" (DI288).

In assessing this situation psychologically, one that must have been an example of social intellectual fellowship for Kafka, it is surprising that his notes include no word of judgment or analysis, and also no reference to Max Brod. Nothing reveals the slightest annoyance about the trick Brod had just played on him. In fact the opposite is the case; to a great extent he seemed to enjoy the situation. The sentences in which he sketches his impressions and the changing scenes are short and curt. The style is that of a protocol and in this regard not any different from his travel notes. Most noteworthy is his observation of the person of Ernst Rowohlt: "Rowohlt: young, red-cheeked, beads of sweat between his nose and cheeks, moved only above the hips" (DI288). Kafka himself is depicted as the exact opposite in the memoirs of Pinthus, who describes him as a "long, thin, very pale and very shy person who said almost nothing" (RaII80). As was the custom, the group moved to the elegant Café Felsche, also called Café Français, after the meal. Here the conversation took place which Kafka later summarized: "Publishers' personal obligations and their effect on the average of the present-day German literature" (DI289).

If Franz Kafka said nothing or very little on this day, Brod did so all the more in his name. "Brod assured everyone that Kafka was a great writer but that he had a difficult time deciding to publish anything," Pinthus recalls. Brod was immediately successful, for Kafka was encouraged "to submit a manuscript" (RaII80). Ernst Rowohlt started things off. He knew how to address Kafka in a way that led him to write contemplatively and surprisingly in his travel diary (in a typical and reservedly optimistic tone): "Rowohlt was rather serious about wanting a book from me" (DI289). Brod made note of the publisher's seriousness as well: "R. asked him in earnest for a book."[18]

On the one hand, even if Rowohlt could find little in common with the rather reserved Kafka, it is all the more meaningful to see how, on the other, Kafka was attracted and fascinated by this person who differed so much from him. Weeks later he expressed this thought almost hymnically in letters about the publisher. On the backdrop of his biography, of that direct split between actual and imagined life, one observes how much Kafka was drawn to strong, assertive personalities his whole life long. Rowohlt was certainly one of these. That Kafka believed Rowohlt and Rowohlt Publishing would help ameliorate his divided life can also be gleaned from a hope-filled letter he wrote to Brod two weeks after the encounter: "The generous, smart, diligent Rowohlt! Leave, Max, leave Juncker, with all or as much of what you have written. He has held you back, not from yourself but from the world for sure." What Kafka recognized as an opportunity here for his friend, had now, by virtue of Rowohlt's request that he submit a manuscript, meaning for himself as well: Rowohlt is the only one who can "come along and wrest you out of your office" (L79).

Kafka did not react negatively to Brod's meddling in his personal affairs; instead he thanked Brod for introducing him to the publishing industry. It can be stated with certainty that Kafka would not have had the strength or self-confidence up to this point to have dared to venture into public on his own or even with the friendly, supportive prompting of his friend. For several months he had been working on his first major novel—initially he considered his writing a success and it gave him great satisfaction; but when about one hundred manuscript pages were complete, he thought that the whole plan of "Der Verschollene" ("The Man Who Disappeared"), as he intended to call his *America* novel, was too nebulous and that the original concept was digressing into irresolvable rambling. How could Kafka have thought of publishing his work in June 1912, since, besides a torso of a novel and several fragments, he had only several delicate, and in large part already published, small prose sketches whose republication made little sense to him. But Rowohlt opened up new horizons, and Kafka promised to submit the manuscript. Following the conversation in the Café Français, Rowohlt accompanied Kafka and Brod back to his offices in order to introduce them to his companion Kurt Wolff before they continued their trip. Only after Kafka's first meeting with a publisher had ended with the promise of submitting a manuscript did he meet the man who a short time later would become known as "his publisher."

In Kurt Wolff's memoirs about his author, Franz Kafka, which were presented exactly fifty years later during a radio broadcast series, a broad interpretation is given to this first meeting.[19] Wolff commented: "How many times I met with Kafka I don't know. But I remember the first meeting with eerie clarity. It was June 29, 1912." While Wolff can recall this date exactly because of his diary entry (cf. Wo104), his recollection of what was said during this short meeting remains clouded and has to be reviewed carefully at critical points. He continues:

> In the afternoon Max Brod, who already had ties to the publishing house, brought Kafka to the rundown publisher's offices . . . Ernst Rowohlt—we went our separate ways a few months later—and I greeted the both of them . . . from the first moment I had an indelible impression: the impresario presents the star he has discovered. Naturally, it was that way . . . Oh, how he suffered. Taciturn, clumsy, tender, sensitive, shy like a schoolboy before his exams, convinced of the impossibility of being able to fulfill the expectations of the impresario's praise. And above all, how could he have agreed to let himself be presented like some commodity to a buyer? (Wo68)

It is curious that the prior meeting of both authors with Ernst

Rowohlt and the others is not mentioned—as is typically the case in Wolff's "memoirs" (Wo75) where he attempts to eradicate the traces of Rowohlt's presence in the publishing house during the years 1910-12. In the case of Franz Kafka this censorship of the past and Wolff's stylization of himself as Kafka's sole publisher are closely linked.

A comparison of the extant notes on the meeting in Leipzig may serve to correct this distortion: Wolff's detailed presentation of the first meeting with Kafka stands in inverse proportion to the extensiveness of Kafka's notes. While Kafka sketches the conversation with Rowohlt in detail in his travel diary, he makes no mention of meeting Wolff. The note at the conclusion—"In the publishing house" (DI289)—is pithy and was added as a kind of afterthought to ensure completeness of the travel diary. A look at Max Brod's parallel diary confirms this impression; following a detailed description of what had preceded this event stands only the note: "With Rowohlt once again." Similarly, Kurt Pinthus' memoirs for that afternoon make no mention of Kurt Wolff.

The conversation at the publisher's was brief: Brod and Kafka wanted to continue on their way to Weimar that same afternoon. At the departure—the train was already leaving at five o'clock—Kafka made the well-known remark passed on by Wolff: "I will always be more thankful to you for the return of my manuscripts than for their publication" (Wo68). This sentence, uttered during the first conversation of a writer with his future publisher, is really quite unique. Subsequently it has all too often been interpreted too narrowly. The version transmitted by Wolff has often been expanded to suggest that Kafka generally would have preferred not to have any of his works published. This line of thinking is endorsed by Kafka's Eckermann, Gustav Janouch, who has Kafka say: ". . . all my friends always take possession of something I have written . . . and so it all ends in the publication of things which are entirely personal notes or diversions. Personal proofs of my human weakness are printed . . ."[20]

But one does not approach the meaning of the sentence with this facile interpretation, or, moreover, with a sentence, which in the fifty years until it was written down, had taken on an anecdotal character. Counterbalancing Kafka's hope for an edition of the book was simultaneously his reservation that the publisher could have no conception of the manuscript, which had been requested exclusively on Brod's forceful recommendation. Kafka felt compelled to make some restrictive remark and balance the embarrassing praise given by his friend. He had to reduce the weighty expectations burdening a manuscript that had not even been finalized.

At the same time Kafka made it clear to Rowohlt that he would be disinclined to make any artistic concessions regarding the possible publication of a book. He would only publish completed works of the highest quality and never anything of poor quality, something that would be abhorrent to the author and might hinder him from further writing. This statement is Kafka's hint to the publisher that he should not rely solely on Brod's assessment of the quality of his work. Moreover, it should not be forgotten that Rowohlt was also courting Brod on this day. Kafka's statement that afternoon about the personal "obligations of the publishers" can very well stem from a fear that he, i.e., his publication, was the price for which Brod entered an exclusive contract with Rowohlt. Kafka drew attention to this duplicity of obligation and challenged the publisher to utmost honesty in exchange for the submission of a manuscript.

From this new perspective Kafka's comment about the return of his manuscript is understandable in a different and new light. Returning the manuscript—though a negative action—would demonstrate a recognized publisher's serious consideration of his writing, which had been previously only promoted by friends. Here too for the first time one sees the typical mixture of truth and strategy, a paradigm for future negotiations with the publisher. Kafka's pessimistic manner of argumentation for his work will still require further discussion.

2. Work on the Manuscript *Meditation*

Kafka was at a disadvantage during the Leipzig conversation, which "quite by chance" (F132), as he later relayed to Felice Bauer, resulted in the publication of his first book. How could he—totally unprepared for the encounter with Rowohlt—promise his publisher-to-be a manuscript that simply did not exist? His "impresario," Max Brod, for whom the Leipzig negotiations were tailor-made, very probably had a clear conception of Kafka's first book and had aroused certain expectations in Rowohlt, thereby committing his friend to a certain degree. With his comprehensive knowledge of Kafka's literary work and his familiarity with what was on hand, the experienced writer Brod saw no problem with putting together a manuscript: "The publishers had already expressed their readiness—these were happy days!—after seeing the specimens I had taken with me to Leipzig. It was only up to Franz to submit a definite manuscript" (FK125).

But a tortuous chasm opened up for Kafka while working on the manuscript for his first book. In looking through his prose pieces with an eye toward imminent publication, Kafka had serious reservations alongside his enthusiasm for everything that the "good, clever, and competent Rowohlt" (L78) was prepared to risk as a publisher for Brod and for him. He considered himself "unable . . . to complete the remaining pieces" (L83) in Jungborn, where he had gone to a natural spa to relax after spending the week together with Brod in Weimar. As a foundation for the selections he certainly had what was published in the first number of *Hyperion*, yet no other piece seemed refined enough to be chosen for the book. Quantitatively amassing enough material for a book, would, as Kafka feared, point out gaping qualitative holes; he did not want to subject himself to this sort of compromise.

From Jungborn he pleaded with Brod to let him publish something short this one time and appealed to his friend's conscience: "[W]ould you really advise me . . . to have something bad published with my eyes open, something which would disgust me, like the 'Conversations' in *Hyperion*?" The anticipated size was actually hopelessly meager, and, Kafka continued:

> . . . is probably not sufficient for a book, of course; but after all, is going unpublished—and are even worse outcomes—not far less bad than this damnable forcing oneself? . . . This artificial working and pondering has bothered me all along and makes me needlessly miserable. We can allow bad things to remain finally bad only on our deathbed. (L83-84)

Despite this unambiguous rejection of compromise in his own work, Kafka continued to file away on what was imperfect; the "damned straightjacket," however, robbed him of strength and inspiration and actually inhibited further work on his novel. For several months he had been writing this first great novel, which he had even hoped to complete in Jungborn where he was free from the constraints of the office and could energetically push the work forward during arduous nighttime sessions. This plan, in which he had placed so much hope, failed because of the work on the manuscript for *Meditation*.[21]

Everything that Kafka had previously written now seemed poor and inferior to him, as if "written in a lukewarm bath"

(L82). He complained to Brod that he had "never been the sort of person who carried something out at all costs" and that he had "not experienced the eternal hell of real writers . . ." (L82). But Brod, the advocate of the book, remained firm and insisted on its publication. Brod's persistence and suggestions to Rowohlt, who apparently questioned Brod a number of times about Kafka's manuscript,[22] led to a real test of their friendship after Kafka returned to Prague. It developed into a confrontation between their very divergent conceptions of the profession of writing. "[P]iecing together these 'worthless' old fragments" (FK125) was now hindering him from producing better works; *Meditation* was for him nothing more than a minor step toward more substantial things. And observing the volume of his friend's literary productivity, Kafka wrote in his diary: "In any event, now, after the publication of the book, I will have to stay away from magazines and reviews even more than before, if I do not wish to be content with just sticking the tips of my fingers into the truth" (DI266).

During the disagreement with Brod, Kafka's doubts about the whole purpose of his writing intensified. Brod was a writer who conceived his books with an eye toward a prospective reading public to whom he had something to say and whom he wanted to influence. Kafka's inclination was the opposite, as he himself judged it; he was more inner-directed and more comprehensive than Brod. He tried to clarify his existence through literature, he wanted to write his autobiography; any thought at all of an audience was foreign to him during the writing process. But this egoism was also the invisible cloak of its direct opposite, of the demand for general truth and validity, which he had never been successful in formulating to his satisfaction. Why should he now force a publication? After exhausting work at night, Kafka reworked entire pieces and honed orthographic details, yet after the first text revision on August 7, he wrote to Brod that he could not "clear up the little pieces that still remain" and will therefore "not publish the book" (DI265). Resigned, Brod had already noted in his diary: "So many manuscripts he has not published."[23] But he later summarized his successful struggle for the promised publication straightforwardly in the following way: "The book had to be completed and was completed."[24]

On August 13 the manuscript was finally assembled: eighteen short prose pieces, among them those eight pieces from the first number of *Hyperion* and *Reflections for Gentlemen-Jockeys*, published in 1910 in *Bohemia*. Exactly half of the pieces selected had been published previously; Kafka even retained the heading *Meditation*. Elsewhere Kafka labeled this manner of putting together the first book his "Quarry practice."[25] Brod, who would have liked to have seen all of these pieces published, wrote some time later about the "amount of material chosen by Franz" (FK125) from a wealth of stories in his diaries and manuscripts: ". . . we don't know why the author considered one worth publishing and kept back the other" (FK106).

On the evening of August 13, Kafka was at Brod's with the completed selections in order to discuss the sequence of the pieces with him, something to which he had paid no attention up to that time (F14). He was not prepared for the fact that Brod had a visitor and was initially "rather annoyed" (F14) that Brod was unavailable to him. His friend introduced him to a close relative from Berlin, a certain Fräulein Felice Bauer, who had stopped off in Prague while on a trip. This encounter—from the moment Kafka joined the little circle in Brod's apartment, he had "an unshakable opinion" about her (DI269)—was to prove to be a fateful one for both of them. Instead of pursuing his original intention, he looked at the photographs being passed around with a certain delight and took an active part in the conversation. He even sketched out travel plans with Felice, whom he had only gotten to know a few minutes earlier! He was able to discuss the manuscript he had produced under duress with Brod only very briefly in private.

Kafka even managed to complicate the actual submission of the modest manuscript. Brod, who was immensely pleased by the finished manuscript (FK127), did not want to let the definitive version out of his hands, since he had struggled for so long to acquire it. (It was possible that his friend would reconsider the text overnight and destroy everything.) Therefore, Brod suggested to Kafka that he himself look at the collection in peace and quiet again and then himself forward the whole thing to Rowohlt the next day. This seemed a plausible suggestion to Kafka, since Brod was not only an exceptional reader but also an employee of Prague's main postal administration. Thus Kafka left the manuscript *Meditation* with Brod to read on this evening. Brod undertook his task with a certain satisfaction for his part in the matter: "Then I read 'Contemplation' [*Meditation*] once again. Divine" (FK127).

Meanwhile, Kafka actually harbored renewed doubts during the night. In looking through the copies, Kafka discovered some mistakes and places that unquestionably needed revision, and he was dissatisfied with the punctuation. He hurried to have a messenger deliver a letter to Brod first thing the next morning in which he carefully inquired—since "yesterday" he was surely "under the young woman's influence"—if "some silliness" had not resulted or if he had come up with "perhaps only a secretly comic sequence." The conclusion of the letter, however, is worth noting; at the time when Kafka's intense work on the manuscript had been completed, he informs his friend: "Please look it over once more and let my thanks for that be included in the *enormous thanks I owe you*. Yours, Franz."[26]

This is more than just a friendly gesture on Kafka's part.

Would he also have owed Brod thanks, if the publication of his small pieces had been thwarted? Kafka knew that the edition of *Meditation* at this point in time was necessary and proper. At the moment when he was working on a promising novel, he needed a publisher's support, and he could establish such a linkage now with this completed manuscript. Kafka's struggle to put together the manuscript for *Meditation* was surely the story of an inner struggle against literary compromise, a test of his friendship with Max Brod, who so obstinately pressed for publication, and a story in which everything that was remotely connected with the book became a problem. But the disagreements were overcome and the manuscript lay ready. As an expression of his sincere thanks, Kafka added the dedication to the book: "For M. B."[27]

On the same day, August 14, 1912, Brod sent the manuscript of *Meditation* to Rowohlt Publishing, and Kafka drafted his first letter to his publisher, Ernst Rowohlt.

3. First Excursus: The First Rowohlt Publishing Company

Ernst Rowohlt

The upstart Rowohlt Publishing Company with its young publisher, who had so impressed Kafka at their first meeting, had only been in existence for a short while. Ernst Rowohlt himself cited 1908 as the year of its establishment, the year in which he "published" his first book with modest means. But the inconspicuous printer's notation: "Printed for Ernst Rowohlt, Munich 1908" points to the fact that there was still no publishing company at this time. The first book was a thin, exquisitely formatted, deluxe bibliophile edition—Gustav C. Edzard's poems *Lieder der Sommernächte* ("Summer Nights' Songs")—which Rowohlt had printed on credit with W. Drugulin Printers in

Leipzig in 270 hand-numbered copies on hand-made paper. The connection to Drugulin proved to be significant in the years that followed. Rowohlt took personal responsibility for the distribution of the first book from his "Schwabinger Bude." His clientele were primarily his friends and relatives and those of the author, who was a young law student and friend.

Rowohlt's unwavering desire to become a publisher pervades his youth and appears as the major course to which future events can almost consistently be linked. Nevertheless, the publishing profession was not one with which Rowohlt was familiar. Born on July 23, 1887, as the only son of a middle-class family from Bremen, Ernst Hermann Heinrich Rowohlt was more enthusiastic early on about books and bookstores than about his father's business as a securities and stock broker, which his father planned for him to take over one day. After his failure in school at the *Gymnasium*, he began a bank apprenticeship at his father's behest. During this time he began to acquire a self-made, fundamental knowledge of literature and became a passionate reader "of the modern poems of Karl Henckel, [Detlev] Liliencron, [Stefan] George, and [Hugo von] Hofmannsthal."[28]

Rowohlt was deeply impressed by Samuel Fischer's publishing house, which dominated the entire publishing landscape at the time, and as a seventeen-year-old he made up his mind to "establish a publishing house that would at least rival Fischer Publishing."[29] Through regular attendance at the literary events in his hometown, he became more and more involved and interested in literature and the theater. In Anton Kippenberg, a friend of the family and the head of Insel Publishing he so admired,[30] Rowohlt finally discovered in 1907 the mentor who would play a decisive role in his future. Having been publishing for three years already, Kippenberg recognized the young Rowohlt's great talent during his first conversation with him and was surprised to encounter such comprehensive knowledge of literature and especially of the publishing business on the part of this not yet twenty-year-old.[31] Kippenberg encouraged Rowohlt to become a publisher and also convinced Rowohlt's parents of their son's new calling. Kippenberg initially provided the idealistic young man a very basic training: as a typesetter, engraver, and printer, and later in Munich as a retail bookseller. In addition, he made it possible for him to round out his apprenticeship abroad by working in a Paris bookstore. "There are enough dilettante publishers in Germany, and I don't want to see you increasing their numbers,"[32] Kippenberg wrote to Rowohlt in 1909.

In March 1909 Rowohlt returned to Leipzig from Paris. For a short while he worked as a volunteer with Insel Publishing and subsequently accepted the position offered him as manager of the bibliophile *Zeitschrift für Bücherfreunde* ("Journal for Book-Lovers"). He had already become a member of the *Gesellschaft Münchener Bibliophilen* ("Munich Society of Bibliophiles") established by Franz Blei, and therefore, although his main interest had always tended toward modern literature, had to a certain extent embarked on the path of bibliophiles.[33] The beneficial ties to W. Drugulin Printers—the *Zeitschrift für Bücherfreunde* had just joined the Leipzig printer—and the honorarium offered him had led Rowohlt to this decision despite the express advice of his mentor Kippenberg. From then on he resided in the front part of the printery where three small rooms were placed at his disposal; here he worked, lived, and continued to unfurl his publishing plans. These quarters were shortly thereafter to become those of Rowohlt Publishing.

While in Paris he had "published" a second book, this time with the somewhat prouder notice: "Paris-Leipzig. 1909. Ernst Rowohlt. Under commission with W. Drugulin in Leipzig."

From his "fictional Paris publishing house"[34] Rowohlt had come into contact with Paul Scheerbart, whom he knew as a writer of humorous and cosmic fantasies and of scurrilous publications in the magazines *Simplicissimus* and *Jugend*. The writer, who was plagued by chronic financial difficulties, submitted a convolution of older poems, entitled *Katerpoesie* ("Hangover Poems"), for which he had been seeking a publisher unsuccessfully for years. Given his personal financial position, Rowohlt paid an astonishingly handsome honorarium. He sent Scheerbart the advance sum of 100 marks and had 800 copies of the work printed by Drugulin in Leipzig from where he had them distributed.

Rowohlt's energetic second attempt to establish a publishing company without a financial basis included sending out 250 [!] review copies, something that had a distinctly positive effect on the critics but did not help sales. The sales of *Katerpoesie* were sluggish, and the work was still listed in the publisher's catalogue years later. With the setback caused by this failure (a financial one as well), it was not possible to consider any further publications, and up until the summer of 1910 the great project continued resting in the thoughts of Rowohlt, who was pondering new possibilities.

On July 30, 1910, Rowohlt entered Ernst Rowohlt Publishing into the commercial register of the city of Leipzig. A notation there explains the sudden awakening from a state of slumber: a silent partner was mentioned, the independent man of private means and student, Kurt Wolff. Rowohlt had apparently finally found the person who would be able to place his publishing plans on a secure financial footing. The history of Rowohlt Publishing begins on this day.

Kurt Wolff

Only a few months older than Rowohlt, Kurt Wolff was the exact opposite of his future partner in lifestyle and personality. Apart from the same year of birth, the two shared no other common denominator when they first met beyond their interest in literature. A straight and conscious course leading to a publishing career, as can be established from the biography of Ernst Rowohlt, did not exist for Kurt Wolff. The parental home and milieu of the young Wolff were vastly different. He came from a very tradition-conscious family of musicians in Bonn. His father was a musician, university professor, and academic music director; his mother came from an established, well-to-do Jewish family. Wolff recollects his childhood: "The most beautiful and essential things were passed on to me by playing chamber music in the house, which also brought me into contact with the entire literature from Bach to Brahms" (Wo103).

Wolff's youth was overshadowed by the long suffering of his seriously ill mother, who left her son a considerable estate upon her premature death in 1904 and thereby rendered him entirely independent financially. After completing the *Abitur*, he studied German language and literature in Marburg but interrupted his studies during his first semester to fulfill his military service in Darmstadt. There he came into contact with the tradition-minded Merck family, the owners of the chemical company by the same name, and became engaged in the fall of 1907 to the family's daughter, Elisabeth Merck, whom he married two years later. This marriage opened up numerous social contacts for Wolff; the Merck family cultivated ties to the upper echelon of the German Empire. Through the Mercks, Wolff also came into contact with Stefan George's circle, became acquainted with Karl Wolfskehl, and was a long-time personal friend of Friedrich Gundolf (Wo81).

Kurt Wolff's parental house and the early orientation toward things traditional and to the family's values did not fail to exert their influence on his subsequent activity as a publisher. Very early on he exhibited gentlemanly airs and related tendencies. A supporter of *l'art pour l'art* in his youth, the aristocratic aesthete had no precise plans for his future. He did not seem concerned about it and attempted merely to invest his inheritance from his mother wisely. From São Paolo, where he completed an internship at the German Bank that had been mediated by the Merck family upon completion of his military tour of duty, he wrote unconcernedly to his mother-in-law Clara Merck: "You will have to laugh if you were to imagine me in a business environment. But I find it quite nice and pleasant to get an idea about it in a short time in this way; this might be useful for my whole life."[35]

Kurt Wolff was an intellectually inquisitive person; along with his musical inclinations he most certainly possessed a love for books and an interest in literature. "I was an impassioned reader, already as a boy. I loved books, beautiful books too, and attempted to collect them, already as half a child and as a student,"[36] he commented later on. An inclination toward beautiful bibliophile books was typical of the demanding youth and the taste of the upper middle class during the first decade of the twentieth century. Wolff's passion for reading found expression in his passion for collecting; within a few years he had amassed a library of approximately 12,000 volumes [!] consisting predominantly of expensive first editions and dedication copies from the age of Goethe.

Along with his bibliophile interests he revealed a definite proclivity toward research in literary history during his early years as a student; presumably he considered a university career at the time. From 1908 a few small pieces by Wolff appeared in the *Zeitschrift für Bücherfreunde*, in which he represented a distinctly bibliophile position.[37] During 1908 he also joined the bibliophile group *Gesellschaft der Bibliophilen*. With the editing of two posthumous literary works from the age of Goethe that were in the possession of the Wolff and Merck families, he demonstrated a talent early on for assembling editions and offering knowledgeable commentary. This fact motivated Anton Kippenberg, the publisher of both editions, to solicit Kurt Wolff's aid in collaborating on the Goethe bibliography he was planning at the end of 1909.[38] Accepting the invitation, the recently married Wolff moved with his wife to Leipzig to complete his studies and to work at Insel Publishing. The aristocratic, upper middle-class life-style of the young couple befitted their backgrounds. The generous hospitality of their household became a new focal point for the upper circles of society in Leipzig.

An Outline of the History of Publishing 1910-1912

In arranging Kurt Wolff's biographical chronology, his second wife, Helen Wolff, writes: "In the winter of 1908, he was at that time a twenty-one-year-old student of German in Leipzig, Kurt Wolff became a publisher: He entered Ernst Rowohlt Publishing in Leipzig, at first as a silent partner."[39] Helen Wolff bases her remarks here on a statement by Kurt Wolff; however, this dating of the beginning of Wolff's publishing activity is incorrect, for Wolff and Rowohlt did not meet for the first time until the winter of 1909-1910 at a meeting of the *Gesellschaft der Bibliophilen* in Leipzig. At that time Kurt Wolff, to whom Rowohlt with his sense for the opportune made the suggestion to help finance one of his private publications, became a partner in the new Rowohlt Publishing Company.[40]

In this manner, with Rowohlt as the experienced book dealer

with a wealth of ideas and with Wolff as the financial backer and occasional literary advisor, the activities of Rowohlt Publishing began, a house "whose first and primary goal was to promote Eulenberg."[41] And when Wolff noted in his diary on July 30, 1910, that: "The company Ernst Rowohlt Publishing has been entered into the commercial register," he could add the notation: "Goethe's Tasso in print."[42] This work was the first volume of a new series, the Drugulin Prints—Editions of World Literature in exquisite, almost bibliophile format at an extraordinarily low price, which would be made possible by a relatively large sales volume.

The calculated need for high volume, however, cast the program of the series in the direction of tested older literature, namely, the classics. The firm achieved a certain degree of recognition among critics and the public with this series. In the *Zeitschrift für Bücherfreunde* there was already a statement in 1910: "A new publisher announces itself with the allure of a private press."[43]

As accidental as its selection for it may have been, the publishing city of Leipzig was important for the rapid development of the young publishing firm. Compared to the café culture of Berlin's literary scene and the bohemians in Munich's Schwabing district, Leipzig was a city that, though certainly not an intellectual center—Gottsched and Gellert were the last poets worth mentioning who were productive there in literature— became instead a center for the book and publishing trade. By the end of 1910 eighteen titles had already appeared in the new Rowohlt Publishing Company; in 1911 thirty-four additional titles were released. Along with the bibliophile editions, which were obviously modeled after the format of Kippenberg's books, Rowohlt also tried to seek out modern literature at the same time. Conscious of the financial risks for a new company and simultaneously limited by the influence exerted by his financial backer, Ernst Rowohlt could in no way have begun with avant-garde intent, and instead turned to more mature authors in accord with contemporary tastes.

Rowohlt's difficulties in counteracting the firm's staid bibliophile reputation, which existed even beyond just the first year, as well as in introducing modern literature can be easily demonstrated by the example of Christian Morgenstern. Morgenstern, who was asked by Rowohlt as early as 1910 to submit his work to his company, experienced the strong reaction of his publisher, Reinhard Piper, who wrote to him about Rowohlt's offer: "This publisher has only made available unnecessary new editions of existing literary works in good print." Changing publishers would offer "not the slightest advantage"[44] for Morgenstern. Rowohlt's other attempts to lure away prominent modern authors to give his company respectability and an established group of authors came to nought. The main authors of Rowohlt Publishing and its financial basis up until 1912 were Paul Scheerbart, Max Dauthendey, Herbert Eulenberg, and Carl Hauptmann.[45]

A decisive factor for the publisher's future was also the redirection toward a young generation of writers who began to cohere as such after 1910. A new emphasis ensued with Georg Heym, from whom Rowohlt requested a manuscript. Rowohlt had read a sonnet by this unknown poet in the journal *Der Demokrat* ("The Democrat"). *Der ewige Tag* ("The Eternal Day"), the "first work" by Heym that Rowohlt printed in April 1911, drew the attention of literary circles in Berlin. In the author's letters to the publisher the pace-setting phrases *Neue Generation* ("New Generation") and *Jüngste Dichtung* ("Contemporary Literature") first appeared. Since most of Germany's larger publishing houses were not receptive initially to this literary movement, and those houses that first published expressionist literature—primarily Alfred Richard Meyer and Heinrich Bachmair—could not have any far-reaching effect because of their financial base, the involvement of the attractive and financially sound and young Ernst Rowohlt Publishing Company did not go unnoticed for long.[46] The young literary generation, which like no other before it was inclined toward publicity and quick distribution, soon flocked to Rowohlt in Leipzig. Kurt Pinthus, theater critic and reviewer, as well as the first editor for the publisher at the beginning of 1912, described this period in his memoirs: "The most surprising thing was that we did not need to search at all; the authors were simply there . . . and they brought along others with them" (RaII78).

Simultaneously Rowohlt sought ties to Prague's literary circle, which having made a name for itself through Brod and through Werfel's *Der Weltfreund*, seemed at that time to be a literary ace-in-the-hole. Paving the way for connections to Brod, the head of the Prague group, was an expression of Rowohlt's will to integrate Prague's recent German literature into his publishing program. For Franz Kafka the timing of this first meeting with Ernst Rowohlt could not have been more opportune.

4. Acceptance and Publication of *Meditation*

In his first letter to Rowohlt on August 14, 1912, Kafka announced the "short prose pieces you wished to see." After the torment of putting together the collection, which the writer did not refrain from mentioning, he was again totally committed to its publication. But knowing that his thin thirty-one page manuscript would first have to be accepted by Rowohlt, he wrote a solicitous letter with all the typical Kafka modesty. Given the fact that Kafka wrote this letter in his diary, i.e., his place for reflection on his existence, we can draw a conclusion as to its significance. At the same time this letter is one of the most beautiful documents in the correspondence of an author with his publisher:

Dear Herr Rowohlt,
    I am herewith transmitting to you the short prose pieces you wished to see. They might well make a small book. While I was assembling them for this purpose I sometimes had the choice between appeasing my sense of responsibility and my eagerness to have a book of my own among your fine books. Certainly my decisions have not been perfectly pure. But now, of course, I would be happy if you liked the things only to the extent of your publishing them. Ultimately, even with the greatest experience and the greatest keenness, the flaws in these pieces do not reveal themselves at first glance. And the personal mark of each writer consists in his having his own special way of concealing his flaws.
                    Yours sincerely, Dr. Franz Kafka

Manuscript follows separately by parcel post[47]

When Kafka received no reply from the publisher after a week, he questioned his decision anew. Preparing himself for a negative reaction from the publisher to his manuscript, he wrote in his diary: "If Rowohlt would send it back and I could lock it up again as if it had all never happened, so that I should be only as unhappy as I was before" (DI268). The manuscript was accepted by the publisher; however, it was a confusing detail for Kafka that it was not Ernst Rowohlt, who communicated this to him, but Kurt Wolff, whom Kafka had hardly taken notice of during the talks in Leipzig. Wolff then asked in a friendly tone whether the author had any special wishes with regard to the contract or the printing (WBr25). Brod had also received his first letter from Kurt Wolff shortly before, which ended with the note: "Rowohlt will write to you about the business arrangements."[48]

Unsure of where he stood, Kafka avoided a personal form of address in his reply and employed a more detached "Dear Sir." He declared himself in agreement with all the publisher's conditions for what he considered a dismally hopeless publication from a commercial point of view. At the same time, however, and although he had already left all decisions "respectfully" to the publisher for the external fate of the book, he made definite statements on the format and expressed his desire for the largest type possible for the book that the publisher might conceive.[49] Kafka's idiosyncratic way of dealing with the publisher, with his mixture of thoughtful and polite reserve and surprisingly precise demands, comes clearly to light. By giving the book little chance of success and simultaneously leaving all decisions respectfully up to the publisher, he normally reached the point of having his suggestions considered; the pessimistic argumentation, balanced between "truth" and "strategy," was perhaps a refined and more successful way of getting his ideas through than any other could have been in Kafka's case.

At the end of September the publishing contract was signed, and Kafka wrote with obvious relief to Felice: "My book, booklet, pamphlet has been accepted at last" (F7). Kafka was enthusiastic about the first type sample Wolff sent him. He later described this gigantic typeface in which his manuscript was set to Felice as a "little too consciously beautiful" ('strategically'?); the type "would be more appropriate to the tablets of Moses than to my little prevarications" (F33).

In accord with Kafka's wish for the largest possible type size, the publisher was happy to comply for technical reasons; by doing so a ninety-nine page book resulted from the thirty-one page manuscript. This simultaneously determined the cover and the binding; the type corresponded to the bibliophile format. The publisher even agreed to the publishing deadline for which Kafka then impatiently pressed. Following Kafka's last corrections on November 3, the Leipzig printers Poeschel & Trepte immediately ran off *Meditation*—"Rowohlt wagered only 800 copies," Kurt Pinthus recollects—and the *Börsenblatt* ran a full-page ad on November 18, 1912, announcing its publication.[50]

Max Brod explained Kafka's hopes with regard to the publication of his first book in a letter to Felice:

> If his parents love him so much, why don't they give him 30,000 gulden as they would to a daughter, so that he could leave the office, go off to some cheap little place on the Riviera to create those works that God, using Franz's brain, wishes the world to have.—So long as Franz is not in a position to do this, he will never be entirely happy. His whole disposition cries out for a peaceful, trouble-free existence dedicated to writing . . . A fine book of Kafka's is about to appear. Perhaps he will be lucky with it and can start a life devoted entirely to writing. He is also writing a long novel, has reached chapter 7, and I think it promises to be a great success. (F57)

Kafka had thus published his first book upon the serious request by Rowohlt, a book which surely would not have materialized had it not been for his conversation with him. For Kafka did not put forth the effort to assemble this book because Brod wanted it, but primarily because in Rowohlt he saw the possibility of developing a promising relationship with a publisher. The security of a relationship with a publisher was important for his future work as well as for increased independence from Brod's literary tutelage. In Rowohlt's attitude toward him, Kafka saw himself strengthened in his writing as well as in his life's desire.

The *America* Phase (1912-1913)

> The tremendous world I have in my head. But how [to]
> free myself and free it without being torn to pieces. And
> a thousand times rather be torn to pieces than retain it in
> me or bury it. That, indeed, is why I am here, that is
> quite clear to me. (Diary, June 21, 1913)

*T*he path to a publisher was paved. Kafka seemed relieved
and sanguine during the following days in Weimar. He then
wrote enthusiastic letters, dealing specifically with Rowohlt, to
Brod from Jungborn. A second element was added to his
prospects in Prague; on the evening of August 13, holding the
definitive manuscript of the first book in his hands, he had met
Felice Bauer. From that point on Kafka's life centered on these
two interests. On August 14 he delivered his manuscript to
Rowohlt; a day later he mentioned Felice for the first time in his
diary. As soon as the book had actually been accepted, Kafka
decided immediately to reorganize his schedule more rigorously
so as to allow as much time as possible for writing. One of his
sisters married, and his friend Max Brod was to marry in
September 1912. Remarkably, the day Kafka sent his first letter
to Felice (September 20) was the day on which he had received
his first publishing contract.

The coincidence of such important events in Kafka's life
engendered a state of immense inner excitement. Having written
the story *The Judgment* in one eight-hour sitting during the night

of September 22-23, 1912, he achieved a "final break-through" (FK126). For the first time he had met the success in writing that had been eluding him for years.[1] This moment represented the ideal of the creative process Kafka sought.

1. Drafting *The Judgment* and Kafka's New Consciousness as a Writer

Writing and "the special nature" of his "inspiration" (DI45) must always be discussed in a twofold way in relation to Kafka, i.e., as condition and as result. Kafka's periods of concentration from the beginning of 1911 on, or at least from the beginning of 1912, signified an almost planned training as a writer,[2] which was only partially governed by his own will. The painful recognition of his own individual impotence dates back to his early childhood. Having been brought to doubt by stubborn, independent parents, he viewed his personality as weak and deformed. Kafka internalized his defiance into his innermost self. In societal and social relations he assumed thereafter the pose of a "living dead person" in the overpowering environment he experienced: he adjusted to personal pain by turning away from the living, vital world.[3]

Thus the decision to turn away from the world of the living developed into a conscious defensive position opposed to the bourgeois *vita activa*. Writing became the typical protective shield. Weakness, an apparent acceptance of susceptibility to sickness and the frequent and then final flight into illness, rigorous rejection of sensual pleasure, and near ecstatic insight into the permanent impossibility of externalizing any of his abilities were the result of planned "training." Kafka intended to resolve this perceived weakness and social inferiority internally. At about the age of twenty Kafka took leave of the world of appearances of youth on the Laurenziberg outside of Prague:

> I went over the wishes that I wanted to realise in life. I found
> that the most important or the most delightful was the wish to
> attain a view of life (and—this was necessarily bound up with
> it—to convince others of it in writing), in which life, while
> still retaining its natural full-bodied rise and fall, would
> simultaneously be recognised no less clearly as a nothing, a
> dream, a dim hovering. (DS292)

In removing himself from the real laws of the active world,
Kafka came close to transforming his existence into myth; he
reduced himself to his "pure self" and stylized it into a parable.[4]

Kafka's perception of his unsuitability for life had become a
condition *sine qua non* for him. "There may be a purpose lurking
behind the fact that I never learned anything useful and—the two
are connected—have allowed myself to become a physical
wreck," Kafka wrote in retrospect in his diary of 1921. "I did
not want to be distracted, did not want to be distracted by the
pleasures life has to give a useful and healthy man." At this point
Kafka viewed how he "systematically destroyed" himself as "a
purposeful action" (DII194-95). The realm of his "fantastic" life
became a "buffer zone between solitude and community;"[5] his
creative power emerged from this contradiction in the basic
structure of his thinking. It was precisely from the ambivalence
of Kafka's dialectical, non-synthesizing thinking[6] that he garnered
that terrifying energy that had to be mustered anew at every hour
for him to confirm his artistic existence.

Though Kafka sought repeatedly to sketch the creative
process conceptually and figuratively, he harbored the essential
element, his inspiration, in an inviolable, almost mystical
darkness. In this connection, he spoke of clairvoyant conditions,
of wrenching, gripping, opening and exciting moments, in which

he was capable of anything. Only at such a "time of exaltation" (DI152) was something deeper released from the recesses of his being—something deeper that precedes inspiration or is synonymous with it. For him, writing entailed conjuring up ghosts, magic, and devil worship as well as birth, sensuality, and even prayer. Kafka did not attempt to explain his inspiration; in the end he formulated once again only new incantations of his creative circumstances in these circumlocutions. For amid all the uncertainty of Kafka's writing one thing was certain: the condition in which he found himself writing had to exist at any price.

Far removed from any reflective, sovereign control over his material, far removed from the constructive mental state of setting stone upon stone and arranging ideas in an architectonically measured whole, Kafka viewed the poetic process as something distinct from and independent of his guiding will. The mere attempt to write in a calculated manner or to structure his texts logically or analyze them rationally would have destabilized his "inspiration." The creative process, the writing experience, gave Kafka a clearer sense of success than the resulting finished text.

In order to write Kafka had to create this condition of "inspiration." Initially he used the diary;[7] even in those moments of greatest failure he clung to his desk and wrote his notes: "Hold fast to the diary from today on! Write regularly! Don't surrender! Even if no salvation should come, I want to be worthy of it at every moment" (DI233). The diary contains a great number of such affirmations and incantations; most of the time the actual beginnings of prose texts were part of them. The multiplicity of the fragments contained in the diaries must be considered attempts to create conditions for the correct creative process and to find a point of departure that would unleash the flow of that dreamlike power. Most often the result was only an initial sentence, which paradigmatically becomes the double fragment with a slightly modified perspective. All too often Kafka made notes like the following after breaking off his attempts to write: "Only this everlasting waiting, eternal helplessness" (DII29). Kafka left himself open to the "initiative" of what he was writing. If the initial sentence, however, did not catapult him into the narrative mode and did not elicit the creative condition, he would break off immediately.[8]

But Kafka did not plot and construct with words. An apparent recognition of his writing preceded the purely artistic requirement: he saw his task as writing down that which could be brought into total parallel with his innermost self. "This is no artistic yearning" he added to this reflection (DI173). The result of his writing had to possess the same certainty as the conditions during the actual writing itself. In this second examination of his work he had to demonstrate to himself whether the transfusion of the fullness of the images had been successfully transformed into a linguistically fixed form, whether the life of the material that had no life in itself proved successful in the inspirational stage. If words—given life by Kafka—found an inner sense of belonging to sentences as to a homeland, then Kafka felt a unity with what he had written.

In recounting the various events that preceded the drafting of The Judgment, it becomes clear to what extent Kafka's life had taken shape by September 1912. On the one hand, during the preceding months Kafka had written more and better things than ever before; on the other hand, his personal isolation intensified all the more. His struggle between bourgeois occupation and writing became more and more polarized; some form of resolution became increasingly necessary. Felice Bauer was able to break through his isolation on one front; the feeling of intimacy, perhaps of marriage, unsettled him, even if it expressed secret desires. He found his real intentions supported by Ernst Rowohlt, who opened up the possibility for Kafka to become a writer during their meeting in Leipzig. Kafka's inner struggle had at this point reached a new, more concrete dimension.

The rapid sequence of events and their concreteness had a catalytic effect. Without interruption he wrote the story *The Judgment* directly into his diary during an eight-hour period. At this turning point in his literary life he discovered the writer's consciousness for the first time. The diary entry after *The Judgment* reads:

> September 23. This story, *The Judgment*, I wrote at one sitting during the night of the 22nd-23rd, from ten o'clock at night to six o'clock in the morning. I was hardly able to pull my legs out from under the desk, they had got so stiff from sitting. The fearful strain and joy, how the story developed before me, as if I were advancing over water. Several times during this night I heaved my own weight on my back. How everything can be said, how for everything, for the strangest fancies, there waits a great fire in which they perish and rise up again. (DI275-76)

The writing of *The Judgment* had just as indubitably run its course as the "indubitability of the story was confirmed" (DI278) when he delivered it the very next day to Oskar Baum. Like "a real birth, covered with filth and slime" (DI278), he described the story which, raised from the depths of his being, developed almost independently of him. With this story he had reached his postulated ideal and simultaneously set the standard for his future literary creativity: "Only *in this way* can writing be done, only with such coherence, with such a complete opening out of the body and the soul" (DI276).

The First Printing of *The Judgment* in Max Brod's Literary Annual *Arkadia*.

With the completion of *The Judgment* Kafka saw his literary possibilities realized for the first time; the sense of security at having been successful registered immediately. Uncharacteristically he read his story to his sisters immediately after writing it down in his diary—and to his friends during the days that followed. In contrast to all his previously exhibited reservation, Kafka considered the story's immediate publication as he was writing it. During this phase when he drew closer to Felice, simultaneously the phase of production of his first book and the continuing confirmation of his success in writing, Kafka opened up noticeably to the outside world. In November—without hesitation, and even with "great pleasure"—he accepted the invitation of the editor of the *Herder-Blätter*, Willy Haas, to an authors' evening in Prague where he planned to read *The Judgment* (L92). At about the same time he sent the small piece *Great Noise* to Haas for the *Herder-Blätter*. He then published another small piece, *Children on a Country Road* from *Meditation* in the Christmas supplement to *Bohemia*.[9] While still writing *The Judgment*, Kafka pondered with "joy" having "something beautiful for Max's *Arkadia*" (DI276). A definite regularity, which determined his relationship to publication, was evident in the spontaneous preparation of a story just written for the yearbook his friend was in the process of preparing for Ernst Rowohlt. In the past Kafka had withheld his smaller prose pieces at least a year before releasing them for publication. When Brod returned to Prague on September 29 from a short trip, Kafka surprised him at the railroad station with the news that he wanted to submit a recently completed novella to *Arkadia* (FK128).

Meanwhile, the format of the literary yearbook *Arkadia* had taken its final shape after Rowohlt's definitive approval. Rowohlt had given Brod free rein with the editing, and by the beginning of August Brod had already assembled a list of contributors. The yearbook's basic concept was clear: Brod saw it as a necessary supplement to the new literary movement in Germany—*Arkadia* also attempted to delineate literature anew along purely geographical lines. In it Prague authors writing in German had a new avenue open to them. Brod's conception of the program for the first edition is important for his personal development. After his early sketches, which were influenced by impressionism, a phase of nihilism, and indifference, and after a short phase of toying with expressionism,[10] Brod struck a new path far removed from the sphere of societal protest: he reflected on his Jewishness and turned above all to the theme of a higher community in coming to terms with this new interest. In turning to Herzl's Zionism he found himself strengthened not least of all by looking towards those who shortly before had celebrated him so exuberantly after his novel *Schloß Nornepygge* ("Nornepygge Castle") appeared and who now in passionate protest against bourgeois saturation had broken into the formerly rather tranquil literary life of Berlin. Behind this expressionistic movement Brod suspected the chaos and divisiveness of a confused youth, which, following a mistaken belief in community, drove it into the clutches of a collectivism that destroyed all creativity.

With his *Jahrbuch für Dichtkunst* ("Yearbook for Literature") Brod intended to serve pure poetry along the lines of his *Smetana-Essays*[11] without a superimposed program and thus contribute to a free unfolding of poetry without programmatic restrictions. In 1912, amidst the explicitly programmatic art of expressionism, that meant a clear rejection of the art of the most recent writers, whom he had previously supported. Brod conceived *Arkadia* in direct contrast to what he called *Großstadt-*

dichtung ("literature of the metropolis"). Once again (insofar as one includes Brod among the editors of *Hyperion*) it was a question for him of rescuing true poetry. Whereas the younger generation had been comprised mainly of lyricists, *Arkadia* was to present a broader overview of contemporary literature, and prose writers were to receive prime consideration. Critics and readers understood this distinction. No "criticism, no economic or sociological observations, no politics, and of course no literary politics and no illustrations" is the way Brod conceived the contents of the yearbook (SL73). The selection criteria for the texts were set very high. A letter by Brod to Richard Dehmel states in rather grandiose terms: "The temperate, the established, the unobtrusive and the inherently calm-artistic-blissful is what in my view should be collected in *Arkadia*."[12]

Brod's idea was supported by the entire group of Prague authors who came to *Arkadia* from the then disbanding *Herder-Blätter*. The circle of Prague writers thus became the focal point. Ten of the eighteen coworkers on *Arkadia*—who wrote thirteen of the twenty-three contributions—were former contributors to this Prague journal, whose last number appeared in October 1912. Noteworthy among the list of contributors were Robert Walser, Max Mell, and Kurt Tucholsky.

Brod's yearbook was certainly peripheral, if not an open contradiction, within the framework of Rowohlt or of Kurt Wolff Publishing, whose commitment to the literature of the younger generation became more and more evident. After months of delay *Arkadia* first appeared after the Pentecost holidays of 1913.[13] That the publication came about at all is linked to the early contract agreement from the summer of 1912 when Rowohlt sought to lure the young Brod to his publishing house. It is linked as well to Wolff's general openness toward subsuming divergent directions in his program. The yearbook received little public attention when it appeared, drawing modest if divided comments from the critics. Nevertheless, Brod's intent was noticed. Eduard Korrodi, for example, questioned "whether the prose writers found in *Arkadia* would be able to raise German literature up by its bootstraps." He added that despite the inarguable expressiveness of the literature of the young generation perhaps those really on the rise are not those who are promoting the rascal-type so enthusiastically.[14]

Certainly Kurt Wolff assured Brod at the beginning of 1913 that *Arkadia* would continue its tranquil and happy existence for a long time,[15] but the publisher did not intercede for this project in the future. Increasingly he replaced the yearbook with the annual almanac, which appeared from 1914 on and which seemed more homogeneous from the publisher's perspective. Brod's classicist-religious program and the conception of "his" arcadian literary fields separated him from Wolff's rising house-authors and led as much to the failure of the almanac, which was originally planned to run for several years, as did the power struggles between Brod and Wolff over the acceptance of a contribution by Franz Blei. The publisher's aversion toward continuing the periodical increased when he found out that Brod in his preface had launched hidden attacks on Karl Kraus about which Kraus conveyed his deep annoyance to Wolff.[16] The copies of this very expensive edition, which probably did not number more than one thousand, were totally unmarketable; after the first edition the publisher distanced itself from the undertaking.[17]

The publication of *The Judgment* marked Kafka's entrance into the public arena with a longer, more unified story. He himself never entered into personal negotiations with the publisher—the acceptance of his contribution was never in question at any point—but Brod had probably conferred with him about the selection of the contributions. Again and again Kafka queried

Brod about *Arkadia* (L80ff.). In his second letter to Felice he stated that Brod will now "thrust upon your Germany an enormous literary yearbook" (F7). Kafka was happy to be able to submit such a successful piece as *The Judgment*. The molding of the work, the temporal sequence of events following it, the successful breakthrough in writing, and the publication of a text in a forum compatible with Kafka, meshed in ideal fashion with the first printing. *The Judgment* is thus a unique example among the works Kafka published during his lifetime; it was a success on all levels (only *A Hunger Artist* would approach the same success, although Kafka's experience with it was not as positive). But a shadow fell over this publication as well; *Arkadia*, no longer supported by the publisher, remained a pretentious collector's item, which for all practical purposes had no literary impact and no real readership. Even this publication, then, did not enable the writer Franz Kafka to direct any attention to himself.

2. Franz Kafka—Ernst Rowohlt's Author?

Kafka's establishment of this initial relationship with a publisher, which has literary-historical significance, encouraged him at first. The single meeting with Ernst Rowohlt temporarily gave him the secure feeling of support for his literary objectives and the hope of achieving status as an author with Rowohlt Publishing. Although Kafka must have already known at this time that Rowohlt Publishing had "two bosses,"[18] Kurt Wolff's entry into the existing agreement irritated him, and perhaps even soured him; his friend Brod, on the contrary, continued to correspond personally with Rowohlt. Thus Kafka wavered anew between the uncertain joy over Rowohlt's acceptance of his little book, which otherwise had little chance in the literary world, and the fear that the publisher had only arranged everything as a favor to Brod. Only from our present-day perspective is it possible to suggest that Max Brod was not the focus of Rowohlt's negotiations in 1912.

Kafka's ambiguity is evident in his second letter to the publisher. He of course desired the publication—he had gotten accustomed to the idea meanwhile—but he no longer turned to Rowohlt or to Wolff. His reaction reveals his shy, fragile reservation. In its typically businesslike tone and sober style, the correspondence that followed stood in stark contrast to the very cordial and personal opening letter.

Among all the authors Kurt Wolff published, it was Franz Kafka who brought him his greatest reputation. To that extent it seems justifiable that Wolff is "appropriately credited elsewhere with discovering Kafka." The passage continues:

> As unequivocally as [Paul] Scheerbart, [Max] Dauthendey, [Herbert] Eulenberg, Carl Hauptmann and Gustav Meyrink were Ernst Rowohlt's authors, since he discovered them for the publishing house, so was Kurt Wolff justified in claiming Franz Kafka as *his* author, even if the attempt was made to list Kafka as a Rowohlt author.

Besides the fact that "discovery" and "care" were probably confused here (in the further course of this study the question is raised as to whether one can even talk of discovery after Brod's offer), the proposed view of Rowohlt's accomplishments on the one hand and those of Wolff on the other comes up short. For what good does it do an author to be discovered, if the publisher's care and supervision are withheld later on?[19] Another question must also be answered: Why did Kurt Wolff replace Ernst Rowohlt from this point on as Kafka's publisher?

3. Second Excursus: Rowohlt Publishing, the House of Kurt Wolff (1912-1913)

The End of the (First) Rowohlt Publishing

Kurt Wolff, whose capital investment with Ernst Rowohlt in the summer of 1910 affected him little, pursued the idea of a purely literary profession "with increasing joy," as he expressed it in a letter to Insel publisher Anton Kippenberg; this included his study of German language and literature and his review and editing activities.[20] He had his name entered in Kürschner's calendar of scholars in 1910 and prepared himself for a university career. During this phase of his collaboration with Rowohlt, Wolff had no intention of becoming a publisher.

To what extent Wolff took part in the day-to-day operations of the company during the first two years of its existence can be documented only sketchily. As the partner with more training in literary history, he ostensibly assumed responsibility for the selection and supervision of the successful Drugulin series and showed himself to be the advisor closely tied to the bibliophile tradition because of his interest in rare editions and in forgotten literature. The parallels to the program of Insel Publishing are quite obvious. However, the view of many book-trade histories, which presents Kurt Wolff in the role of program developer and Ernst Rowohlt in that of practitioner and administrator, must be contradicted. It is more plausible to assume that Rowohlt viewed Wolff primarily as a financial backer whom he tolerated as a publishing dilettante. Up until the summer of 1912 Wolff considered his publishing activity, which was founded on his early interest as a bibliophile and on classical literature, as a useful adjunct preparation for a future professorship. This profession was disproportionately more respected in the social circles in which Wolff moved.

While the publishing house steadily expanded its list of authors and gained attention among readers and critics, Wolff prepared to complete his degree. From 1911 on he worked intensely on a dissertation about the Swiss doctor and natural scientist Albrecht von Haller. His work, however, was rejected by the university in March 1912. From that point on it is quite obvious that Wolff developed a more serious interest in Rowohlt Publishing. The failure of his university career and a sense of being "unproductive"[21] in things literary marked the point of departure for a new motivation. From then on he turned more decisively to the operations of the publishing company, whose financial risk he ultimately bore. On September 1—only a few days before the first letter to Kafka—Wolff confirmed this step by formally and legally becoming a partner; with the renewed investment of a considerable sum of money, he became the branch manager of Rowohlt Publishing.[22]

The collaboration that followed between two such inherently different personalities from contrasting backgrounds quickly led to tensions. Probably the mere increased physical presence of a Kurt Wolff in the tiny offices (in which Rowohlt also resided) was cause in itself for uneasiness. It was inevitable that attempting to share responsibility in such an individual literary publishing house would in the end lead to considerable tensions, a fact not overlooked by contemporary observers. Rowohlt, who had probably also taken the "literary advice" (WV563) of his educated financial backer for diplomatic reasons, saw his original flexibility restricted. After Wolff sealed his participation legally, he—although technically only "branch manager"—incontestably held the strongest position in the company. The inner tensions between the two partners became so intolerable within a short time that after minor arguments and disagreements an outright fight developed just a few weeks later.[23]

The vehement escalation of the disagreement precluded any productive cooperation between the former partners; in the end they could only communicate with each other through a lawyer and by being separated physically. Wolff acted accordingly and released Rowohlt on November 2, 1912, with a cash settlement of 15,000 marks; feeling wronged, Rowohlt left "his" publishing house. All the books published by Rowohlt Publishing since its inception as well as the exclusive right to use the company's name for a considerable time thereafter were transferred to Kurt Wolff. It was a separation marked by one-sided hardheadedness, which was how the literary public also understood it.

The Establishment of Kurt Wolff Publishing

Assuming sole responsibility for the publishing house was certainly not Wolff's intention at that time. Most evidence indicates that the dispute with Rowohlt came rather inopportunely for Wolff.[24] Faced with the Christmas deadline, critical in the book trade and demanding exceedingly intensive work, he had to find an immediate replacement for the departed Rowohlt. A new business manager, Arthur Seiffhart, joined the company in December as technical director. The path for the literary program was already laid by the end of 1912. By virtue of its eagerness and openness to explore new ideas, the young firm became a magnet for young authors. At the time Rowohlt left his company, he had "assumed leadership for the publication of new litera-ture."[25] The fact that Kurt Wolff retained all the publishing rights had a definite effect on the relationships that had been forged. For it was precisely Ernst Rowohlt's last act as publisher, that of accepting the Prague circle of authors around Max Brod and Franz Werfel, which proved decisive for the house's activity during the following years.

Since Rowohlt had no immediate possibility of establishing a new house and accepted a position with S. Fischer in Berlin, the friends Walter Hasenclever and Kurt Pinthus remained with Wolff as valuable literary advisors and preserved a sense of continuity. However, with the initiation of talks between the publisher and the young Werfel, the decisive though totally unintended step by Wolff that determined his future publishing effectiveness and the literary development of his firm occurred. Since the appearance of *Der Weltfreund* contemporaries had been taking notice of Werfel. He became the standard for what the young literary generation viewed as the embodiment of expression and form in modern poetry. After the initial difficulties that Wolff had with Werfel's then still unpublished poems (which had previously led him to reject *Der Weltfreund*), he became "the poet par excellence" in Wolff's eyes a year later (WV610).

During the summer of 1912 Wolff explained in lengthy letters why he had rejected the Prague poet earlier and simultaneously made him an offer, which resulted in Werfel's finally agreeing to come to Leipzig in October. In consideration of the concerns Werfel's father had for the financial future of his underage son, a *pro forma* contract as editor-at-large was concluded. The contract guaranteed Werfel a salary independent of his literary productivity—a generous move for the young publishing company to take with regard to sponsorship, since the position did not obligate Werfel to perform any duties in the publishing house. Werfel's years in Leipzig, from the end of 1912 until the outbreak of World War I, were in fact marked by great artistic productivity. Simultaneously, however, and something no one anticipated, Werfel became the most influential and leading co-worker on the staff of the new publishing house at that time.

Wolff now became fascinated with Werfel's power of

expression. Their relationship, developing into one of friendly understanding, led the publisher during the first year of his sole proprietorship to direct and then to shape the whole profile of the newly established Kurt Wolff Publishing along the lines of Werfel's work and influence. Werfel, who had just turned twenty-two, became not only the premiere author of the house, but was also considered by the publisher to be his most important literary advisor, ahead of even Hasenclever and Pinthus.

Intensive collaboration with a chosen circle of thinkers and advisors was a prominent trademark of Wolff's publishing activities. From the very beginning he granted his associates considerable free rein for their own initiatives. In a German publishing landscape characterized by specialization and expansion at the beginning of the twentieth century, Wolff was a modern example of a well-advised publisher who, moreover, demonstrated his general openness and willingness to integrate divergent literary tendencies into his program. Wolff recognized the importance of a strong team of advisors and, as a curious aside, occasionally had more editors employed in the firm than technical staff. The break with Ernst Rowohlt did not lead to immediate changes in Wolff's program. The books they had planned during their partnership, including Kafka's and Brod's, were produced and also distributed under the signet of Rowohlt Publishing. But Wolff soon made it clear that he would probably take a new direction with future publications to express his individual tastes.[26] Franz Werfel was the person who steered the publisher's attention in a "new direction."

Der Jüngste Tag—The Book Series of a New Epoch

When Wolff decided to rename Rowohlt Publishing to Kurt Wolff Publishing effective February 15, 1913, the plans for a new series of books had already been laid. The series was to demonstrate in exemplary fashion the activities of Kurt Wolff Publishing and establish it as the publisher of the literary avant-garde. Werfel's position as the most important author and advisor was already evident at this point: the series that was to come to the fore as the publisher's prize undertaking was conceived and overseen by Werfel. He wrote the famous four-page publisher's prospectus with the programmatic announcement and justification for a new literature. Werfel's book appeared as the first volume in the new series, and a line from one of his poems became the title for the entire undertaking.

While Werfel was the prime author and essential developer of *Der Jüngste Tag*, the conception of this new undertaking as a series of inexpensive editions originated with Wolff. The tendency toward inexpensive books was a correctly calculated move on the publisher's part and was recognized accurately by him. Books that one could "put in one's pocket" had of course been around since the beginning of the sixteenth century. But the concept only became popular during the nineteenth century, when Carl Josef Meyer introduced his pioneering *Groschen-Bibliothek der Deutschen Classiker für alle Stände* ("Groschen Library of German Classics for the General Public"), and forty years later in 1867 Anton Philipp Reclam began to build up his *Universal-Bibliothek* ("Universal Library"), which he offered at the sensationally low price of twenty pfennigs per volume. Thereafter, more and more such undertakings of popular series appeared; however, they increasingly accepted less demanding popular literature and distanced themselves from Meyer's and Reclam's original idea of providing the highest literary quality at the lowest price. In 1912 there were at least 412 different series of literary books with a total of 21,357 titles.[27]

At the height of his publishing fame in 1911, Samuel Fischer wrote in the almanac for the twenty-fifth anniversary of the company that, based on his publishing experience, a large new audience for literary works could be tapped and that the masses for whom books were still a luxury today could be captured for the book market. This development moved in the direction of inexpensive books, which would assume a special position in the market. Fischer's move, however, went further: "Today it is the inexpensive book; but tomorrow the readers of these books can already move into the ranks of more demanding book buyers, because whoever starts bringing books into his house enters into the cultural class of book buyers."[28] Fischer's involvement with the "inexpensive book" (already in his own company) was labeled by Hans von Weber, whose *Zwiebelfisch* ("Onionfish") took up the subject of the "inexpensive book" in two numbers at the end of 1912, as the "great publishing act."[29]

In June 1912 Anton Kippenberg introduced the first twelve volumes of his *Insel-Bücherei* ("Insel Library"). With their remarkably low price of fifty pfennigs, these Insel books were a sensational and unequaled success; during the first year Insel Publishing produced nearly one million copies. Kurt Wolff was present when the plans to establish this series, in which Insel wanted to incorporate the idea of Goethe's "world literature," were discussed in January 1912 at Anton Kippenberg's (WV575).

Wolff's considerations leading up to the establishment of his book series are apparent. It conveys the image of a coherent whole, an intellectual profile in serial form. If the success of a discriminating title were to come about to a certain degree by chance in comparison with that of the non-discriminating book as a marketable article, the series would demonstrate strength and inner coherency, which would be an advertising advantage amid the general confusion of the increasingly clouded book market. In conceiving the series the publisher had the greatest opportunity within the entire firm of expressing his views and of finding and enhancing his line of thinking. In clear contrast to the programs of well-known publishers, Wolff saw himself strengthened through Franz Werfel in giving his own distinctive profile to the new firm at this moment by publishing works of a young literary generation. It was initially through the publication of this literary avant-garde that Wolff's firm became the famous enterprise of later years.

Kurt Wolff's new series was quite obviously conceived as a counterpoint to Kippenberg's Insel books. This fact is also established in the memoirs of Kurt Pinthus, in which he talks about the inauguration of the series:

> In early 1913 Wolff, Werfel, Hasenclever, and I sat together at a bar. We decided to begin a new series of small volumes of literature, each of which was to be written by a young and unknown author in contrast to the already flourishing Insel Library. What should it be called? On the table lay the corrected galleys of Werfel's new volume of poems "Wir sind." A pencil was stuck into it and the last line of the manuscript opened to page 116 began "O jüngster Tag!" Thus the representative series "Der jüngste Tag" developed for the emergent, upcoming literature. (RaII82)

While the high-volume titles of the Insel and Fischer Publishing series consisted almost exclusively of reprints of already "proven" texts by predominantly well-known authors, Kurt Wolff dared to till fresh publishing ground with his series. He extended Samuel Fischer's theoretically sketched principle of 1911, which Kippenberg brought to reality a year later, namely, the idea of publishing demanding literature in a "popular," inexpensive series of books, to the new publications of unknown authors for the first time. Only Alfred Richard Meyer had previously undertaken such a risky publishing venture; his

Lyrische Flügblatter ("Lyrical Pamphlets"), appearing since 1907, had only several pages and very limited circulation. This "first serial journal of expressionism"—Meyer did not plan a book series—stood out from the flood of journals inspired by the most modern of literature only by its monographic character, since each author was presented in an individual publication devoted entirely to him.

Kurt Wolff Publishing embraced this modern literature at precisely the moment when it was searching for a focal point. Amid the muddled market of literary journals the publisher could offer a central intellectual forum to this still diffuse movement: "Without becoming bogged down in the tangle of smothering journal articles, what our day has to offer in the way of powerful literature, regardless of its type, is to be presented here in worthy form."[30]

On May 2, 1913, the six titles of the first series were introduced in the *Börsenblatt für den Deutschen Buchhandel*, the German book trade journal; the library *Der Jüngste Tag* became incontestably the most significant undertaking in the history of Kurt Wolff Publishing. It formed its intellectual center and soon became "synonymous with the publisher's production" (WV576). As was the company's intent, the series actually became the unique forum of its day. Today it is regarded as the most unified and representative collection of literary expressionism.

4. *The Stoker*

The Failure of the Novel *America*

After completing *The Judgment*, Kafka felt relaxed in his relationship with Felice too. A correspondence ensued and increased steadily so that by October he was already writing her daily. He had a veritable "letter machine"[31] directed toward her; these were letters in and with which he attempted to get closer to her, letters in which he disclosed above all the contradictions of his own existence, and which simultaneously serve as analytical pre-studies of complex literary creation. These letters, in which he actually speaks only of himself and of his own problems with an unrelenting rigor, were the essential source of his writing and could provoke the necessary creative conditions.[32] The absence of return letters only intensifies this impression. Kafka developed an incredible creative desire with the letters to Felice (whom Kafka got to know as a writer): in November 1912 he described his writing as a "business which, incidentally, is highly voluptuous" (F58). Within only a few weeks Kafka brought himself to the height of literary mastery, and he himself recognized the value of what he had written.

In Felice's eyes Kafka was a writer, and the more intimate his letters to his lover became, the clearer this picture was to her and to him. His *Meditation*, the book which joined them secretly together after the evening of August 13, was received favorably, as the second letter indicates. But it contained the proviso: "But it is not very good; better things will have to be written. And with this verdict I bid you farewell" (F7). On September 25, eighteen days after the first book was accepted, and precisely on the day when his first publishing contract was returned signed, he finally began with the great task, a larger composition, on which he had unsuccessfully been attempting to work for some time. Kafka knew that his *Meditation* was so meager in size that it could only be effective in public as a forerunner of some longer work. With renewed self-confidence Kafka now attempted to bring this major work to fruition. He began the second draft of his America novel, which he labeled "The Man Who Disappeared" (F35). About it he wrote: "I want to spend every ounce of myself on my novel" (F35) and was determined "not to show my face until I had finished the novel" (F71-72).

Brod, who before his marriage remained in close contact with Kafka, understandably viewed this development with pleasure. His diary entries describe his friend's great productivity. September 29 reads: "Kafka in ecstasy, writing the whole night through. A novel set in America"; October 1: "Kafka in unbelievable ecstasy"; and October 2: "Kafka continues to be very much inspired. One chapter finished. I'm very happy about it" (FK113). Up until November 17 Kafka wrote almost uninterruptedly. Amazingly, he took pleasure in reading the completed chapters to his friends and did so frequently.[33] On November 17 he interrupted his work out of an inner need to begin a small story that he initially hoped to write down in one sitting as he had *The Judgment*. However, this "little story" began "quietly developing into a much bigger story" (F57-58) and occupied him fully for three weeks. Only during the night of December 6-7 did he put the finishing touch on the longest of his stories to date, *The Metamorphosis*. When he tried immediately "to return to the novel" (F89), he was not able to write "much" and found it "very mediocre" (F96). From then on the lament in his letters to Felice predominated; on December 17 he wrote: "what I wrote is pretty poor" (F109); on December 19: "there won't be any more writing" (F112); and on December 22: "I have not done any writing for far too long and feel somewhat cut off from it—i.e., in a void" (F119). Kafka did not again return to freely productive writing; *The Metamorphosis* had constricted the inspired flow of writing the novel.

Office deadlines and business trips had doomed his attempts to write continuously in the past. ". . . [T]he extent to which these cursed interruptions harm my work," he wrote to Felice at the beginning of December, "is very depressing" (F96). His aversion to the office took concrete form in this poor writing. Even the planned public reading of *The Judgment* was depressing him by this time. The interruption in his ability to write successfully undermined his self-confidence as a writer.

At exactly this point Kafka's first book, *Meditation*, appeared. On December 11 he sent the first, long-awaited copy of it to Felice, which Brod had written to her about so enthusiastically and which she probably anxiously anticipated as "her" writer's literary debut. They had not seen each other again since their first meeting; the physical separation, however, had been bridged by daily correspondence. In it Felice had surely experienced the alienating as well as the enticing elements of Kafka's writing and of his personal inner strife. Felice was surely shaken by her artist's high demands and lack of artistic compromise and became fearful at the accompanying storms of despair, thoughts of suicide, and the unconditional sacrifice of everything which signified life for her. Being otherwise accustomed to reading popular novels, she was obviously disillusioned by Kafka's slender book.

Kafka sent it to Felice with a note and a premonition: "Please be kind to my poor book! It consists of the very pages you saw me putting in order that evening" (F100). Two days later he wrote with confirmation: "I am so happy to think that my book [*Meditation*], no matter how much I find fault with it (only its brevity is perfect), is now in your possession" (F104). Kafka waited in vain for whatever reaction he may have expected from Felice. It is quite apparent that Felice made no mention of *Meditation* at that time in her letters. Two weeks later Kafka received a letter with an elusive, cryptic reference; disappointed he reacted: "Oh, if Frl. Lindner only knew how difficult it is to write as little as I do!" (F120). Fräulein Lindner was a coworker of Felice, who probably only read *Meditation* for the first time two years later.[34]

The wait for Felice's reaction, for her "judgment" about his book, crippled Kafka's continuing desire to write and turned him against writing and what he had written. Most of all he would like to "pick up all I have written of my novel and throw it out the window" (F104). Moreover, he discovered now that in his lover's letters more and more mention was being made of other writers about whom Felice thought she had to ask Kafka. Initially Kafka commented on the content of these letters with some indignation, that somebody like Werfel was capable of "miraculous" things but had entirely different, namely, "blissful" conditions for writing (F102), and that even someone like Eulenberg received a salary of over 12,000 marks a year from Rowohlt and therefore had sufficient time for writing. After waiting in vain for three weeks, Kafka unleashed a violent outburst of jealousy: "I am jealous of all the people in your letter," he attacked Felice, of the "business people and writers (writers above all, needless to say)" (F129). On the following day he stated bluntly: "By the way, now I know more precisely why yesterday's letter made me so jealous: You don't like my book [*Meditation*] any more than you liked my photograph" (F132). Kafka's defeat, the "sad evening's sad mood" (F138), shows through these lines. If Felice, who at least had some personal connection to his first work, did not acknowledge it, then who would? Resigned, he added to his letter to Felice: "no one will know what to make of it, that is and was perfectly clear to me" (F132).

Felice's indifference to and even rejection of *Meditation* brought Kafka to a state of utter helplessness. On top of this, he had had no contact with Rowohlt Publishing for over two months. The positive cycle of concrete hope (marriage and publication) and grandiose creative success, this divine circle, was broken and once again the vicious cycle of permanent doubt set in. His

writing had encouraged him for only a few months; now he stood
before the abyss again: "To have to atone for the joys of good
writing in this terrible way!" (F76). Now he could not even
accept his friends' approbation as meaningful. For quite some
time he did not want to hear from Brod and his other friends, for
they praised and lauded in the most enthusiastic way almost
everything that he wrote; their judgment—even their reviews of
his first book—he considered embarrassing: "valueless in their
exaggerated praise, valueless in their comments, and explicable
only as a sign of misguided friendship" (F194).

By retreating to the past, Kafka, in typical fashion, immediately questioned and retracted everything he had achieved: "The
edition came about by chance," he wrote in bitter consequence,
hiding his and Felice's disappointment; "I would never have
planned such a thing intentionally." If one believes his letter, then
the publication of his first book was a complete failure solely
because of Felice's silence. It was Brod alone who desired it and
Ernst Rowohlt who had assumed responsibility for everything.
Could his text really be so worthless, if two men so well versed
in literature had supported its publication? And perhaps with one
last hope for an objection from Felice, Kafka explained his book
again (in totally strategic interest):

> It really is full of hopeless confusion, or rather there are
> glimpses into endless perplexities, and one has to come very
> close to see anything at all. And so it would be quite under-
> standable if you did not like the book, but hope would remain
> that at some favorable and weak moment it might yet entice
> you. In any case, no one will know what to make of it, that is
> and was perfectly clear to me; the trouble the spendthrift
> publisher took and the money he lost, both utterly wasted,
> prey on my mind too . . . we belong—or so I thought—
> together; I may not like a favorite blouse of yours as such, but
> because you are wearing it, I will like it; you don't like my

book as such, but insofar as it is I who wrote it you will
surely like it—well, then one should say so, and say *both*.
(F132)

At the end of January 1913 work on *America* came to a
complete halt. Attempts to recapture his creative inspiration by
writing other stories failed. Up until July 1914, or precisely the
day the first engagement between Felice and Kafka broke off, he
wrote nothing. The most productive and creative period of his
life, and therefore the happiest, came to a close.

The Fragment *The Stoker* as Volume 3 in the Series *Der Jüngste Tag*

On October 19, 1912, as the typesetting for *Meditation*
began, contact with the publisher broke off; Kafka was not to
receive any further news for a long time. Rowohlt Publishing had
other concerns following Wolff's dispute with Rowohlt: preparation for the Christmas season, personnel reorganization, the
establishment of Kurt Wolff Publishing, and the planning of a
new series of books. *Meditation* appeared on time before the
advantageous Christmas deadline, but in response to his inquiry
on December 24, Max Brod learned from Arthur Seiffhart, the
new manager, that up to that time the publisher had not considered sending out review copies. This was something that was
otherwise taken for granted as advertising policy. When nothing
was done during January 1913 either, Brod had to compile a list
of reviewers himself.[35]

In February and then again at the beginning of March, it was
through Brod that Kafka received the first galley proofs from
Arkadia for which he thanked Wolff very cordially. At the latest
he must have found out about the split between Wolff and

Rowohlt in January 1913, for at that time Franz Werfel visited Prague for a month. Upon his departure Kafka wrote to Felice: "I like that young man better every day" (F161). Werfel's presence in Prague can also be established for February; he read some of his new poems to Kafka. Brod, Kafka's closest friend prior to this time, had withdrawn more and more from him since his marriage and was no longer as freely accessible to Kafka as before. Kafka sought new friends and found them temporarily in the bachelors Franz Werfel and Otto Pick. Significantly, almost every one of Kafka's close friends has a bibliography to his credit.

Closer association with Werfel naturally had consequences for Kafka's relationship with the publisher. Through the influence the young poet had in the meantime come to exert in Leipzig, Wolff first turned again to Kafka on March 20, 1913; as in the case of Karl Kraus, Werfel seems to have motivated the publisher with "urgency" and "conviction" to this three-line letter:[36] "Mr. Franz Werfel has told me so much about your new novella—The Bug?—that I would like to see it. Would you like to send it to me?" (WBr28). Kafka's reply was just as short, but, obviously pleased with Wolff's invitation, he spontaneously held out prospects for the manuscript: "Pay no attention to what Werfel tells you. He does not know a word of the story. As soon as I have a clean copy made, I will of course be glad to send it to you" (L95).

Apparently Werfel was not actually familiar with Kafka's story, for by December 23 Kafka had clearly mentioned the title in a letter to Felice: "It is called *Metamorphosis*" (F58). From Brod's diaries, however, we know that although he enjoyed reading the story, Kafka left his friends in the dark as to the title. Thus Brod had noted on November 11, 1912, that Kafka read his marvelous novella about a *vermin* at Oskar Baum's (the first part of the story), and a few days after completing the story Kafka read the whole *bug tale* on December 15; again on March 1, 1913, when Kafka reread *The Metamorphosis* at Baum's, Brod mentions the *insect story*.[37] It is therefore totally plausible that Kafka had read the story to Werfel in Prague and had jokingly christened it "The Bug." From this perspective and in light of Werfel's prominent position as new advisor to Kurt Wolff, Kafka's desire to publish seems to be quite strong at this time.

In February Kafka decided to travel to Berlin for the Easter vacation in order to alter decisively the course of his faltering relationship with Felice. He feared having to put an end to it: "I am going to Berlin for no other reason than to tell and show you—you who have been misled by my letters—who I really am" (F226). This first meeting in over seven months remained in doubt up to the last day. "Still undecided" (F228), he wrote to Felice on March 22; when he arrived in Berlin the following day, Felice had long since given up on his coming. Left unprepared, she could only meet him for a few short moments. However, she made full use of the time: she freed Kafka from all doubt and gave him new hope for the future of their relationship. Happy about this unexpected pleasant development, Kafka let Otto Pick introduce him to the literary figures of this lively metropolis. Kafka had traveled together with Pick to Berlin, who "knows, and is going to see, half the Berlin literary world" (F227). These events transpired in complete contrast to his original intent; wanting to keep his distance from everything in Berlin, he was now interested in its environment, and even curious to get to know a few literary colleagues after the meeting with Felice.

Here again regularity enters into Kafka's writing and publishing: not actively writing at the time, he sought proximity to Felice as well as publication. The postcard on which Kafka cheerfully and unreservedly promised to send the publisher *The*

Metamorphosis immediately is significant. He wrote the card on that very afternoon in Berlin, when he, together with Pick, met with the Berlin authors. "Best wishes from the full assembly of your fellow authors" reads the heading in Pick's handwriting; it was signed by Albert and Carl Ehrenstein, Paul Zech, and Abigail Basileus III (Else Lasker-Schüler), among others. This promise of the longest of his texts by far was the positive message Kafka sent to his publisher. Although approaching many of those present was comparatively problematic, Kafka now felt like one of Kurt Wolff's authors in this community.

The crowning moment of his stay in Berlin was the agreement to have a newspaper printing from *Meditation*; on March 31, 1913, three pieces appeared in the *Deutsche Montags-Zeitung* with the heading: "From the Marvelous Sketchbook of a New Author."[38] This publication was agreed to on the afternoon of March 24 in Berlin, presumably as the assembled literary circle considered how Kafka's first book could be promoted among the public. Kafka's self-confidence as a writer grew incrementally within a day; now he possessed that certain power of responsibility, which was a precondition for his texts and without which he had no desire to publish anything.

At the end of this trip Kafka may also have met his publisher. Kafka and Pick apparently made a stop in Leipzig on the way back to Prague; there were reasons for the stop: Kafka's friend Jizchak Löwy, an actor from Prague was performing there, and Franz Werfel was working there. Nothing indicates that a meeting between Wolff and Kafka had been discussed in any way whatsoever—it would have been the second and the next to last; the few clues merely hint at a casual, accidental meeting, perhaps in the publishing house, as Kafka and Pick were looking for Werfel. That such a meeting could have taken place can be deduced from a letter at this time from Wolff to Kafka, which concludes apologetically: "Hopefully we'll see each other again soon and under more favorable circumstances than recently in Leipzig."[39]

Kafka himself never mentioned a word about such a meeting. However, with a feeling of renewed self-confidence, he could have told Wolff of his writing, especially of the novel he had abandoned, since "of the entire book only the first chapter stems from an inner truth" and "out of some 400 large pages only 56 . . . remain" (F218). Only a few days thereafter the publisher asked him "very cordially and very urgently" to submit this "first chapter of your novel, which both you and Dr. Brod think might well be published individually." In this regard it is also important to recognize that the publisher did not ask Kafka to submit the entire novel but was only concerned with a short text. In an equally friendly but urgent way Wolff repeated his wish to see the manuscript—or even a handwritten copy—of the "bug story"; he would consider it a special courtesy, if Kafka would send him both texts as soon as possible (WBr29).

Scarcely had the decision about a new series of books been made in February and March at Kurt Wolff Publishing when the first series of the *Der Jüngste Tag* was to be introduced to the public. On March 28 Wolff wrote to Franz Blei: "I hope to bring out the first six little volumes in April" (WBr74). Before embarking on a two-month vacation abroad, the publisher wished to have the first six titles in print. But besides the somewhat imprecise beginning at establishing a forum for new, expressionistic literature with this series of books, there was no program until the end of March. The only authors who had been decided upon to that point were the publisher's editors Franz Werfel (Volume 1) and Walter Hasenclever (at his own wish, Volume 2). No decision had been made regarding the acceptance of other titles. Many authors reacted indignantly to the publisher's suggestions that original publications appear initially in an inexpensive series. The rush and urgency with which Wolff requested Kafka's manuscripts on April 2 is therefore also related to the difficult situation in which he found himself.[40]

Wolff's account from 1962, which maintains that he already had a close relationship with Kafka at this time, is therefore questionable:

> In May 1913 Kurt Wolff Publishing began issuing a new series. It was important to me that a contribution by Kafka be among the first publications of the series to appear under the title *Der Jüngste Tag*. I asked for and Kafka suggested the first chapter of a novel that he never wanted to publish, as an independent story; it was *The Stoker*, the first chapter of the novel *America*. I asked—apparently very urgently—for the manuscript. (Wo72)

Such an account has naturally fostered the image of a fortuitous relationship between Kafka and the publisher. Wolff's statement has to be contradicted here: there was no original intent to include a work by Franz Kafka in the initial publications of Kurt Wolff Publishing's famous avant-garde series.

Since Wolff planned to travel abroad shortly, Kafka, upon receiving the publisher's letter, felt it was impossible to "get the manuscripts to you by Sunday even with the best will in the world." But the urgency of the request moved Kafka to respond to the cordial letter. He in fact sent the first chapter of the abandoned novel by return mail and promised to forward *The Metamorphosis* as soon as the copy was ready. However, he did this with his customary, rhetorical reservation: "To be sure, I cannot see in what way or what sense these manuscripts could be a favor to you, but for that reason I ought to send them all the more readily." Kafka was obviously surprised and moved by the unconditional nature of Wolff's request. He responded positively to Wolff's serious offer as well as to the publisher himself, whom he now wrote and addressed by name. A clear parallel to his relationship with Rowohlt was evident. And although Kafka questioned whether *The Stoker* was suitable for publication as a fragment, he convinced the publisher in the same sentence of the opposite: "It is a fragment and will stay that way; this prospect gives the chapter what coherence it has." The fact that Kafka was quite sure his manuscript would be accepted at that time is revealed in the suggestion he made at the end of the letter: "Perhaps later on these two pieces and the 'Judgment' from *Arkadia* will make up quite a decent book whose title might be *The Sons*" (L96).

The publisher responded to Kafka's renewed pessimism as the author had hoped. "I have to contradict you heartily," Wolff wrote back, "it seems well-rounded and attractive to me and I would like to publish it in *Der Jüngste Tag*" (WBr30). With the rather meager one-time honorarium of 100 kronen for the edition, Kafka was "fully and happily in accord"; at this early phase in his collaboration with the publisher he was never interested in financial matters. The publisher, however, did not respond to the *suggestion* of a collection. Kafka continued in clear-cut fashion: "I have only one request, which I have already mentioned in my last letter." And then he formulated his page-long conditions for publishing *The Stoker* in *Der Jüngste Tag*: "You see, I am just as much concerned about the unity of the three stories (i.e., *The Stoker*, *The Metamorphosis*, and *The Judgment*) as I am about the unity of any one of them" (L96-97).[41] Kafka abandoned his otherwise respectful reserve so that the publisher would not miss the perhaps somewhat hidden reference. But he soon returned to his friendly negotiating tone, when he received Wolff's binding explanation from Paris (WBr31) and responded: "I was already beginning to fear that I was asking too much and here you have so kindly granted all I asked without even considering whether my request made sense. My warmest thanks" (L97).

After the failure of his novel, which was supposed to be the major independent publication with which he could satisfy the promise made at the time of the publication of *Meditation*, Kafka now wished to pursue the collected volume. In it he saw the simultaneous possibility of publishing his *Metamorphosis* and especially *The Judgment*, which meant so much to him because of its inner connection to Felice but which was overlooked in *Arkadia* because of the other contributions by mostly better known authors. But he considered a separate publication of the latter story impossible in light of the first printing in Brod's *Arkadia* (which had not yet appeared).

An essential detail is that Kafka immediately forwarded Wolff's letter urgently requesting submission of *The Stoker* and *The Metamorphosis* to Felice. Elias Canetti makes special note of this: "It had the effect of rekindling his hope of being regarded by her as a writer."[42] With reserved pride Kafka thereby pointed to his close relationship with his publisher: "By the enclosed letter, you can see what a charming publisher I have. He is a very beautiful man of about 25, to whom God has given a beautiful wife, several million marks, the inclination to be a publisher, and a certain aptitude for the publishing business" (F237).

Werfel, who had taken over the business in Wolff's absence, hastily printed *The Stoker* in mid-April as the third volume of *Der Jüngste Tag*. A number of minor typographical errors caused Kafka to demand a corrected version, and he repeated his express wish for the subtitle "*A Fragment*" (L97). Although Werfel introduced the first volume of the new series in the *Börsenblatt* on May 2, it was not delivered until the end of May; only on May 24 or 25 did Kafka receive the twenty copies stipulated in the contract.[43] Kafka was "at first alarmed" by the illustration the publisher included without his knowledge, for the picture, a steel engraving from the mid-nineteenth century "refuted" him on the frontispiece, since he "had presented the most up-to-date New York." But he considered the picture an enhancement for his book (Wolff hastened to inform him that it was Werfel and not he who had come up with the idea). With polite irony he noted that in this way "strengths and weaknesses" had been exchanged between book and picture and that he was "glad" about the unexpected illustration, for he himself would certainly not have approved it (L98).

The writer took a consciously appreciative and receptive tack not only with regard to the illustration but also in general. Thus he wrote that *Der Jüngste Tag* seemed to him—although he naturally could not judge it commercially—"in and of itself . . . splendid." If one compares this judgment with a later one about the printing of *The Stoker*, Kafka's cordial attitude toward the publisher is clear.[44] And as to the programmatic line of *Der Jüngste Tag*, Kafka dared a negative comment only to Felice: "It [*The Stoker*] will appear in an inexpensive series which Wolff is publishing and which will be given the somewhat ludicrous title 'The Day of Judgment,' 80 pfennigs each volume. I rather dislike the whole idea, as I do any useless contrivance of a unity that isn't really there." Then at the end of the same letter Kafka tried to give a reason for making *The Stoker* available in this series: "But first of all I am indebted to Wolff, secondly he practically wormed the story out of me, and thirdly he was kind enough to guarantee to publish 'The Stoker' later on, together with your story and another in one larger volume" (F250).

5. *The Metamorphosis*

In July 1913 Kurt Wolff sent greetings and a message to Kafka via Max Brod that everything was "[g]oing well with the Stoker,"[45] but the publisher did not mention again the other story, *The Metamorphosis*, which he had requested prior to *The Stoker*. Moreover, the correspondence between Wolff and Kafka had broken off entirely, just as it had after the typesetting of *Meditation* began. It would be two years before the publisher would contact Kafka again.

Kurt Wolff's almanac, *Das bunte Buch* ("The Colorful Book"), which first appeared in October 1913, included a text by Kafka, who had already prepared two books for the publisher. Kafka received his author's copy of the complete 64-page catalogue of over 180 titles, which included excerpts from the authors. The low-cost edition (206 pages for .60 marks) became the publisher's first real success. The first edition of 10,000 copies sold out quickly and the demand was so great that the title was reprinted just a few months later. Kafka's prose piece *Reflections for Gentlemen-Jockeys* from *Meditation* had been selected;[46] to lend support the first review by Brod was printed with it. The review was so "exaggerated" in its praise that Kafka wrote to Felice upon its appearance: "This afternoon I could have done with a hole to disappear into"[47] (F194). Several excerpts from Albert Ehrenstein's equally positive review of *Meditation* were printed as well.

Die neue Rundschau and S. Fischer Publishing

Kafka was still awaiting a letter from Kurt Wolff that would finally make good on his promise and request *The Metamorphosis* for the collected volume, when he received a letter from Robert

Musil in February 1914. In it Musil asked the author to submit a contribution to *Die neue Rundschau,* which spawned a brief, hope-filled period that, nevertheless, ended all the same in failure for Kafka.

Musil, who had attempted in vain to establish himself as a writer in Berlin after completing his dissertation there, was forced to return to Vienna, where he unhappily accepted a modest position as a librarian. From that moment on he sought a publisher who might free him from his pitiable official position by providing a monthly salary so that he would be able to write his great novel. Blei, Musil's friend and literary promoter, told Wolff in April 1913 that Musil was working on a marvelous novel and was seeking a publisher for it (WBr75f.). Werfel, with whom the publisher then consulted, was delighted at the proposal: "of course you should take on Musil," he wrote back, "in my opinion, no matter what it takes" (WV612). But Wolff couldn't make up his mind about the author, even after a meeting with him in December 1913.

However, Robert Musil found a place with Samuel Fischer in Berlin. Fischer, the "Cotta of Naturalism," as he had been called for some time, had reason to be concerned about the literary future of his once revolutionary house when he observed how quickly the young Kurt Wolff Publishing Company became a focal point for the literary avant-garde.[48] In Musil Fischer saw the person who could pave the way for joining the publisher to the intellectual movement of the modern generation. Of his own accord Musil had already proposed that the publisher create a distinct new forum for the young generation of writers within the old *Rundschau* by organizing a literary supplement. This journal, once so radically and polemically linked to the naturalistic movement, had become obsolete over the decades, despite the continuing high niveau of the contributions, and was therefore unacceptable to a young generation of writers. Along with Oskar Bie (managing editor since 1894), Musil was summoned by the publisher for the express purpose of bringing new blood to the editorial staff of *Die neue Rundschau*. Fischer's decision proved to be well-founded; a letter from his first editor and literary *alter ego*, Moritz Heimann, reads: "Musil is a winner in any case because he keeps Bie on the move." Just prior to that, in January 1913, Heimann had written to Fischer: "*Mr. Musil is without doubt a man of unusual qualities*: educated, knowledgeable, of deep and strong intelligence, highly talented, and also smart and straightforward in a social sense."[49]

During the very first month of his employment with Fischer, Musil invited Kafka to work on *Die neue Rundschau*. This interesting detail indicates to what extent publishers in the literary industry are dependent on even minor personnel changes. Whether it was Musil's affinity for Kafka, who in his quiet and restrained manner remained an exception within the expressionistic movement (Musil's diaries reveal a certain conservative point of view—similar to Kafka's—to the literature of the day and reject all collective stylistic classifications), or whether Franz Blei, who knew Kafka and Musil well, promoted Kafka, cannot be determined from the available sources. At the very least, Musil had asked Brod for Kafka's address.[50]

Kafka had been familiar with *Die neue Rundschau* since 1903 when he became an avid reader. Up to this point the journal had a greater literary impact on him than books, and he most likely considered it the leading literary journal in the German-speaking world. However, he himself never would have dared to offer a contribution to this journal; moreover, the noble *Neue Rundschau* expressly refused unsolicited submissions. Thus the honor of being solicited by the *Die neue Rundschau* pleased Kafka immensely. It simultaneously troubled him, for "I have nothing," as he wrote in his diary on February 23, 1914 (DII22). The only complete story not yet published was *The Metamorphosis*, which he felt obligated to send to Kurt Wolff. He recalled Wolff's promise to publish *The Metamorphosis* together with *The Judgment* and *The Stoker* in book format. Although the publisher never mentioned it again, this promise obviously was still binding in Kafka's eyes.[51] Not wanting to jeopardize the volume of novellas, Kafka refused Musil's request.

But, as later statements indicate, the author placed great importance not only on *Die neue Rundschau* but also on a speedy publication of *The Metamorphosis*.[52] He wanted his work to be published. At the end of February he had made a surprise visit to Berlin. After the short trip he summed up: "The result of all this was as follows: F. [Felice] quite likes me, but in her opinion this is not enough for marriage, for this particular marriage" (F353); what he meant was a marriage that also included writing. His relationship to Felice had once again "quite definitely reached a dead end" (F373). Kafka knew he had to make a decision. He urgently planned to give up his post and leave Prague in order to "get my foot in on the lowest rung of journalism" in Berlin "without much ambition in that direction" (F373).

Within this career plan, ties to a literary institution such as *Die neue Rundschau* was of course a special opportunity. How better to establish himself in the literary life of Berlin than to publish something there? Furthermore, it seems that Musil had prepared a more comprehensive offer for Kafka than just the printing of a single text. It is conceivable that he offered Kafka a publishing contract with S. Fischer. Kafka's pangs of conscience were great: on the one hand he felt obligated to Wolff (possibly even contractually), on the other, Musil's offer in March 1914 was exactly what he was looking for: "a minor job with some financial support in Berlin" (F373). Kafka decided against Wolff; probably still during March 1914 he forwarded the manuscript of *The Metamorphosis* to *Die neue Rundschau* in Berlin.

The Metamorphosis was accepted, but Kafka had to wait impatiently for over a month for the news. On April 18, 1914, he wrote with obvious relief to Grete Bloch, a friend of Felice:

> I haven't written anything for a year, nor can I, as far as I know. Yet in the last few days I had a stroke of luck . . . : a story, actually my longest, but also my only story (written a year ago) has been accepted by the *Neue Rundschau*, moreover with some further pleasing offers. (F390)

Did Kafka entertain the hope or even the reasonable prospect that Samuel Fischer (with his "other most generous offers") would now somehow replace Kurt Wolff? An embarrassing turn of events unfolded. Around July—it took this long before Kafka received a definitive decision from the editors—Musil communicated to him with regret that the publication of *The Metamorphosis* could only proceed if the text were revised. Musil requested that it be shortened. Indignant, Kafka appealed to Musil and cited the fact that the editors had accepted his *The Metamorphosis* without stipulation. Obviously infuriated, he added:

> And now that months have passed after this acceptance I am being asked to shorten the story by one-third. This is undignified conduct. To tell the truth, dear Herr Doktor, for I know you will admit that I am completely right, if this request had been made to me at the beginning, before the acceptance, you and I would have been spared the present embarrassment. But I would not have shortened the story then any more than I would today. I am sure you will also approve of this stand—there is no other possible course. (L109)[53]

Although Kafka offered *Die neue Rundschau* two possible solutions[54] to the situation, the sensitive author perceived a veiled rejection by S. Fischer Publishing behind this unacceptable proposal to reduce the work, despite his high regard for and inclination toward this journal. As can be determined from his letter to Musil, either Bie or Musil must have requested the changes. Offended, he criticized "this disguised yet clear rejection" in the postscript (L109).

The printing of *The Metamorphosis* in *Die neue Rundschau* did not materialize. Kafka apparently had to totally abandon hope, when Musil—his spokesman with Samuel Fischer—was called back to Vienna after the outbreak of World War I. Yet Kafka's attempt to separate himself at an early stage from his publisher Kurt Wolff in order to establish himself in the publishing world must be emphasized. The failure to emancipate himself and the embarrassment he had to endure were discouraging. Was Kafka merely testing the waters to see what value his name had on the open writers' market and what advantages an eventual change of publishers could have for him? He had tried on his own initiative and failed. Must he not have been convinced that everything he had previously achieved had transpired through the dealings of persons known to him and was therefore pure protectionism? For a year he did not venture to present a single text to the public.

The First Printing in *Die Weißen Blätter*

Fischer had every reason to perceive Kurt Wolff Publishing as a direct competitor and serious threat to the literary future of his house. In September 1913 the publishing house Verlag der weißen Bücher presented the long announced first edition of its new journal *Die Weißen Blätter*. Its title ("The White Pages") was supposed to suggest an unconditional new beginning (approximately in the way Werfel had proclaimed a similar program a few months earlier for *Der Jüngste Tag*). *Die Weißen Blätter* embarked on a forceful, harsh criticism of the older generation of naturalists and judged polemically their literary methods of portraying societal reality. It attacked the archenemy Thomas Mann and the ridiculous Hauptmann[55] and unabashedly viewed itself as the modern counterpart to S. Fischer's journal. In open confrontation the publisher vociferously announced its program: "*Die Weißen Blätter* shall be the organ of the younger generation of writers, just as *Die neue Rundschau* was for the older generation."[56] A disquieting sentence for Samuel Fischer, whose regular authors now were drawn to *Die Weißen Blätter* so as not to be criticized in public as being part of the scrap heap of literature.

The connection of *Die Weißen Blätter* to Kurt Wolff Publishing was a closely knit one, even though it actually appeared in the Verlag der weißen Bücher. Ernst Rowohlt, upon the founding of his house, had planned to edit a literary journal to publish authors who were contractually bound to other houses. From the very beginning Rowohlt's authors, first Georg Heym, then Kurt Hiller, and especially Franz Blei, had made suggestions to the publisher in this vein. But all attempts to start up his own journal had long since failed (as had the mutual project *Fahnenmasten* ["Flagstaff"] of Wolff and Rowohlt at the end of 1912). *Der lose Vogel* ("The Loose Bird"), edited by Franz Blei, remained a temporary phenomenon and ceased printing in March 1913 after twelve numbers (six with Wolff). The impossibility of making a publisher's journal out of *Arkadia* had motivated Wolff to undertake the radically critical semimonthly *Pan II* at the beginning of 1913. But the publisher dropped this plan just as quickly as he did the one proposed in 1913 by Kurt Tucholsky for a similar undertaking (*Orion—Ein Jahreskreis in Briefen*

["Orion—A Year in Letters"]); Tucholsky's intent (Kafka, by the way, was on the list of projected collaborators),[57] through which Kurt Wolff was to become Rainer Maria Rilke's publisher, was abandoned the moment Rilke retracted his initial consent out of loyalty toward Anton Kippenberg.

Also in 1913 Franz Blei brought a young man, Erik Ernst Schwabach, to Kurt Wolff. Schwabach, a twenty-two-year-old Croesus and millionaire, had gained a name for himself as a patron; he owned the Verlag der weißen Bücher and endowed the Fontane Prize for the best modern prose writer. At the time he was looking for the organizational and technical support of an experienced publisher for the literary journal he planned. With a capital investment of 300,000 marks in Kurt Wolff Publishing, he ensured the approval of the publisher, who assumed no editing responsibilities. Blei himself, who maneuvered Schwabach from Axel Juncker to Wolff, skillfully guaranteed himself the position of chief editor, which was originally intended for Otto Flake. Thus *Die Weißen Blätter* began ostensibly as an undertaking of Schwabach and the Verlag der weißen Bücher; however, through the collaboration of Blei and the publishing assistance of Kurt Wolff Publishing, it became his first actual journal. The literary contributions this journal accepted during the following years mirrored Wolff Publishing's production. Gradually Schwabach turned over the direction of the publishing aspects and then of the editing to Kurt Wolff; in matters regarding *Die Weißen Blätter* the authors soon turned directly to Wolff.

This interweaving of *Die Weißen Blätter*, with Schwabach as sole financial backer, and Wolff's publishing program was used advantageously in Leipzig. *Die Weißen Blätter* became the pre-printing organ of Kurt Wolff Publishing, and most of the texts appeared shortly thereafter in *Der Jüngste Tag*. Wolff's series of avant-garde literature could therefore be kept reasonable in price, because the book editions were produced in part with the same typesetting used for *Die Weißen Blätter*.[58] On this basis *Die Weißen Blätter*, along with Herwarth Walden's *Sturm* and Franz Pfempfert's *Aktion*, became one of the most important and encompassing publishing organs of literary expressionism. Under René Schickele, whom Blei replaced as editor after the war began, the journal developed into the leading organ of the expressionistic antiwar movement and supranational pacifist literary center.

In early 1915 Kafka sent Brod the manuscript of *The Metamorphosis*. With little hope that *Die neue Rundschau* would reconsider its original intent to publish the work, Kafka asked his friend to intercede in some other way for the printing of the story. In the enclosed letter Kafka himself made a suggestion: "Now that Blei is no longer with *Die Weißen Blätter*, I wonder if we couldn't try to have the story appear there. I wouldn't care when the story came out, next year or the year after that" (L111).

Kafka had thus discovered that René Schickele had taken Franz Blei's position in January 1915. He did not indicate that because Schickele was now the editor his story would have a chance for publication, but he intimated why no prior chance for publication had existed: the obstacle had been the editor Franz Blei. An apparently totally surprising circumstance, if one recalls *Hyperion* and Blei's efforts on behalf of Kafka's work and believes furthermore—as can safely be assumed—that they were on good personal terms.

But what had happened? A direct consequence of the sudden outbreak of war was its crippling impact on the whole economy. In one fell swoop the normal routine in the German publishing and book trade was disrupted, and the literary publishers noted an abrupt decline in orders and production. Schwabach and Blei, as well as Wolff, were drafted right at the start of the war. The journal, which had begun just a year before with Blei's powerful programmatic article on the nature of the new literature, had to cease production with the delivery of the July/August number. Schwabach, recently deferred from military service, was already considering continuing his journal in September 1914; naturally the plan met with the complete support of Kurt Wolff Publishing. The general crisis, at least psychologically, worked its way to the editorial staff of *Die Weißen Blätter*. As mentioned in a letter by Georg Heinrich Meyer, who in the interim during Kurt Wolff's absence directed the publisher's business, Blei was jeopardizing the journal's future by his influence on Schwabach. Blei had advised Schwabach that in light of the unusual circumstances he should drop *belles lettres* entirely for the second volume of the journal, "because people will only read it now at best in the dentist's waiting room." Although Meyer and Hasenclever immediately objected, Schwabach became tentative. Of his prestigious work he was only able to sell 500 of the 3000 copies printed; in addition, Blei made it clear to him that nothing would be accomplished in *belles lettres* now, and even less than before the war.[59]

Franz Blei, who only a few years prior was the prime literary mover, was not able to establish a bond to the modern expressionistic movement and now hindered the development of this new literature in his role as chief editor of *Die Weißen Blätter*.[60] Without Blei's knowledge, Meyer found a new man, the Alsatian writer René Schickele, who was committed to this literature and who took over the editorship in November 1914. His first letter to Meyer regarding *Die Weißen Blätter* already reveals his powerful entrance: "*Die Weißen Blätter*, which will resume publication again in January, must position itself at the pinnacle of the movement that will determine the character of the times . . .

Fischer is finished; Schwabach can replace him" (WBr198). Hasenclever wished Schwabach luck on his "decision" to begin publishing the *Die Weißen Blätter* again and, as he diplomatically added, "without Blei's hypodermic syringes, therefore hopefully with more aggressiveness and self-confidence."[61]

Kafka thought it possible to have his story printed in *Die Weißen Blätter* for a technical reason as well: the outstanding characteristic of this journal was—and after his experiences with *Die neue Rundschau* Kafka was doubtless cognizant of the advantage—that because of the larger format of the volumes, one could publish dramas and even unedited entire novels. Brod himself strove to have a pre-printing of his large new novel right after Schickele took over the editorship; beginning in February 1915 his *Tycho Brahe* appeared in serial form in the *Die Weißen Blätter* (with the dedication: "To my friend Franz Kafka").

During March 1915 Brod must have forwarded the manuscript of *The Metamorphosis* to Schickele. The new editor reacted promptly to the submission, but, instead of the enthusiastic approval he desired, Kafka confronted the same reservations from this editor as from the prior one. In principle the publisher was prepared to accept the story, but its length was problematic, and Schickele stated that in general he wanted to avoid serials. Once again Kafka suffered a clear setback in contrast to Brod, whose four-hundred-page novel had just appeared in serial form in *Die Weißen Blätter*. Kafka attempted to change Schickele's mind. In his reply of April 7, 1915, he put forth the idea that he was more interested in *The Metamorphosis*'s eventual publication than in a speedy one. "If I nevertheless do not withdraw it of my own accord," he continued forcefully, "my reason is solely *that I am especially eager to see it published*" (L112).[62]

There is no record of a reply from Schickele, nor is there any evidence from other sources to conclude that further contact took place between Schickele and Kafka. Political factors might have played a role here as well, because censorship on political and literary journals in the German Empire had intensified considerably since the outbreak of the war, and because Schickele had decided to go into exile in Switzerland. Whether Max Brod corresponded directly with Schickele during this time (in other studies the suspicion has been expressed that the negotiations leading up to the first printing of *The Metamorphosis* were handled by Brod) is not clear but probably can be discounted, for already in May 1915 Brod had to protest the corrections to his novel appearing in *Die Weißen Blätter* (WBr170). The manuscript of Kafka's *The Metamorphosis* was still with Schickele. Kafka now had to wait in 1915—as in 1913 with Wolff and in 1914 with Musil—for news from Schickele as to whether he would print the story or not.

The Fontane Prize of 1915

From a letter by then director Georg Heinrich Meyer to Kafka on October 11, 1915 (the first letter of Kurt Wolff Publishing to its author after a two-year hiatus),[63] we know that *The Metamorphosis* was accepted for *Die Weißen Blätter*; moreover, in the same mailing Kafka already received his author's copies. Almost hurriedly, so it seems, Kafka's largest work to date appeared in the October number of the journal.[64] Kafka, who placed the greatest importance on the receipt of all corrections for every one of his texts, had seen neither galleys nor page-proofs in advance; he must have been annoyed that this first printing contained errors.

In the same correspondence Meyer suggested to Kafka that his story appear immediately as a single number in *Der Jüngste Tag*: "The small volume could be printed immediately and appear by next month" (WBr34). Meyer lost no time; even before Kafka could have had a chance to agree, he already received the "first signature of the proofs" (L114), i.e., the completed proofs of the book. Kafka commented acridly on Meyer's proposal. In his response of October 15 he maintained that the publisher's questions were actually not questions at all, since *The Metamorphosis* was already being set (L112).

Since 1913, when Kurt Wolff had requested the manuscripts of Kafka's *The Stoker* and *The Metamorphosis*, the publisher had not approached Kafka with any other requests. Why now in October 1915 the publisher suddenly turned again to Kafka, Meyer explained openly and quite candidly: "That a book of yours appear is desirable for the following reason: It is time to decide the Fontane Prize for the best modern writer." But it was not Kafka, but Carl Sternheim—as Meyer had found out confidentially—who had been promised the prize. And with a sympathetic, yet entirely unsatisfactory argument in Kafka's eyes, Meyer added:

> Since, as you well know, Sternheim is a millionaire and one cannot very well give a millionaire a monetary prize, Franz Blei, who is responsible for awarding the Fontane Prize this year, has arranged with Sternheim that the entire sum of, I believe, 800 marks will be given to you as the most deserving recipient. Sternheim has read your things [*sic*] and is quite enthusiastic about you, as you can see from the enclosed card. (WBr34)

Kafka, as Meyer continued, was now the lucky person, for he was not only receiving the honorarium from *Die Weißen Blätter* but also the honorarium of 350 marks from *Der Jüngste Tag* (the highest amount ever paid by *Der Jüngste Tag*), and finally 800 marks as the amount for the Fontane Prize. Good news couched in such terms evaded Kafka entirely: Meyer neglected to mention even a word about the literary honor attached to awarding the money to Kafka as a writer or Sternheim's and Blei's assessment of its quality. No, Kafka was fortunate only because he could expect to receive such a large sum of money.

The Fontane Prize for the best modern writer, initiated in February 1913 by Otto Flake (the endowment was funded once more by Erik Ernst Schwabach),[65] was first awarded by the *Schutzverband deutscher Schriftsteller* ("Society of German Writers"). Previous prizewinners had been Annette Kolb and Leonhard Frank. As the sole juror for 1915, Franz Blei determined already in September of that year that his friend Carl Sternheim should receive the award. (Regarding the relationship between Blei and Sternheim, Musil noted in his diaries: "Sternheim is not only a discovery, but also an education project of Blei.")[66] Sternheim was awarded the prize for his recent novellas in Wolff's *Der Jüngste Tag*: *Busekow* (1914), *Napoleon* (1915), and *Schuhlin* (1916, printed in October 1915). Simultaneously Franz Blei came up with the idea that Sternheim should share the prize and the sum attached to it and therefore a part of the honor as a sign of his esteem for Franz Kafka.

The awarding of the prize could very obviously be traced back to Kurt Wolff Publishing's advertising strategy. The war had begun to become a normal condition and the book market recovered amidst a flood of patriotic war literature. Reports of first-hand experiences at the front became sales successes. With the marketing genius Georg Heinrich Meyer at the helm, Kurt Wolff Publishing profited from this upswing in the German book market. *Der Jüngste Tag* remained the biggest problem child of the house; the extremely modest sales—not even the typical original run of 1000-2000 copies for the first edition[67] found buyers—stood in stark counterpoint to the uncontested high quality of the individual titles and the prestige of the series among the literary public. A glance at comparable contemporary undertakings shows that the titles in Fischer's *Romanbibliothek* ("Novel Library") had first runs of between 15,000 and 30,000 copies by 1909; Anton Kippenberg could count on first editions of at least 10,000 copies in his *Insel-Bücherei*; and the first edition of the legendary Ullstein Books established a starry figure of approximately 50,000-60,000 copies. In comparison with these series of books, the sales figures for *Der Jüngste Tag* fared quite miserably. *Der Jüngste Tag* had previously reached an extremely small readership, which was characteristic of the slow pace with which literary expressionism expanded.

But in Carl Sternheim, the author of an aggressive non-expressionistic prose, who was known additionally through several scandal-ridden theatrical pieces, Meyer recognized an author who could be used to drum up business for *Der Jüngste Tag*; he hoped to gain a larger readership for the literature of the younger generation through him. The awarding of the Fontane Prize simultaneously exercised a positive influence on the overly complicated relationship between Sternheim and the house. Meyer now skillfully employed the Fontane Prize for advertising maneuvers. The fact that Sternheim passed on the prize to Kafka was entirely in accord with the publisher's wishes, for Kafka's *The Stoker* had appeared in *Der Jüngste Tag*. Thus the prize advertised doubly for the series. Now shortly before the official announcement of both prize-winners, nothing was more important for Meyer in October 1915 than to accept another title by Franz Kafka along with a title by Sternheim for the November 1915 edition of the newest series of *Der Jüngste Tag*. Meyer's calculated publishing move and—as he emphatically presented it to the author—also Kafka's advantage was that the imminent awarding of the Fontane Prize would "certainly draw public attention to you." In the same sentence Meyer mentioned the idea of adding a new title to *Meditation*, since the copies were carried for such a long time by Ernst Rowohlt Publishing, and he intended to distribute the book anew as a second edition.[68]

The conditions leading up to the acceptance of Franz Kafka's *The Metamorphosis* in the fifth series of *Der Jüngste Tag* are thus sobering from this perspective. The publisher's readiness to suddenly publish a book by Kafka after the hiatus of relations, the matter-of-factness with which the author's consent was assumed, as well as Meyer's "ardent" efforts to get Kafka to accept the prize despite all his reservations finally point to the publisher's special interest, namely, Meyer's wish to be able to successfully present the fifth series of *Der Jüngste Tag* in the wave of public interest that the awarding of the Fontane Prize in November 1915 would arouse. The full intent of Blei's decision to have Kafka share monetarily in the honor becomes clear for the first time in this context. Blei's decision set the tone for Kafka's reacceptance by the publisher and subsequently for the author's future relationship to this house.

In a separate letter Meyer simultaneously explained the special case of this year's Fontane Prize to Brod, who noted the event tersely in his diary: "10/13: 'Fontane Prize'" (MBA). Later he recalled: "The award of the Fontane Prize . . . was accepted with a certain amount of satisfaction. If I am not mistaken, this is how it all happened; that it was Sternheim, who was really awarded the prize, but handed it down to the 'young writer' for his short story, 'The Stoker,' which had already been published in 1913" (FK154-55). Kasimir Edschmid wrote about the prize later on: "It was one of the three awards that was really an honor, although the sum was ridiculous."[69] Even though it was only the money and not the prize itself that was passed on to Kafka, this was nevertheless the first public recognition Franz

Kafka's work received.

Thus, on the one hand, Kafka expressed "satisfaction" in his reply to Meyer, and was "very happy" about the news, "especially that about Blei and Sternheim." But on the other hand he refused to say why, since he had been insulted by Meyer's tactless communication about the award. Kafka must have felt contempt that he should now consider himself so lucky because of the sum he could expect; an alms recipient he was not. "Kind as such a gesture is," he replied to Meyer, "it raises the question of need. But not of need regarding the prize *and* the money, but need in regard to the money alone." Sternheim had not offered him the prize but just the money. Meyer confirmed his fear; Kafka's letter clearly states: "Important as the prize or a share in the prize would be for me, I would not want to accept the money alone without a share in the prize" (L113).

A further non-extant explanation by Meyer on October 18 also could not satisfy Kafka; his share in the prize was too small. Meyer's reply also seems to have implied that it was exclusively a matter of money. Nevertheless, Kafka wanted to trust Meyer's "general opinion" and wrote to Sternheim as the publisher advised; he pointedly noted: "[I]t is not very easy to write to someone from whom one has received no direct word and to thank him without knowing exactly what for."[70] Almost disparagingly Kafka wrote to Felice several weeks later: "Almost the first I knew about the Fontane Prize was from the papers; the publisher had vaguely prepared me for it some time ago. I don't know Sternheim, neither personally nor by correspondence" (F459).

The Metamorphosis as Volume 23/23 of the Series *Der Jüngste Tag*

The publisher tacitly presumed that Kafka would approve a book edition for *The Metamorphosis*. Pleased at the publisher's new interest in his work but with clear reservations about its business tactics, Kafka declared *ex post facto* his agreement to have his story appear in the next series of *Der Jüngste Tag*. His wish certainly would have been to publish this text together with two others in a larger volume of novellas, but then he reemphasized cordially: "but I suppose in the present circumstances it would be better temporarily to proceed as you have outlined" (L113). Equally politely and veiled, he presented his wishes regarding the printing of *The Metamorphosis*. "As for your proposals," he wrote this time to the publisher, "I completely trust your judgment" (L113); only as an addendum did he express his thoughts precisely.

Kafka criticized the typeface. The print of the first proofs he had already received by October 15 seemed to him too "dark and cramped" in comparison to Sternheim's *Napoleon*, which was set so "pleasantly open and legible" and, as Kafka correctly determined, using the same size letters. Four days earlier Meyer had sent him *Napoleon*, clearly as a sample for *The Metamorphosis*. Although set in the same type and size, Kafka considered *The Metamorphosis* slighted in comparison to Sternheim's *Napoleon*, with whom he had already shared the Fontane Prize so unequally. The spacing inserts between letters during typesetting, which set the distance between lines, was actually a fraction of a millimeter less for *The Metamorphosis* than for *Napoleon*. Kafka demanded the equivalent of Sternheim's text for his: "If something can still be done about that, I would be most pleased" (L113).

Kafka also expressed preferences for the binding. *The*

Metamorphosis should make a better impression than the earlier volumes of *Der Jüngste Tag*. "*The Stoker* was not handsomely bound. There was something sham about the binding which after a while produced a kind of disgust," Kafka wrote to the publisher and added: "So I would ask for another binding" (L113). Kafka's desire for a more open print could not be accommodated, but Meyer agreed that *The Metamorphosis* would have the same (better) binding as Sternheim's *Napoleon*. Kafka was of course in agreement with this (L113).

In the October 18th letter, which has not been preserved, Meyer must have informed Kafka that the illustrator Ottomar Starke was in the process of sketching title pages for the volumes in the new series, including *The Metamorphosis*. The author's fear reached the publisher in an outcry at the end of the month, as *The Metamorphosis* had just been sent over for printing. Imploringly, Kafka wrote to the publisher on October 25:

> It struck me that Starke, as an illustrator, might want to draw the insect itself. Not that, please not that! I do not want to restrict him, but only to make this plea out of my deeper knowledge of the story. The insect itself cannot be depicted. It cannot even be shown from a distance. (L114-15)

The terrible insect/vermin, into which Gregor Samsa finds himself transformed one morning after awaking from restless dreaming, was not to be visible. Kafka made other suggestions for a possible illustration: "the parents and the head clerk in front of the locked door, or even better, the parents and the sister in the lighted room, with the door open upon the adjoining room that lies in darkness" (L115). Starke heeded Kafka's directions closely.[71]

The double volume Number 22/23 of Kafka's *The Metamorphosis*, together with Edschmid's *Das rasende Leben* ("The

Frantic Life"), Schickele's *Aissé*, and Sternheim's *Schuhlin* was delivered at the end of November 1915 as part of the fifth series of *Der Jüngste Tag*; the text of the book edition had been edited by Kafka since the first printing.[72] Immediately prior to the official awarding of the Fontane Prize at the beginning of December 1915, the publisher presented the new titles of its honored authors Carl Sternheim and Franz Kafka, and the publisher Georg Heinrich Meyer skillfully proclaimed *Der Jüngste Tag* in publishers' notices and through press releases as a forum for significant modern literature in the public eye. Even in the case of Kafka this publishing policy proved to be essentially correct. The association of Kafka's name with a recognized literary prize advertised by the supportive publisher developed into a minor sales success over the next three years compared with the previous sales. Approximately 250 copies of the title edition of *Meditation* were sold in the following months;[73] *The Stoker* and *The Metamorphosis* even went to new editions (1916 and 1918 respectively). Kafka's greatest preoccupation, the realization of a collected volume, fell victim to the individual publication of *The Metamorphosis* in *Der Jüngste Tag*. His first major book still remained off in the future.

The *Trial* Phase. Kafka's Struggle for the Novel's Publication (1914-1917)

> "The Stoker," *The Metamorphosis* . . . and "The Judgment" belong together, both inwardly and outwardly. There is an obvious connection among the three and, even more important, a secret one, for which reason I would be reluctant to forgo the chance of having them published together in a book, which might be called *The Sons* . . . I am just as much concerned about the unity of the three stories as I am about the unity of any one of them. (Kafka to Wolff in April 1913)

1. Writing and/or Marriage. His Failed Attempt to Free Himself (Summer 1914)

Kafka's first great creative phase lasted over five months, from September 1912 until January 1913. After the novel he planned failed and contact with his publisher broke off in May 1913, he did not complete another work for one and a half years. During creative voids such as this, the gap between hope and actuality in Kafka's life widened. He was convinced that writing would only become a reality if he could free himself from the necessity of having to earn a living. But he could give up his post only if he were certain that he would be successful as a writer. Next to his writing, the most important element in his life, marriage and starting a family, remained Kafka's highest goal whenever his writing stagnated; he consistently increased his personal contact with Felice during periods when his inspirational powers failed him. Confronted with the uncertainty of his creative potential, Kafka clung to the security Felice provided.

Kafka himself viewed the prospects of combining writing and marriage as unrealistic. He had experienced enough skepticism from Felice with regard to his writing. Nevertheless, Kafka sought understanding and recognition of his literary work from her. He dedicated *The Judgment* to her and sent her the letter from Kurt Wolff in which the publisher so urgently requested further submissions from him. At the times he was courting her, Kafka sought to expand his contact with journal editors and his publisher and displayed a positive attitude toward the publication of his work. At these times he himself offered his texts for publication. Being successful with the public as a writer would have been followed by Felice's (and his parents') recognition of his writing and would have perhaps made marriage possible without the necessity of sacrificing his writing.

But Kafka's unhappy struggle for recognition and confirmation of his existence as a writer by the person he loved was in vain (as it previously had been with his parents). Even in her first letters Felice had advised Kafka to practice "moderation" (F28) in writing. She viewed what Kafka himself considered his authentic existence as a harmful leisure activity. Felice could only substantiate the opinion of Kafka's mother, who in a letter to Felice labeled her son's writing a "mere pastime" in his "leisure hours" (F46). His struggle for justification as a writer and for resolving the contradiction between literature and reality reached dreadful proportions in his letters to Felice. In order to write Kafka needed to be alone, yet the physical and psychological distance from Felice after each separation did not always induce the anticipated literary productivity. The inability to write drove him back again to the security he found in her. Kafka's failure to make a final decision reached a climax in the summer of 1913, when he drew up a list of all the advantages and disadvantages of marriage (cf. DI292ff.). The list resolved nothing, it merely confirmed the view that the arguments neutralized themselves. In August he had decided to commit suicide, but "already on the window sill," so to speak, he mustered the courage to believe that he could "pass the test of marriage in spite of everything" (DI297). Just three days later he informed Max Brod that he had written Felice's father to ask for her hand (FK143).

Kafka's thought process cannot be unqualifiedly labeled dialectical in a three-stage sense; rather it is a never-ending, antithetical one. His manner of courting Felice demonstrated early on the paradox in his position. Relentlessly and almost methodically chastising himself, Kafka apparently revealed his hopelessly divided existence to Felice's father. The letter, in which the prospective son-in-law explains to the father that his daughter would only be unhappy if married to him, because his profession and marriage contradict the sole desire of literature, is unusual. As if wanting to convince himself, Kafka states in the letter to Felice's father:

> Everything that is not literature bores me and I hate it, for it disturbs me or delays me, if only because I think it does. I lack all aptitude for family life except, at best, as an observer. I have no family feeling and visitors make me almost feel as though I were maliciously being attacked.
>   'A marriage could not change me, just as my job cannot change me.' (DI300)

This letter was not sent, because Felice's father had already given permission for them to marry. The certainty that marriage would make him sacrifice his writing forever compelled Kafka to flee; his "wish for an unthinking, reckless solitude," of only being "face to face" with himself (DI288), immediately gained the upper hand. He spent his vacation alone in Riva, where a secret affair with a Swiss woman confirmed his decision to break off entirely from Felice and to resign his post in Prague. But writing did not follow. By November he was reconsidering his relationship with Felice again; Felice's friend, Grete Bloch, acted as a mediator. From their now hardened standpoints they corresponded again and carried on the hopeless discourse on their diverging lifestyles. Nevertheless, despite all the reservations expressed, they became engaged on Easter in 1914; at Pentecost of the same year the official engagement took place amidst a circle of family and friends, under "inauspicious circumstances," as Max Brod cautiously phrased it.[1]

With the wedding set for September, the inevitable happened. When Kafka came to Berlin two months later to meet Felice for the vacation trip they were to take together, the conversation that so distressed Kafka and terminated the engagement took place at the Askanischer Hof. Kafka was later to call this encounter on July 12, 1914, the "tribunal in the hotel" (DII65). Felice, who had arrived with her sister, presided during it, and Grete Bloch played the role of the plaintiff. The writer Ernst Weiß served as Kafka's witness. Kafka was declared guilty. He himself remained silent and took no measures in his own defense.

Kafka subsequently spent his summer vacation with Weiß on the Baltic Sea. He must have reached his decision there, for when he returned to Prague on July 26 with renewed spirit, he wrote his parents a letter that sounded like an early version of the *Letter to His Father*:

> I am younger than I seem. That is the only good effect of
> dependency, that it keeps people young. Though it acts this
> way only if it comes to an end. . . . But as long as I stay in
> the office, I shall never be able to achieve this improvement.
> In any case, not in Prague. Here everything is arranged so as
> to keep me, a person basically craving dependency, in it.
> Everything is offered me so readily. The office is a great
> nuisance to me, and often unbearable, but basically easy. In
> this way, I earn more than I need. What for? For whom? I
> will continue to climb the salary ladder. For what purpose?
> . . . Outside Prague I can gain everything, that is, I can
> become a calm, independent person who is utilizing all his
> abilities and, as the reward of good and truthful work, is given
> the feeling of really being alive and of lasting contentment.
> (O9-10)

The thought of leaving Prague, the embodiment of family
and occupational constraints, accompanied Kafka as a more or
less secret desire since his school days. "Prague doesn't let go,"
he wrote as early as 1902 to his friend Oskar Pollak; "[t]his old
crone has claws" (L5). In the early years of his professional life,
he made the decision to go to Berlin no matter what so that he
could devote himself solely to literature there. Kafka's eye
toward the future is naturally not just a personal phenomenon but
an expression of the striving of his fellow writers as well. In
actuality very few Prague writers remained in their native city.
Mostly of German-Jewish background, these writers lived in
their native city in double isolation. The memoirs of Franz
Werfel convey an impression of the intellectual climate in Prague
before the First World War:

> I left Prague in 1912 at the age of twenty-two. It was at that
> time a semi-conscious attempt to save myself. My instincts for

life rebelled against Prague. For the non-Czech, it seemed to me, this city has no reality; it is a daydream which has no experience, a lame ghetto, without even having the poverty of the ghetto, a hollow world from which only false or no activity springs. Prague can only be born in the stupor of drugs, as a *Fata Morgana* of life, and that is the reason why so many artists have not fled.[2]

On the other hand, Berlin, the metropolitan city and center of literary life, attracted these writers and Kafka like a magnet. In Berlin he felt "the chances of earning a living are best," because, as he said, he could "make best and directest [sic] use of my ability to write, and so find a means of livelihood at least partially suited to me" (DII27). In a certain symbolic sense, his hope of independence and freedom was tied to Berlin:

> April 5. If only it were possible to go to Berlin, to become independent, to live from one day to the next, even to go hungry, but to let all one's strength pour forth instead of husbanding it here, or rather—instead of one's turning aside into nothingness! If only Felice wanted it, would help me! (DII31)

With the failure of his marital plans, the thought of living an independent writer's life intensified in July 1914. As a result Kafka began making plans to move to Berlin. In a letter to his parents he explained how he intended to carry them out. His savings of 5000 kronen would support him for two years without having to work. "These two years," he continued, "will permit me to do literary work and to bring out of myself what, in Prague—where I am hampered by inward slackness and outward interference—I could not achieve in such clarity, fullness, and unity" (O10). Thereafter Kafka intended to live off the royalties from his literary works. Never before (and never again) did he exude such optimism when a weighty decision was to be carried out. This one time in July 1914 he stood firm in his decision to be an independent writer. He sent his "letter of farewell" by messenger to "her parents" on July 27 (DII66).

As so often, defeat soon followed the high point of the liberating decision. World War I broke out suddenly on July 28, 1914, and all borders were closed. The plan to move from Prague to Berlin was thwarted. Kafka did not abandon his plan, but he was forced to defer it for some time. The war spread like wildfire: within a few days the regional conflict turned into a multinational one, and Europe mobilized. Although he had been declared unfit for military service two years earlier, the outbreak of the war had directly impacted Kafka. After his brother-in-law was drafted and his oldest sister Elli moved in with their parents, Kafka not only had to assume management of the factory but also had to give up his room in his parents' home. At the age of thirty-one Kafka was forced to rent his own private room.

Kafka retreated from the political happenings of the day. He hardly takes a position in his personal notebooks and scarcely mentions the historical events of the times. After the fatal failure of his decision he saw himself thrown back upon himself. In sharp contrast to the patriotic parading heard in the streets, the diary notes his "total loneliness" and his agony over the failed marriage. Once again he assumed the role of observer and withdrew from reality. On July 31 he made passing reference to the "general mobilization" but immediately thereafter commented on the "reward for living alone":

> Still, as a consequence, I am little affected by all the misery and am firmer in my resolve than ever. I shall have to spend my afternoons in the factory; I won't live at home, for Elli and the two children are moving in with us. But I will write in spite of everything, absolutely; it is my struggle for self-

preservation. (DII75)

2. The Second Major Creative Period (August to December 1914)

"If I can't take refuge in some work, I am lost" (DII68), Kafka wrote despairingly in his diary on July 28. Two days later he completed the "Joseph K. Fragment," the precursor to *The Trial*. Without a doubt his creative capacity was rejuvenated around the middle of August and his life gained meaning and "justification" (cf. DII79). He simultaneously worked on "three stories" (DII91). In quick succession *Memoirs of the Kalda Railroad* and the first chapters of *The Trial* took shape. The "Arrest and Conviction of Josef K.," which was originally planned as a short narrative work, expanded during the course of writing into Kafka's second attempt at a novel. In order to bring his first major book to fruition, Kafka extended himself to the limits of his creative and physical capabilities; the slow process of self-awareness and the clarifying effect his writing had on his personal being impelled him to work on the novel. Immediately after drafting the first chapters, he noted: ". . . full insight into my situation occasionally" (DII93). Almost as if by pattern and signaling his satisfaction, he began anew reading to his friends. In September he read the first chapter of *The Trial* (ÜFK139) to Brod; subsequent readings followed. In October Kafka took a vacation in order to continue work on the novel, but instead he wrote the last chapter of *America* ("The Man Who Disappeared")—the "Nature Theater of Oklahoma"—and the story *In the Penal Colony*. During this two-week vacation Kafka wrote more than seventy printed pages.

Just as at the end of 1912 when the writing of *The Metamorphosis* interrupted the America novel, so too in November 1914 did the writing of *The Trial* became laborious after he completed *In the Penal Colony*. The extent to which Kafka's life can be described in clearly defined and logically sequential phases is revealed by the fact that he once again attempted to rekindle his relationship with Felice. In November 1914 he wrote a long letter to her in which he explained the reasons for their separation and asked for a reconciliation (F436ff.). As if following some causal principle, the familiar vicious cycle associated with his proximity to Felice unfolded. The tally Kafka took at year's end of the writing he had completed reveals the traces of his resignation:

> December 31. Have been working since August, in general not little and not badly, yet neither in the first nor in the second respect to the limit of my ability, as I should have done, especially as there is every indication (insomnia, headaches, weak heart) that my ability won't last much longer. Worked on, but did not finish: *The Trial*, "Memoirs of the Kalda Railroad," "The Village Schoolmaster," "The Assistant Attorney," and the beginnings of various little things. Finished only: "In the Penal Colony" and a chapter of "Der Verschollene," both during the two-week vacation. I don't know why I am drawing up this summary, it's not at all like me! (DII106-07)

In January 1915 Kafka completely abandoned his work on *The Trial*—this was in fact only a few days after his first meeting with Felice in Bodenbach (DII111). Once again, this second creative phase had lasted five months; once again he would abandon his writing for a period of one and a half years. Kafka described this creative void as "[a] well gone dry, water at an unattainable depth and no certainty it is there" (DII126). Contraposing the deadlocked standpoints in his diary, Kafka summarized the trip to Bodenbach and the first meeting with

Felice since the engagement was broken off: "she, indifferent to every mute request, wants the average: a comfortable home, an interest on my part in the factory, good food, bed at eleven, central heating." But he himself affirmed: "I yield not a particle of my demand for a fantastic life arranged solely in the interest of my work" (DII111). Kafka's courting of Felice ran its course according to the pattern of 1913. Once again he attempted to integrate opposites, once again he defended his writing and sought to please Felice as a writer. Characteristically he opened up toward the outside world again; in order to lend credence to his inclination toward the "fantastic" life of the imagination, Kafka made the effort to have something published.

But now the war shattered these hopes. Shortages of materials and personnel had almost crippled the book industry. Wolff had still not expressed an interest in publishing *The Metamorphosis*. Back in June 1914 when he traveled unannounced to Leipzig, Kafka had attempted to arrange a meeting with him. However, he never met with Wolff. Dejected, he made note of this fruitless trip to Leipzig in his diary: "Failures: . . . pointless trip; by mistake, a local train; Wolff was just going to Berlin" (DII64). Even Werfel had no time for Kafka; he was—as Kafka laconically noted—"appropriated" by "Lasker-Schüler" of all people (someone he did not especially admire).[3] Kafka's ties to his publishing house became even more tenuous when Franz Werfel, the advocate for the interests of all the Prague writers, left Kurt Wolff Publishing after the war broke out. Wolff himself was called up for military service at this time, and a new man, Georg Heinrich Meyer, assumed responsibility for the publisher's business in his stead. For the second time in the brief history of his publishing encounters, Kafka changed publishers without having changed publishing houses.

3. Third Excursus: Kurt Wolff Publishing during the First World War

August 1914—"The Uprooted Intellectuals"

The declaration of war by the German Empire against Russia came as a complete surprise, yet it evoked widespread euphoria. People gathered spontaneously for patriotic rallies; the Germans' hunger for victory seemed insatiable and evolved into a stupefying mass hysteria in which the most diverse viewpoints were joined in general pathos under one banner. Amidst the delirium of the war, intellectuals in Germany experienced a sudden change and a solidarity for the fatherland that would hardly be comprehensible two years later for the majority of those affected by the war. Those cultural and literary leaders who had not already received their orders reported to the front voluntarily to fight together with guns for the monarchical-bourgeois system they previously battled with weapons of the mind. Names like Alfred Kerr, Richard Dehmel, August Stramm, Rudolf Leonhard, and also Ernst Rowohlt are representative. Authors such as Gerhart Hauptmann and Thomas Mann supported the war-frenzied patriotism with their publications. *Die neue Rundschau* turned immediately to this new course. Oskar Bie's almost programmatic article in the September number of *Die neue Rundschau* characterized the mood; in reflecting on "war, art, people," it stated: "Writing appears superfluous. This is a time for action and one reads nothing but reports on the war." This introduction was rhetorical, for Bie convinces the reader of the opposite; in his appeal to the writers of the day he reveals the new task and purpose of literature: "We want to feel this war down to our very bones, until the great decision, that of truth's final victory over decadence, even among our own people . . .

Let the great purification wash over us."[4]

Not only the older generation with Fischer but also the younger writers became infected with the war fever, even if their fascination stemmed from some other more revolutionary ideology. The pathos of expressionism dissolved into the pathos of a great historical moment experienced in common. In a romantically transformed yearning for collective adventure and for a world revolution freeing man from bourgeois restrictions, the war seemed to be the purgatory of a beneficial apocalypse; many of the writers already over twenty years of age perceived the war as the continuation and fulfillment of expressionistic thought with means more encompassing than just literary ones.

"The mood, how it enveloped everything from all sides," is how Musil described his "summer experience of 1914" in his diary; on the mark, he had captured the intellectual climate of his day in the phrase: "The uprooted intellectuals."[5]

Georg Heinrich Meyer—the New Director

Publishers and book dealers found themselves in a severe crisis; *belles lettres* were no longer in demand during this "time of action." Hans von Weber, the keen observer of the literary scene in Germany, reluctantly confirmed this sad reality of fall 1914 in his *Onionfish*: "With one stroke the outbreak of war interrupted business in the book trade. The shops were deserted."[6] Book dealers canceled orders from the publishers, which forced the publishers to make adjustments; fall production was cut almost entirely in most publishing houses.

Kurt Wolff's literary program was reduced to a few titles, and the delivery of books on hand was temporarily halted. This is the situation Georg Trakl encountered at the beginning of September; the publisher was withholding his *Sebastian*, because for the time being the real publishing business was dormant as it had never before been (WBr88). Wolff was caught up in the wave of the initial mobilization and was already on his way to Belgium as a soldier on August 4. The editor Pinthus complained after a brief conversation with the publisher in October that Wolff now had "no longer a spark of sense for literature."[7] Like most Germans, Wolff had initially underestimated the impact of this world conflict and failed to recognize its consequences. There is no evidence to support the view that he left detailed directives behind in case of a lengthy absence upon his rather hasty departure from Leipzig. But Wolff had designated an expert in the trade, Georg Heinrich Meyer, to replace him; for two years he would not be able to directly manage his own publishing house.

Meyer's solitary regime thus lasted for two years. During this period Meyer guided Kurt Wolff Publishing out of its greatest economic crisis into the greatest period of sales in its history. As Pinthus wrote in 1956, Meyer actually remained the leading figure in the house for some time after the war.[8] Meyer's life before 1895—the year he founded his first publishing house—lies clouded amid the haziness of diverse anecdotes. (Anecdotes were Meyer's preferred form for describing his life.) Born on February 27, 1868, in Heidenheim, he once made himself out to be ten years older than he was in order to command greater respect from a younger author he was with. Sternheim called Meyer the "most diligent book dealer" (Wo36) he had ever known; superlatives mark the praise of contemporaries for his comprehensive knowledge of the German book trade. His long journey through the German book business began with his apprenticeship with a Viennese bookseller. When he died on March 22, 1931, at the age of sixty-three, he was the director of Rhein Publishing, which had become famous through James

Joyce and Hermann Broch.

At about the same time as his friend Eugen Diederichs, Meyer established his first company at age twenty-seven with the slogan "Heimat" in the publishing metropolis Leipzig. National art and literature were the leading line of the company, which Meyer, the energetic initiator, intended to pursue in grand style. The company and its activities would certainly have been forgotten, if Rilke's exceptional collection of poems *Mir zur Feier* ("In Celebration of Myself") and its art work by Heinrich Vogeler had not appeared there in 1900. Although this was the only book Rilke published with Meyer, the publisher's fervent desire to produce not just this title but the author's entire *oeuvre* is evident in this early phase. But Meyer overestimated his company's financial possibilities with his program policy. The risks he took (Meyer published, among others, eighteen books by Max Dreyer, thirteen by the Austrian Adolf Pichler, and seven titles by Rudolf Huch) soon proved to be too much for the small publishing house. The creditors forced it into bankruptcy in 1904. The collapse was complete: a letter from Meyer to Diederichs in January 1905 states that his future income was mortgaged for a year and a day.[9]

The will to be independent, however, was not broken. After an interlude with the *Deutsche Verlags-Anstalt* in Stuttgart, Meyer founded the publishing house of Meyer and Jessen, Berlin, in 1910 with a financially strong partner. The company at first picked up on the tradition of "Heimat" literature, but Meyer's new publishing ambitions were evident in his publishing of the authors Anselm Feuerbach, Theodor Fischer, and Paul Ernst, as well as in the plans for an eight-volume selection of Goethe's letters. Meyer's books attracted special attention in the trade; he printed consumer books with bibliophile standards. Especially striking were the simple beauty of his books' artwork and the clarity of their print.

Because of overly ambitious plans, Meyer's second company was also not able to gain a foothold in the marketplace. Increasing indebtedness strained the relationship between the partners and by 1913 led to arguments. Jessen prudently saved himself from impending bankruptcy by simply assigning his interest in the company over to Meyer, who then became the sole publisher in spring 1914, as well as the sole owner and debtor. Meyer's second attempt to establish his own publishing house likewise ended up in court.

For financial reasons Meyer turned to Wolff in January 1914 in the hope of consolidating his own business by issuing the rights to several books. Wolff did not express any interest in this offer; instead he offered Meyer the post of director in his house (disregarding the danger of introducing a certain cultural conservativism into the company). At first Meyer harbored reservations; he knew that his authors would not follow him to Wolff's avant-garde company. But it was precisely these authors who advised him to make a deal with Wolff, and when the demise of Meyer and Jessen's company was evident in April 1914, he accepted the offer.

Overcoming the Shock of War and the Expansion of Kurt Wolff Publishing

The declaration of war and subsequent mobilization struck the German book market at the point of its greatest prosperity. The number of new books reached a record in 1913, and 1914 was expected to exceed that figure. The inner circle of market experts feared the consequences of overproduction with good reason. But paradoxically it was exactly this circumstance that made it possible for the publishing industry to survive the years of crisis unscathed.[10]

In 1915 the book market recovered from the shock of war; businesses gradually got on their feet again. The publishers, who were compelled to sell their books quickly during this period of limited capital, exploited the Germans' enormous hunger for patriotic-chauvinistic literature. "It hailed war chronicles, war brochures, war editions, collections of field-post letters," according to Julius Zeitler, who summarized these "war biblio-philes" in *Die Weißen Blätter*.[11] Yet even publishers like Wolff, who kept their programs generally free of cheap war lyrics and patriotic reminiscences of the front, shared in the economic upturn in the book market. The successful Christmas season of 1915 marked the beginning of a triumphant economic upswing for Kurt Wolff Publishing and signaled the commercialization of Wolff's publishing and the rapid expansion of his publishing houses in the years that followed.

Meyer's predominantly conservative publishing activity for twenty years and his new assignment with Kurt Wolff Publishing and its young generation did not pose a conflict for him. Without a hitch Meyer transformed his endorsement of "Heimat" literature to that of expressionism in the summer of 1914, even though the basic foundations of each were so diametrically opposed. The commercial profile of Georg Heinrich Meyer's fifteen-year employment with Kurt Wolff Publishing is what stands out above everything else. Meyer's task, and his success, was to produce the best possible sales figures for the books entrusted to him. In the area of distribution and sales he proved, above all, as one of his coworkers confirms in his memoirs, that his knowledge of the publishing business could record unheard-of sales for the day, even for books outside the mainstream.[12] Meyer's goals were to solidify economically what had long been a business built on subsidies and to keep the company intact during a time of general crisis.

The demanding publications of Kurt Wolff Publishing brought the company a great deal of respect in literary circles that bore no relationship to the weak sales. Meyer's comment in February 1915 upon seeing the publisher's full warehouse is significant: "Franz Werfel is today the only drop of fat in the empty soup plate of Kurt Wolff."[13] The publisher lacked attractive titles, especially novels. Except for the idea of starting a popular novel library and his involvement with the novelists Gustav Meyrink and especially Heinrich Mann, Meyer's influence on program development was modest. His ability to conduct delicate negotiations through skillful clarification and simplification of complicated bookkeeping matters and his successful efforts to promote sales endeared the publisher to the authors.

Wolff called Meyer "a propaganda genius and a leading sales cannon" and gave him a free hand in most of the publishing decisions (Wo36). From the beginning of their collaboration onward Meyer had entreated his publisher to "advertise, advertise, advertise—that's the only way to sell books." Wolff responded: "We advertised, without any budget, as had never before been done in the German publishing business" (Wo36). Thereafter, the marketing psychologist Meyer undertook what had previously been considered impossible for publishers: he announced books in large columned newspaper ads and placed posters of salesworthy books in large format on the billboards in large cities. Along with this highly visible public advertising Meyer did not overlook winning the allegiance of the booksellers. Unusual special discounts were made available to the book dealers—up to fifty percent of the store price—and Meyer introduced into the book trade that sales philosophy referred to in modern terminology as "inducement."[14]

Meyer failed to see a clear structure or central focus on which Kurt Wolff Publishing could base its programmatic view and which could determine advertising policy. More clearly than ever before Meyer emphasized the literature of the young generation of expressionists. One of his first publishing decisions was to reactivate *Der Jüngste Tag*, which had been canceled at the beginning of the war, as the visible symbol of the literary efforts of the house. The Fontane Prize of 1915 became a fortuitous point of departure for effective advertising for Meyer. It was questionable whether prize winner Sternheim fit in literarily with these younger writers, but for Meyer's needs he was an author tailor-made for the market. Meyer vociferously directed public attention to the honored Sternheim and especially to his three titles in *Der Jüngste Tag*.

Encouraged by the positive results that his entry signified for *Der Jüngste Tag*, Meyer hit upon newer and more impressive classifications of publisher production. Meyer grouped the literature presented under the signet of Kurt Wolff Publishing from now on under two key words: "young" was the first of the major concepts, already introduced by *Der Jüngste Tag* and the *Dichtung der Jüngsten*; "new" was the second term which Meyer established as characteristic for the publisher from 1915 on. A glance at the undertakings Meyer initiated to give the program an inner coherency make this attempt clear and simultaneously promote the key word in public: the fifth series of *Der Jüngste Tag* was dedicated to the "new German narrative writers"; *Der Neue Roman* followed, a series of novels from which Meyer hoped to gain popularity. Series devoted to modern poetry, dramatic stories, and finally the new Drugulin Prints followed. In Meyer's enthusiasm for the young and the new, neither the year of composition nor the author's year of birth were especially important to him. Gustav Flaubert, who died in 1880, was considered a contemporary author, and Carl Hauptmann, age fifty at the time, was listed as one of the younger writers in the publisher's announcements.

Meyer's sovereign policy of propaganda—an expression which described everything related to advertising in the trade as well as in public up to 1933—brought Kurt Wolff Publishing its first great sales successes in 1916. Through Meyer's well-planned campaign, Meyrink's *Golem* and Heinrich Mann's *The Blue Angel* reached six-figure sales within a short time. The previously unsellable literature of the expressionists received a certain degree of publicity through the publisher's strategy of integrating the unpopular titles into the popular series of books. Werfel wrote Meyer in March 1916: "I am very happy that the house has grown so much during the war under your direction. Everywhere one reads and hears about Kurt Wolff Publishing. Your advertising (especially the inserts) was the most intensive that could be imagined" (WBr198).

But the ads alone were not the sole reason for the financial success of Kurt Wolff Publishing. There was also a strong, renewed interest in literature on the part of the public that was founded on the changing experience of the war. The high-sounding expectations at the beginning of the war did not last long. Daily contact with the reality of a war that demonstrated for the first time in global fashion the horror of modern techno-logical capabilities roused those intellectuals who has entered it so enthusiastically with their romantic-nationalistic dreams. After the euphoria of the summer of 1914, the experience a year later was sobering. A period of restlessness and experimentation ensued; the collapse of the old world order induced a societal protest and consequently a new orientation and a search for new values. But who in Germany in 1916 could consider open dissent? Police force and censorship scattered or suppressed all opposition. In historical perspective one of the almost logical consequences in the realm of intellectual life was that the actual widespread acceptance of expressionist literature began at this point. In poems and prose the writers of the generation of 1880-1890 had anticipated the social and individual chaos and the decay of values before the outbreak of the war. Their texts were political, sociocritical, and radical. But only after the experiences of the war persisted did those outside the small circle of expressionists find an objective correlation and a symbolic concretization of their own inner condition in this literature.

Given these circumstances, Meyer was able to effectively intercede for the literature of the younger generation with his practice of propaganda politics, and during the second half of the war Kurt Wolff Publishing reached the zenith of its literary impact.

Meyer's position at Kurt Wolff Publishing remained uncontested during Wolff's absence. Criticism of his "American" business tactics increased, first from other publishers and then from within his own house. Fearing for the literary future of the company, Albert Ehrenstein, who for a short while served as an editor for Meyer, wrote a sharp letter of protest to Wolff in April 1916 in which he commented on the sad, confused state of the house:

> There is no denying the fact that Meyer ruined his own publishing house, but it would be very painful for me if *the sole literary institution available to the generation of today's literary youth* were to collapse through the insufficient adaptability and the sloppiness of an aging person who had overextended himself. This is why I am speaking up . . . With the continuing sole regime of Meyer I could no longer advise myself or my friends to submit larger epic or dramatic works to Kurt Wolff Publishing.[15]

Ehrenstein urged Wolff to utilize Meyer, who was masterful as a technician and as a bibliophile, within the range of his abilities. It is noteworthy for Wolff's position with regard to Meyer that he let Ehrenstein's warning, this first clear indication of the danger of the publisher's literary dehydration, go unheeded and continued to give Meyer complete control. By around November 1915—about the time of new discussions with Kafka —Meyer collapsed under the pressures imposed upon him by his work. The inability to delegate specific tasks as well as a cumbersome and suspect system characterized the reverse side of an otherwise ingenious book-trade technician. Business mail —letters from the publisher's authors—for which Meyer had no time during the twenty-hour days he was working, were put into baskets unopened and locked in a vacant attic. Whether the publisher, who focused on distribution and sales matters, found the time to discuss problems other than technical ones with his authors cannot be concluded from what remains of his correspondence with them. Wolff (who later opened the attic several times without Meyer's knowledge and processed mail) gave Meyer every support imaginable. Not only did he distance himself from Ehrenstein, but upon his return to Leipzig in the summer of 1916 he also sanctioned the decisions Meyer had made.

Without a doubt the results of Meyer's activity during Wolff's absence impressed the publisher; shortly before his return he read in Munich's *Allgemeine Zeitung* (June 17, 1916) that Kurt Wolff Publishing had begun "to become as important for the newest literature as the publisher Friedrich had been for naturalism."[16] Not without pride, the publisher reminded René Schickele in 1921 that his company was the first premiere German publishing house and to a certain extent remained the only one to strive for Ullstein-like sales for literary books (WBr210). Thus upon his return he supported Meyer's costly advertising and endorsed his unusual guidelines for dealing with the authors, such as reducing honoraria to partially finance the advertising campaign (cf. among others WBr210ff.). The enhanced position in the book trade and among the public strengthened Wolff's loyalty to Meyer. More and more authors from other companies, who had no or at least no comparable newspaper advertising from their publishers, offered their new works to Wolff, primarily for financial reasons.

The two years that Meyer represented Wolff were consequently extremely successful for the future of the company. Wolff obviously came home from the war a changed man. His letters to his authors seemed more sober and to the point and give the impression of a restless publisher concerned with the expansion of his company. Wolff accepted Meyer's business practices as guidelines for his own conception of publishing. The publisher's new stance was already clear in February 1916, when he wrote to Heinrich Mann from the Balkans: "I don't intend to be enthusiastic as a publisher, but rather intend to sell books; I want to incorporate your books into my house, not as objects of art; for the hundred readers I want to win over a thousand, I want to make money for you and with you" (WBr222). Wolff's correspondence with his authors after 1916 shows how business considerations were pushed more and more to the forefront. In doing so he confirmed, not without pleasure, that a terrible, ruthless American business attitude (WBr147) had suddenly been ascribed to him in literary circles.

The publishing program for 1917 basically contained no noteworthy literary works. Only the collected works of Heinrich Mann and Meyrink stood in the foreground as literary production was obviously stifled. Wolff's literary advisors and editors, Pinthus, Hasenclever, Haas, and Werfel, were involved in the war. But the publisher made no changes based on his perception, and "the company now had to function entirely without editors." He continued to see "no way out of the situation."[17] This remark seems strange, for a number of his own authors offered to serve Wolff as editors in order to support themselves during the war years; noteworthy among them were: Max Hermann(-Neisse), Felix Braun, and especially Brod, who had been begging for this position since the beginning of 1916. Hence it is highly questionable, as other sources state, that Kurt Wolff Publishing had offered Kafka an editorship.[18] Johannes R. Becher spent a short period in 1916 as editor, but he—just as Ehrenstein, who was peeved at Meyer—left the house after a few months because he felt he could find more favorable working conditions with other publishers.[19] The dismal situation with editors during 1917 was more than an unfortunate circumstance; it was a symptom, for amid this crisis Wolff's new ambitions were already manifest.

In 1917 the publishing trade encountered some delay because of the general economic crisis. Paper was rationed and production costs rose rapidly. Publishers felt compelled to plow back all the profits from their sales into their own businesses. Wolff did otherwise. In response to the question why he began precisely in 1917 to expand, and in part acquired other houses, and partly reestablished himself, the publisher responded after the fact in 1962:

> I wanted—it was a question of being young—to do more and more. And there also weren't too many authors for a literary publisher. Publishing more would have changed, watered down, and detoured in some way the face of the original Kurt Wolff Publishing Company. That was the reason that I looked for other names and new expressions.[20]

In actuality, 1917 marked the publisher's major shift of interest. More and more Wolff concentrated on the publication of expensive, bibliophile editions and perhaps speculated on the public, which at the time wanted to invest its money in goods of lasting value in order to escape creeping inflation. 1917 saw a boom in luxury editions. The entry into the company of Hans Mardersteig, the famous book artist and master of typography, was paradigmatic. Mardersteig not only became Wolff's closest advisor and friend, but also strengthened the house considerably in its plans to form its own art division. The establishment of an art division at the beginning of 1917, however, was only the start of the almost frightening expansion of Wolff's firm in 1917. But it was exactly this expansionism that paved the way for its eventual downfall and forced the publisher to liquidate his businesses entirely after the severe economic crises of the 1920s.[21]

4. "The Sons" and "Punishments"—the Ultimate Failure of the Novella Volume

Power and individual strength as well as humiliation and degradation are terms that bear critical importance for any description of Kafka's life and works. His striving to escape the dominating forces in life in any form and simultaneously his clouded desire to possess power himself prove to be feeble attempts. Elias Canetti held to this idea when he wrote: "Among all writers Kafka is the greatest expert of power."[22] In actuality Kafka confronted things outside the uncontested realm of power (i.e., outside of his own writing) with powerlessness and of course quite deliberately by positing his own failure *a priori* and by taking note of the manifestation of outside force without responsibility as a mere observer and sufferer in his environment. The personal threshold to resignation was quickly crossed.

Kafka expressed to his publisher many times the wish to

produce a volume of novellas that would collect his greatest stories of 1912 under one title. This project is given too little attention today and is generally underestimated when one considers the collected works. But the question of the publication of a collected volume determined in great part Kafka's relationship to his publisher for over three years. The chances for realizing his first great book were initially good, but in the end the publication did not materialize because of the publisher's delay as well as because of its policy on individual works. This circumstance naturally had personal consequences for the author; the inability to have his desires met by the publisher confirmed his own pessimistic estimation of what he had written and triggered his protective mechanisms. Without anyone at Kurt Wolff Publishing suspecting it, Kafka's conviction that he was at the time a scurrilous outsider in a weak position with the publisher intensified in the face of the failure of the novella volume.

The first and the second phases of the discussions about the volume have already been noted. Kafka's idea about a volume including the complete novellas stemmed from early 1913 when he had to abandon hope of publishing "The Man Who Was Lost Sight of." Immediately after abandoning the novel he corresponded with the publisher about the collected volume. Despite a binding promise, Wolff no longer seemed to entertain the possibility after the successful publication of *The Stoker*. In vain the author had waited since summer 1913 for news from his publisher. The volume "The Sons" did not materialize.

The second phase in the history of the novella volume ran parallel to his failure in completing the second novel. This causal relationship must be mentioned again. After working on *The Trial*, which the author had also written with an eye toward later publication,[23] Kafka immediately became obstinate about his novella project in 1915, as the psychological burden of the missing great book continued to weigh heavily upon him. Meanwhile, Kafka wrote *In the Penal Colony* and planned a volume with the title "Punishments." Together with *The Metamorphosis* and *The Judgment*, which had only been published in magazines, the new text justified the publication of a larger volume of novellas. But Kafka lacked the courage to do more than merely hint at this wish in October 1915. At that time the publisher was interested only in an individual publication of *The Metamorphosis*, and therefore this double publication "Punishments" (as befell "The Sons" because of the individual publication of *The Stoker* two years earlier) was relegated to the distant future. Although obviously displeased, Kafka acquiesced to the wishes of the publisher, and the volume "Punishments" never appeared.

Although Franz Kafka had only given up on his novella book with Meyer at the end of 1915 because of "the present circumstances" (L113), which were related to the Fontane Prize, the war, and his peripheral contact with the publisher, he gave up his hopes entirely after the publication of *The Metamorphosis*. A publication focusing on *In the Penal Colony* also appeared senseless to him, since *The Judgment* had already been printed once and *The Metamorphosis* twice. When the discussion entered its third and last phase six months later, it occurred under a different omen. A letter of July 7, 1916, from Meyer—he turned with his request to Brod, with whom he was in close correspondence—includes an important statement about the changed attitude of Kurt Wolff Publishing toward Kafka: "talk to Kafka about bringing out *The Metamorphosis* with the 'Criminal Colony' as a novel volume." The letter goes on to reveal Meyer's strong personal interest in Kafka. Of course the sales of his books in the period following the Fontane Prize had perked up, but the question remains whether that was the only reason why the publisher now tried to pave the way to the lay reader and saw an opportunity with the most recent critics. "Certainly you have read the essay by Walzel in the *Berlin Tageblatt*," Meyer wrote in his letter to Brod, "and I think one needs to exploit this for Kafka."[24]

Meyer's idea of presenting the two stories by Kafka in the company's popular novel series is puzzling for two reasons. First of all, there was the rather happenstance combination (besides Kafka had always insisted on the acceptance of *The Judgment*) and secondly the proposal to place this prose volume in the series *Der Neue Roman* ("The New Novel"). Just two days earlier Meyer had written to Brod that the company's future lay more or less in this series of novels.[25] For this inexpensive, mass-produced series he needed marketable novels, so the question arose whether Kafka's texts should be placed in such a group. Meyer himself reconsidered, and only three days later he reversed this spontaneous decision. A look at the review mentioned by Meyer reveals the basis on which the hasty decision had been made: the famed literary historian Oskar Walzel presented Kafka's prose as a poetological event in the tradition of Heinrich von Kleist and reviewed Kafka's work in great detail (i.e., *The Stoker* and *The Metamorphosis*) and acclaimed it critically. This extensive article appeared on July 6, 1916. Meyer's suggestion to assign a title in his novel series to Kafka, originates from July 7, 1916.[26]

In a letter of July 10, 1916, which like other negative letters has not been preserved, Meyer personally retracted his offer to Kafka. The reason is not known, but it can be concluded from Kafka's reply (since the novella book was not suited to the novel series because of the sales expectations) that the publisher asked for a different, larger work. The tenor of the letter must have been Meyer's wish to be able to present to the public a "market-able" title by Kafka.[27]

Only after great delay Kafka received Meyer's letter at the end of July. When he wrote to Brod in mid-July that he did not want to contact the publisher, "for it is not so urgent and he too sees no urgency[!]" (L118), he made reference to Meyer's earlier proposal. Since July 3 Kafka had been in Marienbad together with Felice, who had agreed to spend the summer vacation with him after their long separation. The days between July 3 and 13 were apparently the happiest for them during the course of their five-year relationship. Renewed trust and renewed hope emerged; Kafka described the changed situation in a letter to Brod:

> Now all that has changed and is good. Our agreement is in brief: to get married soon after the end of the war; to rent an apartment of two or three rooms in some Berlin suburb; each to assume economic responsibilities for himself. F. will go on working as she has done all along, while I—well, for myself I cannot yet say . . . Nevertheless, in this there is calm, certainty, and therefore the possibility of living. (L118)

When Kafka thereafter speaks of *his advantage*, it is charac-teristic of his changed, secure life at this moment; in an almost matter-of-fact way he set forth the problem of his writer's exis-tence: "It is not such a good idea after all to come out with a collection of three novellas, two of which have already been published. I would do better to keep still until I have something new and complete to present. If I can't do this, then better for me to keep still permanently."[28]

To that extent Kafka's opinion meshed with the publisher's, even if his position, as he also communicated it to Meyer on July 28, was "necessarily more radical" (L124). He could not offer him the longer work Meyer wanted to publish instead of the novella volume. The question about the "point" of the novella volume ("even if no longish work were to follow in the near future") was deferred to Meyer's "undoubtedly better judgment" (L124), and thus again to the decision-making power of the financial backers. The struggle for the novella volume was Kafka's struggle for a first major publication and for literary recognition. But under the premise of his own weakness, Kafka came only to agree with his publisher's decision not to publish his book of novellas. This meeting of minds—although arrived at from different positions—remained for some time the last in the conversation between Kafka and Kurt Wolff Publishing. The exchange that followed, marked by misunderstandings on both sides that in the end led to the individual printing of only *The Judgment* in *Der Jüngste Tag*, reveals the difficulties of the communication between the author and his publisher.

The Judgment as Volume 34 of the Series *Der Jüngste Tag* (1916)

In August 1916 a relatively lively correspondence took place between Meyer and Kafka. After the Fontane Prize and at the latest after Walzel's laudatory critique, Meyer indeed wanted to publish a book by Kafka. Via Brod he suggested again that under the present circumstances he would accept *In the Penal Colony* by itself for *Der Jüngste Tag* and drop the idea of a novella volume. Kafka was in accord with the latter suggestion and wrote: "it is most unlikely that this book will represent the salable book you want"(L125). But he added that *The Judgment* would also have to appear along with *In the Penal Colony* in *Der Jüngste Tag* as an individual volume. For this story, dedicated to Felice, had regained its original importance for Kafka after the happiness he had experienced with her in Marienbad. This reconciliation with Felice was precisely the reason for withdrawing the plan to publish *The Judgment* together with *The Metamorphosis* and *In the Penal Colony* under the very harsh common title of *Punishments*. At this time Kafka wanted to publish *The Judgment* individually:

> . . . each story in its own separate volume. This latter type of publication offers the advantage over the novella collection that each story can be seen individually and have its individual effect. Should you agree, I would ask that "The Judgment," which means more to me than any of the others, appear first; "In the Penal Colony" could follow at your discretion. (L125)

Of course for Meyer such an inner connection between the literary text and the author's biography would not have been evident. It is understandable that the well-versed book dealer, who still wanted to publish a best-seller, argued against the idea immediately, since *The Judgment* had comprised just thirteen pages in the *Arcadia* format. When Kafka then decisively rejected the publisher's next proposal on August 14 to combine *The Judgment* with *In the Penal Colony* in one volume ("In that case I would prefer the bigger book of stories" [L125]) and furthermore requested the publisher to do him a favor and accept his story "in a separate format" (L125), Meyer referred to the insurmountable technical difficulties. According to the publisher, using "giant typeface" would be entirely inappropriate for this text—something that Kafka questioned in a letter (L126). Meyer then asked Kafka to outline in detail all his desires to the publisher once again. Kafka complied with this request, probably with some annoyance—the letter once again was impersonal—in a two-page letter of August 19. The logic of his argumentation for the individual printing of *The Judgment* is astounding:

Initially there was no talk of issuing them in *Der jüngste Tag*
series, but only of a volume of stories, *Punishments* (containing "The Judgment"—"Metamorphosis"—"In the Penal
Colony"), which Herr Wolff projected a long while ago.
These stories have a certain unity and as a group would
naturally have bulked up to a more substantial volume than
any of the numbers of *Der jüngste Tag*. Nevertheless, I would
gladly give up the book if I saw the possibility that "The
Judgment" could be issued as a separate work. (L125-26)

Viewed from this perspective, abandoning the "more
substantial" volume of novellas that had been promised represented a concession by the author to the publisher. In return he
demanded a small, inexpensive volume that would reach thirty
pages. On the basis of this return favor Kafka believed that the
publisher could very well do him "the favor . . . of publishing
the story by itself" (L126).

The correspondence of the ensuing months appears incomplete, but Wolff must have personally turned to Kafka around the
beginning of October. (Since June 1916 the publisher had been
active again in Leipzig and was thereafter in direct contact by
mail with Brod. The supervision of the publisher's dealings with
Kafka though had long been left to Meyer.) To this letter, the
first that Kafka had received from Wolff since *The Stoker*
appeared in May 1913, the author reacted especially cordially;
he was pleased to be back "near" the publisher again ("Though
these days there is little difference between being near and being
far.") From Kafka's reply one learns that "'The Judgment' is
going to appear separately, thanks to your kindness" (L127).
Kafka certainly could not have been sure about this publication
at the time, for on October 30 he wrote to Felice about the fate
of her story: "But Wolff—incidentally without having let me
know—again seems to be trying to suppress it" (F531). The flow

of information between the author and the publisher was interrupted again, since unbeknownst to Kafka, *The Judgment* had already appeared at the time he was complaining to Felice.

For on October 20 *The Judgment*, together with the newest series of *Der Jüngste Tag* (*Gehirne* by Gottfried Benn was also part of it), was announced in a large double-sided ad in the *Börsenblatt* and printed as the 34th volume in the Wolff Library.[29] It was most likely delivered to the bookstores at the end of October. In this ad the publisher proudly made reference to the new editions of several titles from *Der Jüngste Tag*. Also announced was the second edition of *The Stoker* and *The Metamorphosis*; it is possible, however, only to verify a second edition of *The Stoker* at that time. The announcement of a second edition of *The Metamorphosis* may have been only an advertising trick, some more trumpery by Meyer, with which the publisher hoped to dispose the book trade favorably toward the successful Kafka titles.[30]

The Expressionistic Misunderstanding of Contemporary Kafka Reception

With the publication of *The Judgment*, the final chapter on Kafka's novella volume closed. Apparently remembering the promise he had made, Wolff certainly offered to make good in his letter of October, but the news came too late, for Kafka did not want to hear anything more about this senseless publication after the individual works had already appeared (cf. L127-28). The history of this failure can be divided into three phases, each of which ended with the publication of one of the stories in Wolff's *Der Jüngste Tag*. Kafka had never pressed for these individual publications. His wish for a large first book conflicted with the publisher's policy, which had other interests, a policy which in its spontaneity points more to a capricious rather than continuous nurturing of its authors. Moreover, it was an unintentionally misguided policy, since the reception of Kafka's work went astray to a large extent as the result of it. The publication of three titles in the avant-garde series was a signpost for Kafka's reception during his lifetime. By mistake, Kafka, the quiet author from Prague who was not constrained by any preconceived literary notions, became in public view one of the exemplary figures of that avant-garde expressionistic literature that scarcely anyone of his contemporaries knew how to describe or separate from other types of literature. For Kafka this meant a reputation and an expectation to which he—standing entirely outside the literary activity of the day in both thought and action—could naturally not do justice.

One could criticize Meyer for having cast Kafka into this dilemma by not clearly distinguishing between sales tactics and genuine literary promotion in the presentation of *Der Jüngste Tag* and by publishing *The Metamorphosis* for obvious advertising motives. Wolff's series of books was already synonymous with the literary expressionist movement by the end of 1915 (as shown by the literary criticism). One could reproach the opportunistic Meyer for taking advantage of this expressionist connotation with his advertising campaign and, therefore, for having fostered the persisting impression that Kafka was an expressionist; in announcing Kafka's *The Metamorphosis*, the publisher spoke directly of the "hurried sense of life, characterizing the new German writers, which is brought out with consciously new means of heightened representation."[31] Meyer could certainly call on the contemporary critics (Meyer did not view his role as embracing matters related to editors), who naturally belonged to the circle of Wolff's authors, Werfel and Pinthus, Schickele, and doubtless even on the most knowledgeable Kafka expert, Brod, who in July 1913 in a review of *Meditation* had written: "The directness with which Kafka establishes his unique style of writing instead of reality, joins him to the expressionistic direction in modern painting."[32]

For the publisher and his circle there was no doubt that Kafka—although unjustified on the basis of his work—belonged to literary expressionism.[33] Even the modest sales success of his books in 1916 following the publicity of the prize turned inevitably against the writer. Those who bought them, thus the potential readers of the newest literature, did not find Kafka a true expressionist. And because of his affiliation with Kurt Wolff Publishing and having been labeled an expressionist because of *Der Jüngste Tag*, other more conservative groups did not pay attention to him or take him seriously. He was not read and thus he could not break out into wider arenas. Owing to this misidentification, the already weak reception of Kafka was disadvantaged even more. Literary opinion worked against Kafka; here too he was forced into a borderland.

5. *In The Penal Colony*. Rejection by the Publisher (1916)

After the novella volume failed to come about, the first printing of *In the Penal Colony* was still outstanding. Kafka tolerated this fact in deference to *The Judgment*, but perhaps also because he thought that he would be able to have this novella printed in *Die Weißen Blätter*. After alluding to this possibility in an "offer" in a letter to Meyer,[34] he probably believed he would receive an invitation from Schickele. But he received no proposal to publish in *Die Weißen Blätter*. Moreover, Kurt Wolff Publishing retreated from its earlier willingness to publish *In the Penal Colony* as a single work.

In a non-extant letter from October 1916, Wolff must have

personally expressed his deep dislike for this novella by Kafka.
His polite rejection, which he apparently clothed in friendly
words about the manuscript, was based on the "painful"
elements of the story. Kafka reacted with surprising forcefulness
to this objection by Wolff, the first clear-cut, direct rejection of
one of his works by the publisher. If during the preceding years
he had argued for the publication of his texts from a purely inner
justification (which was additionally veiled by his own pessimistic manner of argumentation), he now directed the defense of his
work toward a general, public dimension. In his answer of
October 11, 1916, he wrote:

> Your criticism of the painful element accords completely with
> my opinion, but then I feel the same way about almost
> everything I have written so far. Have you noticed how few
> things are free of this painful element in one form or another?
> By way of clarifying this last story, I need only add that the
> painfulness is not peculiar to it alone but that our times in
> general and my own time as well have also been painful and
> continue to be, and my own even more consistently than the
> times. God knows how much farther I would have gone along
> this road had I written more or better, had my circumstances
> and my condition permitted me, teeth biting lips, to write as
> I longed to. (L127)

Quite obviously this affirmation of Wolff's opinion was
purely rhetorical. With this harsh note that the books from his
pen previously appearing with Wolff's consent were not any less
painful than the manuscript now under discussion, Kafka not
only placed Wolff's competency as a publisher in question but
modified Wolff's negative judgment. The explanation Kafka
directed to the publisher that in this story his particular painfulness culminated with the general painfulness, that the story thus
had application of a general nature through its direct time

reference, must be seen as a further explicit measure by the author to have *In the Penal Colony* published. The harshness of the letter and the wounded irony point to Kafka's deep disappointment. The defensive nature of the letter is increased when the writer begins to speak of his writing. In these lines one can sense Kafka's annoyance and simultaneously his helplessness vis-à-vis the publisher, who was now maneuvering to suppress *In the Penal Colony* after having done the same with the novella volume.

However, despite his clear preamble and his protest against the publisher's opinion, Kafka willingly withdrew from the publication promised him. Once again this agreement with the publisher shows itself to be rhetorical, for he wrote in the same letter:

> I also agree entirely that the story should not appear in *Der jüngste Tag*. I suppose it is also inappropriate for a public reading, though I am scheduled to read it in the Goltz Bookshop in November and I mean to do so. (L127)

Kafka underscores his failure and intensifies it by agreeing with Wolff's rejection and continuing to talk of failure and making reference to the imminent public lecture of *In the Penal Colony* in November. Thus there was complete failure on all levels, and one cannot avoid the impression that the responsibility for it in some form or other was the publisher's. Kafka's letter had a method to it. But with his pessimistic argumentation on the one hand and the skillful reference to the invitation of the well-known Goltz Gallery for a reading of that novella on the other hand, Kafka's letter fell upon deaf ears in Leipzig. Wolff's decision to withdraw the printing of *In the Penal Colony* can surely not be separated from his general desire to dissociate the literature published in his firm from any antagonistic theme or one that might result in censorship—which illustrates especially his turning to art and things bibliophile, areas that in the following years dominate the publisher's program more clearly. The novella written in November 1914—also the only complete text by Kafka not in print at this time—remained unprinted, despite the author's various suggestions for its publication. Comparable to his almost hopeless attempt to publish *The Metamorphosis*, Kafka viewed the publication of *In the Penal Colony* as a struggle against the literary industry that was weakened during the war years and sworn to other literary idols. He could not establish a foothold in the industry and remained on the periphery as a writer.

The *Country Doctor* Phase and the Change in Life (1917-1920)

> I will give up my job . . . will marry and move away
> from Prague, possibly to Berlin . . . I do hope that you,
> dear Herr Wolff, will not quite desert me, provided, of
> course, that I halfway deserve your kindness. In the face
> of all the uncertainties of the present and the future, a
> word from you at this point would mean so much to me.
> (Franz Kafka to Kurt Wolff in July 1917)

1. The Creative Period of Winter 1916-1917

*I*n September 1916 Kafka was invited by the Munich gallery "New Art—Hans Goltz" to read from his work as part of a "course entitled 'Evenings for Modern Literature'" (F502). This series of lectures had an outstanding reputation in literary circles in Munich; the names of well-known contemporary German writers were already on the list of participants. Kafka was pleasantly surprised by the invitation. Without a doubt he initially considered it an honor and a recognition of his artistic existence and work by a still very distant public. How great his disappointment must have been when he discovered that it was again Max Brod who had arranged for the invitation. It had originally been sent to Brod, who then expressed a desire to participate together with Kafka in one of these literary series.[1]

Nevertheless, Kafka accepted. Before he found out that Brod was responsible for the invitation, he had already proudly told Felice about it and even asked her to travel to Munich so that she could be there for his debut. Kafka used this invitation to Munich in an almost demonstrative manner to defend his existence as a writer. A trip from Prague to Munich during the war was not easy. It required much of Kafka's time and energy to complete the necessary border formalities and surmount the considerable "passport difficulties" (F502). In addition, there was the incalculable factor of "Munich censorship" (F529), an authority to whom his manuscript had to be delivered for examination before the reading. On the evening of November 10, 1916—immediately following his ten-hour train trip—he was finally able to read *In the Penal Colony* in the lecture hall on the second floor of the gallery before approximately 50 listeners; to begin Kafka read several poems by Brod, who was unable to obtain furlough from duty to participate in the reading.[2]

Kafka attentively studied the audience's reactions (especially that of the writer colleagues present: Max Pulver, Gottfried Kölwel, Eugen Mondt, possibly even Rainer Maria Rilke) and waited for the critical reaction to the lecture, before concluding that this entire trip to Munich was an "actual grandiose failure" (F536). With very mixed feelings, those present listened to *In the Penal Colony*; the alienated public, as one newspaper account read, could in part not endure "the excessive straining of nerves." (According to Pulver's memoirs, three women fainted.) The reviewer could not refrain from characterizing Kafka as a "sensualist of terror." Two other newspaper reports were scarcely more positive.[3] With self-tormenting certitude Kafka confirmed the complete failure of his Munich appearance, this passing two-day ordeal of his anonymity as a writer. He blamed himself for the "incredible impudence" of reading in a far off place, while "for the past year and a half" he had not read anything in Prague, even among his "best friends" (F536). It remained his only public reading outside of Prague.

Since private and public spheres in Kafka's life cannot be separated, it happened that, parallel to the failure of his literary debut in Munich, another disagreement arose between Kafka and Felice that led once more to a break in their relationship. For only four months, from the bliss in Marienbad during summer 1916 to Munich, had the period of closest understanding and new hope for a life together endured. A sudden argument with Felice (who had expressly come to Munich for the lecture of "her" writer) came to a hasty end in "that ghastly pastry shop" (F534).

Nevertheless, Kafka returned from Munich to his hometown "with renewed courage" (F541). During his absence from Prague he had made a decision and resolved to see it through. His separation from Felice resurfaces as part of the plan, for as in the summer of 1914 after the termination of their first engagement, the distance from the woman he still loved led Kafka into a new phase of creative work. The inner release from the idea of an imminent marriage gave Kafka the strength to begin writing once more and opened an avenue of inspiration for him. Kafka's failure as a writer during his Munich lecture actually led him to a contradictory conclusion: instead of retreating into a passive resigned position again, he resolved unconditionally to begin writing again. After the failure of two novel projects, after an almost two-year standstill in his literary production, after the unsuccessful public appearance, Kafka decided to muster his creative capabilities anew.

Kafka's commitment to work was uncompromising; the fact that he went looking for a room immediately upon his return supports this view. He found his working apartment in a small house in Prague's Alchimistengasse (F542). During the ensuing winter months he lived there for the exclusive purpose of writing. He continued to eat dinner at his parents' apartment; to sleep he returned to his own apartment in the Lange Gasse, where it was too noisy to write. He was able to isolate himself almost entirely from the outside world. The bond with Felice was broken; contact with Brod and other friends from Prague was infrequent. The seclusion of this "bachelor's life" (DII79), even at this time the requisite for successful writing, became more intense because of the unusually harsh winter of 1916-1917. Hunger and coal shortages accompanied the cold, public services came to a standstill, streetcar lines were hardly maintained, theaters and cafés remained closed.

During these months, from the end of November 1916 until the end of February 1917, the prose pieces that later formed the core of the volume *A Country Doctor* evolved: *The Bucket Rider*, *Jackals and Arabs*, *The New Advocate*, *A Country Doctor*, *Up in the Gallery*, *A Visit to a Mine*, *A Horseman*, *The Brief Time* ("The Next Village"), *A Fratricide*, and also the later version *Murder of a Brother*, *The Neighbor*, as well as other prose pieces and fragments such as *The Bridge*, *The Crypt Guard*, and *Hunter Gracchus*.

Kafka did not pursue larger literary forms but wrote again in the style of *Meditation*; the texts are short and concentrated and more artistic and complete than the early prose. Kafka's utilization of the parable characterizes this creative phase, which differs from the previous ones in its new narrative perspective.[4] In their own way the surviving documents establish the transformation: Kafka abandoned the *Quarto Notebooks*, which had long served him as diaries, and began the *Octavo Notebooks*. These works are smaller than those of the *Quarto Notebooks*, but also less rambling, more concentrated, and at times parablelike. One can venture the guess that, since Kafka had failed at the expansiveness of novel writing and at the impossibility of spanning a plot to the end, he now pursued his literary possibilities in short prose works he could complete.

2. New Publication Plans: The Volume of Stories *Responsibility*

The *Octavo Notebooks* contain listings of the newly written prose works; the first list from the end of February 1917 is placed at the end of the first *Octavo Notebooks* (actually the second, cf. sy80) and contains eleven texts (DF400). From this as well as from other lists one can conclude that Kafka was concerned about the ordering and possible sequencing of these texts. Early on there was an express desire to have the eleven prose pieces collected and printed in a single volume. Even during the actual writing process, Kafka's desire to have them published is evident; one must assume that he expressly wrote these works with an eye toward eventual publication—his Munich plans would seem to support this.

In a diary entry Brod recounts having visited Kafka once in his working apartment. On Sunday, February 11, 1917, Brod notes: "With Kafka in Alchemists' street. He read aloud beautifully. The monastic cell of a real writer" (FK156). Kafka was once again pleased enough with his writing that he read to Brod from it—he had not done so since 1915. Apparently he read his prose piece *Eleven Sons*, for Brod recounts that Kafka explained this text to him: "The eleven sons are quite simply eleven stories I am working on this very moment" (FK140). The list at the end of the first *Octavo Notebook* includes exactly eleven titles!

The list is in no way the result of the author's fleeting fancy. It points much more to an ingrained view, as the third *Octavo Notebook* (in the correct chronological order) proves. (Brod mistakenly labeled this notebook the sixth in his editing.) At the end of this volume there is another summarizing list, which once again shows Kafka's intention to make some minor changes. The titles here are: "*Ein Traum* (A Dream), *Vor dem Gesetz* (Before the Law), *Eine kaiserliche Botschaft* (An Imperial Message), *Die kurze Zeit* (The Short Time), *Ein altes Blatt* (An Old Manuscript), *Schakale und Araber* (Jackals and Arabs), *Auf der Galerie* (Up in the Gallery), *Der Kübelreiter* (The Bucket Rider), *Ein Landarzt* (A Country Doctor), *Der neue Advokat* (The New Advocate), *Ein Brudermord* (A Fratricide), *Elf Söhne* (Eleven Sons)" (DF404). Kafka, who had written new pieces in March and April,[5] modified his table of contents: instead of the previous eleven, he now planned twelve texts for the volume. He artistically made the last text, *Eleven Sons*, an epilogue in the form of a story, for it is actually an enumeration. Developing this connection between content and outward form, critics have attempted to identify Kafka's tendency toward intentional mystification in the story *Eleven Sons*. The interpretation is that this story relates to literary objects, even if it is carefully veiled. Malcolm Pasley's analysis is plausible. The text begins "I have eleven sons," and continues "I, his [the] father" (PC162). Immediately following that, Kafka characterizes these eleven sons sequentially in short sentences. Pasley's attempt to match up the identity of these eleven sons with the eleven stories leads him to the conclusion that Kafka proceeded to work here with artistic design, because in *Eleven Sons* he was probably commenting on the preceding eleven stories in summary fashion.[6]

This fact is not surprising: the writer who his whole life long brought his writing into visible connection with the procreative process, the pregnancy of woman, the birthing stage, and the growth of the infant, expressly viewed his literary creative power as "analogous to his father's creative power," as Brod communicates (FK140). Kafka's wish to be a father cannot be denied. Yet the pre-conditions and peripheral factors of real fatherhood were mired in doubt—such an attempt had just failed again miserably. Did Kafka now literarily procreate the sons which reality denied to him? The planned publication of a collected volume with the piece *Eleven Sons* as the concluding twelfth text supports such a position.

The publication did not materialize in this form. One may assume that the author felt that such an artistic trick was too obvious. Thus he veiled his original intention, changed the sequence, and added other small stories to the collection. Under what title he then intended to have the collected volume printed, Kafka disclosed only a short while thereafter in a letter from mid-April 1917 to Martin Buber: *Responsibility* was to be the title for his new book.[7] All signs point to the fact that Kafka was very pleased with what he had written (in so far as Kafka was ever satisfied with his work); his intention to have it published was quite clear in the spring of 1917. But a direct link to his publisher, to Kurt Wolff Publishing, was missing, and his personal "relationship" to Wolff was "much too tenuous and without influence" (L130), as Kafka commented in a letter from the beginning of 1917, for him to turn to the publisher with the manuscript on his own. His work and position as a writer seemed too insignificant to him to undertake such active measures.

Although the manuscript of *Responsibility* was surely ready by mid-April 1917, Kafka could not bring himself to deliver it without first receiving a personal and binding invitation from the publisher. One may identify a lack of self-confidence in Kafka here, but it was certainly above all the lack of any type of literary self-understanding (not of artistic!) that maneuvered him into this position. He needed the security of someone who was willing to assume complete responsibility for the future of his work. In early 1917 Kafka was merely waiting for a sign from the publisher before sending off the completed manuscript.

3. 1917—The Year of the Small Prints

Kafka had become passive with regard to the publisher, but on another level he exhibited a remarkable activity. When his writing began to falter in April 1917 (again this phase of inspiration lasted five months), he advantageously employed short literary forms. The possibility of widespread individual publications, renewed indications of his desire to reach the public, and repeated parallels to *Meditation* are revealed here. This is the year in which several journals were to list Kafka's name among their steady contributors: *Der Jude*, *Die Selbstwehr*, *Marsyas*, *Die schöne Rarität*. The *Prager Tagblatt*, as well as anthologies and publishers' almanacs, included texts by Kafka. The publications of brief stories by Kafka reached their incontrovertible high point around 1917 amidst the crisis of World War I.

Der Jude

The presentation of Judaism as a living ethnic entity and the discussion of the question of the Eastern Jews were the basic themes of the monthly *Der Jude* ("The Jew") which commenced publication in 1916. Brod, whose literary development into a Jewish-Zionist writer became ever more clearly drawn, participated in the goals and fate of this journal with increasing activity. He argued especially with its editor, the Jewish writer and philosopher Martin Buber, and advocated expansion of the program to include a literary section. In 1916 he wrote to Buber: "You should place the best writers next to our best social thinkers in the revue; the youngest generation includes Werfel, Kafka, Wolfenstein, etc."[8] Upon Brod's insistence, Buber was introduced to Kafka (the Fontane Prize winner) in November 1915 and asked him at that time for a brief manuscript for the first numbers of *Der Jude*. Kafka politely rejected the offer by saying he was "far too burdened and insecure to think of speaking up in such company, even in the most minor way" (L115).[9] A year later Brod sent Buber "a little original by Kafka," whose "begging," as the accompanying letter stated, had bothered him greatly. Brod's double efforts became obvious: on the one hand, he attempted to win over Buber for the publication of a Kafka text, on the other, he hoped to interest Kafka in working on *Der Jude*, and for Brod that meant working for Judaism as well.[10] The small original (the brief piece *A Dream* from *The Trial*) was rejected by Buber "in a letter more complimentary than any ordinary letter of acceptance could have been" (F506), as Kafka almost surprisingly emphasized.

At the beginning of 1917 Brod referred the editor of *Der Jude* to his friend's recently completed stories. Upon Buber's invitation Kafka sent him his texts immediately on April 22 to make a selection for a publication. "I am sending twelve pieces . . . All these pieces and some others are to be published sometime in the future as a book, collectively entitled *Responsibility*" (L131-32).[11] Thus Kafka hoped to publish them as a book and continued to work on arranging this collected volume. He was able to offer Buber a preprint from the future large book; this explains his confidence. From the bundle Buber chose two pieces: *Jackals and Arabs* and *A Report to an Academy*. For the heading he proposed "Two parables." Kafka replied:

> Many thanks for your friendly letter. So I shall be published in *Der Jude* after all, and always thought that impossible. May I ask you not to call the pieces parables; they are not really parables. If they are to have any overall title at all, the best might be: "Two Animal Stories". (L132)[12]

Both these stories by Kafka thus appeared as first printings in the same year under this heading in the October-November number of *Der Jude*.[13] As the first story lay in print before Kafka, he had to "draw fresh breath from outbursts of vanity and complacency." This notebook entry from mid-October 1917 continues: "The orgy while reading the story in *Der Jude*. Like a squirrel in its cage. Bliss of movement. Desperation about constriction, craziness of endurance, feeling of misery confronted with the repose of what is external" (DF64). Here Kafka sketches the gap between writing and publishing, the problem of his literary existence.

Die Selbstwehr

In an announcement in one of the first numbers of *Der Jude* the publisher of *Die Selbstwehr* ("Self-Defense") named Kafka one of the collaborators for the 1916 volume. *Die Selbstwehr*, a weekly with strong Zionist views aimed at Bohemian Jews, had been appearing since March 1907 in Prague. Franz Kafka had belonged to its readership since 1911.[14] The author's association with this journal, which focused on local problems and concerns of Judaism related to life in Prague, was established through Brod. Early on Brod was quite active in it, for many of his early short works and essays appeared there, and he became the closest advisor of the editor, Siegmund Kaznelson, during the war years. In 1915 Kaznelson published a Kafka text in the New Year's commemorative number of the journal, dated September 7. He probably received the manuscript through Brod; Kafka's legend from *The Trial* entitled *Before the Law* was published there for the first time. Although the later printings reveal major changes, Kafka certainly had a part in plans for this printing. Several times during the course of 1915 he had read his little "doorkeeper story" (DII112). Exactingly, he had made note of the "greater attention" that Felice paid to this text when he read it and others to her in January 1915 in Bodenbach (DII112).

Kafka's *A Dream*, rejected by Buber for *Der Jude*, found its way to the editors of *Die Selbstwehr*. The publisher of the *Die Selbstwehr* was planning a collected work for the year 1917. Buber, himself co-editor of the volume, was able to recommend the publication of *A Dream*, even though he had rejected it for publication in *Der Jude*. Included in this collected work *Das jüdische Prag* ("Jewish Prague"), edited by the staff of *Die Selbstwehr* and appearing in December 1916, was Kafka's *A Dream*.[15]

Franz Kafka's views on Judaism were very discordant and cannot easily be outlined in brief. Characteristic of his position is the remark he made in a letter of June 1914 to Grete Bloch: "I admire Zionism and am nauseated by it" (F423). More positive, but equally as contradictory, were his remarks associated with the views of practicing Jews. Remembering his father, he despised the non-believing Jews. But in spite of all the contradictions in this area of his life, no other journal is mentioned so frequently in Kafka's letters as the Jewish-Zionist *Die Selbstwehr*. A possible reason was that Kafka viewed this journal as the work of his friends and—as he indicated in a letter to Felix Weltsch—as their personal message to him during his absences from Prague (cf. L235). It is therefore difficult to defend Brod's standpoint that Kafka's publications in *Die Selbstwehr* represent the author's "acknowledgment" of Judaism (ÜFK271). Another of Kafka's friends, Otto Pick, noted in the aforementioned collected work, *Das jüdische Prag*, that Kafka had in no way disclosed his beliefs.[16] And as late as 1922 Kafka sketched for Brod the "absence of any firm Jewish ground beneath my feet" (L349).

The editors and collaborators of *Die Selbstwehr* were and remained his friends. Kaznelson and the journal's subsequent editors—Nelly Thieberger (from 1917) and Felix Weltsch (from 1918)—belonged to Kafka's inner circle in Prague. Thus the group that had formed around the Jewish journal *Die Selbstwehr* was in certain respects a familiar one for Kafka. Precisely because of this personal relationship, Kafka presented other short texts in later years for printing in *Die Selbstwehr*: *An Imperial Message* appeared in September 1919, *The Cares of a Family Man* in December 1919, and *An Old Manuscript* in 1921. It is worth noting that Kafka took part each time in a special commemorative number.[17]

The *Marsyas* and other Journals

The publication of three prose pieces in the exclusive Berlin bimonthly journal *Marsyas*, unlike those in the *Die Selbstwehr*, cannot be traced back to Kafka's personal contacts. The literary-artistic journal appeared from 1917 on as a luxury print on handmade paper in folio format; the small edition (235 numbered copies) and the very high price (600 marks, and 1500 marks for the special edition) characterized it as a rather esoteric-artistic undertaking from the start. Its editor, the then twenty-six-year-old Viennese writer Theodor Tagger (better known during the 1920s as a dramatist under the pseudonym Ferdinand Bruckner), outlined the programmatic philosophy in his announcement of May 1917—in a manner that Kafka could have fully endorsed at the time: "Its goal is precise and limited—to present the best and richest the times have to offer after the most careful selection."

For *Marsyas*, the journal that conceived its basic task as the preservation of values, Tagger accepted exclusively original literary contributions and graphics—politics was excluded. The connection to *Marsyas* surely came about because of Brod, who had published several contributions in it. Kafka was already listed as a contributor of the subsection *Notes—Chronicle of New Literature and Graphics* in the announcement of the first number of *Marsyas*. But, as can be seen from the announcement of May 1917, the plan was that he have a larger contribution for the next numbers: "the novella *In the Penal Colony* by Franz Kafka,"[18] that story for which Kafka had unsuccessfully sought publication, was to be published. Two of Kafka's small prose pieces lay before Tagger in April 1917. By all appearances Kafka was not particularly interested in publishing them; also in April, he wrote to Buber: "The New Advocate and A Country Doctor are at present with *Marsyas*. If, however, precisely these two pieces should seem to you usable, I can recall them from *Marsyas*; that will probably not be too difficult" (L131-32).[19] Placing them with Buber's *Der Jude* was without a doubt more important than the publication of his work in *Marsyas*. Only after Buber had selected the "animal stories" did Kafka forward other texts to Tagger for selection; the editorial decisions for the July-August edition were to be made by June 17. In this first edition of *Marsyas* Kafka's *An Old Manuscript*, *The New Advocate*, and *A Fratricide* appeared as original editions.[20]

The printing of the more significant *In the Penal Colony* in the main part of the journal never materialized. Since reading *In the Penal Colony* in Munich, Kafka had reservations of another kind; his lasting impression was that it was his story's conclusion that was most heavily criticized at that time. When Kafka set out to revise the ending of *In the Penal Colony* for publication in *Marsyas* at the beginning of August 1917, he was unsuccessful. Despite the fact that he put forth the greatest effort, the attempts to begin again and again are contained in his diary (DII175ff.). During the night following his last attempt at revision, his lung illness broke out. Kafka then abandoned reworking the conclusion of his story.

The period during 1917 was without a doubt the high point of Kafka's own initiative on behalf of the publication of his work. One can say that his will to have manuscripts printed and to present the work to the public was never so clearly defined. In a letter of November 1917 Kafka states that any [!] magazine "seem[s] tempting enough at the moment" for the publication of his work (L167). Up until the end of 1917—corresponding to his biographical rhythm—Kafka attempted to publish.[21] Thus Kafka's name stood on the list of contributors to the first numbers of the literary-artistic journal *Die schöne Rarität* ("The Beautiful Rarity") from its inception in July 1917.[22] Another journal published a Kafka sample in a new announcement; whether the literary journal from Bremen *Der Orkan* ("The Hurricane") planned to reprint a future Kafka story is unclear.[23] Kafka intended to offer two of his prose pieces to the theatrical and literary monthly *Das junge Deutschland* ("Young Germany"), edited by his acquaintance from his early Prague days, Paul Kornfeld; *An Old Manuscript* and *The Bucket Rider*, however, did not appear there.[24] He actively took part in the journal plans of the psychoanalyst and student of Freud, Otto Gross; the *Blätter zur Bekämpfung des Machtwillens* ("Papers on the Struggle against the Power Seekers"), however, never got beyond the planning stages.[25] Kafka seriously sought a publication in *Daimon*, a journal from the circle of new Austrian and Bohemian writers. The *Prager Tagblatt* reprinted *A Dream* on January 6, 1917, in its entertainment section. Also a reprint —this time unauthorized—*Jackals and Arabs* and *A Report to an Academy* appeared in the *Österreichische Morgenzeitung* ("Austrian Morning News").[26] During the course of 1917 Josef Körner had received Kafka's agreement to a literary contribution for the literature section of the *Donauland* ("Danube Country"), which he edited. In December Kafka retreated from this hasty promise because the Austrian-nationalist family newspaper seemed to him an "unmitigated lie," as he indicated "frankly" to Körner; he naturally did not want to participate "voluntarily" in "something patently untruthful" (L179). For the same reasons Kafka declared emphatically to the editors of *Anbruch* ("New Dawn") in December that he "would not contribute" (L182).

This phase of opening up to the outside ceased abruptly at the end of 1917. Since the majority of the journals previously mentioned could only resume their work after 1918, there were no further publications of texts by the author. Undeniably Kafka's position stands in direct relationship to the outbreak of his serious illness. After he was diagnosed with lung tuberculosis, he rejected all publication as a rule. In a letter that Kafka sent to Johannes Urzidil, the co-editor of the monthly for culture *Der Mensch* ("Man") at the beginning of 1918, the basic tenor of the following years is sounded. The answer encompasses just one sentence: "Many thanks for your kind invitation and the copy of your magazine but I must ask you not to expect any contribution from me, at least for the present, since I have nothing I could publish "(L205).

Contributions in Publisher's Almanacs and Anthologies

Franz Kafka was a regular and avid reader of the literary almanacs and catalogues that the well-known German book publishers put out yearly to promote their new books and to define their programs. The early diary entries establish Kafka's interest. Brod recalls that "Kafka enjoyed reading publishers' catalogues and almanacs (Insel, S. Fischer, Georg Müller, A. Langen) and let the mere titles run wild with his imagination."[27] According to a theory by Pasley, Kafka even once took a Kurt Wolff almanac as the point of departure for his poetic imagination in writing *A Visit to a Mine*.[28] After editing his first almanac, *Das bunte Buch*, at the end of 1913, Kurt Wolff described the purpose and meaning of the undertaking in a letter to the author, Countess Mechtilde Lichnowsky, whom he sought to attract: "My intention with this book is for the first time to give a picture of my proposed publishing house in some kind of a collection other than a catalogue "(WBr157).

In *Das bunte Buch* Wolff gave examples of the poetic creativity of his authors; he presented a representative cross-section of the company's activity. Although the publisher was actually intent on accepting only original contributions, i.e., first printings of his authors, in contrast to the literary journals, the almanac was supposed to advertise the titles available from the publisher. Kurt Wolff thus addressed himself to the future's youthful audience with whom the modest, inexpensive books also had their greatest success. *Das bunte Buch* was the house's first real bestseller, and the subsequent high sales of the almanacs did not lag behind.

From the start the publisher included an original contribution by Kafka in each of the almanacs. The sales of Kafka's works were slow and his books were among the "most available" from

Kurt Wolff over the course of the years. His small prose pieces were suited marvelously for individual printing. Thus in December 1921, at a time when Kafka was already certain of not wanting to appear any more under the Kurt Wolff imprint, the publisher turned to Brod with the following request: "We are preparing an almanac. In this almanac we would like to include primarily unpublished texts. Naturally we cannot leave out Kafka. Perhaps you would be so kind as to help us acquire a small, characteristic, and beautiful contribution by Kafka."[29]

As has already been mentioned, Kafka's *Reflections for Gentlemen-Jockeys*, in print two times previously, had already been accepted at that time for *Das bunte Buch*. At the beginning of 1916 a new almanac appeared. In the course of the advertising campaign for *Der Jüngste Tag*, Meyer had proposed an almanac that would have a broad impact. After initial reservations—at the time Wolff was considering a collection dedicated to his biblio-phile-historical program (WV708)—the publisher agreed. Meyer could then communicate to Werfel: "Kurt Wolff likes the idea of an almanac . . . Understood: it should be an almanac of *Der Jüngste Tag* . . . that is, of new writers in the context of *Der Jüngste Tag*."[30]

Meyer delegated determination of the almanac's content, *Vom Jüngsten Tag—Ein Almanach neuer Dichtung*, to the publisher's sole literary advisors available during the war years, Werfel and Brod. Kafka's *Before the Law*, which was first published in the September 1915 edition of *Die Selbstwehr*, was accepted. The 280-page almanac, which consciously selected works of the expressionistic generation, was a considerable public success; in November 1916 a second edition (10,000 additional copies) appeared in somewhat different form and bearing the date 1917. *Before the Law* was published here for the second time with different page numbers.[31] If Meyer had channeled the publisher's efforts toward *Der Jüngste Tag* at the beginning of 1916, the change of interest toward commercialization in the direction of the novel was now evident. *Der neue Roman* ("The New Novel") was also the name of the almanac of Kurt Wolff Publishing for the year 1917; it appeared in an edition of 30,000 copies and was supposed to promote the sales of the series that came on the market in summer 1916. While the publisher could of course in this instance not accept any contribution by Kafka for it, the author was immediately represented by two texts in the almanac of the following year, *Die neue Dichtung* ("New Literature").

The history of publication of Kafka's two contributions to the 1918 almanac deserves closer examination. Far more important than previously thought were the consequences for the relationship between Kafka and Wolff that developed from this printing, consequences that had a subsequent effect on the relationship during the course of the typesetting of Kafka's collected volume *A Country Doctor*.

The typesetting of Kafka's prose works, *The Murder* and *A Country Doctor*, occurred in the almanac of Kurt Wolff Publishing in 1918 in a way other than previously thought. *The Murder* must be regarded as an early version discarded by Kafka immediately after he wrote *A Fratricide* that was first printed in *Marsyas*. Contrary to earlier assumptions, the origination of this pre-version can be fixed with reasonable certainty on New Year's Eve 1916 (datum ante quem). On this day Brod, following up on Wolff's invitation from the same month, sent the publisher "two contributions for an almanac," one of his own poems and "a prose contribution by Kafka."[32] Wolff agreed to both contributions and thanked Brod and especially Kafka for the submission. In the same letter, however, he had to clear up a misunderstanding. At that time he had only requested texts for his almanac *Der neue Roman*, for which of course only excerpts from novels would be considered. But the publisher added: "Nevertheless, I will gratefully keep the both submissions for a new almanac of *Der Jüngste Tag*, which is now being prepared and which should appear at the latest by the end of the summer."

A closer examination of the context reveals that the mentioned prose contribution by Kafka could only have been *The Murder*. Analyses of the texts proves that *The Murder* is an earlier stage of *A Fratricide*, a fact also confirmed by a later Kafka document (cf. L207). *A Fratricide* already appeared in the first listing of his works in the *Octavo Notebooks*, that is, before the end of February 1917 (DF404). In addition, the new text was the version used for the printing in *Marsyas*. Consequently it would have been impossible for Kafka to have sent *The Murder* to the publisher after February 1917; the assumption that Kafka had made this just-completed text available in response to Wolff's hasty invitation of December 1916 is plausible. The manuscript of *The Murder* remained with Wolff in Leipzig and was forgotten, since a new almanac of *Der Jüngste Tag* did not appear. The following account documents how little personal contact, how superficial the author-publisher relationship between Wolff and Kafka actually was, and how superficially Kafka's works were read at Kurt Wolff Publishing, for the similarity of the two texts, *The Murder* and *A Fratricide*, was apparently not recognized by either Wolff or Meyer. When Kafka presented the publisher his manuscript for *A Country Doctor* in July 1917, the assumption in Leipzig was that these were two entirely different prose pieces, because the titles were different and the texts varied (though very insignificantly). This mistake, which borders on the embarrassing, was only cleared up later, at the end of 1918, by a rather peeved Kafka.

But before matters reached that point, the question of a

contribution by Kafka for the almanac *Die neue Dichtung*, planned for Christmas 1917, still remained. In the meantime Wolff had received the manuscripts of thirteen prose pieces by Kafka. In order to advertise this forthcoming publication in his almanac, the publisher decided to print the title story, *A Country Doctor*, with the note: "From a collection of unpublished stories." Only at this time did Wolff recall the small prose piece that Kafka had sent him via Brod at the beginning of the year and that was expressly intended for publication in a publisher's almanac. Without further consultation with Kafka, Wolff printed the old version of *A Fratricide*. Through this mistake a text long discarded by Kafka, *The Murder*, was printed; the publisher placed the following note in his almanac after this second contribution by Kafka as well: "From a collection of unpublished stories."[33] This disquieting note points to the ensuing misunderstanding.

Moreover, Wolff failed to send the author his usual copy. Kafka had received both almanacs of *Der Jüngste Tag* (1916 and 1917) from the publisher, and most likely the almanac *Der neue Roman*. But he certainly did not receive the other almanac, *Die neue Dichtung*, which appeared at the end of 1917, before 1920. Only at this time did Milena bring the publication to his attention, for at the first hint by Milena, Kafka could still jokingly answer in April 1920: "I did not write any novella entitled 'Murderers' (although this was apparently advertised in a catalog)—there is some misunderstanding, but since it's supposed to be the best one of the lot maybe it's mine after all" (M20).

In the publication of three prose pieces in the *Almanach der neuen Jugend* ("Almanac of the New Youth") as well as in two anthologies of the publishers Furche and Rowohlt, no direct participation by the author can be documented. It is, nevertheless, important to mention these contemporary collections that prematurely accepted Kafka's works, even if only briefly. That his short prose pieces, as much as they were predestined to it because of their length, found no place in other anthologies of the time, likewise documents Kafka's peripheral position as a writer within the complex literary world. No contribution by Kafka was even accepted for Oskar Wiener's collection *Deutsche Dichter aus Prag* ("German Writers from Prague"), which appeared at the end of 1918. Publications of his works in anthologies, especially in ones which could have garnered him a new, expanded circle of readers, remained extremely rare right up until his death.

In this regard the *Almanach der neuen Jugend* of 1917, edited by Heinz Barger, can be singled out because Kafka's *A Dream* was accepted for it. In strict chronological terms, this was the first printing.[34] The almanac of the Berlin publishing house *Neue Jugend* appeared toward the end of November 1916. Its publisher, Wieland Herzfelde, who had recently turned twenty, renamed his firm Malik Publishing a short time later. It was also Herzfelde who had prepared and proofread the almanac until "fall 1916" (RaII229), when he was drafted in early November to serve on the western front. Barger, cofounder of the *Neue Jugend*, which had been bought up by Herzfelde at the beginning of 1916, exploited this opportunity for himself—he apparently took the galleys prepared by Herzfelde and added "some" of his own selections to them; in the publisher's note he referred to himself as the sole editor of the almanac. According to a statement by Herzfelde, the texts Barger added were "old pieces" by Annette Kolb and Martin Buber.

Herzfelde later reported in a letter that he himself accepted Kafka's story *A Dream* for the almanac, but he did not disclose how he had gotten hold of the short prose piece.[35] Since it definitely involved *A Dream*, another possibility contradicting

Herzfelde's account is plausible: Barger had reaccepted a text by Buber with whom he was subsequently in contact. Buber had just rejected Kafka's prose piece for the October number of *Der Jude*, so it is conceivable that he passed on the manuscript —along with his own text—to the *Verlag der Neuen Jugend*, and that *A Dream* was thus accepted by Barger for the almanac through Buber's mediation. In any case, this almanac introduced Kafka to a wider, more significant circle of readers, since the book was one of the few intellectually attractive titles which, in spite of its politically sharp tongue, was able to escape censorship from Berlin for a time. (Hans Reimann recalls that the almanac was "too deep for the Berlin watchdogs and therefore they had approved it, the blockheads."[36]) Many of Kafka's later great admirers (such as Walter Benjamin and Bertolt Brecht) were first introduced to him there.

In the summer of 1918, Kafka's story *Jackals and Arabs* from *A Country Doctor* appeared as a second printing in the first volume of a larger anthology, *Neue deutsche Erzähler* ("New German Writers"), which was edited by J. Sandmeier in the series *Liebesgaben deutscher Hochschüler* ("Special Gifts of German Students"). The source information ("*A Country Doctor*. Short Stories not yet published, Kurt Wolff Publishing, Leipzig") as well as an editorial notice in the second edition ("authorized by author and publisher") leads to the suspicion that Kafka was not actively involved in the publication.[37]

Kafka hunts through the "darknesses of the moment," according to the short description of his prose by Max Krell in the preface to *Die Entfaltung. Novellen an die Zeit* ("The Unfolding. Novellas to Time"), the anthology he edited in December 1920. Appearing in the same house (Ernst Rowohlt) and in a comparable design, this anthology of modern German prose was supposed to tie in with the success of Kurt Pinthus' important collection of poems, *Menschheitsdämmerung* ("Dawn of Man"). Krell accepted Kafka's *A Fratricide*, which, if one counts the printing of the earlier version *The Murder*, is among the most frequently published of the author's texts during his lifetime. Details point to the fact that Kafka learned of this publication only after the anthology was edited and that he did not participate in its planning.[38]

No further publications of texts in anthologies, publisher's almanacs, or other literary collections occurred during Kafka's lifetime. During the course of his entire career as a writer, Kafka appeared only eight times in such a publication, at a time when he was struggling to have his works published. It is exactly these types of publications that would have been important vehicles to facilitate broader public access to his work and to attract new readers. Even despite the fact that this period was a lyrical one and that the greatest part of literary anthologies was devoted to poetry, the eight listings seem shamefully scant, especially if one considers that Kafka's short prose pieces were well-suited for exactly this type of publication.

4. *A Country Doctor*. The Three-Year Story of Publication

For quite some time Wolff was unaware of his author's renewed period of creativity or of his wish to edit a volume of collected stories. It was only after being prodded by Brod in a letter that the publisher personally contacted Kafka again on July 3, 1917. The reserved manner in which Wolff couched his request that the recently completed work be forwarded reveals his uncertainty about wanting to reestablish personal ties after a gap of so many years. It was Wolff's second letter to his author since the publication of *The Stoker* in May 1913. With his request for a new manuscript Wolff had not only hit upon the right moment, but also upon the correct tone with its sense of urgency and readiness to oblige. Kafka, who had been waiting for news of this sort from his publisher since April, forwarded thirteen prose pieces by return mail. But in his accompanying letter he could once again not avoid playing down his hope for publication with his pessimistic manner of reasoning; once again he belittled his work on the surface but actually promoted it and left the burden of responsibility for a decision to the publisher: "I am most happy to hear from you directly once again. I had an easier time of it this winter, which in any case is now well behind us. I am sending some of the better work of this period, thirteen prose pieces. It is a far cry from what I would really like to do" (L133).

Much in the style of Kafka's reasoning, Wolff then convinced the author of the opposite; he himself found the pieces "extraordinarily beautiful and accomplished" and offered Kafka, as he wrote, a "commercial publication" (WBr43). Wolff's decisive assent—and with it the acceptance of a degree of responsibility for publication—gave Kafka a "certain reassurance," and he immediately seized the opportunity to raise an issue that had now (after his second engagement to Felice in the summer of 1917) come to the fore and that had been weighing on him for a long time. Rejuvenated in his literary intentions by the previous productive phase, he planned to give up his post, marry, and move to Berlin in order to earn a living as a writer, although he indicated an "oppressive fear" of doing so. The letter to the publisher continues: "I do hope that you, dear Herr Wolff, will not quite desert me, provided, of course, that I halfway deserve your kindness. In the face of all the uncertainties of the present and the future, a word from you at this point would mean so much to me" (L134-35).

Wolff immediately dispelled the fears Kafka expressed:

"Most sincerely and most gladly I declare my readiness to give you, even after the war, continuous material support" (WBr44). But matters did not end with this obliging gesture on the part of the publisher, for after a personal conversation between Wolff and Brod in Leipzig a further welcome suggestion, unexpected by Kafka, followed. Wolff now wanted to simultaneously publish individual editions of not only *A Country Doctor* but also of *In the Penal Colony*. Kafka was particularly surprised that Wolff, despite the crises of the day, planned the same type of expensive bibliophile edition for both volumes, in which *Meditation* had previously appeared (WBr45). Kafka could not restrain his enthusiasm at the publisher's attentiveness: "I could not wish for a finer proposal for the *Country Doctor*. Of my own accord I would certainly not have dared to choose type of that size . . ." (L136). Of course, Wolff retreated from publishing *In the Penal Colony* on artistic grounds. But Kafka's enthusiasm at the publisher's decision led him to the concluding remark: "Besides, should my powers halfway hold out, you will receive better work from me than the 'Penal Colony'"(L136).

Quite obviously a significant interaction between author and publisher had taken place here. From Wolff's preceding letters, Kafka could see that the publisher now apparently had faith in his literary future and intended to support him. This new dialogue with the publisher, which began so positively, produced immediate results; after his publisher's personal, accommodating signal, Kafka spontaneously promised a work he had not yet written! This moment marked the start of fruitful cooperation between Kafka and Wolff, the essential element for a successful author-publisher relationship.

Kafka's delight at the promising new beginning in his relationship with his publisher did not last very long. After Kafka delivered the manuscript, outlined the title and exact order of stories for the book for the publisher,[39] and then signaled "better work" for the future, the correspondence from Leipzig broke off without comment. If Kafka had believed he could count on Wolff's support for his work as a result of the attentive overtures that were now finally forthcoming, and, furthermore, if he had counted on continuing and, above all, more personal attention from the publisher, he was left disappointed. His letter of September 4 went unanswered. After a new creative phase and with the certainty of several publication commitments from magazines, the surprisingly generous offers from the publisher and, last but not least, his second engagement to Felice, Kafka found himself incontrovertibly at the high point of his life during the summer of 1917. With unrelenting consistency, the setbacks then followed.

August 13, 1917. The Turning Point in His Life

At the end of his letter of September 4 to Wolff, Kafka made an almost offhanded remark: "The disease which for years now has been brought on by headaches and sleeplessness has suddenly broken out. It is almost a relief" (L136). This letter to the publisher was written on the very day that a specialist's diagnosis confirmed Kafka's suspicion that he had tuberculosis of the lungs. For Kafka, who from the outset was more certain of his tuberculosis than all the doctors examining him, this outbreak of the disease signified a break in his life that was both corroborating and frightening. It represented a comprehensive change in his life, though not the one he had hoped for. As Kafka knew, there was no hope of recovery from the nocturnal "gush of blood" that heralded the disease.[40]

A new period in his life began. Marriage to Felice was now impossible for objective reasons; Kafka's illness officially caused their final separation in December 1917. By the beginning of September 1917 Kafka had requested his pension. But being only thirty-four and presumed to have "lung disease," he merely received an extended leave of absence, which he began several days thereafter. The following months were spent with his sister Ottla in Zürau. His life's pattern was totally changed by this move to the country. The incontestable reality of the disease configured a new intellectual constellation. He now wanted "to follow with utmost resolution the lines of [his] previous life" (L166). Facing the likelihood of certain death, Kafka began to confront life philosophically. The aphorisms, Kafka's meditations, which Brod later printed under the often misunderstood heading *Reflections on Sin, Suffering, Hope, and the True Way*, were the result.[41] The prose pieces *An Everyday Confusion*, *The Truth about Sancho Pansa* and *Felice, The Silence of the Sirens* emerged. In his diary at the end of September 1917 he noted in a manner characteristic of his new intellectual make-up: "I can still have passing satisfaction from works like *A Country Doctor*, provided I can still write such things at all (very improbable). But happiness only if I can raise the world into the pure, the true, and the immutable." (DII187)

The "Feeling of Misery at the Calm of the Outer World"

Kafka continued to wait for news from the publisher in response to his letter of September 4. At the beginning of November—already somewhat vexed—he wrote in a letter to Brod: "Today I received the statement from Wolff on 102 copies of *Meditation* for '16-17, amazingly high sale, but I haven't received the statement he promised you he would send, nor the one for *A Country Doctor*" (L164). Of course Kafka was awaiting the promised news from the publisher about the fate of the *Country Doctor* volume. In the meantime, he inquisitively asked his friends Brod and Felix Weltsch and also Oskar Baum about how Wolff proceeded with the editing of their books (cf. L160, 165, 184, 188). But in no way did he personally dare break the silence himself. His posture of waiting—already one of principle—was formulated clearly in a letter to Josef Körner in January 1918: "At the moment I am out of touch with him, and my last letter, in response to an urgent one of his, has gone unanswered for some four months" (L192).

In the same letter he indicated several apparent reasons for the publisher's disinterest: the situation within the publishing industry was difficult, the "paper shortage" great, and the publisher's time taken up with various matters outside the company. Especially dear to the publisher's heart was his new undertaking, *Der Neue Geist Verlag*. Kafka also jealously took note of the publisher's new non-literary interest. But now Körner had specifically requested Kafka to put in a good word with Wolff for him, a request that Kafka of course had to decline. Nevertheless, he advised Körner on what tactics to use to introduce himself to Wolff. Summarizing his prior experiences with Wolff, he added with obvious resignation at the end: "One has to shout if one wants to be heard by such a publisher who is besieged by authors. I would be very glad if this succeeded" (L193).

Upon Kafka's request (cf. L165), Brod must have asked in Leipzig at the beginning of 1918 whether the interest in Kafka's *A Country Doctor* had dissipated, for only in response to such a protest did Wolff inform him that the production of the book had been "delayed considerably." The publisher bore no responsibility for the delay, since the sole reason for the footdragging was that the type planned for the book was being used for another work and just now became available (WBr46). In actuality, Kafka received the first galleys for *A Country Doctor* just several days after this correspondence. In a sharply worded letter with the characteristic salutation "Dear Sirs," he then commented on the typesetting and requested in addition a dedication page with the inscription: "To My Father" (L193-94). The next day Kafka made a point of thanking Brod for reminding Wolff about him (L195). The four-month waiting period was, however, not without consequence. Trust in his publisher had been put to a difficult test, and in a letter to Brod on January 28, 1918, Kafka expressed his suspicions regarding his present relationship to Wolff:

> It is so much pleasanter to have this done through you than to remind him myself (providing that you don't find it unpleasant), because he can then be frank when he doesn't want something or other, whereas otherwise, at least this is my impression, he does not speak frankly, at least not in letters. Face to face he is much more candid. I have already received proofs of the book (L195).

Without a doubt Kafka sought a close personal relationship with his publisher, but Wolff's letters, those that came with promises, and those that did not come at all and thus cast doubt upon what had been promised, disappointed him. "How on earth did anyone get the idea that people can communicate with one other by letter," Kafka later wrote to Milena; it "is, in fact, an intercourse with ghosts" (M229). Wolff sent cordial thanks for the return of the initial galleys, and again obligated himself with intentional politeness to carefully adhere to all of the writer's instructions and promised to send "revisions soon" (WBr47). Kafka then received a cordial book gift as an author's prize from the publisher. At that point the correspondence broke off again, and the announced revision of course never arrived.

At the beginning of March Kafka turned to Brod because he had received nothing more from Wolff after the first galleys but had received "a friendly invitation" from Reiss Publishing (L200). Brod intervened immediately with the publishers for Kafka; in the middle of March he informed Wolff that Kafka desired to see further galleys.[42] Kafka was obviously annoyed, for after the decision to dedicate *A Country Doctor* to his father, he was committed to the speedy publication of the text (L201). Kafka decided to take a drastic measure; he seriously considered changing publishers and wrote to Brod: "That is why—since Wolff has cut me off, doesn't answer, sends me nothing, though this one is probably my last book—I wanted to send the manuscripts to Reiss, who made such a friendly offer" (L201).

Kafka did not avail himself of this invitation, which Johannes Urzidil had probably secured from the Jewish publisher Erich Reiss. To be sure, he had already sent off his "ultimatum"[43] to Wolff, but Brod's intervention in Leipzig had been successful; in the meantime new corrections and revisions had been sent. Unsure of himself, Kafka declined Reiss Publishing's offer and wrote to Brod: "Thanks for interceding with Wolff"; but he appeared again to regret having declined Reiss' offer. In the meantime he had received an invitation from the publisher Paul Cassirer ("How, by the way, does he know my Zürau address?") and indecisively Kafka turned to his friend for advice regarding his book: "But should I after all go elsewhere?" (L201). But at the end of March 1918 Brod had only "bad news" for his friend; the disarray in the publishing industry was widespread and for the time being he did not recommend changing publishers at all.[44] Kafka's attempt to intervene for his own work was brought to a halt by Brod. He remained with Wolff—and continued to wait for news from the publisher.

At the beginning of May 1918 Kafka had to start working again for the insurance institute in Prague. But he still had to wait until the end of the war for any communication from the publisher, at which time Meyer presented at great length the reasons for the delay of the publication in September 1918. The manuscript for *A Country Doctor* had been sitting now for over a year at the publisher's:

> You are certainly not unaware of the difficulties of manufac-turing books. To dissect and explain the details to the lay person would not be very easy. How it happens, for example, that it is possible to print books more easily in very big editions than in normal runs, etc. etc. (WBr47)

At the very beginning of the letter Kafka was informed that *A Country Doctor* could still not appear, and, on the basis of Meyer's not very felicitous comments, he could conclude that his book was put on hold because the publisher was apparently now interested in authors whose titles promised higher sales. To be sure, Meyer said in conclusion that consideration was now being given to publishing Kafka's book in a subsidiary in Vienna (still only in the planning stages), whose founding Wolff had negotiat-ed in order to circumvent the difficult paper market in Germa-ny.[45] This letter only rounded out the negative picture that the author had of his publisher, for only at the end of the two-page letter (in which Meyer spoke less of Kafka than of his own "difficulties") was Kafka's book briefly mentioned. Without any explanation he said that "the printer could not begin work because there was not enough print of this type available" (WBr48). But equally annoying was the list of selections for *A Country Doctor*, which the publisher, "following Kafka's directives," had completed for the page-proofs: in the first position stood the long discarded piece, *The Murder*, which must have been totally incomprehensible to Kafka. Carelessly, the publisher (as is clear from Meyer's handwritten note on an original Kafka letter) had placed the outdated version of *A Fratricide* at the front of the entire book without even asking Kafka about it! Correctly Kafka had to conclude that the publisher's editors were ignorant, since the old and the new versions of the same story appeared next to each other in the same volume.[46] The manuscript of *A Dream*, Meyer indicated, had been lost somewhere internally.

Such errors and capricious actions on the part of the publisher apparently occurred several times during the course of the printing of *A Country Doctor*. The title page, covered with handwritten corrections by Kafka, shows most clearly how little attention the publisher paid to the author's very precise and carefully considered ideas on the printing. In imitation of Kafka's first book, Wolff had printed: "A Country Doctor. New Meditations." But these stories were not meditations in the manner of Kafka's first book. A different narrative tone and a totally new perspective point to a substantial transformation. In a letter of April 20, 1917, Kafka had established the definitive title as *A Country Doctor. Short Tales.* Wolff, who also wanted to make the association with *Meditation* by using the same typographical features, the large classical Walbaum-Antiqua, preempted Kafka's wish and demonstrated little sensitivity to the writer's development since the first book. Furthermore, Kafka apparently had to request the title page continually during the proofreading; the proofreading of this page accordingly never took place. Did the author at this time not have reason to fear that he was not being taken seriously by his publisher?

In reply to a letter of Meyer, Kafka sent a new clean copy of *A Dream* without comment and corrected the publisher's mistake very curtly in a subdued tone. Kafka's complete response to Meyer's letter reads:

Dear Sirs,

Many thanks for the information. If I understand your remark about printing, I am not to receive any proofs. That would be a pity. The order you list is correct, except one mistake which cannot stand: the book must begin with "The New Advocate." The piece which you have down for the first item "A Homicide" [*A Murder*], is simply to be discarded, since, except for trivial differences, it is the same as the later piece correctly entitled "A Fratricide." Please do not forget the dedication of the whole book "To My Father." I enclose the manuscript of *A Dream*."

Very truly yours, Dr. Kafka
(L207)

Kafka's bitterness comes through quite clearly in this very impersonal letter. Lacking the security provided by an inspired period of writing and being seriously ill, Kafka felt doubly burdened by his publisher's unconcerned behavior. His novels, the focus of all his literary hopes, had failed as a whole; in surveying his accomplishments in literature, he had, in the true sense of the word, completed nothing. Seeing himself at an end-point in his writing because of his illness, he was obviously bewildered by the unexpected difficulties in the printing of his last book. This continual waiting for news from the publisher basically led Kafka to doubt the purpose of publishing or of pursuing a writer's existence. Kafka's note of October 1917 is called to mind, when he read one of the *Country Doctor* stories in print:

Always first draw fresh breath after outbursts of vanity and

complacency. The orgy while reading the story in *Der Jude*.
Like a squirrel in its cage. Bliss of movement. Desperation
about constriction, craziness of endurance, feeling of misery
confronted with the repose of what is external. (DF64)

A New Offer by the Publisher (1918)

What kind of impression a new and very generous offer by
the publisher made on Kafka at this moment of doubt can be
surmised. For instead of dealing straightforwardly and persistently with the completion of *A Country Doctor*, as Kafka most
urgently hoped, Wolff turned again to a new book project. In an
especially cordial and friendly letter Wolff suggested in mid-
October 1918 an edition of *In the Penal Colony* in a deluxe
individual printing. The manner in which the publisher turned to
Kafka after a conversation with Brod in Leipzig is worth noting:

> I would actually like to suggest to you that we publish this
> work which I love very much, even if my love is also mixed
> with a certain horror and fright at the terrible intensity of the
> terrible material. It would appear in the framework of a small
> group of new literary pieces, which are to appear as the
> "Drugulin Prints." I would also like to note that this group of
> fine books has no fixed serial character . . . and that I will
> soon be publishing works by Werfel, Francis Jammes, Péguy,
> and Březina in the near future alongside your wonderful story.
> (WBr49)

This very warm and cordial letter from Wolff, who did not
refrain from complimenting the literary quality of Kafka's story
(after he had rejected it a year before), could be used to confirm
the opposite of what has been said up to now. But even Wolff's
negotiating style had its method, and there were recognizable
motives behind his promises. It is hard to overlook the great

friendliness and charm of Wolff's correspondence with his authors when he sought to have a manuscript submitted. As background to the surprising suggestion made to Kafka in view of the drastic economic situation is Wolff's purchase of the famous Leipzig Offizin Drugulin in 1918. In the course of expanding his company, the publisher had acquired the printing company and was now looking for the initial titles for a series of modern literature, which, by association with Rowohlt's Drugulin Prints, were to tap into the famous tradition of the press with decidedly bibliophile editions. For two years already the manuscript of *In the Penal Colony* had been with Wolff; first Wolff rejected it, and afterward Kafka vetoed its publication. Now Wolff was in need of a title for the series and this seems to be the reason for the publisher's urgent, obliging tone. The analogy to the publishing history of *The Stoker* is quite close. In order not to jeopardize this new contact with Kurt Wolff Publishing, Kafka sent word through Brod at the beginning of November 1918 from his sickbed (for a month he had been suffering from the life-threatening Spanish flu) that he was quite in agreement with everything, but that he wanted to rework the manuscript once before it went to press. This time the revision was less of a problem than in the previous year. He shortened the end of the novella, about which the critics whom Kafka knew said—after his reading in Munich—that it just slowly ebbed away (Bo121). He returned the manuscript to the publisher immediately. At the point of abbreviation, three pages from the end, he requested a "largish space should be inserted, to be marked with asterisks or some other means." The letter that he sent simultaneously with the manuscript without a personal salutation to the publisher, reads pithily: "I fully concur with Herr Kurt Wolff's plans for its publication" (L208).

After this letter, from about the middle of November 1918

until February 1920, no further correspondence between Kafka and his publisher has been preserved. A letter by Kafka to Brod reveals that the manuscript of *In the Penal Colony* was lost in the mail and then was probably sent again (the same manuscript?) to Wolff (cf. L209). A year later *In the Penal Colony* appeared; *A Country Doctor* did not appear until the summer of 1920.

In The Penal Colony (Initial Publication 1919) and *A Country Doctor* (First Edition 1920)— Dates in the History of Publication

Kurt Wolff had suggested the bibliophile formats of both Kafka books at a time when he was not totally aware of the full extent of the crisis in the book trade. All of the negative effects of the political and economic developments came to bear on *A Country Doctor* during its three years of coming to press. On the contrary, *In the Penal Colony* had the advantage of being an added "bonus" within the larger framework of a new series and was hurried along by Wolff. But both of Kafka's deluxe editions appeared very late and at a time when there was no longer a market for bibliophile editions; in their deluxe formats these books were at the time of their appearance too expensive for modern literature and remained unmarketable.

No correspondence between Kafka and the publisher during this difficult phase of collaboration is available; the few letters that were probably written between November 1918 and February 1920 have been lost. Therefore, the course of publication and the problems connected with it remain for the most part obscured today. Because of the lack of other reliable source material, previous attempts to reconstruct the history of the publication of these two books have resulted in misunderstandings, especially in the determination of an exact date of publication. However, if one carefully separates the author's previously published comments and those of his circle of personal acquaintances in connection with the presentation and events in the book industry in general and at Kurt Wolff Publishing specifically, a clear picture emerges that permits a new, precise dating.

In his account of the publication of *In the Penal Colony*, Klaus Wagenbach associates the imprint note in the first edition of the novella with the date of publication; he lists *In the Penal Colony* as the fourth book of the new series of Drugulin Prints in May 1919. Other studies have utilized this dating suggestion.[47] Actually, however, *In the Penal Colony* appeared only later, in October 1919. The following data support this finding: a notice in the *Prager Tagblatt* of September 28, 1919, reveals that the book that was announced had not yet appeared.[48] An often reprinted letter from Brod to Kafka on August 1, 1919, does not refer, as has been assumed (cf. sy119), to *A Country Doctor* but to *In the Penal Colony*; the letter states: "I spoke a lot with Wolff about you; the printing of your book is almost complete; the copy editor who failed to deal with it properly has been fired (not just for that)."[49]

Even if *In the Penal Colony* had been set in May 1919 there would still have been a delay until the beginning of August 1919 because of the negligence of a proofreader. *In the Penal Colony* was probably then printed immediately but could not be delivered, since a book dealers' strike in Leipzig crippled the trade during the months of August and September. The latest possible date for the appearance is Kafka's trip to Schelesen at the beginning of November 1919. There in his *Letter to His Father*, with the impression of the appearance of *In the Penal Colony* fresh in his mind, he described his father's "proverbial way of hailing the arrival" of his books: "Put it on my bedside table!" (DF176). The assumption that the book appeared toward the end of October 1919 is further substantiated by an announcement of Kurt Wolff Publishing; on October 29, 1919, the first series of the New Drugulin Prints were announced in an ad in the *Börsenblatt für den Deutschen Buchhandel* with the note: "The first volumes, which are ready for shipment, are indicated here." Kafka's *In the Penal Colony* is among the books listed.[50]

The publication date of Kafka's last book with Kurt Wolff Publishing, *A Country Doctor*, can be determined in a similar way, even if somewhat more problematically. Since Brod's letter mentioned above had long been thought to refer to *A Country Doctor* and not to *In the Penal Colony*, his remark of August 1919 ("Your book is almost ready") was considered the most important reference for the dating of the text. But not until months later, actually in May 1920, could *A Country Doctor* have been delivered. A note in the imprint: "Copyright: 1919 by Kurt Wolff Publishing"—even amidst this period of crisis—is only an apparent contradiction to this assumption; Kafka himself removed the year 1919 on the original title page while making corrections and did not enter a new date. Ludwig Dietz takes the position that Kafka saw only the first two corrections (i.e., the first correction and the one revision), that is, those small mailings of the publisher from January and March 1918. This is probably incorrect, for much information supports the view that Kafka had undertaken corrections several times later;[51] on the other hand, one can assume with relative confidence that Kafka did not receive several corrections and that the publication can only be viewed as "partly authorized." Kafka had the last datable correction at the end of 1919 during his stay in Schelesen.[52]

Actually then, the book could have appeared in December 1919 or January 1920 (at this time *A Country Doctor* was prematurely announced by Kafka's friend Felix Weltsch in *Die Selbstwehr* as having appeared), but the rather chaotic condition at Kurt Wolff Publishing, which was in the process of moving from Leipzig to Munich and could begin with their actual publishing work only in the first months of 1920, prevented this earlier publication date. While the imprint lists the place of publication as "Leipzig and Munich," the correction of the title page shows only "Munich."

Probably *A Country Doctor* was not ready until April 1920, for when Milena was attempting to acquire all of Kafka's published books at this time, she was able to get everything except *A Country Doctor*. Thus at the end of April Kafka requested Wolff to send a copy directly to Milena, because she, as one of the following letters supports, apparently had not received it right away.[53] A further point makes this dating more plausible: the first notation in the *Wöchentliches Verzeichnis der erschienenen und vorbereiteten Neuigkeiten des deutschen Buchhandels* ("Weekly Catalogue of New and Forthcoming Books of the German Book Industry") that *A Country Doctor* had appeared dates from June 3, 1920. These points support dating the publication in May 1920. The first (and only) review of *A Country Doctor* appeared thereafter at the end of October in the *Prager Tagblatt* (cf. Bo102). The publisher himself did not announce Kafka's new title until Christmastime (December 12, 1920) in a large format announcement in the *Börsenblatt*.[54]

5. Fourth Excursus: The Last Years of Kurt Wolff Publishing (1918-1930)

A direct consequence of the treaty of 1918 was the struggle over a new division of political power. In Vienna revolution broke out at the end of October and Austria-Hungary disintegrated. Two weeks later, on November 9, the Republic was proclaimed in Germany. Economic crisis and political disorder now exerted a direct influence on the publishing industry. Paper prices rose to starry heights; raw materials for cloth and leather bindings were effectively unavailable from the end of 1918 on. Printers could not find qualified help. Moreover, book manufacturers had to limit their working day to several hours, since electricity was in short supply as a result of the coal shortage. In March 1919 the young republic suffered its first general strike.

The publishers reacted accordingly; programs were tightened and capital was used very cautiously. This was not the case with Wolff, who amidst the widespread crisis in the book industry maintained unfaltering optimism as a publisher and businessman. During the summer crisis of 1917 he independently proposed to Kafka a giant typeface (16 point, tertia), the finest hand-made paper, and half-leather binding for *A Country Doctor*, while other publishers could only print narrow lines on poor, woodpulp paper. At first Wolff enjoyed success with his business policy: a glance at publishing statistics reveals that Wolff produced 48 new literary editions for the book trade in 1915, 83 the following year, 91 in 1918, and 135 titles in 1920.[55] Wolff employed new workers and purchased a palace in Darmstadt, which he had renovated at great expense for the company headquarters. After the abdication of the Archduke Emil Ludwig of Darmstadt, Wolff sold the palace at a substantial loss and finally moved his publishing house to Munich at the end of 1919.[56] Relocating had a devastating effect on the daily publishing operations and turned out to be more problematical than anticipated, not least of all because of the book dealers' strike that crippled the industry for two months late in the summer of 1919 (WV839). The strike came at the time when preparations for the move were also bringing the normal course of business to a standstill. It took until the beginning of 1920 before bookkeeping and distribution operations were functioning normally again (WV839).

The splendor of Kurt Wolff's publishing house dedicated to art and literature did not last long in Munich. Prices for raw materials rose daily, and the books printed with the publisher's highest bibliophile standards became increasingly difficult to produce and to sell. The boom in expensive deluxe editions, for which Wolff had openly hoped, faded quickly.[57] And when inflation set in after the increase in the cost of living in 1921, the publisher encountered difficulties arranging financing for his expensive publishing operations because of rising personnel and production costs.

To consolidate the company, Wolff sold individual operations and looked for new partners; finally in November 1920 he decided to relinquish his independent status. The publisher acquired a broader financial base by forming a stock company, but the efforts came too late. The occasionally considered merger with S. Fischer Publishing failed because of the incompatibility of the two publishers' personalities (Wo33).

Even before this "difficult period" (WV839), Wolff's ambitious policies had eroded the financial base of his company. However, he in no way wanted to become dependent on the manufacturing sector or on antagonistic creditors, as other publishers had during the worldwide economic crisis.[58] Wolff adjusted his book prices to the demands of the marketplace too late; inflation caught the publisher totally off guard.[59]

The actual decline of Wolff's publishing business had begun very much earlier. Even before the inflationary period authors began to cut their ties to Wolff and seek out other publishers for their books. Of course, financial considerations were at play. The sudden change of policy became portentous for the publisher; the transformation from a recognized publisher of avant-garde literature into a publisher of art and bibliophile editions was undertaken too quickly and caught the authors completely by surprise. Not only Wolff but also the long-time editor Pinthus, who had set a new standard for the waning expressionistic movement with the editing of the poetry collection *Menschheitsdämmerung* (in Ernst Rowohlt's newly founded house!) had lost faith in contemporary literature. Wolff's personal circle of acquaintances surely influenced him, including Karl Kraus, Franz Muncker, Rilke, Brod, and probably many others, who were skeptical of the expressionist movement after the end of the war.[60] Wolff sought other names, other forms of expression,[61] but from 1917 on the complaints about the lack of young authors increased. In April 1919 the publisher wrote to Fritz von Unruh: "We are so depressed that this new period has not blown a single page toward us from which a young new talent with a good future speaks" (WV864).

The previously mentioned editor crisis had existed since 1914; after 1916 Wolff effectively had no functioning editorial department at all. The crisis of conscience that the publisher experienced together with his expressionist authors, as well as his disappointment with the most recent avant-garde, especially with Dadaism, led him further and further from things literary. His closest advisors now became Hans Mardersteig and Carl Georg Heise. Instead of guaranteeing his literary authors monetary support as in the past, immense sums flowed into art publishing. A letter by Wolff to Werfel from August 24, 1921, reads: "I sense more and more strongly . . . that your generation, which I may also claim to be my own, has no young, rising creative talent; despite the greatest attention to what is around me, I at least do not see anything, and find that writing in German today has sunk to an indescribably low level" (WBr344).

Wolff's position led to an exodus of his authors, who could

only assume that they would no longer be represented literarily by the publisher. Since 1917 all of the important authors had left the publisher. The magnetic effect of what was previously a center for contemporary literature lost its attractiveness; inflation drove the remaining authors from the house.[62] With the exception of the young Alfred Brust no new authors were published. Unsolicited manuscripts (submissions by Oswald Spengler and James Joyce among them) were rejected by the editors. The publishing house experienced a slow process of disintegration. The number of new literary works decreased steadily; after 1928 no literary title appeared in Kurt Wolff Publishing. In June 1930 Wolff wrote to Werfel:

> Publishing, it seems to me, is a speculative business in which the risks are minimized for those possessing enough capital and skilled management. I have been able to find no other prior conditions which would have made continuation possible or even have allowed it; we have muddled along enough recently and to continue indecisively in this untenable interim situation seems undignified and senseless to me. (WBr552)

At approximately this time, 1930-1931, Kurt Wolff Publishing was completely liquidated. It was, as Franz Werfel had written to the publisher in March 1930, "the literary instrument of the last poetic movement that took place in Germany" (WBr350).

6. Franz Kafka—Kurt Wolff's Author?

With the publication of *A Country Doctor* in May 1920, Kafka's collaboration with Kurt Wolff Publishing had come to a close. During the eight years of this relationship, six books by Kafka had been published—if one counts *Meditation* which appeared with Ernst Rowohlt—each an individual publication.

After the correspondence took a final modest upturn again (Kafka requested the publisher's help at the beginning of 1920 in looking for a room in a Bavarian hospice), no further personal contact between Kafka and Wolff took place; the publisher's increasing interest in Kafka was answered by the author with silence. Discouraged, and obviously resigned after the experiences with the publication of his last two books, and perhaps disappointed with the meager public response,[63] Kafka began to withdraw from the publisher. The timing of his retreat from the publisher overlaps chronologically with the peak of the exodus of Wolff's authors.

In Göbel's detailed standard critical investigation of Wolff's impact as a publisher, one point stands out: to the question of Wolff's outstanding author relationships, two names are mentioned, Kraus and Kafka. The author defends his choice: "With these authors, Kafka and Kraus, the missionary element of Wolff's publishing is most strongly evident and his ambition to promote authors among the public, whose works he was convinced of, even if he had to overcome the opposition of the public and that of the authors themselves" (WV794).

Though this characterization may be true for Kraus, it is incorrect in the case of Kafka. What then was the nature of Kafka's resistance to his publisher? Does Göbel perhaps mean the fact that Kafka could not complete his novels and held them back from the publisher until after his death? Or phrased another way, what resistance had Wolff actually overcome with Kafka? One draws here too superficially on the obvious, i.e., on the bias of an "impossible author" already subsumed in the name Kafka, who would rather burn his texts than hand them over for publication. Not a word is mentioned about the publisher's resistance or of Kafka's struggle for years for the publication and for his recognition as a writer and publisher's author.

In the course of developing a commonly held picture of Kafka, it was not known that Kafka's earlier general resistance to the publication of his writings in June 1912 ended with his first contact with the publisher. At that time Rowohlt was able to overcome Kafka's obvious resistance. With the publication of *Meditation* Kafka gave up the anonymity he had long thought it impossible to overcome. His desire from that point on was to have his completed texts printed, for according to Kafka, "the test of the writer is in his works" (L204); his hope of living a pure writer's existence would have to be nourished by publications. Brod reminds us that Kafka could feel joy at literary success, even if there was "generally a deprecatory smile there at the same time" (FK61).

Kafka's "resistance" was directed his whole life long against the publication of artistically incomplete works and is the mark of a true artist. Here he was truly scrupulous: he did not want anything incomplete or adventitious to be presented to the public; he struggled against the temptation to improvise and against premature feelings of success, against the "pride," as he called it, which the publication of each of his texts brought him. Such a satisfaction, he feared, would hamper him from producing better work. The author's extreme sensitivity to the publisher's "sloppiness" about faulty or missing corrections points already in this direction.[64]

It remained Kafka's misfortune that he never found a mutually functioning author-publisher relationship after a promising opening of contacts that then failed because of the direct effects of the personnel changes at the publishing house and of the war. In Wolff he encountered a publisher who printed his books with a kind of silent matter-of-factness, but who he then had to conclude cut him off gradually (L201), "suppress[ed]" (F531) his publication wishes, and did not "speak frankly" in his letters (L195). Kafka could do no more than confirm Wolff's resistance; he did not attempt to break through this resistance from his side. Kafka could not force his way through ("shouting," as he wrote) to make the publisher, who was "besieged by authors," take notice of him (L193). He left that to others, who in his eyes were "real" writers. The many encouragements that he gave fellow writers for the correct approach to the publisher speak for themselves. He wrote to Weltsch at the end of 1917 (when he himself was urgently waiting for news from the publisher): "Don't be daunted by Wolff. He has to play it coy. How many writers are bombarding him! Overwhelmed as he is, he cannot sort things out" (L160).

At about the same time he recommended that Josef Körner force his way into Wolff's circle and judged a failure of Gottfried Kölwel as follows: "I am not surprised that you have difficulty publishing; you neither startle nor frighten" (L130). But Kafka himself failed in formulating and following through on his demands for publication and for being treated as a writer. In order to do so he would have needed a closer relationship with the publisher within which it would have been possible to resolve misunderstandings.

Wolff later remarked that he certainly did not know a great number of the authors publishing with him at all, but that there were a few with whom he had a close personal relationship. He reminisces about this with particular fondness because, he states, there were personal contacts beyond the publisher-author relationship in the case of Kafka![65] In light of what has been stated previously, this characterization by Wolff from the year 1964 is astonishing. At this later point in time Wolff could no longer remember how often he had met Kafka (cf. Wo68). The results of this investigation reveal that at most the publisher, who published six of Kafka's books in his house, had seen Kafka during the course of the entire relationship twice for sure and possibly three times: on June 29, 1912, perhaps on March 25, 1913, and on June 30, 1914. Each time the author came to Leipzig, each time he was accompanied by a friend; never did the author and the publisher speak alone, and they saw each other for only a few minutes each time. A further reminiscence of Wolff, also from 1964, is thus equally astounding: "To be together with Kafka in a group made no sense at all. He would be silent, and the others would talk, talk, talk . . . that was not being together with Kafka, that was like being with a crew."[66]

How then, one must ask, did this special personal relationship between author and publisher come about, a relationship which was based on three short, insignificant group encounters and on a meager correspondence, which Wolff himself labeled as "scarce and sporadic" (WBr54)? Thus Wolff's reference to the fact that he had accommodated the writer's wish by dealing directly with Brod as a mediator in publishing matters related to Kafka seems to be a late justification for neglect. The expectations attached to such a statement are in no way fulfilled by an examination of the wealth of Wolff's unpublished letters to Brod from the period 1912-1924.

The essential points in the publication history of Kafka's books are entirely clear from the writer's own correspondence. As a "mediator" Brod functioned in a somewhat different way, namely as a proposer to Kurt Wolff Publishing for matters related to Kafka. Especially during the period between 1917 and 1920 Brod was specifically requested by Kafka, whose habit it was never to write twice and to expect a direct answer from the publisher to his letters, to remind the publisher of him. Although Kafka had a strong lobbyist at Wolff Publishing in the influential Brod, he resisted Brod doing anything more than reminding Wolff of him and guarded against using his friend as a literary mouthpiece.

Wolff's early publishing impact was characterized by his idealism, generosity, and the general openness in his program. Personal contacts with authors remained extremely rare. A reason for this may be the fact that social class separated the rich and aristocratically-minded Wolff from his authors. In examining the correspondence between Wolff and his authors (in comparison to that of Samuel Fischer), it is also striking that the initial intensity in the interplay between author and publisher was not maintained over a longer period of time but remained limited to short periods. These periods were sporadic, episodic, and above all reactive.

Wolff's sporadic and reactive interest in his authors (although there are also examples of continued collaboration with authors like Werfel) becomes especially evident in the case of Kafka. Wolff appeared concerned not with the process but rather with the results of literary activity; he never inquired about the progress of a work or about difficulties in writing and never attempted to exert any sort of influence on the work with respect to its completion. If the author did not signal the completion of a work, there was no contact from the publisher about it. Wolff once expressed the thought to Alfred Döblin that his interest in an author stood in direct proportion to the author's interest in him (WBr154); this is perhaps an indication of why Kafka remained for years at a time without further news from the publisher. Kafka had already spoken to his publisher in 1913 about a novel; but only years later, apparently only in 1921, when Kafka's interest in his publisher had already eroded measurably, did Wolff mention the novels of his own accord.

Wolff's interest in Kafka developed in indirect proportion to the author's interest in him. In 1920 Kafka wrote to Brod: "for much as I might be interested in the publishing house, it would be a passive interest" (L237). In the years after Kafka's retreat from Kurt Wolff Publishing the actual involvement of the publisher on behalf of his author began; this subsequent involvement can also be considered reactive. During the period around 1921 the publisher was searching in vain for new literary authors; there was scarcely a new literary edition in his house. Thus the publication of a Kafka novel would have certainly meant success for the publisher, as Wolff wrote to Kafka in 1921, not to mention that this success would simultaneously bolster promotion of his earlier published works as well (WBr54). Sales for *In the Penal Colony* and *A Country Doctor* were sluggish in the first years after they appeared; even copies of *Meditation* were still available at this time. At the beginning of the 1920s, however, Kafka had become known, though certainly not through the sales of his books or through the literary voice of journalistic articles. Rather he had become a prospective luminary who would remain in the public eye for a long time: Kafka was promoted as a writer for writers. In the process of establishing genuine literary fame, such status is an effective element, even if it is not especially quick.

Along with Brod, who from the beginning of their collaboration constantly encouraged his publisher to publish "Germany's greatest living writer," the number of important literary personalities of the day who referred Wolff to Kafka grew steadily. Thus the change in opinion of Wolff's highly regarded Franz Werfel was surely not missed by the publisher; Werfel grew to respect Kafka's work more and more. After the publication of *A Report to an Academy* in 1917, he expressed the view that Kafka was for him "the greatest German writer."[67]

Wolff's decision to write his first major letter of solicitation to Kafka (November 1921) came as a direct result of his meeting with Ludwig Hardt, the marvelous elocutionist who, himself inspired by Kafka's publications, made a habit of reciting texts by Kafka during his readings and thus became an important factor in the writer's later fame.[68]

Hardt got to know Kafka's work through Kurt Tucholsky. Under the pseudonym Peter Panter, Tucholsky, who had known Kafka personally since 1911, wrote an enthusiastic review of *In the Penal Colony* in which he placed Kafka in the tradition of Heinrich von Kleist. And in December 1921 Tucholsky wrote about Hardt's evening lectures: "Franz Kafka. Who he is we unfortunately know too little . . . He writes the clearest and most beautiful prose being written at this time in the German language."[69]

A few days before Wolff sent his second letter to lure Kafka (March 1922) (Wo70), he had received a letter from Rilke, who thanked the publisher for sending him some books, among them Kafka's *A Country Doctor*. Rilke commented:

> I have lined the books up for my next period of reading—but the one by Kafka I already perused yesterday evening even though I was occupied with other things. I have never read a line by this author which did not affect me in the most personal way or amaze me. Please be so kind as to send me especially anything you have by Kafka in the future. I am, I may assure you, not his worst reader.[70]

References from authors—especially those whom Wolff respected, like Werfel and Rilke—were used by the publisher to plan the literary orientation of his program. Thus Wolff's behavior was again reactive when he assured Kafka of his further inclinations after receiving Rilke's letter. But when he ended his letter for the first time in their ten-year relationship with the closing "Your Publisher" (WBr55), his efforts came too late. The publisher had neglected to transmit to Kafka the feeling of a continued and meaningful relationship during the preceding years. After the unfortunate experiences Kafka had with the publisher, he now wanted to refrain from becoming involved anew in 1922. His distrust of Wolff's promises had become too great.

The dilemma in the conversations between Wolff and Kafka reveals a dual one-way communication; the necessary interaction and adjustments in the differing points of view were in essence disrupted. By nature Kafka was trapped in a state of personal immobilization and could not on his own initiative break loose from his normal situation of suffering. However, in order to be able to write properly and to create the possibility of complete poetic development, he planned to give up his profession. When he therefore, despite all reservations, dared to request some financial assistance from his publisher, it was "happily" granted to him. But Wolff never followed through on the promise he had made, and Kafka himself did not dare and was probably too proud to approach the publisher (four years his junior) a second time with the request. Wolff, on the other hand, waited for the request (the "interest") from him for financial support, just as he waited for his author to signal the completion of a book in order to begin the "publishing evaluation," as he once wrote to Kafka (WBr43). The initiative had to come from somewhere else, if not from Kafka or Wolff; actually for each of Kafka's book publications such an initiative from the outside (not just with Wolff's solicitous letters to lure Kafka) can be established.

Selling himself, and thus expressing "interest" in the publisher in Wolff's terminology, seemed to Kafka a vain venture that would undermine his writing. The sole possibility of vying for the publication of his work without being obtrusive was, in Kafka's mind, his "pessimistic manner of argumentation"; this element, too, is demonstrated in the history of each of his books. Kafka was thoroughly conscious of this strange way of dealing with the publisher (which too frequently seemed to him to express Kafka's indifference toward his own work). The pessimistic way he delivered his manuscripts—Kafka called it his "self-denigration"—he depicted unequivocally as his "strategy" in a letter to Brod from June 1922: "My self-denigration has two aspects. On the one hand there is truth . . . then . . . also inevitably a strategy, which, for example, makes it impossible for Wolff to agree with it, not out of hypocrisy which he surely does not have to practice toward me, but because he is forced to by the strategy" (L326).

This unrelenting criticism of his own writing on the surface, which basically determined the nature of the correspondence with the publisher, matched Kafka's real view only in part; his criticism of himself was his "strategy" directed toward winning over the publisher. As confirmation Kafka added the self-reflection: "[T]ruth produces no successes; truth only shatters what is shattered" (L326). Part of his method of dealing with the publisher involved waiting, for only when an urgent invitation by the publisher arrived could he formulate his own demands; only on this basis (of exchange) could Kafka express his wishes. Kafka noted in his diary in 1922: ". . . there is a middle ground between 'doing' and the 'opportunity to do' . . . a practice I have unfortunately followed not only in this but everything." This "tempting" resembles, as he continues, "dallying with the idea of conquest" (DII204-05).

Kafka revealed intentional understatement in his communications with the publisher—on this level of argumentation he demonstrated a devout air praising the publisher. But this understatement necessarily created the impression that the writer himself was not interested in the publication of his work. Wolff shared this impression, when at the end of 1921 he directed his first letter to entice Kafka:

> Our correspondence is seldom and sparse. None of the authors
> with whom we have contacts approaches us with so few
> questions and wishes as you, and with none do we have the
> feeling that the external factors of published books is such a
> matter of indifference as it is to you. Therefore, it appears
> appropriate if the publisher from time to time says to the
> author that this lack of participation on his part regarding the
> fate of his books will not deter the publisher in his belief and
> trust in the special quality of the publications. (WBr54)

Of course Kafka's inhibition against approaching the publisher
directly with his work lay deeper than Wolff could suspect.
When the latter continues to state in his correspondence that
every manuscript that Kafka submits to him will be published
with "affection and care" and that it is moreover a "personal
joy" for him, the publisher perhaps for the first time struck upon
the correct negotiating tone. For the writer's pride and his
idiosyncrasy of not wanting to force himself as the pleader,
resulted from his own special situation: as a "part-time writer"
he was, on the one hand, not dependent upon his writing for
income,[71] on the other, his works developed on the basis of his
double life under such psychological pressure that he himself—since no real financial emergency existed—only wanted to
deliver them up to the outside world after the highest personal
recognition was evident. If one now applies this interpretation of
Kafka's pessimistic strategy of argumentation to the letters to his
publishers, it is clear how the writer sought to elicit the publisher's reaction; in the end he indirectly orchestrated the direct
personal recognition of his work by the publisher. Kafka required such massive praise before he could muster the strength
of conviction to enter the public arena with his works.

In hindsight Wolff expressed the problematic nature of his association with Kafka:

> As soon as one happened to meet Kafka, one could only love him. But one sensed already the deer-like shyness, the fright, the embarrassment, so that one got the feeling that you can easily prove your friendship to him by a gesture, by a friendly line, by many trifling things. But don't protect him or take him by surprise.[72]

The extent to which an author's commercial importance to a publisher determines the intensity of conversation between them need not be elaborated on here. Wolff was involved with the very marketable Nobel Prize winner Rabindranath Tagore and sold 150,000 copies of Meyrink's *Golem*, while *Meditation* (800 copies) was still available after twelve years. Wolff wrote in his first letter to Heinrich Mann that he did not just want to be "enthusiastic," but also wanted to "sell books" (WBr222). That Wolff remembered the interests of the day differently fifty years later is understandable. However, despite the questionable nature of a subsequent change in the fame of writers in view of Kafka's overpowering future fame, this later statement by Wolff supplies an important clue to a probable early misunderstanding on the part of the publisher: it was exactly this reservation and protective stance by the publisher that Kafka had least expected. On the contrary, he sought a certain institutionalized authority in his contact with the publisher—replacing paternal authority—with whose help he could have established his existence as a writer. He needed such an integrative point for his hopes. Little was gained for him with a mere "gesture," a "friendly line," or some "trifle." Wolff defended his passive position with regard to this author in a radio broadcast from 1962 dedicated to Kafka: "While I frequently tried to encourage other authors orally or in writing regarding their work, and sought manuscripts from them, I felt inhibited with regard to Kafka and not prepared to penetrate into his world" (Wo70).

It is clear from the foregoing statements how much Kafka waited for openness and commitment, for influence or pressure from outside, in order to be able to trust in his uncertain literary future. Without such recognition his mistrust could only grow and foster the idea that Wolff Publishing was publishing his books only because the influential Brod had interceded for him. In order to present something for publication himself—without the requisite invitation—would require, as he wrote to Carl Seelig in 1923, "a certain ability to assume responsibility" (L380), which he could actually not conjure up from within himself. Thus for him in the years of his relationship to the publisher only that "feeling of misery confronted with the repose of what is external" remained (DF64); this led him to sense with greater and greater clarity the hopelessness of his position within the literary world and, therefore, the hopelessness of his desire to give up his bourgeois occupation.

Establishing Kafka's independence (and also supporting him financially) naturally could have been and perhaps should have been the publisher's overriding task. But the publisher did not consider engineering such a decisive change in Kafka's life. Wolff's fascination with his author Franz Kafka was obviously not comparable to his actual enthusiasm for (the infinitely more successful) Franz Werfel. Not without envy did Kafka follow the publisher's response to this young writer from Prague. But also in comparison with other authors of Kurt Wolff, Kafka came off badly. He not only received no form of financial assistance (thus no advances, no loans, none of the invented honoraria paid to editors or advisors), but also no moral support and—after the publisher did not mention again the once promised support—no sense of trust either. Thus his ties to the publisher could in no way promote his writing.

On the contrary, because of this relationship marred by misunderstanding and neglect on the part of the publisher, his literary productivity was first made uncertain and finally was noticeably hampered. This process culminated in the outbreak and the psychic consequences of his disease and can be traced back as well to these negative interactions between him and the publisher. Conditioned by his upbringing, he quickly reached the point of resignation anyway. Kafka did not possess Brod's fighting spirit. Brod assessed his friend accurately, when he wrote in his review of *Meditation* in 1913: "It is his characteristic not to want anything that is limited or deficient. This extremely passionate, unwanted rigor influences each of his activities in life. If he can't achieve perfection or the most ecstatic happiness, he yields completely" (Bo25).

How insecure his "financial and intellectual existence" actually was, the writer depicted in one of his last letters to Felice at the end of 1916: "And even supposing I do one day accomplish something (my restlessness won't let me write a line), it is quite possible that even people who are well disposed toward me will turn me down, and the others of course all the more so" (F506). That was, however, not only his "official's typical apprehension," but the fully blossomed fear that governed and repressed him in the face of the failure of his ideal existence as a whole. In his life plan everything—his attempts at solutions as well as his attempts at integration—was a failure. His will to live hinged solely on the projection of the lingering hope for a future literary existence; the failure of the critical publisher relationship caused him to forfeit the greater part of this will, whereby he lost the belief in the meaning of publishing works no one wanted. Herein lies a very basic reason why Kafka did not establish that literary discipline that could have brought his writing, especially his writing of novels, beyond the level of fragments.

Even the quantitative side of Kafka's publications is not depicted accurately in Wolff's memoirs. He was too capricious with his consistent talk about Kafka's limited marketability (during his lifetime). Certainly there were no large sales—the author's net proceeds from all of his literary work during the entire ten-year period of his association with Kurt Wolff Publishing may have perhaps reached a modest four-digit amount. Wolff's naming Kafka, in response to a questionnaire which Herbert Eulenberg sent to leading German publishers in 1927 on the question of their biggest flop, was uncalled for.[73] It is only a half-truth that everything published by Kafka, as Wolff recalls, was not publicly accepted (Wo74). His whole life long the publisher was uninformed about the true figures for printings and sales of Kafka's books. Thus Wolff asserted in this vein in 1963: "We never printed a second edition."[74] He was well aware of the fact that the second edition of *Meditation* involved merely a change in title with a new publishing signet (Kurt Wolff instead of Rowohlt). Moreover, in 1963 Ludwig Dietz already established the existence of genuine second editions of *The Metamorphosis* (ca. 1918-1920) and of *The Judgment* (ca. 1920), and even of a second and third edition of *The Stoker* (1916, 1917-1918). After a thorough investigation of the series *Der Jüngste Tag*, he estimated that each of Kafka's three stories had reached a maximum edition of about ten thousand copies![75] Wolff himself had written Brod in July 1924 that the sales figures for these volumes were not essentially higher than those of the expensive books.[76] Even if Dietz's estimate is very inflated, it reflects a substantial difference from the editions of Kafka's bound books: *Meditation*: 800, *In the Penal Colony*: 1000 and *A Country*

Doctor: (at most) 2000 copies.

With a more precise publication policy the publisher could have promoted the popularity of Kafka's works during the author's lifetime. Unfortunately this is shown in a negative way by the bound books. Presenting the first work of a young newcomer in such an unquestionably beautiful bibliophile but expensive format was a daring move. The price and, above all, the grandiose print had to scare off potential buyers of modern German literature. Wolff, who in the fall of 1912 had only been fully involved in the publishing business for a few days, acted like a bibliophile connoisseur and not like a publisher by not advising Kafka better on the format of his first book. No sales success could be expected in this way. (This is a significant parallel to Robert Walser, whose deluxe editions of 1913 and 1914 by Kurt Wolff Publishing were complete failures.)

After Werfel's entry into Kurt Wolff Publishing, Kafka was presented a few months later in the first series of the new avant-garde literature. Thus the public was served a bibliophile, esoteric Kafka and simultaneously an avant-garde, expressionist Kafka. The question remains as to how far such an early confusion of the readership influenced the reception of Kafka.

Additional labels such as "writer of the Prague Circle" or the variation propagated by Brod of "Jewish writer" could only compound this confusion. For sales reasons, Meyer maintained the term "Prague writer" for *Der Jüngste Tag*. Because of these almost random individual publications in that expressionist magazine, which—because of its associated readership—brought the quiet author into the wake of the lively contemporary literary scene and absorbed him, the great novella book he hoped for was doomed to fail. The problem of not being able to present the public this more comprehensive publication continued to persist.

Wolff's retreat from literary expressionism caused another

change in the reception in 1917: with his new advisors Marder-steig and Heise, Wolff decided to re-promote Kafka's books "traditionally" in bibliophile, expensive style. At that time in 1917, sales of deluxe bibliophile editions were flourishing as never before, yet Wolff did not recognize the signs of looming crisis. But soon one had to recognize that materials such as leather and handmade paper were unavailable for the production of deluxe editions, that the size of typeface for *A Country Doctor* was not available, and that typesetting firms lacked skilled personnel. Already in October 1918 Wolff informed Hasenclever that the balance of payments for bibliophile editions had become so bad that he considered future efforts in this direction futile. When *In the Penal Colony* and *A Country Doctor* appeared nevertheless in 1919 and 1920, the boom in deluxe editions had already long subsided; in the economically difficult postwar period the book market had turned to inexpensive productions. Wolff had speculated unwisely; the two expensive Kafka editions could not be stocked in bookstores at the time they appeared.

"Every good book," Wolff once said, "must be published at the right time, with the right publisher, and with the right enthusiasm, otherwise it is hopelessly lost."[77] But Kafka's books appeared at the wrong time, and the writer's true importance was only clearly recognized publicly after the release of the entire posthumous work. Even if published with the "right publisher" and with the greatest "enthusiasm," those works Kafka himself authorized would not have been easy to sell at that time. Kafka's work fell outside the parameters of expectation of contemporary reception and thus did not find a public. The success of a book among the public is measured by the relationship between the work and the circles to which it is addressed; to influence this relationship and to define it is the task of literary mediation. In the case of Franz Kafka, however, not enough attention was paid to "creating a value for the work"[78] in the public eye. Of course Kafka was a problematic author, but in view of the manner in which the publication of his work was handled during his lifetime and in view of the type of care he received from his publisher, it is clear that scarcely any effort was made at that time. Such an effort was critical for the author to have a chance to transmit his work to the public. The history of Kafka's publications shows that other obstacles than merely the wrong times opposed the modest possibility of Kafka's success as a writer.

The Castle Phase and Kafka's Last Publications (1920-1924)

> For the rest, I repeatedly have the same experience: the test of the writer is in his works . . . I don't know whether such principles are valid; I'd gladly disclaim them if I could; a world is conceivable to me that is governed by a living idea, a world in which art has the place it deserves, which in my experience it never has had. (Kafka to Brod, April 1918)

1. Withdrawal from Literary Life

With the breaking off of relations with Kurt Wolff Publishing, Kafka's life as a writer reached an absolute low point. After the appearance of *A Country Doctor* ("probably my last book," as he wrote in 1918 [L201]), Kafka refrained from the futile attempts to publish his work. The break was total: after *A Country Doctor*, or more exactly since Spring 1917, no further work intended for publication was produced until Spring 1922. A short burst of writing in Fall 1917 seemed to be a reflex reaction to the strong surge of the earlier years. In addition, the aphorisms came to fruition (only later was Kafka to gather them for a possible publication) and in November 1919 the *Letter to My Father*, which was surely not intended as a literary piece.[1] The break did not just occur in his literary life: his illness had freed him from the constraints of his bourgeois profession, which previously no other power could do. Although not pensioned, he received extended leave. First from September 1917 until May 1918, then again from October 1918 (he was severely ill with the Spanish flu), and a large portion of the years 1920 and 1921 he spent in treatment outside of Prague. In Zürau he found enjoyment in the work and gardening of country life with his sister Ottla. He immersed himself totally in the works of Tolstoy and (from the beginning of 1918) in those of Kierkegaard. He no longer seemed to be interested in writing; even personal notes and letters were reduced to a minimum. With Ottla, he lived as in "a good minor marriage" ("marriage not on the basis of the usual violent high currents but of the small windings of the low voltages" [L141]), but the loneliness of eternal bachelorhood obviously depressed him. A renewed attempt at marriage failed: the third engagement, to Julie Wohryzeck, failed because of his father's opposition and—despite his literary distance—because of his writing and "what is connected with it" (DF192). The separation from Julie failed to influence his literary productivity. But a new, passionate relationship developed from a casual acquaintance that Kafka made at the end of 1919, almost according to the pattern with Felice, and led to a new emotional problem in his life.

Milena Jesenská, a young translator and journalist, was a Christian Czech from a Prague family. Unhappily married in Vienna, she had approached Kafka with the request to translate his works into Czech. The correspondence between her and Kafka intensified (a parallel to 1912) at a breathtaking tempo. As Kafka recuperated in Meran, the first of Milena's translations (*The Stoker*) appeared in the Czech journal *Kmen*.[2] Already at the beginning of May, Kafka wrote to Brod in Prague of his insomnia: the reason "perhaps is my correspondence with Vienna. She is a living fire, of a kind I have never seen before"

(L237). Kafka experienced a new happiness in his love for a woman who lived and felt intellectually ("Since I love you . . . I love the whole world" [M136]), yet he was always haunted by the fear that Milena might reject him. Despairingly he observed Milena's relationship with her husband, who openly and continually was unfaithful to her, as she related to Kafka, but whom she nevertheless loved. Kafka, who wanted to believe her sole dependence on him was financial, offered her money so that she could live independently of her husband, but she rejected the idea.

The relationship became a test of strength, for Kafka's suspicion seemed to be confirmed: despite all assurances of her passion for Kafka, Milena did not want to leave her husband (M160); the vivacious young woman did not consider herself in a position to share Kafka's ascetic life in Prague (cf. FK238). This had a negative effect on their relationship. As Kafka's complaints gained the upper hand, Milena instigated a meeting in the middle of August 1920. It resulted in "misunderstandings"; Kafka felt nothing but "shame, almost indelible shame" (M223). Milena made no confessions and saw "no hope," (M222) so he ended the "torture" (M224). In dissolving the relationship, Kafka confirmed for himself again his incapacity for real love ("Only I am at fault . . . This pitcher was broken long before it went to the well" [M220-21].) Resigned, he later described his inability to love in a letter to Brod:

> As long as she withheld herself from me (F) or as long as we were one (M), it was only a menace from far away and not even so very far; but as soon as the slightest little thing happened, everything collapsed. Evidently on account of my dignity, on account of my pride (no matter how humble he looks, the devious West European Jew!), I can love only what I can place so high above me that I cannot reach it. (L273)

The recognition Kafka experienced was the "kernel" of that "monstrously swollen whole that even includes 'fear of death'" (L273). But now he attempted—as after his separation from Felice—to anchor his existence again in writing; actually for a short while his literary will-power manifested itself. From September until December 1920 he wrote the texts: *The City Coat of Arms*, *Poseidon*, *Nights*, *Community*, *The Rebuff*, *On the Question of Laws*, *The Drafting of Troops*, *The Examination*, *The Vulture*, *The Helmsman*, *The Top*, and *Little Fable* (cf. sy83 and KI241-52). But this productive surge proved unfulfilling. If he had been certain during 1913 that his whole being was directed toward literature, at the beginning of the 1920s he was quite unsure of the value of this writing. He bemoaned his "isolation from life" (DII216) and observed "[h]ow happy . . . the married men, young and old both, in the office" without a doubt are (DII210); the value of marriage at this time seemed to stand disproportionately higher for Kafka than that of writing.

2. A Major New Period of Creativity (February-September 1922)

In October 1921 Kafka handed over all his diary notebooks to Milena ("Did you find in the diaries some final proof against me?" [DII205]). Since the turning point in his life in 1917, he had refrained almost entirely from these personal notes. Now, however, when his diaries were with Milena, he asked himself whether he was "still able to keep a diary" and, if so, about what or whom he should then write (DII193). Promptly on this day the diary entries began again:

> I could probably write about M. [Milena], but would not willingly do it, and moreover it would be aimed too directly

at myself; I no longer need to make myself so minutely conscious of such things, I am not so forgetful as I used to be in this respect, I am a memory come alive, hence my insomnia. (DII193)

Other self-judgments from the following years are clearly different from the earlier ones. As his disease pressed on and on—in the summer of 1922 he was finally pensioned—Kafka's wish to be 'realistic' grew. He did not attempt to conjure up his inspiration (or love) any more as earlier; he no longer projected his hope and his strength onto a future utopian existence but made the effort to assess his actual status without any illusions. The questions of what he had accomplished and where it had gotten him were driving forces in Kafka's thinking since the caesura of 1917. After the previous failed attempts to integrate himself into active life, he had to give an account of himself and thus redefine himself. On the one hand, he viewed his failure as "fate" (DII196); on the other he saw "a purposeful action" (DII195). It was both the result of his human weakness and of his will ("I did not want to be distracted" [DII194]). More and more, family and office seemed "imaginary" (DII197) to him, and loneliness and childlessness were his realities (DII204-05). An exaggerated entry of January 1922 depicts the result of this life:

> Without forebears, without marriage, without heirs, with a fierce longing for forebears, marriage and heirs. They all of them stretch out their hands to me: forebears, marriage and heirs, but too far away for me. . . . There is an artificial, miserable substitute for everything, for forebears, marriage and heirs. Feverishly you contrive these substitutes, and if the fever has not already destroyed you, the hopelessness of the substitutes will. (DII207)

But even if Kafka was thinking here of his writing as the "substitutes," he could not question the "value" of his writing again in January 1922. It was not his "comfort" (DII212), nor was it a substitute for life; it was the sole content of his life, his very life. For because of it his other life failed. For the sake of writing he had sacrificed marriage, family, and children. Kafka's diary for January 22, 1922 contains the note: "Nocturnal resolve" (DII207); two further entries from January 27 and 29 signal the new creative phase. Apparently after this date he was working on his new novel.[3]

He was still rather reserved with his statements and provided no commentary in his diaries or letters. Only to Robert Klopstock, a young medical student whom he had gotten to know the previous year, and with whom he had become friendly, did he write a careful allusion: "Lately I have begun to write a little in order to preserve myself from what is called nerves" (L322). On March 15 Kafka then read Brod "the beginning of *The Castle*" (FK185, cf. also 221). Simultaneously in the spring of 1922 the texts *First Sorrow*, *The Break*, *Intercessor*, and *A Hunger Artist* were completed (cf. sy83 and KI252-61).

3. Renewed Readiness to Publish (1922)

As a result of the sudden outbreak of his illness, Kafka had lost the strength to present his works to the public. Not until 1921 did this resistance begin to mellow. On April 3, 1921, a small prose piece from *A Country Doctor*, *In the Gallery*, appeared in the *Prager Presse*; the editorial note leaves the question open as to whether Kafka took an active part in the publication.[4] The collaboration with the new Prague daily, whose editorial staff included his good friends Otto Pick and Oskar Baum, grew in the period that followed. In September *Unmask-*

ing of a Confidence Trickster appeared in it, and in December 1921 it even published an original, *The Bucket Rider*, which at that time was taken from the *Country Doctor* material.[5] Simultaneously Kafka submitted *An Old Manuscript* to *Die Selbstwehr*, headed by his friend Felix Weltsch.[6] It is interesting and important to observe how Kafka mustered renewed courage to publish and how he now—probably with a view toward his foreseeable retirement and then a possible unencumbered writer's existence—tested the waters by releasing a few small pieces to assess the impact they would have. The German literary industry had in his experience remained closed to him; in order to break out of the anonymity that he had suffered, greater efforts would have to be expended. Kafka therefore chose a path via his closest friends for this gradual new beginning: through his friends' experience he did not confront literary business as a tenacious opponent, for with them there was no alienation.

First Sorrow in Genius

When one understands as a process the systematic effort that the writer required for a publication, it is not surprising that Kafka found renewed courage after small publications in Prague to consider publishing outside of Prague. If the small publications had in their own way prepared the new creative period and spurred him on to new, cohesive writing, then the texts that he wrote about in this way formed the basis of a greater power of responsibility.

At the beginning of May 1922 Kafka sent a handwritten copy of a new prose piece to Mardersteig for publication in *Genius*, the representative journal for avant-garde and traditional art. An exchange of letters between Wolff, in whose house the journal had appeared since 1919, and Mardersteig, who together with the art historian Carl Georg Heise had founded *Genius*, illustrates how sudden Kafka's leap from rejection to acceptance could be. Wolff, now an art publisher very much involved with Ernst Ludwig Kirchner, asked Mardersteig to intervene at the end of 1921. The latter informed him that Kirchner would probably want to illustrate another book ("He would not again do a portfolio") and that it would have to be a modern work such as a Kafka, for to have him illustrate something old would be unfortunate (WBr385). Wolff, who then contacted Brod, answered with little encouragement on January 26, 1922: "From Kafka, who is continually struggling with his health—as Max Brod writes to me—nothing is forthcoming despite all my efforts. For years there has not been a single manuscript page from him and he apparently doesn't intend to have anything printed in the future" (WBr389).

Brod must have passed on this negative information to the publisher in January 1922.[7] Even the longer second letter by the publisher on March 1, 1922, to entice Kafka fell on a deaf ear. The writer had published several small pieces over the course of the years and had experienced a marvelous, new writing phase, and his diaries reveal that he had ended his retreat from literature. But Kafka did not respond with even a line to the urgent, amicable requests of 'his' publisher. Now however, in May 1922, together with an accompanying letter that was supposed to excuse his long silence and that Wolff himself characterized as alluringly beautiful, he sent off a new text to Munich.[8] In view of his recently recovered creative power—and the greater power of responsibility connected with it—did Kafka desire to renew the contact with the publisher with whom his entire work had been published? This is a rhetorical question that must be denied categorically. The writer most recently had decided to break off any contact with his old publisher after the unfortunate printing of *A Country Doctor* and since then had consistently shunned any personal contact with Wolff. A causal connection—as theorized elsewhere—between Kafka's submission and the publisher's long letter to entice him does not exist.[9]

Kafka sent his prose text *First Sorrow*—originating at the beginning of his last writing phase—not to Wolff but personally to Mardersteig at the address of *Genius*. He already knew this journal well. Back in 1918 Meyer had invited him to collaborate; it was entirely due to Meyer's arrival that *Genius* had a literary section at all.[10] Despite Meyer's solitary advocacy of a literary section, it was quite minimal in comparison to that for the visual arts, something paradigmatic for the revised programmatic viewpoint of Kurt Wolff Publishing. Quite perturbed, Werfel expressed his opinion about the first edition of *Genius*; he wrote to Meyer (not to Wolff) that the poetry supplement seemed to him rather thrown together and incoherent. At such an expense one would certainly have to achieve more unity and quality (WBr332).

Certainly Kafka had a high regard for this splendidly designed, expensive, and exclusive journal (the editors did not consider it necessary to send out review copies), which, according to announcements, placed itself in the tradition of *Pan*, *Hyperion*, and *Marsyas* (cf. WBrXL and WV874). Precisely these three journals were drawing cards for Kafka. Mardersteig himself, after Meyer's proddings, several times requested a contribution from Kafka. One such letter, of November 18, 1921, has been preserved. In its intensity and amicable courtesy it is unmatched in the history of Kafka's relations to the literary world.[11] Only with this special kind of invitation can it be explained that, despite his continued reticence to publish again in Kurt Wolff Publishing, Kafka submitted a small manuscript. Delayed considerably by the production difficulties of the day for deluxe editions, the second book of the third volume of *Genius* appeared with Kafka's contribution as a first printing in fall 1922.[12] But here too there was a hitch: in *First Sorrow* Kafka merely released to *Genius* the work (of the two newly written pieces) of which he himself had reservations. Kafka planned to fulfill a wish he had cherished for years with the other, "better" story.

A Hunger Artist in *Die neue Rundschau*

Kafka quickly regretted submitting the manuscript to *Genius*, for it was not the editor Mardersteig, to whom Kafka had written, but rather Wolff, who thanked him for the submission—and in an exuberant manner. Kafka considered this unplanned renewed encounter with the publisher "disconcerting" ("His letter makes me wince"). He would now be happy—as he wrote dejectedly to Brod—if he could remove "the repulsive little story out of Wolff's [not Mardersteig's!] desk and wipe it out of his memory" (L326). Analyzing Wolff's excessive praise with a certain degree of melancholy, Kafka drew the conclusion that the publisher had not evaluated his writing honestly, and that he could do nothing other than praise the little text "because he is forced to by the strategy." Only in this pessimistic manner of argumentation had he been able to experience this praise by Wolff for what was without a doubt a bad text. Kafka called it "gossamer successes" (L326). Brod did not follow up on this resigned reflection of Kafka; he contradicted the equally and very methodically pessimistic explanatory thesis of his friend in a pointed manner: "Enclosed letter of R. Kayser will interest you . . . I would really like to know how you will explain the enthusiasm of Dr. Kayser, who is certainly unscathed by your method."[13] Kafka calmed his friend, who obviously thought he had been speaking so deprecatingly of *A Hunger Artist*. He was not referring to this story, but rather to "the story sent to Wolff, which an unprejudiced person cannot be in doubt about." Kayser's letter had of course "pleased" him—"how need and vanity lap such things up." "But he is not unmoved by my method," he wrote to Brod; besides, the story he sent to Kayser is "bearable" (L329)—presumably the most positive description the author could elicit in evaluating his own work. Probably already in May Kafka had prepared the manuscript of *A Hunger Artist* for publication. At the latest by the end of June 1922, at the time of this exchange between Brod and Kafka, the text was already lying on the editor's desk of *Die neue Rundschau*.

Rudolf Kayser, a literary scholar born in 1889, wrote his dissertation on Arnim and Brentano. He joined S. Fischer Publishing in 1919 and at the same time remained active literarily as a writer and editor. Initially an assistant to Samuel Fischer and then changing over in 1921 to Oskar Bie at *Die neue Rundschau* upon the departure of its long-time editor, he took over the journal as its chief editor with the January 1922 number. The situation paralleled that of 1914, when Musil was supposed to bring new blood into the editorship. In 1922 Fischer was also concerned with modernizing his journal, whose reputation as a liberal European organ during the war years had suffered badly. *Die neue Rundschau* had become "genuinely poor" and Fischer's own authors considered their own in-house organ for preprinting fatigued, obsolete, and ready for dissolution.[14]

Kayser—simultaneously Fischer's foreign expert—was the appropriate European-minded individual to establish the ties to the intellectual tendencies beyond Germany that had been neglected since 1914. The programmatic considerations were buttressed by a visual change in the journal's format: beginning with the January number of 1922, *Die neue Rundschau* no longer appeared in the former conservative German script, but in unpretentious Latin antiqua, which was more liberally cosmopolitan and more readable abroad.

Kafka's personal connection to *Die neue Rundschau* had not changed since 1914. Also after the distressing failure of the collaboration initiated by Musil and irrespective of its conservativism, it remained the literary journal that the writer treasured most highly his whole life long and of which he was a regular reader and a longtime subscriber. In contrast to the avant-garde journals of expressionism that attracted his own younger generation, *Die neue Rundschau* was the most appealing to Kafka, who was conscious of enduring values and dominated very much by tradition. His opinion, however, is similar to that of his Prague friends: *Die neue Rundschau* embodied German literature for the circle of German writers from Prague; for them it was the institution that in a certain sense was concerned with the continuation of German literature (after Goethe).

After the incident with Musil, Kafka would have probably refused to collaborate further. The row two years later between Brod and *Rundschau* editor Oskar Bie was another reason for Kafka to avoid collaboration.[15] Between 1917 and 1920, the period when he wrote *A Country Doctor*, he had not considered working with the house journal of the competing publisher. Although Kafka was probably always interested in publishing in *Die neue Rundschau*, for external reasons this had previously never been possible.

A parallel to 1914 and to Musil's activity in the editorial office of *Die neue Rundschau* is that Kayser requested a contribution from Kafka during the first months he was chief editor. But the connection between Kafka and *Die neue Rundschau* came about with relative certainty because of Brod's efforts. Already in 1916 Brod had promoted with Wolff a young Berlin writer, this same very Rudolf Kayser, who at the time was quite apparently a great admirer of Brod's books. During Brod's frequent stays in Berlin the bond between them probably solidified. And when it was clear in the fall of 1921 that the Czech selection of Kafka's works proposed by Milena would not materialize, Brod was able to send the foreword he had written for it to Kayser; this article appeared in 1921 in the November number of the *Rundschau* as the first great praise of Kafka.[16]

Elsewhere the assumption has been made that the printing of this very comprehensive article was part of a promise to publish on the part of the writer himself. Actually it was common practice for *Die neue Rundschau* to present an author to the public in this way before the publication of a larger contribution. But the reference to the long unknown original purpose of Brod's Kafka essay at least modifies such speculation. It must also be kept in mind that Kafka's new creative phase began only at the end of January 1922 and that he therefore could not have promised any text at all in fall 1921. But the fact that the article was printed, which was more laudatio than critique, is extremely important for another reason: for Kayser, the new editor of *Die neue Rundschau*, came to appreciate the writer Franz Kafka, and Kafka emphatically demonstrated that he was now open to publication in this journal. It is thoroughly conceivable that this article by Brod helped to unleash Kafka's new creative phase, for now the possibility of publishing in *Die neue Rundschau* was real for him. Such a possibility was presumably a great impetus for Kafka.

A Hunger Artist appeared in the October 1922 number of *Die neue Rundschau* at approximately the same time as *First Sorrow* in *Genius*. With it Kafka clearly underscored his retreat from Wolff: the worse story (he wrote "repulsive") he had made available to Wolff's *Genius* because of Mardersteig's friendly invitation, but passed on the successful ("bearable") one to Kayser for printing in Kafka's highly esteemed *Neue Rundschau*. That the writer played a part in this story is revealed by a parallel printing of *A Hunger Artist* in his hometown *Prager Presse*.[17] With *A Hunger Artist*—actually only comparable to *The Judgment*—it was a question of publishing a text whose quality was obviously quite clear to him, in a place where he personally felt comfortable. Writing *The Judgment* in September 1912 had revealed a new ideal to him; the publishing of *A Hunger Artist* in 1922 also signified a landmark in the history of his publications: Kafka's self-esteem as a writer had changed again. The year 1922 brought a new—and final—great shift in his conception of writing. He began his actual life as a writer.

Seclusion in his Existence as a Writer (1922-1924)

The repeatedly manifested cycle of writing and non-writing to which Kafka was subjected his whole life no longer took place after the outbreak of his disease, neither in its earlier exactness nor in its eruptive form. Only in summer 1922 after a writing phase that lasted longer than ever before did a break in the pattern that has been described as both a vicious circle and as its divine opposite become evident. The different phases of the pattern not only alternated, but actually generated each other. After his retirement in July 1922, Kafka's productivity was no longer subjected to these abrupt and sharply defined phases. His writing was now more than ever before dependent on his will. Although weakened by illness, Kafka was more even-tempered and resolute. When work on *The Castle* had to be abandoned in September (cf. L357), his will was not stifled nor was his ability for creative writing.

His decision to leave Kurt Wolff Publishing in order to publish in S. Fischer's *Rundschau* did not signify an attempt by Kafka to reorient himself within the literary industry. The new literary consciousness made possible for the first time by regular productivity and freedom from the oppressing routine of office life, was accompanied by no new hope of bringing his work successfully before the public. Since the summer of 1917 Kafka had geared himself toward a private existence (not including writing), but only *after* the task of *The Castle* in 1922 did he radicalize—in the self-judgment of his writing—the position that he had taken until he met with Rowohlt in Leipzig in 1912: the conviction of the total futility of accomplishing anything with his work in the literary industry and the intentional refusal to publish. But now a decade later, it was not a matter of simply falling back into the anonymity of merely being a writer as earlier. What Kafka had expressed negatively up to 1912 about his own writing in the sense of a retreat in case of failure, of the lack of success of a publication, and what was expressed between 1912 and 1917 as a pessimistic argumentation serving to protect him and to advertise his own work, now became truth for him.[18] The quiet, unobtrusive, and therefore entirely unnoticed struggle carried on relentlessly by Kafka between 1912 and 1917 for the publication of his work and recognition by the outside world had been thoroughly obscured amidst the turmoil of wartime and the stormy situation of contemporary literature. The public's awareness of Kafka had reached its high point in October 1915 with the awarding of the Fontane Prize and since then had steadily declined. The publisher's advertising efforts for him had noticeably waned after this event. Kafka's first small book *Meditation* received in its day more critical attention than *In the Penal Colony* and *A Country Doctor* together after 1919! What Kafka had already postulated in 1907 after the first mention of his name among the literary public in a letter to Brod turned out to be true: "This name will have to be forgotten" (L23).

During these years Kafka wrote his "first will and testament" in which he assigned Brod the task of "burning completely and without remnant and unread everything in my remains (or in the bookcase, wash closet, desk at home or in the office or anywhere else anything was carried on and occurs to you) of my diaries, manuscripts, letters, of others and myself, sketches and so forth."[19] At this moment, since the world had begun to forget him, he wanted to eradicate any trace of his own existence. And after the failure of the third novel it was no longer that earlier patient and methodical coquetry when he wrote in July 1922 about the uncompleted manuscript of *The Castle*, which he had delivered to his friend to read: "I know that it exists only to be written in, not yet to be read" (L343).

At the moment, therefore, when he was freed from the office work he despised and when the writer's life he had been desiring for over a decade finally became possible, Kafka withdrew from the public. A possible reason for this may be that the financial importance of publication—only the financial profits from his publications would have perhaps been able to make his profession unnecessary—disappeared the moment he retired. Contradicting this idea is the fact that Kafka always kept his profession separate from his writing and never wanted to be dependent on the income from his writing; this was something about which he was most fearful. His rejection of the literary public, therefore, had other, deeper reasons. A single publication could no longer help him now when everything else was rendered insignificant because of his worsening illness. His main work was artistically "incomplete, incompletable, and therefore unpublishable," as he remarked.[20] He could not expect to realize more than a single publication from his future writing. Why then torment himself with that thought, especially after his negative experiences with the literary industry? His "concept of the 'writer'" (L344) changed under these conditions: its purpose was now only self-preservation, his writing became private without that earlier longing or hope for something outside. About this new purpose, this new "value" of his writing the author drew a bold picture in a letter to Klopstock:

> [T]his writing is the most important thing in the world to me (in a way that is horrible to everyone around me, so unspeakably horrible that I don't talk about it)—the way his delusion is important to the madman (should he lose it, he would become "mad") or the way her pregnancy is important to a woman. This has nothing to do with the value of the writing—I know that value only too precisely, just as I know the value it has for me. (L323)

4. Palestine and Berlin (1923-1924)

Serious illness overshadowed all the activities of the following months. Again Kafka was dependent upon the care of his family as outbreaks of fever and insomnia, which drove him to despair, made the winter of 1922-1923 a torment. Only the spring brought more than a passing improvement and spiritual and moral renewal. No longer tied to Prague by his job, he now planned, as he indicated later to his sister Ottla, "something altogether radical" (O84)—emigration to Palestine.[21] While bedridden he had read a lot, above all Jewish, Zionist authors in order to intensify his "national feeling" (M213). As his letters to Milena reveal, Kafka meanwhile had been very much influenced by Zionist thought. Repulsed by the growing anti-Semitism of everyday life in Prague (and naturally considering the much more tolerable—for him—Mediterranean climate), he pondered emigration. How serious he was about it is demonstrated by the Hebrew studies that he regularly undertook during the first half of 1923. But when he got to know Dora Diamant, the Eastern Jewess from Berlin, while he was spending the summer vacation at the Baltic spa Muritz—he had accompanied his sister Elli's family there in July—he immediately canceled the Palestine trip planned for October. For "in view of the possibilities in Berlin," as he expressed it in a letter to Klopstock in September, his emigration was now not "urgent" (L380). Kafka had hoped to forge a new life for himself in a total community in Palestine. Just as earlier the myth of a free and liberating America had existed for him, Palestine was in 1923 more than a strip of land—it was a principle and had become a new culminating point for his hopes. After his futile attempts at integration, he no longer believed he was capable of having a personal relationship with a woman. Now, as he expressed to Brod, "loneliness" was his "sole aim," his "greatest temptation" and "opportunity" (L359). Brod countered at that time rather bluntly: "you avoid women, you attempt to live entirely without them. And that won't work."[22] However, after the unexpected encounter with Dora, the myth of marriage and family regained its earlier power to integrate all hope. Without mentioning Dora's name, Kafka reported at the end of September 1923 to Milena:

> I began considering the possibility of moving to Berlin. At the time this possibility was not much more real than the Palestine plan, but then it grew stronger. To live alone in Berlin was of course impossible, in every respect, not only in Berlin but for that matter anywhere. For this, too, a solution—surprising in its special way—offered itself in Muritz. (M236)

Berlin was the most lively opposite of Prague. Whereas his native city symbolized dependency and perennial bachelorhood for him, he saw in Berlin a "vitality" (L246) and—remembering Felice—independence and family. In a certain regard Berlin was a city of fate for him, but something that remained an unattainable goal. When he had come to the decision in July 1914 to begin his life as an independent writer in Berlin, the First World War began (precisely on the day of his planned departure). And when he communicated to Wolff three years later that he was going to give up his job in order to write and "marry and move from Prague, possibly to Berlin" (L134), his illness broke out (only several days thereafter). In such a fateful way Kafka's otherwise infrequent decisions were shattered. Now in July 1923 these hopes reemerged. But it was no longer Berlin as the capital of the German literary world that attracted him and in which he thought as in 1914 and 1917 he could best keep up his literary work. Now Berlin was the place where he would live with a woman.

Previously Kafka had been advising his friends, not himself, to settle in Berlin: "Prague is of questionable worth," he wrote in the summer of 1922 to Klopstock, "Berlin is a medicine against Prague" (L361). Kafka interceded on Klopstock's behalf for connections and associations so that his young friend could at least continue living in Berlin; he himself no longer believed he would find the strength for such a radical change. At that time he found contacts, above all, through Ernst Weiß (cf. PK133f.) and Brod (L361-62). At this time the latter could be found almost more frequently in Berlin than in Prague, since—as Kafka somewhat ashamedly communicated to Klopstock—"for a special reason" Berlin had become a "second home" for him. For years Brod had been having an affair in Berlin and himself toyed for a while with the idea of "moving" there (L246). Financial considerations—he did not want to risk his post in Prague in these difficult times before he had found another one in Berlin—prevented him from taking this step. Through his letters from Berlin, Kafka experienced the greatness and liveliness of this city, its pulsating activity and the productivity of its people. With fascination Brod once summarized his impression of the city as follows: "things get done."[23] Kafka responded: "You imagine that your letter did *not* make me hot?" (L246).

Several times Brod had invited his friend to accompany him on trips to Berlin where he could "meet new people and enter new relationships." Brod envisioned Berlin as a salvation for his friend ("you must break this bond to Prague. Only the first steps are difficult.")[24] If at that time the thought of being alone in the city of his failed attempts at marriage, alongside Brod and his female friend, made him shy away from the trip, his friend's letters and stories expanded in a positive way his perspective on Berlin. Thus Brod had already laid the groundwork; only a catalyst was now needed for Kafka to make the final decision. The acquaintance with Dora kindled the flame. After Brod's report Kafka returned in August 1923 changed and "full of high courage" from his summer vacation:

> His decision to cut all ties, get to Berlin, and live with Dora stood firm—and this time he carried it out inflexibly. At the end of July he left Prague, after offering successful resistance to all his family's objections. From Berlin he wrote to me for the first time that he felt happy, and that he was even sleeping well—an unheard-of novelty in these last years. (FK197)

Given his condition, he viewed his trip—he actually, as Brod recounts, did not travel to Berlin at the end of July but on September 24, 1923—as "foolhardiness" and only comparable to "Napoleon's march to Russia" (L382), a statement that clearly indicated Kafka's anxieties. He moved into an apartment with Dora in the Berlin suburb Steglitz. With one stroke his whole mood improved; he was, as Brod reports, "happy with his companion" and had "become a new man" (FK198). Again he began to write, "with enthusiasm," as Brod emphasizes, and now read again to his friend what he had written (in October: *A Little Woman*, later some passages from *The Burrow* [FK198]). Kafka's days were again firmly ordered; everything was done with a view toward writing.[25] Since he found his friend so changed and reborn, Brod viewed himself again as the designated intermediary in literary matters. When he introduced Kafka at the end of 1923 or the beginning of 1924 to a director of the publisher *Die Schmiede*, he noted to his satisfaction that his friend was apparently in agreement to publish a new book.

5. Fifth Excursus: The Publishing House *Die Schmiede*, Berlin

In the absence of a monograph or bibliography about it, the history of the publishing house *Die Schmiede* still remains essentially clouded today. The publisher is not forgotten, however, since its books have survived; among them are sophisticated and literarily noteworthy publications that advanced *Die Schmiede* to one of the most important literary publishers in Germany shortly after its establishment. Knowledge about the publishing house is, nevertheless, out of proportion to its literary significance at the time. Thus until today the problematic external situation of the publisher of predominantly Jewish and

Marxist authors at the beginning of the National Socialist era has been most emphasized[26]; the books of *Die Schmiede* were considered "entartete Kunst" ("degenerate art") in the 1930s and were destroyed as such when on the night of May 10, 1933, the fanatical campaign "Against the German Spirit" reached its climax with the book burning. Long before, the authors of *Die Schmiede* had been persecuted, expatriated, or had themselves chosen exile. The correspondence, publishing records, and archives of *Die Schmiede* did not escape the wave of destruction of National Socialism. The situation with regard to source material is paltry.

What remains are the books: about 100 of *Die Schmiede*'s titles could be identified for the period between 1922 and 1927; two titles followed in 1928, and only one was printed in 1929. For exactly five years then, from 1922 until 1927, the publishing company was active. This short period of existence stands in contrast to its literary reputation. From its inception the young firm had been the most demanding and ambitious representative of modern German literature. For a while it was exceedingly successful, when measured by the reactions of authors, publishers, and the press. Most resolutely, *Die Schmiede* assumed Wolff's inheritance of the expressionistic movement and became the major publisher of post-expressionism. The publisher also became famous for its involvement with primarily contemporary French novelists. Following German first editions of Balzac's works, the novels of Francis Carco and Raymond Radiguet and since 1926 the first volumes of Proust's *In Search of Time Lost* appeared. Walter Benjamin was among the translators. But in proportion to the growth of the literary significance of its works among the public, open contradictions emerged from the day-to-day publishing practice. The apparently clear conception of the publisher ebbed into bungling attempts. Even the political line became unclear. Supported by a bourgeois press, *Die Schmiede* published noteworthy socialist and revolutionary authors, which even amazed the leftist oriented *Neue Bücherschau*. For this journal, *Die Schmiede* was certainly among the group of most important literary and art publishers, but its basis and production seemed to be in total contradiction: "Many books of this bourgeois publisher lack the spirit of the bourgeoisie so much that, if it weren't for prices hardly within the means of the proletariat, one might assume that they were publications of proletariat publishers."[27]

The business practices of the directors soon led to an explosion. None of the authors remained with *Die Schmiede* any longer than contractually required. Tucholsky summarized the rage of many of *Die Schmiede*'s authors toward the publisher in a pamphlet that appeared—not under a pseudonym but under his real name—in the *Weltbühne* in February 1929: "Let's hold our noses and enter." This very prominent publisher, according to Tucholsky, never had a face, and never could one have said: "This book could only have been published by *Die Schmiede*, for almost anything could appear there." But how did it happen that Tucholsky—himself the author of one of *Die Schmiede*'s books—now demanded that the owners be "pilloried," that they be given a piece of one's mind, that their desire had disappeared to do business in the domain of literature where they have no business? How did it happen that this publisher, distinguished by its splendid books, gave the protective association of German writers (*Der Schutzverband Deutscher Schriftsteller*) more to do than eight major publishers together?[28] At a time marked by general resignation and even depression, many authors had placed great hopes in this publishing house, hopes that were bitterly disappointed.

Die Schmiede—A Rumor in the Confused
Literary Landscape of 1922-1923 in Germany

The First World War took a great toll on the writers of the young, expressionist generation. Many of those under thirty did not return home in 1918, among them: Alfred Lichtenstein, Ernst Wilhelm Lotz, Ernst Stadler, Georg Trakl, August Stramm, Reinhard Johannes Sorge, Gustav Sack, and Wilhelm Runge. After the end of the war, Wolf Przygode drew up the balance sheet with his *Buch der Toten* ("Book of the Dead"), which he edited for Roland Publishing. His intention was to gather in a collection of poems by those talented young poets who died at the beginning of their promising literary careers, and with whose extinction present-day art suffered deep losses.[29] The destruction exerted a powerful impact on the literary world. Already in 1916 Albert Ehrenstein—at that time an editor with Kurt Wolff Publishing—was not able to report to the publisher, who was on the battlefield, about any newly received exceptional manuscripts, because, according to Ehrenstein, the talent may have died on the battlefields (WBr235).

The intellectual culture prior to 1914 disintegrated during the war. Additionally, amid the political and social crises of the postwar period, the belief in the meaning of literature was broadly shaken; new hopes now came about through much more concrete utopias. Many of the previously engaged authors of the expressionistic movement were totally resigned when they learned of the failure of the "German Revolution." A sense of helplessness marked the literary scene in Germany from 1919 on.

The literary scene at the beginning of the 1920s was dominated by the generation of writers in their fifties: Thomas Mann, Gerhart Hauptmann, Hugo von Hofmannsthal, Hermann

Hesse, and Rainer Maria Rilke, Otto Julius Birnbaum, and other bourgeois writers stood at the pinnacle of their fame. Kurt Wolff Publishing, up to that time the watershed and hope of avant-garde literary movements, abandoned the literature of the younger generation entirely. Pinthus—as Wolff's editor he had been the specialist in what the young writers produced—was at that time not prepared to follow Wolff to Munich; he was drawn to Berlin, to Rowohlt. Here he edited the most famous anthology of literary expressionism, *Menschheitsdämmerung*. But the "Symphony of Young Literature," which the subtitle promised, was already its final symphony, for expressionism as a literary movement had exhausted itself. The preface by Pinthus alluded to this end:

> As one who stood in their midst, tied to them by friendship and a love of their works, I step forward and call out: Let this be enough, you who were not satisfied with yourselves, for those for whom the old man is not enough; let it suffice because this divided, inciting, confusing poetry may not be enough for you! Let it not suffice! But rather help, all of you, to create a simpler, clearer, purer being in the future for the will of humanity . . . Friends, not these sounds! Let us ring out other more cheerful ones![30]

Other so-called necrologies in 1920-1921 joined this clear retreat of the one-time mentor of expressionistic literature. Kasimir Edschmid wrote about the situation of expressionism in 1920: "One thing however is certain: the generation is used up. Surprise will only come from achievement, not from confrontation."[31] And Kayser wrote in the prologue of his *Verkündigung. Anthologie junger Lyrik* ("Pronouncement. Anthology of Modern Poems"), edited in fall 1920, of a literary epoch coming to an end.[32] All the comprehensive anthologies of expressionism were only compiled after the end of the actual movement. However, since wide reception followed the avant-garde with some delay, the expressionists' books now had good sales; in the years between 1918 and 1922 they reached the high point of their popularity. As soon as one could list "expressionism and the prosperity of mankind as assets on the balance sheet," a critical account of 1927 read, then the literary retail trade burgeoned en masse in all of Germany's major cities, and publishing companies rode the popular wave.[33] Publishers and editors opened up now more than ever before to budding young literary talent from outside the major cities. A widespread epigonal era flooded the literary scene in Germany.

The internal political situation in Germany was very complicated as extremism from the left as well as the right intensified. Fears of a civil war mounted. But above all the young republic fought against the collapse of its currency. For the publishers as well, the inflation that spread in August 1921 had fatal consequences. Book production was reduced to a minimum, and the trade could only be kept afloat through emergency measures. At that time the financially powerful publishing houses pressed forward: the giant Ullstein attempted to lure authors away from S. Fischer Publishing; and Zsolnay Publishing, founded at the beginning of 1923, became a stiff competitor for Kurt Wolff, since this Viennese publisher paid in stable currency (Wolff, who had come upon economically difficult times, first saw Werfel and then Brod, two of his most lucrative authors, switch over to Zsolnay). But also in Berlin, in the midst of economic depression and political uncertainty, there was a new literary center that openly defied the inflation problems. When Arthur Schnitzler had a falling out with his publisher, Samuel Fischer, because of the increasing drop in prices and enlisted a friend, the translator

Hans Jacob, to keep an eye out for a better paying publisher for him, he received the tip: "[I]n case you really intend to go to another publisher, I could recommend to you in good conscience *Die Schmiede*."[34]

This example is not an individual case; many other writers whose honoraria had been devalued by inflation thought as Schnitzler did. In September 1922 Weiß, who had also come upon financially hard times, turned to his publisher Wolff and let him consider seriously that he (Weiß) had just received a very generous offer: "I have just completed a small novel which is called *Die Feuerprobe* ["Ordeal by Fire"] . . . A publisher will print it in a single small edition of 500-600 copies and pay me, who am now suffering considerably from financial strain, 70,000-80,000 marks" (WBr381). Wolff could not offer his author such a large advance. While Schnitzler did remain with Fischer, *Die Feuerprobe* appeared in 1923 with the publisher Weiß mentioned, *Die Schmiede*; three further titles of Wolff's authors were listed in the publishing program of *Die Schmiede* in the years 1923 and 1924.[35] The publishing house fulfilled two essential conditions in this difficult time: first, it had the reputation of paying its authors quickly and generously, and second, as a young house, it promised to become a new attractive publishing center amidst a decaying and tired landscape of publishers. Pinthus had given the reason for the initial successes of the young Rowohlt/Wolff Publishing house with the rumor: "Because everybody knows they do things and have money" (WV646). The same was true ten years later for *Die Schmiede* —a similar rumor was afloat about this publisher.

A Sketch of Publishing History between 1922 and 1930

In 1923 *Die Schmiede*, Ltd., Berlin, was listed for the first time in the directory of the German Book Trade. The Berlin trade register sets the exact founding date as November 23, 1921 (with a supplementary contract on April 28, 1922). The directors of the company, which had to be consolidated as a result of the high inflation and changed into a stock company, were Julius Berthold Salter, who previously worked in his father's theater agency, and Fritz Wurm, who had a degree in economics. Besides his father Norbert, Salter's sister Lilly and his older brother Georg were involved in the company. Through Georg Salter, who worked primarily as a stage designer between 1920 and 1927, but who also was known for his book graphics and individual volume designs, the young house developed a unified, characteristic line with its book design. There were two separate entities in this family business: the theater and the book publishers. From the beginning they had concentrated mostly on the editing of plays as well as on the administration of lucrative theater rights. The family, with its bent toward the theater, knew how to promote quickly an economically successful stage business; it became the primary financial basis for all the further literary endeavors of the concern. The house name apparently goes back to "Offizina Fabri," in which more than likely the first actual title of *Die Schmiede—Die Feuerprobe* by Weiß—was published.

With the takeover of the literary division of Roland Publishing, the actual literary activity of *Die Schmiede* began at the end of 1922. The small publishing house of Roland (Munich), headed by Albert Mundt, distinguished itself by its efforts to provide new impetus to the expressionist movement after the war ended. The company had claimed a degree of literary fame through its yearbooks and literary collections, which were closely tied to the history of late expressionism. Przygode's *Buch der Toten* appeared there in spring 1919; it was labeled the first special print of Przygode's journal *Die Dichtung*, which also appeared with Roland in the first year. In 1920 *Der Anbruch* appeared, a "yearbook of new poetry" edited by Otto Schneider and Arthur Ernst Rutra. In 1921 Rudolf Kayser edited his exemplary late-expressionistic lyric anthology *Verkündigung* with Roland. But Roland's greatest undertaking was its book series *Die Neue Reihe* ("The New Series"). This collection of *Dichtungen der jungen Generation* ("Literature of the Young Generation"), which appeared between 1918 and 1921, presented especially the generation born after 1890 that formed the basis of the avant-garde literature after World War I, in a total of 25 volumes.[36] A second series, the *Kleine Rolandbücher*, became available through *Die Schmiede* from 1922 on.[37] With the acquisition of the publishing rights of Roland Publishing, the latter's authors switched to *Die Schmiede* as a group. Authors of Roland Publishing who later published with *Die Schmiede* included: Rudolf Leonhard, Kurt Heynicke, Georg Kaiser, Max Hermann (-Neisse), Otto Flake, Ivan Goll, Alfred Wolfenstein, Rudolf Kayser, and Heinrich Mann.

The second group of authors who later published with *Die Schmiede* came directly from Kurt Wolff. The late expressionistic generation of writers had only found temporary domicile with Wolff; at the latest after the end of *Der jüngste Tag* in 1921, a whole group of authors had to reorient themselves. The list of authors who changed from Wolff's *Der jüngste Tag* to *Die Schmiede* is impressive. There were thirteen authors in all, by whom twenty titles had appeared in Wolff's series: Rudolf Leonhard, Leo Matthias, Carl Sternheim, Walter Hasenclever, Johannes R. Becher, Gottfried Benn, Alfred Wolfenstein, Ivan Goll, Karel Čapek, Rudolf Kayser, Max Hermann(-Neisse), Karl Otten, and Franz Kafka. Thus there is the picture of a typical rotation: after Wolff turned away from modern literature, a definite circle of his literary avant-garde writers left his house in order to go to Roland or directly to *Die Schmiede*. But also those of Wolff's authors who were never able to tie themselves totally to a publisher and found themselves on a merry-go-round in the publishing landscape, such as Heinrich Mann and Weiß, decided on *Die Schmiede*. With the acceptance of the authors from Roland and Wolff, however, *Die Schmiede* essentially concluded its recruitment of its own group of authors. Remarkably, this publisher paid little attention to the cultivation of new literary blood with its non-literature oriented publishing team of Salter and Wurm. No noteworthy first work of a young German writer appeared in *Die Schmiede* (with perhaps the sole exception of *A Hunger Artist*).

While other literary publishers encountered great economic difficulties during the inflationary period that crippled the book industry, *Die Schmiede* was able to expand considerably. In the first year of publication from fall 1922 until fall 1923 the following titles appeared: Becher's *Verklärung* ("Transfiguration"); Flake's *Deutsche Reden, Erzählungen, Nein und Ja* ("German Speeches," "Stories," "No and Yes"); Weiß's *Die Feuerprobe, Olympia*; Kayser's *Die Zeit ohne Mythos* ("The Time without Myth"); Wolfenstein's *Mörder und Träumer* ("Murderers and Dreamers"); Kaiser's *Flucht nach Venedig* ("Flight to Venice"); Haas's *Das Spiel mit dem Feuer* ("Playing with Fire"); and Leonhard's *Die Insel* ("The Island"). The business élan of *Die Schmiede* was promoted through a sympathetic press that commented attentively and very positively on the work of the upstart publisher. Furthermore, the books of *Die Schmiede* were attractive in their full-blown, artistically demanding form and gave a uniform impression, as did the program policy. *Die Schmiede* promised to become the most successful literary press of the 1920s.

The *Kleine Rolandbücher* and the Balzac series acquired from Roland were points of departure for an apparently clearly defined policy for series that largely determined the profile of the company. Thus in Fall 1923 the first volumes of the much heralded series *Romane des zwanzigsten Jahrhunderts* ("Novels of the Twentieth Century") (16 titles until 1927) and from 1924 the series *Die Außenseiter der Gesellschaft* ("The Outsiders of Society") edited by Leonhard (14 titles until 1925) appeared.[38] In addition to the young Walter Landauer, *Die Schmiede* was able to win over Rudolf Leonhard himself as editor. To a certain extent Leonhard became the company's literary drawing card between 1923 and 1926.

Yet the prosperity of the house did not endure for long. Already in 1924 it was reorganized into a stock company and shares were sold. The fiscal year 1924 showed considerable losses. Although in spring 1925 renewed rumors of a collapse of the press circulated,[39] this year proved to be the high point of the publisher's production. Twenty-three titles appeared in 1925. Among them were Leonhard's *Das nackte Leben* and *Segel am Horizont* ("Naked Life," "Sail on the Horizon"), Daudistel's *Das Opfer* ("The Offering"), Matthias' *Ausflug nach Mexiko* ("Excursion to Mexico"), Otten's *Der Fall Strauß* ("The Case of Strauss"), Wolfenstein's *Der Narr der Insel* ("The Fool of the Island"), Goll's *Germaine Breton*, as well as translations of the French writers Radiguet, Carco, and Châteaubriant. The following year produced Becher's poems *Maschinenrythmen* ("Machine Rhythms"), Wolfenstein's play *Bäume in den Himmel* ("Trees into the Sky"), several publications of and about Georg Kaiser, Barbusse's novel *Kraft* ("Power"), the first volumes of Proust's *In Search of Time Lost*, and in 1927 titles by Kisch, Klabund, and Tucholsky.[40] With the exception of these titles, however, the once ambitious program leveled off noticeably. The publishing steered into more and more conventional directions and tended subsequently toward a broader-based consumer population.

Intellectual belletristic literature was no longer in demand in crisis-ridden Germany; interest in literature dissipated. Book business was generated by other types of literatures, and most of the publishers had to follow this development because of their economic crisis. In the middle of the 1920s fantasy literature reached sales records, as grotesques, ghost stories, and utopias of all sorts became the most popular reading matter. There was also a market for the genre of documentary literature imported from America. Through the *Außenseiter der Gesellschaft*, a collection of the best documentaries and investigations, *Die Schmiede* had already followed this development. The more sensationalist *Berichte aus der Wirklichkeit* ("True Reports")[41] and a collection *Klassiker der erotischen Literatur* ("Classics of Erotic Literature")[42] then followed. Even the *Stachelschwein* ("Porcupine")—Hans Reimann's satirical journal appeared with *Die Schmiede* from the end of 1926 until the end of 1928—must be viewed as an indication of a change in literary direction.

The commercialization of production came too late for the publishing industry itself and was a particular surprise to the literary authors of *Die Schmiede*. Confronted with a new publishing policy, by which *Die Schmiede* was no longer willing to do anything of its own accord for its literary authors, but would not openly release them from their contractual obligations, the authors fought with the company's management. Charges came to light: the option clauses were too harsh (most of the times the authors had to obligate themselves to the publisher with several titles); the publisher was not doing anything for the authors' books, did not advertise adequately, and set the prices too high; the publisher was blamed for not selling more copies.

Actually the publisher missed out on a trend of the time, for in the 1920s cheap, unbound books claimed the greatest successes. Even the advertising activity of *Die Schmiede* must have seemed too conventional to Wolff's former authors. But the company did not answer these charges, and thereby confirmed the "lack of conscience" of the entrepreneurial-minded publishers whom Tucholsky attacked. The publishing team of Salter and Wurm, who always co-signed letters to the authors, no longer responded to the complaints raised by them, and were "negligent," and kept their business intentions "hidden."[43] At the same time they insisted on their rights and—there is a good suspicion—suggested to their authors who were bound by well-defined option contracts that they write marketable documentary literature for the publisher's book series.

When the publisher encountered liquidity problems and could no longer cover its debts to the paper manufacturers, irregularities also crept into the payment of author honoraria. The store price (on the basis of which the author honoraria were calculated as a percentage) was subsequently raised and payments were delayed or totally ignored. Arnold Zweig, who at the last moment backed out of his contract with *Die Schmiede*, reports of the "greed of the publisher" extending as far as "extortion maneuvers."[44] Even Joseph Roth, who was the sole literary discovery of *Die Schmiede*, expressed his visible displeasure at the beginning of 1925: "In the middle of February I had a novel ready. I was bound by contract to *Die Schmiede*. I admit to you candidly . . . that I wasn't satisfied with the propaganda, the honorarium or the design of the books. I also do not believe that *Die Schmiede* will be willing to accept my new demands."[45]

Roth had to honor his contract. In 1927 his book *Juden auf der Wanderschaft* ("Jews in Migration") appeared in the series *Berichte aus der Wirklichkeit*. A further title by Roth, *Fall*

Hofrichter ("The Case of Hofrichter"), which was already announced in 1925 as volume 32 of the series *Außenseiter der Gesellschaft*, did not appear with *Die Schmiede*.[46]

Once again in 1926 the bankruptcy threatening *Die Schmiede* was averted. The apparently flourishing stage business (which previously was covering the losses from the book business, whereby the stage authors had to sacrifice a substantial portion of their royalties) restored the credit-worthiness of the entire undertaking. But the prior positive attitude of the authors of *Die Schmiede* had been totally reversed. The authors who had come to *Die Schmiede* primarily because of its financial attractiveness attempted to secure release from their contracts. The protective organization of German writers received a flood of written complaints. Probably in 1926 Leonhard left the firm; the former editor vented his anger to Tucholsky at the insensitive business practices of *Die Schmiede*: "What has been messed up in this firm . . . has happened because of one postcard, which was not written at the decisive moment."[47]

Seventeen further titles appeared in 1927, whereupon *Die Schmiede* ceased production. In 1928 and 1929 combined, only three small theater scripts appeared. In June 1928 *Die Schmiede* began to sell off its publishing rights. The German rights to Proust were sold to Piper Verlag and—in August 1928—the rights to the entire theatrical work of Hasenclever were sold to Propyläen-Ullstein for 6000 marks. The remaining theatrical rights probably went to heirs of Felix Bloch. In 1929 a legal proceeding was initiated to declare *Die Schmiede* bankrupt. In February 1929 Tucholsky declared with satisfaction the end of the provincial, "unreliable" publisher, which had only made itself noticed by "staggering through the labyrinth of literature," whose publishers first showed "false haste in establishing relationships" and then "unseemly obliviousness to the fulfillment of its obligations." "*Die Schmiede* is gone," Tucholsky prophesied in February 1929, "may it rest in peace in its bankruptcy."[48] In February 1930 the firm *Die Schmiede* finally went into total liquidation.

6. The Last Publication: The Novella Collection *A Hunger Artist* with the Publishing House *Die Schmiede* (1924)

On exactly what date and under exactly what circumstances Kafka came to *Die Schmiede* cannot be verified. The conditions and climate in which he was able to opt for this young Berlin publishing company, however, are known.[49] It is plausible to interpret Kafka's choice of *Die Schmiede* as the publisher for his last book as a sign of his approval of the program of the primarily Jewish-Marxist literature published there. Many of the authors who published books with *Die Schmiede* between 1923 and 1924 were personal friends of Kafka and could have instilled a feeling of trust for this publisher in him because of their proximity to it. Brod boasts of having introduced Kafka to the directors during one of his visits to Berlin at the end of 1923 or the beginning of 1924:

> When I introduced him to the manager of the publishing firm *Die Schmiede*, he agreed, without much need of long arguments to persuade him, to the publication of four short stories as a title for which he took the name of one of them, "A Hunger-Artist." From all these circumstantial indications of his interest in life, I then later gathered the courage to regard as no longer valid his written instructions to me—written long before this period—which forbade the publication of any of his posthumous papers. (FK198)

Is this a parallel situation to that of June 1912 when Brod introduced his friend to Rowohlt? Brod's intimation of a "principal change" in Kafka's attitude toward the publication of his work is, upon closer observation however, quite questionable. For in his justification for "poorly executing the will as written," Brod makes no mention of his friend's continuing urgent need, which was in the end the basis for his decision to publish again.

Also during the second half of 1923 Brod's insinuation of Kafka's will to publish again is not present—or at least not in any sort of verifiable measure. Thus the common view derived from Brod, which represents the writer's path to *Die Schmiede* as the conscious expression of a principal change—thus in a certain sense an ideological one—must also be contradicted.[50] Since the outbreak of his illness, Kafka had undertaken no further futile steps into the public realm, and his "concept of the 'writer'" remained constant after the summer of 1922 (L344). In September 1923 he rejected a decidedly attractive offer by the Viennese publishing house E. P. Tal. The editor, Kafka's esteemed Carl Seelig, had turned to him with the request to submit an unpublished work for his collection *Die zwölf Bücher* ("The Twelve Books"), which appeared monthly in a limited edition. For it, as Brod recalls, "the sum of one thousand Swiss francs, a fortune in those days of inflation, would be offered" (L488). Kafka turned down the offer with the following explanation: "To respond to either [the demands of Seelig] would call for a certain ability to assume responsibility, and at the moment that is beyond me" (L380). Kafka did not possess such "ability to assume responsibility" to complete a book after the experiences he had had with a tough, non-receptive public. On the contrary, his "scribbling" was more than ever before of purely personal "value." Writing was to keep him going, and, as he wrote at the beginning of 1924, to help him "stiffen his neck" (L405). Nevertheless, he soon thereafter published again.

At that time in September 1923 Kafka had actually come to Berlin for only a few days. But he quickly decided to separate himself forever from Prague and from his "lack of independence" there. To build a new life with Dora in Berlin was a decision that he immediately saw as his life's greatest challenge; he now wanted to protect this new life from any sort of attack. But as with all of Kafka's previous major decisions, this one also came to a futile conclusion. By changing residences, he encountered the turbulent price spiral of the German economic crisis when he was already quite desperate. Kafka had made his decision to move to Berlin thinking exactly the opposite, in so far as the material side of his life was concerned. Even if he hardly expected any honoraria for the six books with Kurt Wolff[51], he was conscious at that difficult time that the small amount of money he was to receive would be almost totally devalued in Prague by the poor exchange rate against the German currency; at the beginning of the 1920s the Czech krone was very stable. Brod had been confronted with this fact when only a few days before Kafka's departure for Berlin, he received on September 15 the rather lapidary excuse from Meyer on September 15 for his outstanding royalties: "Living in Prague, you are understandably more seriously affected by the bankruptcy of the German economy than our other authors."[52]

Any honoraria to come from Wolff in the future could only have worth for Kafka in Germany. The pension that he was paid in the more stable Czech currency naturally commanded much more in Berlin. Kafka, this "overly anxious official" (cf. also F493 and DII163), who at the time was extremely worried about how he would get along financially, made the decision to move to Berlin with these financial considerations in mind: "A further factor in my decision, finally, was the hope of being able to get along on my pension more easily in Germany than in Prague" (O87). Even Dora, his companion for the brief six months in Berlin, said that Kafka came with great expectations to the city that had long remained inaccessible to him: "For a while he thought that Berlin would be his life's salvation; a personal solution for the inner and external turmoil. He wanted to feel like an average human being, with a few small desires and needs."[53]

In Dora, who in a positive sense was undemanding and unintellectually natural, Kafka thought he had found the right partner for such a peaceful life. In her youthful openness she admired him and was attracted by his eccentricity, which made him an enigma to her. Kafka himself did not seem inclined to ask any basic questions regarding their living together and their growing happiness. The inflation, however, immediately provided a bitter pill to the greatest and most liberating of his life's decisions. What transpired was what Kafka in all the years before, in light of the possibility of a free writer's life, had most feared: the total uncertainty of his material existence.

The spiral of inflation, which Kafka never fathomed, escalated relentlessly, with the consequence that the intended advantages of life in Berlin—almost precisely to the day of his arrival—turned into the exact opposite. Thus the first days in his new surroundings revealed to him, as he ironically noted, "a severe fit of numerical obsessions" (L383-84), instead of the free atmosphere he had perhaps hoped for.

The rent for the first small apartment, already too expensive from the start, went up sixfold within only a few weeks, and soon he had to look for new accommodations. There were even more oppressive rates of inflation for groceries and winter clothing and above all for heating fuel, which had grown scarce as the severe Berlin winter began to set in. One "manage[d] only by the most extreme stringency" (O88), is how Kafka understated his extreme material need. But only after his pension check was two weeks late did Kafka dare to ask Ottla for a little money. Yet he simultaneously wrote his parents an encouraging letter ("I am continuing well" [O82]). Also providing for Dora, who herself was without means of support, he refrained almost fearfully from admitting to his family and especially to his parents the true measure of his poverty; he considered this life he himself had freely chosen as his highest treasure, no matter how much self-denial it now required. Financial difficulty was the price he had to pay for the freedom he had just attained.

Because of the relentless rise in prices and the growing "difficulties in changing money" (L388), the young couple had to refrain more and more from any sort of luxury and subsequently from many necessities. However, Kafka lived these difficult moments together with Dora without obvious despair. In situations that seemed irresolvable, he asked the calendar on the wall for advice with occasionally stoic calm.[54] He countered the protests of a crotchety landlady that he was using too much electricity at night by buying a kerosene lamp, by whose light he began to write more intensively. (He portrayed the landlady—in spite of the artistic distortion—in a very clear fashion in the story *A Little Woman*, which he wrote in October 1923.)

Little is known about his writing during these months. Aside from *The Burrow* fragment and *A Little Woman*, nothing has been preserved; Dora had to burn the larger portion of the manuscripts according to Kafka's directions, and others fell into the hands of the Gestapo in April 1933. One of Dora's memoirs leads to the conclusion that Kafka remained true to the principle of only writing for himself, a decision reached in the summer of 1922, and that he wrote in order to keep the "ghosts" away. Yet despite all his reservation and the withholding of his writing from the public, there was some joyful hope in him. In the midst of the dire situation in Berlin, he indicated that this "goal remains . . . to be able some day to do without the pension entirely . . ." (O84). Dora's memoirs also points to his future intentions: "What he really wanted to write was to come about only when he had attained total freedom. For him literature was something holy, absolute, uncompromising, something great and pure."[55]

Kafka could not gain this freedom in Berlin any longer; on the contrary, his degree of dependency increased day by day. In his letters to Prague, in which he only hinted at his actually hopelessly dire straits, an almost joyful frivolity can be heard. Thus he was able to write to Ottla about the growing expense of renting a room that caused him anxiety as follows: ". . . prices are climbing like the squirrels where you are. Yesterday I became almost a little dizzy from it . . ." (O78) and about the impossibility of his earning some money in this foreign city as an ill retiree: "If there is a moving men's school where everybody can be turned into a mover, I would enter it with passionate eagerness. So far I haven't yet found the school" (O82). The family, which could only surmise his desperate need from these comments, sent packages of food that he only reluctantly accepted and wanted to pay for ("We'll settle up for it . . ." [O78]). Kafka expressed himself somewhat more openly to Brod, from whom the true nature of the situation in Berlin could not have been hidden anyway, because of his contacts there. "[T]he rise in prices," he wrote to Brod after the first month, "is really enormous and it's impossible to buy anything aside from food" (L392).

Kafka had an invincible fear of the "Berlin excitements" (L388) and of the "dangers" (L383) of this city in a state of emergency; "profoundly grateful," he resided in the quieter suburb of Steglitz:

> My "Potsdamer Platz" is the Steglitz Town Hall square; two or three streetcars pass through it, there is also a small amount of traffic, Ullstein, Mosse, and Scherl have branches there, and from the front pages of the newspapers on display there I absorb the poison that I can just manage to bear, sometimes momentarily cannot bear (just now there is talk in the anteroom about street battles). But then I leave this public place and lose myself, if I still have the strength, in the quiet autumnal avenues. (L388)

Kafka was "afraid of the city" (L384) itself and because of his generally poor condition and the costs involved, he scarcely left the house; he returned exhausted and "miserable" (L388) from the few excursions he took into the nearby big bustling city. As he wrote to Ludwig Hardt a short time later in February 1924, he had not been "out of the house in the evening throughout these four months in Berlin" (L408). The winter made the situation worse; in addition to the cold it brought a "mad inflation" (L399), and Kafka must have been afraid that the "miracle of getting along" on his small pension would not "be repeated" (O90). Clearly the apartment could no longer be adequately heated during the winter. During the Christmas season he suffered from a lung infection and was confined to bed for four weeks. At the end of the year he again attempted to illustrate lightheartedly the severity of the situation in a letter to Ottla: "Cooking is so easy. Around the New Year there was no alcohol; nevertheless, I almost scalded myself while eating; the food was warmed on candle stubs" (O90).

Kafka did not recover from his serious illness. He not only lacked the money for adequate food and for satisfactory heating of his room, but also for the necessary medical care. Because of high medical costs he had long refrained from any type of professional care for his acute illness. Only once did he call in a doctor for treatment of a severe relapse ("high temperature, chills and fever" [L403]), but he did not recover from the bill for quite some time. "[T]he figures of the doctor's fee," he wrote to Brod, "float in fiery letters over my bed" (L404). At the same time the deathly ill Kafka was given notice to vacate his room; he and Dora were to be evicted as of February 1, 1924, from their "wonderful apartment" as "poor foreigners" (L404). The situation became desperate; the means available to them were insufficient for another apartment. "If only I could earn something!" Kafka wrote to Klopstock at the end of January 1924, "[b]ut nobody is paying wages for lying in bed until twelve" (L406). Dora was able to find an apartment just in time. Freed from the fear of being forced onto the street during winter in Berlin, and again in better spirits, he reported to Klopstock about a similar case, which he had just read about in *Die neue Rundschau*: "Incidentally, he has Hamsun saying—it's crude and clumsy fiction, obviously put in solely to comfort me—that the winter in Paris took a great deal out of him, that his old lung disease has flared up again, that he has to leave for a small summer sanatorium way up in Norway, and that Paris is too expensive anyhow" (L410).

Kafka mentioned Hamsun's similar illness, because receiving treatment in a clinic threatened to become more and more unavoidable due to his rapidly deteriorating condition ("100.4 has become my daily bread" [L409]). When his uncle, Siegfried Löwy, a country doctor from Triesch, finally traveled to Berlin at the end of February 1924—having being sent by the concerned family—he found his nephew in terrible physical condition; he was able to convince the obstinate Kafka of the necessity of entering a sanatorium in Davos, if possible. At the beginning of March with the proximate end of his independence in sight, the writer called his disclosure in a letter to Klopstock his "Davos surprise." Unhappily he added with an eye toward the imminent sanatorium costs: "How hard all this is, and what frightful sums I shall have to squeeze out of others for myself" (L411).

Only a few days later, on March 7, 1924—a fact that should not be viewed in isolation—Kafka concluded a contract with *Die Schmiede* for the collection *A Hunger Artist* in the series *Romane des zwanzigsten Jahrhunderts* ("Novels of the Twentieth Century"). For this contract, by which it was agreed to publish three novellas, namely *The Hunger Artist*, *First Sorrow*, and *A Little Woman*, in an edition of 2000-3000 copies, Kafka received an immediate advance of about 800 marks.[56] By assuming that overriding financial reasons existed for this publication, we can see why this very same Franz Kafka, who had vigorously rejected publishing any book since the outbreak of his serious lung illness, was now able to come forth with a book without any essential "philosophical" change. If one views the writer's decision as a kind of concession, then there is no contradiction with the fact that (*simultaneously* with this entry into the public realm, which can be used to unequivocally document the author's wish to circulate his work) Kafka demanded that his companion Dora burn before his very eyes everything he had written during this time in Berlin.[57]

Even if such a renewed readiness to publish does not attest to a changed position on writing and on the literary industry, the choice of *Die Schmiede* as a publisher for *A Hunger Artist* was by no means accidental. The circle of authors around *Die Schmiede* played a significant role. A large number of the authors publishing with *Die Schmiede* during the years 1922-

1924 were known to him personally and met him in the period when there was certainly an opportunity to talk about the new and then highly regarded publishing house. At the end of 1922 Kafka met Alfred Wolfenstein during one of his visits to Prague; at that time Wolfenstein had just joined with *Die Schmiede* with which he published after 1923. In the spring of 1923 the future house author of *Die Schmiede*, Georg Kaiser, visited the bedridden Kafka at his apartment in Prague (M226-27). Kaiser, whose first book with *Die Schmiede* had just appeared in recent weeks, was on particularly personal terms with the publisher of *Die Schmiede*, Julius Salter, and occasionally procured new manuscripts for him.[58] Kayser's volume of essays, *Die Zeit ohne Mythos* ("A Time without Myth"), also appeared with *Die Schmiede* in 1923, and Kafka was in contact with the editor of *Die neue Rundschau* several times during his stay in Berlin. On one of his visits to Kafka during the winter of 1923, Kayser brought along Haas, the former editor of the Prague *Herder Blätter*, who, although like Kayser still active with S. Fischer at the time, was similarly writing for *Die Schmiede*. Haas's prose writings *Das Spiel mit dem Feuer* ("Playing with Fire") was published by *Die Schmiede* in 1923. Later there were Sternheim and Tucholsky, and even Brod was mentioned as a future contributor in a pre-announcement of the *Außenseiter der Gesellschaft* ("Outsiders of Society").

Finally, a special point that attracted Kafka to *Die Schmiede* was his acquaintance with Ernst Weiß. This friend from his earlier days in Berlin, when Kafka had sought advice about Felice in the summer of 1914, had remained the idol of the literary life he had longed for since that time. In Kafka's eyes Weiß led the paradigmatic life of an independent writer. He lived modestly in a wild marriage to an actress in a cheap Berlin garret. Weiß had already persuaded him in the summer of 1914 to give up his professional career and to move to Berlin (which was not possible at the time because of the outbreak of the war). At the end of 1922 Kafka apparently sought to renew the friendship that had waned during the war years. At the end of 1922 Weiß's novel "Ordeal by Fire" appeared in a bibliophile edition with *Die Schmiede*. Weiß presented him with this book, which was very much to Kafka's liking (L406), after a visit in October 1923. Like Weiß, who had three further titles published with *Die Schmiede* up until 1924, other writers from *Die Schmiede* with whom Kafka came into contact could report only positive things to him about the infant publisher, up until the spring of 1924. Such a climate of trust may have been an essential reason for the author's decision for *Die Schmiede*, aside from the decidedly financial reasons.

Having returned to Prague, Kafka had to be cared for against his will in his parents' apartment. Despite all the care he received there—as Brod reports—he perceived this fact "as the shipwreck of all his plans for being independent, as a defeat" (FK203). On March 19 he informed his former employer that he was now going "to Davos";[59] but there were financial difficulties involved in addition to the border formalities, so that in the end he remained in Prague. He wrote daily to Dora in Berlin; he did not want her to accompany him to Prague, since he did not want to bring her into contact with his Prague past.

Kafka's last work was written under these circumstances, the wonderfully complete story *Josephine the Singer*, in which the existential anxiety of the artist striving for perfection is engulfed by the illusion and void of the art that is practiced; the artist finally gives up art and strives to forget. When Kafka completed *Josephine* in the beginning of April 1924, he noticed a burning sensation in his throat that temporarily caused him to lose his voice. Still joking, he remarked to Klopstock (similar to the way he had referred to the outbreak of the disease with the flesh wound, as he had described it shortly before in *The Country Doctor*), that with *Josephine* he had probably begun "to investigate that animal squeaking at the right time" (L495). When this burning in the throat intensified, Kafka "grew worse and worse" (FK203). He was taken to a sanatorium, where he was diagnosed as having laryngeal tuberculosis (L411). The illness had progressed to such a degree that it was already impossible for the doctors to operate. After another examination in a Viennese sanatorium, he was finally sent upon Dora's and Klopstock's prodding to a friendlier, brighter hospital outside of Vienna, to Kierling near Klosterneuburg. A specialist who had been summoned informed Dora that Kafka was expected to live only about three months, but she rejected the idea of returning him to Prague, so that he would not suspect the hopelessness of his situation.

The very day his laryngeal tuberculosis was first diagnosed, Kafka had requested Brod to conduct some literary business on his behalf; he wrote from the sanatorium on April 9:

> Dear Max, It is expensive, might very well be frightfully expensive; "Josephine" must help out a little, there's no other way. Please offer it to Otto Pick (of course he can print whatever he likes from *Meditation*); if he takes it, please send it to Die Schmiede *later*; if he doesn't take it, then send it *right away*. As for me, it's evidently the larynx. (L411-12)

Josephine, which apparently was supposed to appear first in *Die neue Rundschau*,[60] was, like the previous texts of Kafka, immediately accepted by Pick, the editor of the *Prager Presse*; the Easter supplement appearing on April 20 was suited for this purpose. For his part, Brod was able to pave the way for the one remaining complete text, *A Little Woman*, for he had been just recently employed in the editorial office of the second largest Prague newspaper, the *Prager Tagblatt*. *A Little Woman* appeared on April 20, likewise in an Easter supplement.[61] An unmistakably material motive also lies at the heart of the publication of these two late texts in the *Prager Presse* and the *Prager Tagblatt*.[62] This is, of course, not to say that Kafka was entirely indifferent to the publications; just as before, he wanted to see the texts in print. He complained to Brod that the *Prager Tagblatt* was not sent to him ("be so kind and inter- vene—perhaps the Easter issue could still be sent to me" [L413]). Kafka must have had contact with *Die Schmiede* at the beginning of April while he was still in Prague—he probably corresponded with Rudolf Leonhard[63]—to tell the publisher about a recently completed fourth novella and to request that it be added as a supplement to the collection. The previously rather meager volume was greatly enriched by the addition of *Jose- phine*, which contributed marvelously to the overriding theme of the hunger artist and the artist's fate.[64] One can assume that Kafka had second thoughts again about the meager size of the volume, for immediately after drafting *Josephine*, he offered it to *Die Schmiede* as a supplement.

At this time Brod again took a very active part in promoting Kafka. In addition to handling the Prague publications, he also entered contact with *Die Schmiede*. In contrast to Kafka he corresponded directly with the publishing team of Salter and Wurm. Reporting on the serious physical condition of his friend and his urgent treatment in a clinic, he asked for a further advance in Kafka's name. At the same time he sent back to *Die Schmiede* the original of the story *A Little Woman*, which has been preprinted in the *Prager Tagblatt*,[65] so that the publisher could begin immediately with the production of the book. On April 20 Kafka thanked his friend for "all the laborious literary affairs" that he had "so splendidly taken care of" for him (L413). But he could not have known that his new publisher had not yet typeset *A Hunger Artist* (because of the long absence of Mr. Wurm)—something which took place at the earliest on April 28. Thus Kafka was waiting impatiently for the first proofs, when Brod came to Kierling for a visit in the middle of May. At that time Kafka was not allowed to talk; he communicated with written "conversation slips," of which a few have been preserved.[66] One of these directed to Brod around May 11 or 12 shows how much Kafka was still wrangling with the present publications, even on his sickbed:

> . . . now, since no proofs are available, the book will probably not appear before the end of the year at best. Either they boast or they remain silent. The story is to get a new title/ Josephine the Singer/ or/ The Mouse Folk/ Such titles with "or" are not especially pretty but here it perhaps has a special meaning, it balances things out.[67]

Perhaps already suspecting his imminent death, Kafka wanted to complete the production of his last book as quickly as possible. He had not reckoned with the lax procedures of *Die Schmiede*; the brief relationship to the publisher already seemed to be developing in an unsatisfying way. The remaining conversation slips also allude to this fact and, though when taken out of context, they document Kafka's intense occupation with the editing of his last book.

When the proofs finally arrived, he wrote angrily: "Here, now, with what strength I have am I to write it? They have waited so long to send me the material" (L419). Kafka himself undertook the proofreading very carefully; the note, "A third deleted from the middle" (L418) alludes to the fact that he must have read at least two sets of proofs, for in the extant excerpt of the page-proofs corrected by him, there is no indication of such a deletion. This drastic cut (probably it was a matter of the first galley proofs[68]) was an exception; otherwise Kafka only made minor corrections. "Let the bad remain bad" he wrote on one of the slips during the correction, "otherwise it will grow worse" (L419). During this proofreading work Kafka was obviously moved in this "reencounter" with what he had written. Klopstock, who was present, commented with surprise:

> At this time Kafka's physical condition and the whole situation of his literally starving to death were truly ghastly. When he finished the proofs—working on them must have been a tremendous psychological effort and a shattering intellectual reencounter with himself—tears rolled down his cheeks for a long time. This was the first time I ever saw any expression of emotion of this kind in Kafka. He had always shown a superhuman self-control. (L494)

Although probably hounded by Brod to hurry, *Die Schmiede* did not send the page-proofs to Kierling until May 27. The printer's mark on the first sheet of the typeset copy, "2nd Corr." establishes with finality that a first proofreading must have taken place.[69] Kafka was obviously dissatisfied with the work. Probably after seeing the galley proofs Kafka had given the directive to move *A Hunger Artist* to the third position; now he found it again in the first. He had to delete the subtitle (totally nonsensical in the singular) "Story by Franz Kafka" (which he did without replacing it); in addition, he corrected several other minor printing errors.[70]

Kafka was able to rework only the first of the five and a half sheets of the page-proofs. He wrote to Dora, who was devotedly assisting him, on one of the notes: "How many years will you be able to stand it? How long will I be able to stand your standing it?" (L419). After a brief struggle Kafka died on Tuesday, June 3; he was buried in Prague on June 11, 1924.

———————

The book in which Kafka had placed his art in the central position of his life as in no other before, and therefore had given death more room with the sequence of the stories, appeared only after the writer's death. However, *A Hunger Artist* is not a posthumous work.[71] Each of the stories contained in the volume was authorized by the writer during his lifetime and appeared individually; moreover, Kafka had read all the galley-proofs for the book edition. Brod no longer recalled this detail when he wrote: "He had corrected the first pages of the 'Hunger Artist' one day before his death, I had to take care of the remaining proofreading."[72] Certainly Brod endeavored to ensure that Kafka's wishes were carried out during the publishing phase that followed. On the original of the corrected page-proofs he made the handwritten note about the "reversal" of the novellas in the sequence known today and requested revision. Already on June 20, 1924, the change in the sequence was legalized—together with the addition of *Josephine*—in an "amendment to the contract of March 7, 1924." After the successful revision Brod had to counter energetically the subsequent attempts of *Die Schmiede* to change the title. It remains unclear to whose suggestion the subtitle "4 Novellas" is to be traced, which *Die Schmiede* later changed to "Four Stories" on its own.[73] It is not known whether Kafka—who had stricken the inappropriate sub-title without replacement on proofreading the page-proofs—wanted a subtitle at all. The book appeared in mid-August 1924, two months after Kafka's death.[74]

Kafka's Literary Estate (1924-1939)

> It would be very nice, if you could talk to Meyer some-
> time—he has mentioned several times that he would like
> to make a sensational success out of a novel by you. I
> will tailor your Trial to the end on my own! (Letter by
> Max Brod to Franz Kafka from August 1, 1919)

1. An Overview of the Problem of Editing

*A*n introduction into the problem of Franz Kafka's literary
remains has already been treated elsewhere.[1] The following
overview of the actual handling of publications from the author's
literary remains is essentially restricted to a chronological
presentation of new research and material. In the center stand the
complicated dealings of the administrator of the literary estate,
Max Brod, with different publishers and the multiplicity of
publishing contracts that were concluded up until 1939 for one
and the same work.

The editing of Kafka's literary legacy was Brod's domain.
No one else would have been as suited for this task, no one else
would have worked in this self-sacrificing way for its completion. From the very start of his efforts to help his friend to
posthumous fame, Brod never hid the fact that this task was
terribly complicated. "We can allow bad things to remain finally
bad only on our deathbed" (L84), Kafka had written to him with
self-tormenting consistency in June 1912 during the work of

assembling the prose pieces for the first book. But on two remaining notes, the so-called "testaments,"[2] he categorically ordered the unconditional destruction of his entire literary remains, of "writings" and "sketches" (T328), and not excluding the letters he sent from this decree. As precise as his directive was, even more so was the incomprehensibility (and with a certain disloyalty toward Brod) that the choice should go to his friend to carry out his last will. Brod could of course not carry out the "holocaust" [herostratic act] (T329) assigned to him; almost everything that has been preserved of Kafka's writing up to today has appeared "against" Kafka's will.

However, the pangs of conscience for having disregarded the last will of his friend, as Brod mentions them several times—most clearly in the summer of 1924 on the occasion of his report about Kafka's literary remains in the *Weltbühne* and then in 1925 in the afterword of the first edition of *The Trial*— are hedged by a rhetorical reservation. The great decision of conscience that Brod discussed was actually none at all, since he himself had explained to Kafka while he was still alive that he would never be able to follow such a directive.[3] Thus Kafka's choice corresponded exactly to his innermost state of mind at the moment he chose Brod to be precisely the one to carry it out: it clearly reveals his attempt to integrate and balance contradictory elements. Very logically Walter Benjamin considered this disregard of the wills as "honest loyalty toward Kafka" and in a very sensitive plea defended Brod against public criticism, which based itself on 'ethical' principles first elicited by Brod's detailed self-justification. Benjamin wrote in the *Literarische Welt* in 1929:

> The author's shyness with regard to the publication of his works sprang from the conviction that it was incomplete and

not from the idea of keeping it secret. That he was guided by this conviction in his own practice is just as understandable as it was that it did not apply to his friend . . . [Kafka] had not only known: In view of what has not developed in me, I have to hold back that which has, but he also knew: the other will rescue it and save me from the pangs of conscience, give it the imprimatur himself or have to destroy it. Here Welk's disarming will know no bounds. To cover Brod by ascribing to Kafka Jesuit tricks, a reservatio mentalis! To ascribe to him the deepest intent that this work appear and at the same time the author's word against its appearance! Yes, we are saying nothing else here and add: honest loyalty toward Kafka consisted in the fact that this happened.[4]

If Brod showed conflicting "loyalty" toward his friend's last wish, he rigorously pursued the execution of another directive. By Kafka's statement that he *destroy* "all writings and sketches which . . . others possess; and ask those others for them in my name" (T328), Brod was given a pretext to acquire all retrievable manuscripts and letters. Kafka's parents gave him his personal effects, he received a sketchbook from Dora (T333), and the manuscript of *The Burrow*; from Milena Jesenská "fifteen large notebooks," containing the diaries and the handwritten manuscript of *America*; from Klopstock several sketches and letters, as well as the manuscript of *Josephine*.[5] As described in the postscript to *The Trial*, Brod had already obtained *The Castle* and *The Trial* in 1920 and 1923 (T333, cf. ÜFK190). By these methods (by such a partial fulfilling of the last will and testament), the entire literary remains of Kafka were gathered in the shortest of time into one hand. Already on July 17, 1924 [!], Brod announced the state and expanse of the remains in the *Weltbühne* and made his intention clear to publish from that point on not only the literary texts but also the documents of Kafka's.[6]

2. The "Difficult Case of the Collected Works of Kafka"—The Publishing Contracts up to 1939

Already on June 19, 1924, Brod had worked out the edition of the remains with Kafka's copyright owners. The "main contract" was validated with Kafka's parents and sisters on July 11.[7] "After his death," Brod recalls, "it was not easy to find a major publisher who would undertake to bring out a posthumous edition of Kafka's work. I had to go to a different publishing house for almost each successive volume" (FK214). The interest that tied Brod to the edition must have been a double one: he wanted to make Kafka's work known to the public and, additionally, relieve those of his friends (on his own wish?) from the apparently considerable debts that they had incurred from Kafka's sickness and hospitalization. Brod accomplished his "first task" by putting together a very readable text; he partially compiled handwritten manuscripts, in order to be able to present a normal reading edition (as much like a novel as possible, and therefore more popular) and free from minute and pedantic details (SL71). With regard to his "second task," he sought a large, financially strong publisher.

Looking for maximum efficiency, Brod's offer was directed to all the major literary publishers in German-speaking countries. Already on the day of Kafka's funeral in Prague, Haas, representing *Die Schmiede*, called on Brod to talk about the posthumous works; the publisher clarified its offer in writing on June 14: "We have the greatest interest in acquiring the literary estate."[8] Already on June 10 Rowohlt Publishing had responded to Brod's offer by stating that Rowohlt was naturally interested in Kafka's posthumous novel or novel torso and recalled that he "was the first to publish Kafka years ago."[9] On June 20 Wolff informed him he was "terribly interested in becoming familiar with the posthumous works" and mentioned the fact that Wolff was in the end the only publisher who could be considered appropriate for the publication of the posthumous works of Kafka.[10] On July 4 Kayser wrote: "I succeeded in interesting Herr Fischer in it"; Kayser added on July 11: "He [Samuel Fischer] asks you to send the manuscripts. The question of an honorarium can of course be discussed only after the manuscripts are here and Herr Fischer has made a decision."[11] And on July 12 the Viennese Zsolnay Publishing made known its interest in looking at the posthumous works of Kafka.

But the financial conditions Brod proposed seemed disproportionately high to most of these publishers. In this economically critical situation the edition of a complete collection of Kafka's works that would involve several volumes in an edition of three thousand copies each, together with a rather demanding honorarium in advance, posed too great a financial risk. Furthermore, Brod would not send Kafka's manuscripts to the editors under any conditions. In light of the high demands by Brod, Rowohlt was "extremely pessimistic" and had to decline with the "utmost regret."[12] Even S. Fischer and Zsolnay retreated in light of Brod's financial demands. Wolff declared himself prepared to proceed with an edition but wanted to discuss Brod's terms. *Die Schmiede*, however, reiterated its unreserved readiness. Brod quickly gathered detailed information through the credit bureau about the solvency of the publisher. Although the information was less than encouraging,[13] and although Wolff, by return mail, threatened to withhold the rights to *The Stoker* (and therefore blocked Brod's first planned edition of *America*), Brod concluded the contract with *Die Schmiede* on July 31, 1924, for the works from the estate of Franz Kafka, edited by Max Brod.[14]

Also on July 31 the concluding of the contract with *Die Schmiede* was announced in the *Weltbühne*.[15] Shocked at this public announcement, Arnold Zweig turned angrily to Brod:

> Today I just want to warn you quickly: I read in the
> Weltbühne which publisher has acquired Kafka's posthumous
> works. I have had dealings with this publisher that go well
> beyond what I am able to repeat; it goes so far as clear-cut
> extortion practices, and only because of the exorbitant greed
> of these people, whom they blindly turn loose to stalk prey,
> was I able to escape the trap. Please ask what experiences
> Meidner and Ernst Weiß have had with these fellows and back
> out of your contract, if you still can. You will have *only*
> trouble and no royalties for Kafka's heirs but will help these
> gentlemen to new respect with Kafka's name and his work.
> Naturally I have proof for everything I have said. With
> dispatch, Zweig.[16]

Zweig's warning came too late; but Brod considered himself
protected by a release clause that was subsequently added to the
contract: he retained the right to be released by the publisher if
just one of the scheduled monthly payments from the publisher
was overdue.[17] He then punctually received the further corrections and revisions for *A Hunger Artist*; the volume was finally
to appear in the middle of August. When Wolff declared himself
unwilling to release the rights to *The Stoker* for the actual first
volume of the posthumous works for the *America* volume[18]
—although *Die Schmiede* had apparently invested a great amount
of effort—Brod then went about editing the almost illegible
manuscript of *The Trial*. This "novel" by Kafka was probably
typeset in the fall of 1924.

Brod viewed his tie to *Die Schmiede* as basically a business
one—he perceived the financial support of Kafka's heirs as his
responsibility. Thus Brod showed his dissatisfaction in his
negotiations with *Die Schmiede* over the cash honorarium,
adjusted percentages, and retail prices. He pressed the publisher

for greater efforts at advertising for *A Hunger Artist* and demanded a greater activity in the placing of preprints of *The Trial* in newspapers and journals (which would at the same time advertise it and produce revenue). Several such prints, as well as publications from the remaining posthumous works (the *Aphorisms* are mentioned in the *Weltbühne*) appeared in the second half of 1924.

Brod paid off Kafka's medical costs and could now think about directing income from his successful editing to the benefit of the heirs; Dora—as Klopstock before her—had urgently requested a share of Kafka's honoraria by referring to her personally dire situation.[19] But *Die Schmiede* fell behind in its contractual payments—nothing came for over four months, and the publisher did not respond to Brod's protests. In January 1925 Brod then turned again to Wolff. He found out that *Die Schmiede* was at that time not in a position to pay its suppliers' costs.[20] As a counter-move Meyer proposed that under such circumstances Brod consider the contract with *Die Schmiede* null and void and turn over the remaining posthumous works under similar conditions to Kurt Wolff Publishing.[21]

After several requests *Die Schmiede* finally apologized to Brod at the beginning of April, while raising questions about what a difficult author Kafka was to sell, how much money needed to be invested to promote him, and the fact that they actually only had expenses up to now, and practically no income. According to the publisher, they had sold only 551 copies of *A Hunger Artist* up until March 31, 1925, and paying further honoraria was therefore problematic; Brod noted in pencil in the margin of this letter: "Dear Mr. Kafka, I request your opinion on this matter . . ."[22] On April 8, 1925, Brod canceled the contract. He explained this step to *Die Schmiede* later as follows: "I was forced to take this step to ensure further payments to the heirs. I couldn't let Frl. Diamant, Kafka's fiancée, perish. The legacy of my friend was much too valuable to me for that."[23] One day later on April 9 he concluded a new exclusive contract with Meyer, who had traveled to Prague specifically for the purpose.[24]

Die Schmiede appeared more than astonished at the cancellation of the contract. Brod's position was not shared in Berlin; moreover, the publisher considered itself the owner of the posthumous works now as before.[25] If it had been Wolff who had prevented the publication of an America edition the year before, it was from this point on Die Schmiede that blocked Kafka's collected works. Meyer labeled the pretenses of Die Schmiede as "very stupid excuses about which he intended to talk to them,"[26] but the fierce legal battle between Wolff and Die Schmiede would last until into fall 1926. Next Salter and Wurm declared themselves ready to deal with Kurt Wolff Publishing regarding transferral of the posthumous works while fully protecting their interests and rights. But Wolff rejected Die Schmiede's offer to take over both of Kafka's works that had appeared at cost, which for Die Schmiede was proof that Wolff's interest in the matter was not very great.[27]

Despite all the protests, the legal position of Die Schmiede appeared unchallengeable. For quite some time Brod had not agreed to the publisher's proposals (which usually had as their goal the reduction of honoraria), but in January 1926 he had to agree to amend the contract whereby the sum paid out in advance for 3000 copies of A Hunger Artist would be adjusted against The Trial. Only on this new basis, to which a non-reimbursed increase in the store price was added, did Die Schmiede consider itself able to promote Kafka's works. The publishing team of Salter and Wurm forced Brod into a corner: "We especially hope that we will now receive the remaining volumes of the posthumous works, as has been agreed."[28]

Brod had gotten into a difficult position; on the one hand, he had to accept the obviously stronger legal position of *Die Schmiede*, on the other, there was the arrangement with Wolff. In addition, the manuscripts of *America* and *The Castle* had been ready to go to press with Wolff since the end of 1925. Meyer had a very practical solution to the problem: he speculated on the inevitable decline of *Die Schmiede*'s solvency. He was, as he communicated to Brod in May 1926, "today more than ever convinced . . . that—barring a miracle—*Die Schmiede* would scarcely be able to bring out the Kafka edition."[29] But *Die Schmiede* reconsolidated. Before Salter and Wurm turned again to Wolff, to whom Brod had gone over in the meantime, they had offered to sell their rights to Kafka's posthumous works to Zsolnay Publishing; but the wealthy Viennese publisher did not want to agree to the conditions dictated by *Die Schmiede*.[30] In the summer of 1926 Meyer commented on the new demands by *Die Schmiede* regarding the "difficult case of the Kafka edition," which—he wrote apologetically to Brod—"were not even worth discussing and which no publisher in the world would have considered or come to an agreement on."[31]

The readiness of *Die Schmiede* to sell its Kafka rights was tied to a high price. But with its profit-oriented business mentality, *Die Schmiede* had not figured on a Kurt Wolff, who himself could only be very skeptical about taking on a Kafka edition; the extent of the financial emergency in Wolff's business in the middle of the 1920s was simply not known to the literary public. Meyer's letters to Brod reveal an additional problem of convincing Wolff to take the financial risk and become once again the publisher of Franz Kafka; Wolff himself had great "financial reservations."[32] Thus there was never a final (i.e., financial) adjustment made between Kurt Wolff Publishing and

Die Schmiede. But Wolff gave in to Meyer's pressure. On September 24, 1926, Meyer told Brod that *The Castle* was now "at the printers, Poeschel and Trepte." The experienced publisher decided to set Kafka's book in the same format as the edition of *Die Schmiede*, in order to preserve the outward appearance of a collected edition.[33] Meyer proposed that Brod compose a proclamation for well-known writers to sign in order to find subscribers for the collected works of Kafka by this publicity. Meyer energetically readied his propaganda. In December 1926 he proclaimed Kafka's new novel as the "literary Christmas miracle" and as "Franz Kafka's Faust piece."[34]

However, the "sensational success"[35] that Meyer thought he would achieve with his comprehensive advertising methods fell far short with *The Castle*. The sales figures lagged behind all expectations. Wolff now refused to publish *America*. Once again the editor of Kafka's works was in an undesirable position. Brod sought help and found it in Hardt, who answered on February 27, 1927: ". . . everything must appear soon with Kurt Wolff; even if he doesn't want it to. In that eventuality I will cover the costs."[36]

With this support from Hardt, along with his activity with Wolff, he actively promoted Kafka on his reading tours to increase the publicity for Kafka and finally to find subscribers for the novel. Meyer and Brod were finally able to move the obstinate publisher to print *America*. In fall 1927 Kafka's last novel appeared. With it the publication of Kafka's "trilogy of loneliness," as Brod referred to it in his afterword, was complete. But Brod was deceiving himself if he thought he could now relax. At this point Wolff lacked the necessary means to be able to advertise the completed edition properly. Two years later he had to abandon the company entirely. Wolff sold the rights to Kafka's works to his brother-in-law, Peter Reinhold, and the

stock of unsold Kafka books went from the Munich publisher to
the Neuer Geist Verlag in Berlin.[37]

In a letter to the *Literarische Welt* of early 1930, Brod
expressed his resignation about the unfortunate editing of Kafka's
posthumous works. He bemoaned the untenable condition that
those two eminently important books that appeared with *Die
Schmiede* were no longer available and that this publishing house
to his knowledge no longer existed. He bemoaned the "grotesque
circumstance" that "translations of Kafka's works were now
available abroad when the originals in the German language were
not." Conscious of his responsibility as the editor, Brod continues:

> Now you will certainly ask me: When will the complete
> German edition appear which will include in addition to the
> previously published works a whole series of unpublished
> ones? If answering this question were to depend solely on me,
> I would say: Immediately. But that which we desire and deem
> honorable, unfortunately seems to lie off in the future.[38]

As Brod indicates, the publication of the three major novels
from the posthumous works appeared already in 1930 to have
fallen flat (SL194). In view of the public's desire for new
publications, Brod saw no hope in the possibility of further
distribution of the remaining works on hand. Haas, the editor of
the *Literarische Welt*, recommended Transmare Publishing to
him, but Brod had "reservations"; even the Berlin Propyläen
Publishers came under consideration.[39] On April 8, 1931, Brod
finally concluded a new contract with Gustav Kiepenheuer
Publishing in Berlin for the Kafka edition. This contract dealt
only with two unpublished volumes from the posthumous works
and *The Trial*; quite obviously the Neuer Geist Verlag was now
no longer interested in releasing its rights to *The Castle* and

America to Kiepenheuer.[40] In the very same year Brod edited a new volume with this publisher in cooperation with Hans Joachim Schoeps: *The Great Wall of China. Unpublished Stories and Prose from the Posthumous Works*. He additionally issued a proclamation, which Meyer had initiated years before, to be signed by leading personages in literary life, to "make the public aware of this event." The results of these efforts were, however, somewhat discouraging: only one of the authors contacted (Hermann Hesse was the exception) wanted to sign Brod's rather euphoric draft; Gerhart Hauptmann excused himself by claiming unfamiliarity with the name Kafka (SL194-96). No further Kafka title appeared with Kiepenheuer. In light of the increasing national socialist mood, the publisher distanced itself from this "Jewish author."

Brod's mentioning of Schocken Publishing led Peter Reinhold, director of the Neuer Geist Verlag, to enter into negotiations with Salman Schocken in 1934. Reinhold sold the rights, as was emphasized, only "under the pressure of the political climate."[41] After the National Socialist Party seized power, Kafka became an ostracized writer. His collected works were listed a short time later in October 1933 "in List 1 of harmful and undesirable writings."[42] His books were publicly burned, and on April 20, 1933, the Gestapo searched Dora Diamant's apartment and confiscated her remaining personal part of Kafka's posthumous works. Under these circumstances Salman Schocken was able to acquire the entire rights to Kafka's work. On February 26, 1934, Brod concluded an editor's contract for an "edition of the complete works" in six volumes. In the same year a small volume of selected works of short prose pieces by Kafka appeared under the title *Before the Law*, as Volume 19 of the *Bücherei des Schocken Verlages* ("Library of Schocken Publishing"), edited by Heinz Politzer and looking very much like the Insel books. At the beginning of 1935 the first volume of the collected works, *Stories and Short Prose*, appeared; Brod noted in his diary of February 17: "Finally the collected volume of Kafka's short prose had appeared. For years I have been asking all the publishers for it—how much effort it takes to see that what is absolutely right finally takes its final form."[43]

In quick succession the following works appeared in the same year: *America* (Vol. 2), *The Trial* (Vol. 3), and *The Castle* (Vol. 4). However, in 1936 the publisher, who was labeled "Jewish" by the authorities, had to cancel the remainder of the edition; the political pressure was overwhelming, and once again the rights to Kafka's works were sold. The contract concluded on May 23, 1936, with Mercy Sohn in Prague was merely a front set up by Brod and Schocken to continue with the edition. In identical format, but now in Prague, Volume 5 (*Description of a Struggle*) appeared in 1936 and a year later Volume 6 (*Diaries and Letters*). With them the edition of the collected works was concluded. Brod could now devote himself to writing his great Kafka biography, which also appeared with Mercy in Prague in 1937.

Shortly before the outbreak of World War II when the Jewish intelligentsia in Prague no longer felt safe from attacks by Hitler's regime and the question of emigration became more and more pressing, Brod rescinded the fake contract. On February 28, 1939, the notary, who was an insider, transferred the rights again to Salman Schocken, who had been living in Jerusalem since 1934 and emigrated to the United States in 1940.[44] During the night of March 14-15, 1939, exactly one day before the entry of the Germans into Prague, Brod left his home city destined for Palestine; in his luggage were the collected manuscripts and documents of Franz Kafka.[45]

Postscript

Franz Kafka's reticence and reservations about whether to publish his works did not emerge from some basic aversion toward the public within the realm of writing solely for himself. This investigation of the history of the production of the author's works and its relationship to his biography has shown that Kafka was by no means opposed to the publication of his work with the finality with which this is generally presupposed, even in the critical literature. Also a purely egotistical interest that bound Kafka to his writing does not exist—along the lines of the common belief that Kafka freely chose anonymity and generally scorned any public involvement. With his own desire for a life in society, Kafka hoped for support through the public. Up to the point when his life changed dramatically because of the outbreak of his serious lung condition, Kafka recognizably demonstrated the intention of gaining this public for himself as a writer. Only in this way could he create the conditions for the exclusive literary existence he so earnestly desired.

If the question of Kafka's attitude toward his work has in the past been answered for the most part with reference to his will and testament, this study makes it clear that such an approach following this document literally (and emphasizing the destructive negative opinion of the writer toward his own literary creation) is insufficient and misleading when the totality of his life is considered. For in following the former approach one can grasp only one part of Kafka's life: that of Kafka's complete distance from literature during the years 1918-1922. The decision Kafka made at this point in his life to demand in his will that his entire work be destroyed in view of his impending death, could not have validity for the years before, especially not for the important period between the appearance of his first book and the onset of his illness; also the fact that Kafka specifically chose Max Brod to be the executor of his will (about which Kafka could assume he would not carry out his directive) modifies the general validity of this late and apparently so rigid rejection of his own work.

The discretely identifiable periods in Kafka's life reveal the author's clear-cut attitude toward his work. The close interrelationship between events in Kafka's personal life and the sporadic periods of literary inspiration are evident here—as well as their relevance to the relationship of the author toward publication. Within these clearly definable phases (and lasting up until the dramatic change in his life), a cyclical pattern has become evident. Gradually conditioned responses and results alternated with surprising regularity after Kafka's periods of writing and of inability to write. Kafka was subjected to this cyclical pattern, not least of all because of his personal instability; moreover, a vicious circle developed from it, which he described as "this terrible humming top" inside him (F314). With the interruption of the inspired flow of writing that lasted each time for five (winter) months, Kafka then began to doubt seriously the purpose of his writing. Because of this doubt the necessary power to write successfully eluded him; this power alone could have provided him with the continuing hope of establishing his existence as a writer. In its place Kafka's alternative wish entered, supported enthusiastically by his parents: marriage and the founding of a family. His desire for bourgeois responsibility was rekindled and subsequently became the focus of all his hopes. With the failure of his marital plans a new phase was introduced, a time of "inspired" writing commenced again. At the point where these developments intersect, i.e., at the point of direct confrontation between these two alternatives for life, Kafka sought to publish.

A clearly delimited phase corresponds to each completion of such a cycle. One chapter of this study is devoted to each of these phases. Transcending the actual publication history of his work, the fundamental process of development in Kafka's "concept of the 'writer'" (L344) is thereby revealed. This is the process of Kafka's disillusionment, of the constant unsettling of his wish by the world outside, in realizing the goal of his life that he identified so early on—becoming an independent writer.

Kafka's life is inseparably connected to the history of his publications. His path from the hope of becoming a writer and then the decision to do so is shown, via the confirmation of being a writer (which released his creative productivity), to the disappointment of never being able to achieve his goal in life (which in the end painfully crippled his productivity). One of the most important causes of his failure appears to be his peripheral position as a publisher's author. Kafka never established a stable relationship with a publisher and never had a fully productive relationship to the literary industry of his day. Practically overnight he changed publishers three times without having changed his publishing house, before he then left it resignedly. Most importantly, his correspondence with Kurt Wolff was not only very sparse but, through its negative exchanges, fundamentally disruptive. The missing productive dialogue between Kafka and a publisher for six of the seven books he published during his lifetime destroyed the writer's early confidence of having followed the correct path with his writing. Kafka himself did not dare to turn to the publishers with his requests and had an almost exaggerated respect for each decision they made—and even if it was just a matter of financial risk. He employed the "strategy" of pessimistic argumentation only in order to enlist support for the publication of his texts. Sharply criticizing the quality of his own writing from the start, Kafka looked for the publisher to contradict him and thus tried to gain for himself in such an indirect way the direct (kindly) praise which he needed from the outside world in order to give meaning to a publication. The attention that came from his publisher Kurt Wolff, though always cordial, never gave the writer any new perspectives on the significance of his creation; this attention remained sketchy and purely reactive. Both of the publisher's letters that were meant to encourage him arrived too late. Ill and without any realistic prospect of achieving his "genuine life," he had already given up any hope of success. Finally, after 1922, after the failure to complete his last novel, he was on the whole negatively inclined toward any publication of his work. This position did not change even with the publication of his last book in 1924, since here for the first time financial need—based on the writer's distressing situation in life—dominated the decision to publish.

His awareness of his own weakness together with his lack of prospects for a public life as a writer led Kafka to a mystification of his existence. He retreated further into his "borderland" and formulated for himself the condition of a living-dead person, of a pure observer, as his way of rescuing himself. His hopes, however, are directed beyond this land of loneliness. His "desire" to write something which "would be accessible as well to the understanding and feelings of everyone else" (DI181) pointed in the direction of community. But rejected by a literary industry that was dedicated to other idols and in which he found no possibility of expressing himself as he ideally wished, Kafka could not reach this community. More and more he became insecure as a result of experience and saw less and less possibility of mediating between his own ideal and this reality. In 1918 he wrote: "a world is conceivable to me that is governed by a living idea, a world in which art has the place it deserves, which in my experience it never has had" (L204).

Notes

Introduction

1. Cf. Heinz Liepmann, "Ein wahrer Grandsigneur. Erinnerungen an Kurt Wolff" *Die Welt*, Oct. 24, 1963.
2. Paul Valéry, "Inaugural lecture on poetics at the Collège de France." *Zur Theorie der Dichtkunst*. Frankfurt am Main, 1975, 207.
3. Dora Diamant, as cited in Josef Paul Hodin, *Kafka und Goethe*, op. cit., 27.
4. A list of abbreviations for the works cited can be found in the appended materials.
5. As early as 1931 Werner Marholz (*Deutsche Literatur der Gegenwart*. Revised and expanded by Max Wieser. Berlin, 1931, 309f.) referred to the close interrelationship between publishing and literary activity: "One can almost always find a publishing house at the center of the intellectual movements in Germany." This interrelationship is evident to historians of the book industry. (Cf. Herbert G. Göpfert: *Buchhandel und Literaturwissenschaft* and *Wissenschaft vom Buchhandel—Wissenschaft für den Buchhandel*, op. cit., as well as Wolfram Göbel, WV col. 523ff.) Bernhard Zeller [WBrVII] writes: "The history of the large publishing houses is . . . an essential part of German literary history. A presentation of its work and of its development will necessarily reflect literary activity.")
6. See esp. Klaus Wagenbach: *Franz Kafka. Eine Biographie seiner Jugend. 1883-1912* (Wa). There is only limited material documenting Kafka's adult years. This phase of his life is most comprehensively presented by Hartmut Binder (KHI).

Chapter I

1. Cf. RaI and SchI and II. It should be noted that Schlawe's comprehensive listing is based on entries in indices and journal pre-announcements without comparing these to the actual publications. Inaccuracies can thus result, as the example Schlawe

cites regarding Kafka's work on the journal *Die schöne Rarität* reveals. Actually Kafka was only on the list of "permanent collaborators" for the first edition, but no contribution appeared. (Cf. SchII44f.)

2. Cf. (among others) Hans von Weber—one of the sharp-tongued observers of the literary activity of the era—*Der Zwiebelfisch*, vol. 2, no. 6 (Dec. 1911), 213.

3. Rilke's first publication, the poem that begins "Die Schleppe ist nun Mode" ("Dress trains are now in vogue"), appeared on September 10, 1891, in *Das interessante Blatt*; the young poet from Prague had sent the poem to a competition in the Viennese journal, and it was printed there upon the recommendation of the judges. Rilke spoke about the significance of this first publication for him as a fifteen-year-old in a letter to his mother: he now considered himself a "total poet." (Unpublished letter by R. M. Rilke to his mother on July 13, 1891, Rilke Archives, Gernsbach.)

4. Oskar Baum recalls his first encounter with Kafka: "Max Brod arranged it. He brought Franz Kafka to me and read to us on that fall evening in 1904 his recently completed novelle *Ausflüge ins Dunkelrote* ('Flights into Dark Red'). We were at the time a little over twenty years of age" (PK151).

5. PK40—Cf. also SL11 and 18.

6. Brod's dating of the "Wolf's Gorge Letter" as either "1903 or 1904" (L13) is problematic; a later date can be assumed.

7. Klaus Wagenbach has already referred to this (Wa7).

8. As cited in Born (Bo25).

9. Walter Benjamin, *Benjamin über Kafka. Texte, Briefzeugnisse, Aufzeichnungen*. Ed. Hermann Schweppenhäuser. Frankfurt am Main 1981, 48. It is most noteworthy that in almost all of Kafka's friendships literary creativity was placed in the foreground.

10. Cf. KP, especially 99-169. The core of the "Prague Circle," the socalled "inner Prague circle," included the friends Max Brod, Franz Kafka, Felix Weltsch, and Oskar Baum. Later on the somewhat younger Willy Haas and Franz Werfel joined.

11. In an article from 1913 Brod summarized the circumstances of his first publication in a manner very characteristic of his endeavors

on the part of Franz Kafka. After long years of "suffering," in which he did a lot of writing, but nevertheless saw no possibility of publishing anything, the help of Gustav Meyrink, "who took up my case and sent one of my novellas to the *Magazin für Literatur*," was a solution. Brod writes further: "*This one helpful deed sufficed and was decisive* . . . It is predominantly the recollection of these endured sufferings that have motivated me to support a group of budding talent with its first publication." (*Bohemia*, Easter supplement [no. 81], March 23, 1913.) [Author's italics.]

12. In the Berlin literary weekly *Die Gegenwart* (Feb. 9, 1907), Brod wrote that Franz Blei had "the same unsentimental relationship to his creations" "as nature to us humans." From there comes the "healthy, impersonal air, like that breathed on a ship in the middle of the ocean . . . It is a sign of the high level of culture reached by German literature, that we have several who achieve that and decorate the most varying sides of existence with their art and terror. Heinrich Mann, Wedekind, Meyrink, Franz Kafka and several others belong with the author of this piece to this hallowed group." (Review by Max Brod of Franz Blei's *Der dunkle Weg* in *Die Gegenwart* [Feb. 9, 1907, no. 6, 93.] [Author's italics.]

13. L23—*Die Gegenwart*, a weekly for literature, art and general interests, had a consistent printing of 5000 copies in 1906. Hartmut Binder summarized Kafka's reaction: "The recognition seemed to him to inhibit his freedom of movement with regard to the possibility of individual literary effectiveness and to determine his decision from the start" (ZdPh, no. 86, 225).

14. Photographs of the small sketches that have been preserved are in the Max Brod Archives in Tel Aviv (MBA).

15. ÜFK394. Cf. also: Gustav Janouch, *Gespräche mit Kafka* (expanded edition), Frankfurt a. M. 1968, 58 and 180. Brod tried at that time to collect the sketches Kafka had discarded (a repeated sign of his high esteem). He even wanted a sketch on an envelope by Kafka's hand for his first collection of poems *Erotes*, which appeared under the title *Der Weg des Verliebten* ("The Path of a Lover") with Axel Juncker in Stuttgart. Brod had certainly convinced the publisher Axel Juncker of Kafka's

envelope sketch—a vignette, but the plan failed in the end
because of the fact that Kafka's original could not be reproduced
(Cf. L26 and L37-38). Brod, who was still praising Kafka's
sketches in a letter from 1910 (L66 and 436, note 17), speaks
again about "Kafka's great artistic drawings" in his biography of
Kafka: "previously one has only considered them a curiosity.
This opinion will change" (ÜFK213f.). In one of the two
"testaments," Kafka later charged that "everything be burned . . .
diaries, manuscripts, letters, my own and from others, *sketches*,
etc. in their entirety and unread, as well as all written material or
sketches that you or others . . . have" (Cited from the
original—MBA). [Author's italics.]

16. Cf. Hodin, op. cit., 15ff.
17. Cf. PK87, and Siegfried Unseld, *Robert Walser und seine Verleger*, op. cit., 252f.
18. *Opale*, no. III, 39ff.—Cf. also: KP66 and Steffen, op. cit., 115.
19. SL (old version, op. cit.), 380—In December 1906 Franz Blei discussed Brod's first book, the novella collection *Tod den Toten* ("Death to the Dead") in *Deutsche Arbeit*, vol. VI, 200f.
20. SL (old version, op. cit.), 380—The diaries of Max Brod (MBA) frequently note the presence of Franz Blei in Prague between the years 1906 and 1910.
21. Janouch, 53—The personal contact between Kafka and Blei remained limited to several meetings. Blei later wrote about Kafka: "Everyone was a stranger to him and in the end had to remain such." (Franz Blei, *Zeitgenössische Bildnisse*, op. cit., 5.)
22. As cited in Steffen, op. cit., 126.
23. Catalog of Hyperion Publishing, Hans von Weber, Munich 1909, 21.
24. Cf. no. 1 in the Bibliography. Edition size from: Steffen, op. cit., 127.—Although Brod still maintained in 1968 he had, with the agreement of his friend, sent *Hyperion* in 1907 or 1908 eight of his short prose pieces, which he had given the collective title *Betrachtung* (Afterword to *Franz Kafka. Beschreibung eines Kampfes*, ed. Max Brod, Frankfurt a. M. 1969 [II], 149), no such communication can be found, and more than likely should be discounted. Obviously Brod confused Kafka's publication with the following one; Kafka's second publication in *Hyperion*, which

without a doubt came about through Brod's efforts, Brod commented about in the same place: "*Hyperion* produced again two works by Kafka in number 8; this time Franz sent them in by himself" (ibid., 151).

25. To Heymel's question Blei responded in summer 1908: "to answer an earlier question right away: Kafka is not Walser, but really a young man in Prague by that name." (Blei to A. W. Heymel. Undated letter [approximately summer 1908], DLA. As cited in sy8.)

26. *Zeitschrift für Bücherfreunde*, N[eue] F[olge], vol. 1 (1908/09), supplement, 7.

27. Ibid., vol. 2, no. 1 (1910), supplement, 23.

28. Letter from Rowohlt to Kippenberg on Jan. 18, 1909. As cited in Peter Bramböck, op. cit., 583.

29. Cf. also L83-84.—The memoirs of Z. W. Weltsch, the brother of Felix Weltsch, confirm the involvement Brod showed: "It was in the quiet corner [of a Prague restaurant] that I sat together with Kafka, Max Brod, my brother, and Franz Blei. Max had told Blei about the stories Kafka had written and then a struggle developed, since Blei wanted to have the story for his new journal *Hyperion*, but Kafka hesitated somewhat from allowing him to print it. After long debates and many exhortations, he declared himself ready to give Blei two stories for his paper . . ." (Unpublished letter from Z. W. Weltsch to Hartmut Binder on Oct. 26, 1976.)

30. Franz Blei to Max Brod (unpublished, handwritten letter, undated—2nd half 1908—MBA). Blei continues in the letter, which he curiously did not direct to Kafka but to Brod: "Preferably as *one* piece, with a space separating them and with one title—which? Conversations in the Twilight?" In the table of contents the title *Gespräch mit dem Beter und dem Betrunkenen* is listed (107).

31. Cf. no. 2 in the Bibliography.

32. Text of a publisher's announcement. *Zeitschrift für Bücherfreunde*. N[eue] F[olge], vol. 2 (1910/11), supplement, 209.

33. Max Krell, *Das alles gab es einmal*. Frankfurt am Main, 1961, 69.

34. Kafka's review appeared upon Brod's intercession in the theater journal edited for a short time by Herwarth Walden, *Der Neue*

Weg, vol. 38 (1909), no. 2, February 6, 1909. Cf. also Paul Raabe, "Franz Kafka und Franz Blei," sy7-20.

35. *Bohemia*, vol. 83, no. 16, morning edition, Prague, Sunday, Jan. 16, 1910, 33.

36. Kafka apparently only submitted two literary critiques for publication. A third, a review of a volume of Kleist anecdotes edited by Julius Bab (Rowohlt Publishing, Leipzig 1911— Drugulin Printings no. 12), which was among Kafka's favorite books, has only been preserved in handwritten form; attempts to identify an actual printing have long been unsuccessful. Besides these literary reviews, Kafka also published several "professional reviews" (cf. among others L64-65 and L98) and a small article on the "painter Holub" (cf. Wa280f. and L278-79). After 1911 Kafka consciously refrained from writing reviews and critiques (cf. DI266).

37. The publisher Hans von Weber had a complete falling out with Blei, who was the editor of *Hyperion* and the actual initiator and program director of Hyperion Publishing. Ludwig Rubiner (1881-1920) reported to Max Brod in June 1910: "Just imagine, the loyal Hans von Weber . . . is now attacking Blei wherever he can. In the last 'Zwiebelfisch' . . . he declared for example all the books that Blei had edited with him to be huge blunders and regretted editing them, etc." (Ludwig Rubiner to Max Brod, unpublished handwritten letter from June 3, 1910. MBA.) As early as 1910 Hans von Weber sold the remaining copies of *Hyperion* at a deep discount in a Berlin department store.

38. Kafka's general comments are based essentially on the text of the publisher's ads (see above).

39. Kafka's positive review in *Bohemia*, vol. 84, no. 78, morning edition, Prague, Sunday, March 19, 1911. (Reprinted in E316ff., author's italics.) In *Zwiebelfisch*, vol. 3 (1911), no. 1, 36, Hans von Weber reacted to this positive review in a very malicious manner: "In *Bohemia*, no. 78, 33 an interesting article appeared on *the well-known Prague author Franz Kafka*, which closes with the statement that 'the unforgotten *Hyperion* is already beginning to move away from any animosity and in ten or twenty years will simply be a bibliographic treasure.' The publisher requests a shortening of this gallows time."—Paul Raabe finds it

"astonishing" that "Hans von Weber writes here about the 'well-known Prague poet Franz Kafka' who made his debut with only a few small pieces in *Hyperion* (sy9). Raabe though fails to recognize Weber's obvious irony. [Author's italics.]

40. Brod's parallel diaries of his common trips with Kafka are unpublished and are in his literary estate in Tel Aviv (MBA).

41. Cf. Felix Philipp Ingold, *Literatur und Aviatik. Europäische Flugdichtung 1909-1927* ("Literature and Aviation. European Flight Literature 1909-1927"), Frankfurt am Main 1980, 19-27.

42. Kafka too was a reader of the works of Jules Laforgue (cf. DI327, PK157 and SL41).

43. Unpublished diaries of Max Brod (MBA).

44. Cf. no. 3 in the Bibliography. According to James Rolleston ("Die Erzählungen" in KHII248) this publication has been only "slightly" abbreviated in comparison with the original—in comparing the publication in *Bohemia* (225 lines of 50 characters) with the preserved galleys of the complete version from 1913 (435 lines of 50 characters) this author has reached a different conclusion (cf. note II, 13).

45. Unpublished diaries of Max Brod. In MBA (cited as published with slight variation in ÜFK343).

46. Unpublished diaries of Max Brod (MBA). Note from: "Saturday, March 19, 1910—Evening with Kafka, who is unhappy, at Wiegler's" (Cf. L64).

47. Cf. no. 4 in the Bibliography. Max Brod recalls how Paul Wiegler "believed the collective title should adhere to general linguistic convention and had to be changed to the plural 'Observations' ['Meditations']. I recall very clearly how Kafka spoke to me with consternation about this meddling." (*Franz Kafka. Beschreibung eines Kampfes*, op. cit., 150.)

48. ÜFK340—In his travel diary Kafka wrote: "Our idea a poor one: to describe the trip and at the same time our feeling toward each other during the trip. How impossible it is, was proved when a wagon full of peasant women passed by" (DII244).

49. Max Brod, "Zusammenarbeit mit Franz Kafka" ("Collaboration with Franz Kafka"), *Herder-Blätter*, facsimile edition on the 70th birthday of Willy Haas, Hamburg 1962, VIII.

50. Max Brod had warned Kafka, among other things, about writing

passages that were too long, since he viewed the "effect of such writing as somewhat jellylike" (DI170).

51. Cf. DI123—In his diary Max Brod once mentions "Kafka's hopelessness" during their collaboration (unpublished diaries of Max Brod, MBA). In Kafka's notes the name "Robert" is sometimes found instead of "Richard." However, the English version of the diaries uses "Richard and Samuel."

52. Willy Haas, *Herder-Blätter*, Hamburg 1962 (facsimile), VI. Hans von Weber wrote about the elegant first number of the *Herder-Blätter* (*Zwiebelfisch*, vol. III, no. 2, 59) in June 1911: "Printed very nicely in Tiemann-Antiqua at Poeschel & Trepte in Leipzig, it presents a preprinting from the novel *Olga* by the Prague poet Max Brod, essays by Hugo Bergmann, Jules Laforgue, Oscar Baum and the editors, as well as poems by Franz Werfel and Franz Janowitz. It is testimony to the active intellectual life of a small circle centered around Max Brod in the Bohemian capital."

53. The third number of the *Herder-Blätter* did not appear in May, as had previously been assumed, but rather in June 1912. (Cf. note II, 10 and no. 5 in the Bibliography.)

54. It deals with the small text *Großer Lärm* ("Great Noise"), taken directly and unedited from his diary, the publication of which may have taken place without Brod's intervention. When Haas failed to send Kafka corrections for the text that was comprised of only seventeen lines—and author's copies as well—Kafka wrote to him very angrily on July 11, 1912: "That you will become bored with sloppiness is not something I can rely upon at all; once a sloppy person, always a sloppy person, I know that from personal experience. But perhaps, since you have now not fulfilled two responsibilities towards me (copies of the earlier Herder edition and the sending of corrections), I will now by virtue of the number three occupy a special place in your memory." (As cited in Binder, "Unvergebene Schlamperei," op. cit.) The prose work "Great Noise," written in November 1911, Kafka did not include in his *Meditation* because of its very private, personal character. (The manuscript of his first book was already with Rowohlt Publishing at this time.) On November 11, 1912, Kafka wrote to Felice Bauer (apparently Haas had sent him his author's copies immediately after his sharply worded letter):

"No, I don't live completely withdrawn from my family. Proof
of this lies in the enclosed description of the acoustic conditions
in our apartment, which has just appeared in a local Prague
periodical as a mild public chastisement of my family" (F36). Cf.
no. 6 in the Bibliography.

55. In light of the success in writing, Kafka also drew the public in;
such a piece of writing would be "accessible as well to the
understanding and feeling of everyone else" (DI181).

56. Willy Haas reports: "Max Brod read one sketch by Kafka, then
another, and then a third [Brod read the *Conversations* from
Hyperion]. Werfel and I stared at each other in amazement. Then
Werfel said rather excitedly: 'This will never get beyond
Bodenbach!'—Bodenbach was at that time the border stop
between Bohemia and the German Republic—Brod, bitter and
silently fuming, shrugged his shoulders and packed up the
manuscripts. We did not speak any more about it." (Willy Haas,
Die Literarische Welt, Munich, 1958, 30.) After the publication
of *The Judgment* Werfel changed his opinion entirely. (Cf. note
V, 66.)

Chapter II

1. The following appears elsewhere regarding the 'successful'
author-publisher relationship: "Kurt Wolff, who was directing the
production [of *Meditation*], chose at Kafka's wish the largest
available typeface (tertia); thus a real book, which appeared
before Christmas 1912, was made out of the thin manuscript. The
helpfulness of the publisher, *the mutual satisfaction with the book
form arrived at formed a continuous good relationship between
publisher and author that lasted until the author's death*. The fact
that Brod himself remained with the same publisher and that his
activity could therefore often be used by Kafka, without he
himself having to be present at the publisher's, naturally plays a
significant role for him. Also all the remaining books down to the
last one, were to appear with this publisher . . . Kafka's decision
to leave *Meditation* to the publisher, reveals a commitment to the
future." (Ludwig Dietz, *Franz Kafka*, op. cit, 36ff.—author's
italics.) The same author had already previously expressed this

implicitly drawn prejudice about the ideal publisher relationship of Kafka very clearly: "Wolff estimated the possibilities of Kafka correctly and led them to the corresponding success that was possible for them at the time. The first publication already expresses Wolff's (up until his death . . .) constant evaluation: a limited edition for a limited readership and exquisite formatting for lovers of such 'great little works of prose.'—The relationship between Kafka and Wolff always had a clearly definable distance, even though it was cordial; again and again Kafka left Wolff to decide many issues, certainly not only out of innate modesty" (sy94).

2.   There are examples of this, Thomas Mann or Hermann Hesse, to whom Samuel Fischer communicated before the appearance of his first book, that he was the "greatest hope" of his publishing house. Hugo Ball, Hesse's biographer: "This firm will of the publisher, this strong awareness of leadership and worth was perhaps exactly what for Hesse became the condition of constant security. It is very possible that only this publisher could offer the writer that feeling of meaning in his work and that stream of expectation, without which Hesse's work, as we know it today, would perhaps not exist." (Hugo Ball, *Hermann Hesse. Sein Leben und sein Werk* [1927], Frankfurt a. M., 1956, 99.)

3.   Kurt Wolff's radio lecture was broadcast on March 7, 1964 by WDR as part of the series "Kurt Wolff Recollects." The printed text appeared simultaneously in *Sprache im technischen Zeitalter*, 1964, 894-904. Cited in Wo15.

4.   Walter Kiaulehn, op. cit., 52. Kiaulehn's presentation of Ernst Rowohlt's impact as a publisher resulted from his long-standing friendship with the publisher and is—consciously—very subjective. In factual matters, too, the book contains a number of errors.

5.   The published English translation reads: "the literary talk" (DI268). The original German is more closely represented here.

6.   Cf. Karl S. Guthke: "Franz Werfels Anfänge," DVjs, no. 52 (1978), 83.

7.   In a letter to Brod on Dec. 16, 1909, Axel Juncker writes: "I am—I repeat—very grateful to you for the recommendation to Baum, and you will not regret it; I am now very curious about

Kafka." (Unpublished letter, MBA.) Probably Brod then sent Juncker Kafka's Brescia essay (cf. note II, 13).

8. SL33—In an essay on the discovery of Werfel ("Die Entdeckung Werfels") Brod discussed this disagreement: "The publisher [Axel Juncker], who was not exactly famous for his instincts, defended himself in every way possible against the expectation that he edit at that time a book of poems by a still totally unknown author Franz Werfel . . . I was so enthusiastic that I simply overran any resistance by the publisher." (As cited in a typescript by Brod, MBA.)

9. Unpublished letter from Rowohlt to Brod on April 16, 1912 (MBA). The statements of Manfred Durzak that Kurt Wolff first entered contact with Brod (cf. *Dokumente des Expressionismus*, op. cit., 343) as well as of W. Göbel, according to which Brod had offered himself to Rowohlt as an author (cf. WV628) are herein corrected.

10. Max Brod in RaII60.

11. Author's tally from a quarto sheet, that Adolf Brod, the father of Max Brod, kept on the early publications of his son. According to it, Brod published eleven books and 482 texts (poems, essays, reviews, etc.) up until June 1912 in newspapers and magazines (MBA). The last entry before the meeting with Rowohlt in Leipzig on June 29, 1912, was "Richard und Samuel." Since the dating in this notebook is generally very exact, it can be assumed that Brod and Kafka's collaborative work first appeared in June 1912. In comparison with this listing of Brod's publications, the bibliography of W. Kayser and H. Gronmeyer (*Max Brod . . .* Hamburg 1972. Hamburger Bibliographien, vol. 12) is totally insufficient.

12. Unpublished travel diary ("Weimar") by Max Brod (MBA)— entry from June 29, 1912. By the *Smetana-Essay* Brod is referring here to one of his own essays on Smetana, which had just appeared in *Die Schaubühne* on June 10, 1912. Later included in a collected volume: *Über die Schönheit häßlicher Bilder*, Leipzig 1913. The periodical was later called *Arkadia*.

13. Citations by Brod from an unpublished travel diary ("Weimar") (MBA). This conversation with the publisher led to the separation of Brod from his first publisher Axel Juncker and to his long

relationship with Rowohlt and later Kurt Wolff Publishing. He became one of Kurt Wolff's primary authors and published a total of thirty books there up until 1925, including a six-volume selection of his works (1919). It can also be assumed that Brod brought Franz Werfel, who also wanted to leave Axel Juncker, to the attention of the publisher on this day as well. Only four days after Brod's visit to Leipzig the publisher made its first offer to Werfel (cf. WV609, also Wo15). It is possible that Brod also recommended that Rowohlt Publishing contact Robert Walser as well (cf. WBr175).

14.　Brod was able to convince Kafka to have his report *The Aeroplanes at Brescia* accepted by Axel Juncker in his collected volume *Über die Schönheit häßlicher Bilder* along with his essay on the same topic (cf. DI145). Because of Brod's disagreements with Juncker the publication of the volume was delayed until Rowohlt expressed his readiness to publish it in 1912. Brod was "proud of having brought about Kafka's first publication in this way" (although at this point in time Kafka's contract for *Meditation* must have been near completion). After it was typeset and page-proofs prepared, however, the volume proved to be too large and Kafka's Brescia—as well as Brod's corresponding essay—"at the wish of the publisher" had "to be cut out of the final set-up of the book" (FK105). A correction copy of a prepared galley—including Kafka's *Aeroplanes at Brescia*—has been preserved. The printed pages are paginated from pages 249-64 with the printer's imprint: "Oscar Brandstätter, Leipzig—18 March 1913" (MBA). Based on the date, Kurt Wolff had thus voiced his objections to accepting Kafka's article.

15.　Unpublished travel diary of Brod "Weimar" (MBA). Note from June 29, 1912 (cf. Wa171).

16.　Kurt Pinthus in RaII75.

17.　His memoirs continue: "Thus our little circle in Wilhelm's Wineroom in a short time became a collecting point for all sorts of movements and personalities of expressionism, for the whole movement was based here not solely on an active publisher but also on a financially powerful one." (Kurt Pinthus in RaII83.)

18.　DII289 and note of Max Brod from the unpublished travel diary "Weimar" of June 29, 1912 (MBA).

19. The title of the series broadcast by NDR was "Reader of Expressionism. Selected and established by Kurt Wolff." Wolff's recollections about Franz Kafka were broadcast in the third program ("Kurt Wolff—Franz Kafka") on March 10, 1962. The text is printed in Wo67-74.
20. Janouch, op. cit., 23.
21. On August 11 Kafka noted with despair in his diary: "Nothing, nothing. How much time the publishing of the little book takes from me and how much harmful, ridiculous pride comes from reading old things with an eye to publication. Only that keeps me from writing" (DII266).
22. From Jungborn Kafka wrote to Brod: "Of course I am pleased that he [Rowohlt] is thinking about my book, but write him from here? I would not know what I ought to write" (L79).
23. Unpublished diaries of Max Brod (MBA), entry from August 1, 1912 (cf. Wa143).
24. FK124-25. Brod writes with equal calm here: "Kafka's diary is a witness to the resistance he put up against me, but it didn't help him in the least" (FK125).
25. Heinz Politzer, *Franz Kafka. Der Künstler*, op. cit., 148.
26. L84, author's italics.
27. Brod notes at this point that he was not just filling the role of "the one urging publication," while Kafka strove against it (cf. FK127).
28. Ernst Rowohlt, op. cit., 21.
29. As cited in Peter de Mendelssohn, op. cit., 617.
30. As cited in Rowohlt, op. cit., 8 and 11.
31. Certainly flattering for Anton Kippenberg was the fact that the young Rowohlt during this first conversation "was familiar down to the last detail with all the publications of Insel Verlag and knew right away for almost every book the printer and book designer" (Ernst Rowohlt, *Insel Almanach auf das Jahr 1974*, op. cit., 32f.).
32. Letter from Kippenberg to Rowohlt on Sept. 21, 1909 (ibid., 50).
33. Rowohlt, op. cit., 22.
34. Kurt Pinthus, "Ernst Rowohlt und sein Verlag," *Rowohlt Almanach 1908-1962*. (M. Hintermeier and F. J. Raddatz, ed.) Reinbek bei Hamburg 1962, 10.

35. Letter from Wolff to Clara Merck on Nov. 1, 1907 (WV554).
36. Kurt Wolff, "Porträt der Zeit im Zwiegespräch. Ein Gespräch mit Herbert G. Göpfert," op. cit., 2054.
37. In "Von einem Exemplar des ersten *Werther*" the bibliophile stance of Wolff culminates in his identifying with the material, when he uses the term "we bibliophiles." (*Zeitschrift für Bücherfreunde*, vol. 2, NF [1911], no. 2, 232.)
38. The great admirer of Goethe, Anton Kippenberg, planned together with the famous literary researcher from Leipzig Albert Köster—by the way, the future dissertation advisor of Kurt Wolff—a wide-ranging Goethe bibliography, which a close coworker of Kippenberg, Reinhard Buchwald, was then to take over. Kippenberg then sent Wolff to Leipzig for it. Kurt Wolff did not volunteer by chance at Insel, as Göbel maintains (WV556), and was also not, as Salzmann writes (op. cit., 378), only "a volunteer in name with Anton Kippenberg." Wolff came to Leipzig upon the express wish of Kippenberg. Witness to his material work for Insel Verlag is his publication about the problems connected with a Goethe bibliography. (*Zeitschrift für Bücherfreunde*. NF., vol. 1 [1909/1910]. On Wolff's activity for Insel Verlag, cf. *Insel Almanach auf das Jahr 1974*, op. cit., 25.
39. Helen Wolff (Wo104).
40. In a letter from 1961 Wolff described his first encounter with Rowohlt: "At our first encounter, a relaxed meeting of Leipzig bibliophiles, Ernst Rowohlt told me he had just received another Scheerbart manuscript, *Das Perpetuum Mobile*, and made the suggestion I immediately accepted to publish this book together under his name, financing and profit or loss 50/50" (WBrXVI). On July 24, 1910, Wolff wrote to Kippenberg: "I told you at that time that Rowohlt was trying to interest me in becoming involved financially for several of the works his company was planning. At first I thought it would only be a matter of lending R. a small sum for it; in the meantime I met with him several more times and his plans really struck and impressed me (of course it was actually a matter of only a very modest undertaking), so that I did not lend R. the sum in question, but invested it as a share in his undertakings" (RV492). In Kiaulehn's (op. cit., 27) account, the same matter—somewhat altered—reads as follows: "When

Rowohlt returned to Leipzig from Bremen in 1909, a well-to-do young man was awaiting him who was very much interested in giving him some financial support. The young man was Kurt Wolff and was in many respects the image and likeness of Ernst Rowohlt."

41. In a manuscript that fell into the hands of Heinrich Scheffler, the former apprentice at the publishing house Kurt Wolff/Neuer Geist Verlag, the goals of the earlier publishing work of G. H. Meyer were sketched out. It mentions there that Rowohlt and Wolff joined together "to establish a publishing house that should then primarily promote Eulenberg. But soon many young unknown authors turned to the publisher . . ." (Heinrich Scheffler, *Wölffische Lehrjahre*, Frankfurt a. M. 1975, 20.)

42. Wo104—Also in the registry of the German book trade (*Adreß-buch des Deutschen Buchhandels*, 1911, 439) the founding date for Ernst Rowohlt Publishing is listed as July 30, 1910.

43. *Zeitschrift für Bücherfreunde* (NF), vol. 2, no. 1 (1910), supplement, 23. This journal, for which Rowohlt was the business manager, naturally discussed the work of the young Ernst Rowohlt in the most detailed and friendly way. Among others, Kurt Pinthus—already an editor with Rowohlt at the time—here also wrote hymns of praise about Rowohlt's work.

44. Letter from Reinhard Piper to Christian Morgenstern on Dec. 9, 1910. (*Briefwechsel mit Autoren und Künstlern. 1903-1953.* Munich 1979, 108.) Ernst Blass also declined at first an offer by Rowohlt since the publisher of Eulenberg and W. Fred was a little too avant-garde for him.

45. Even turning to those older, more established authors was not a problem for the young Rowohlt Publishing in the period of its establishment—although it was almost entirely a matter of forgotten authors whom Rowohlt signed up. To Rowohlt's inquiry the former Juncker author Max Dauthendey answered hesitantly: "You have to remember that I got involved with a publishing house that offered me no positive guarantees at all, except for a few recommendations. For this I handed over my mature name as a writer." (Max Dauthendey to Rowohlt Publishing, handwritten letter from April 6, 1910. As cited in Durzak, op. cit., 355.)

46. The newest writing, or the new poetry, as one called it when it first came to be known, had great difficulties at the start finding possibilities for publication and most often there was no other way out except to establish one's own journal. Even at Rowohlt Publishing there was no unanimity at first regarding this literature. Against the vote of Rowohlt, Wolff rejected Werfel's first manuscript that later became a sensational success in 1911 with Juncker.

47. L85, as cited from the original, KWA. The characteristic orthographic error in the salutation was corrected during Brod's editing.

48. Letter from Wolff to Brod from Kainzenbad on Aug. 7, 1912 (unpublished, MBA).

49. Both Kurt Pinthus ("The manuscript was so slim that we had to print it in a giant typeface, with the widest margins possible, so that a book of 99 pages could result" [RaII80]) and Max Brod ("When the amount of material . . . turned out to be incredibly small, the publisher decided to have *Contemplation* [*Meditation*] . . . set in unusually large type . . . And thereby, by one of those rare accidents which according to Schopenhauer have nothing accidental left in them, the innermost character of this great prose was after all unsurpassably brought out" [FK125]), fail to remember in their memoirs that it was originally Kafka who expressly requested this size print.

50. Kurt Pinthus (as cited in RaII80). Publisher's notice for *Meditation* in the *Börsenblatt* from November 18, 1912, no. 269, 14607.—The widespread view that *Meditation* first appeared in January 1913—a mistake that is based essentially on Brod's recollections and the predated imprint notice (1913)—must be corrected. The book was already printed during the first two weeks of November 1912, advertised by the publisher on Nov. 18 and—although it can only be shown that Kafka received *Betrachtung* on Dec. 11 (F100)—delivered by the publisher at the end of November, or at the latest at the beginning of December. (Cf. no. 7 of the Bibliography.) Kafka's publishing contract is, like all of those he concluded during his lifetime, not extant. For *Meditation* one can reconstruct the following details:
    Edition: 800 (handnumbered) copies

Price: In Japan brochure: 4.50 marks
                Half leather volume: 6.50 marks
Royalties: Percentage of sales. According to the letter from
                Kurt Wolff Publishing to Kafka (WBr41) on Jan.
                13, 1917, Kafka received ".37 marks per [sold]
                copy."

Chapter III

1. The point in time at which Kafka wrote *The Judgment* is
    generally recognized in the literature as a caesura in his life and
    writing. Kafka's breakthrough with the successful writing of this
    story was recognized as such from the beginning; Brod himself
    was the first to use this term. Compare in this regard (among
    others): FK112, KI123ff., KHI29ff., KHII262-69 and Politzer,
    op. cit., 84.

2. Martin Walser (*Beschreibung einer Form*, Frankfurt am Main,
    1973, 9) points aggressively in his "Versuch über Franz Kafka"
    to the "almost planned training of Kafka as a writer," in that "he
    reduces his bourgeois-biographical personality, even destroys it,"
    in order to come to a "poetic personality."

3. This characteristic that Kafka hypothetically posited for his life is
    most clearly reflected in his diary entry on Oct. 18, 1921:
    "Anyone who cannot come to terms with his life while he is alive
    needs one hand to ward off a little his despair over his fate—he
    has little success in this—but with his other hand he can note
    down what he sees among the ruins, for he sees different (and
    more) things than do the others; after all, dead as he is in his
    own lifetime, he is the real survivor" (DII196, cf. L334f.).

4. Walter H. Sokel points to how in an encompassing sense
    "Kafka's literary and poetic idiosyncrasy grows out of the
    mythification of his existence problematic." (*Franz Kafka. Tragik
    und Ironie*, Frankfurt a. M., 1976, 337.) Kafka was aware of the
    parable nature of his own existence was known to Kafka when he
    wrote in his piece "On Parables": "If you only followed the
    parables you yourselves would become parables *and with that rid
    of all your daily cares*" (S457; author's italics).

5. In his diary Kafka writes for the date October 29, 1921, after a

visit to his parents: "But it begot no intimacy, or whatever trace there was of it was smothered under weariness, boredom and regret for the wasted time. It would always have been thus. I have seldom, very seldom crossed this borderland between loneliness and fellowship, I have ever been settled there longer than in loneliness itself. What a fine bustling place was Robinson Crusoe's island in comparison!" (DII198).

6.   Kafka's entire work can in a certain way be labeled "dialectic." But it is a matter of a dialectic that appears incomplete, since thesis and antithesis are not subsumed into something higher, but continue in variations on the same level *ad infinitum*. (Cf. in this regard Martin Walser's determination of Kafka's "purely rotational dialectic," op. cit., 67 and Walter Benjamin's comment that Kafka wrote "fairytales for dialecticians," op. cit., 15.)

7.   The "means" of the diary through which he hoped to enter into this condition was in this early phase a comparative harmless thrust for his creative power. After his acquaintance with Felice Bauer, Kafka transferred this more and more into his letters, then also to the personal relationship to this woman, then to the certainty of a functioning principle according to which the energies bound up in their relationship had to be released in him as only catalysts (by occasional separation) so that a creative condition could set in.

8.   In case the writing should have some "justification," the text at its beginning would already have to have "the completed organization" (DII104). Only then, imposed by the necessity of that which was to be described, which could be nothing but single-minded, could writing succeed in a more ideal way.

9.   Cf. no. 8 in the Bibliography.

10. Brod's early work had a great influence on the first expressionist writers. Kurt Pinthus viewed Brod's early prose as the first actual expressionistic prose. (Cf. "Zur jüngsten Dichtung" [1915]. Reprinted in Paul Raabe [ed.] *Expressionismus. Der Kampf um eine literarische Bewegung*, op. cit., 75f.) As late as 1924 the "poet" Max Brod was labeled by Heinrich Eduard Jacob as the first of the "chaotic ones," who attacked the proud edifice of Parnassian poetry. In his polemic against expressionism Jacob continues: "Brod's adlatus was the early Werfel . . . Werfel drew

his linguistic material for *Der Weltfreund* from Brod's free work. (Jacob, "Zur Geschichte der deutschen Lyrik seit 1910," ibid., 194-211.) After turning to Zionism Brod himself saw his enthusiasm for expressionism as "a misunderstanding of great scope" for his early work, although he had to admit to himself that "for a while he himself had been something like the pope of the expressionists" (PK206).

11. See note II, 12.

12. Letter from Brod to Dehmel on June 2, 1913 (In the same mailing Brod also sent a copy of *Arkadia*). As cited in *Richard Dehmel: Dichtungen, Briefe, Dokumente* (Paul Johannes Schindler, ed.), Hamburg 1963, 244. As this and a mailing to Martin Buber establish, Brod received the first author's copies of *Arkadia* on this date.

13. Unpublished letter of Wolff to Brod, "Aldych w. c.," from "Tuesday 1913" (MBA). It states there *Arkadia* will "at this time" after the "holidays" finally be able to appear; apparently he was talking about Pentecost.

14. Eduard Korrodi, "Die Jüngsten der deutschen Literatur," in *Neue Züricher Zeitung*, 1914 (771/775/779). (As cited in Paul Raabe [ed.], *Expressionismus. Der Kampf um eine literarische Bewegung*, op. cit., 41.) As Jürgen Born (cf. Bo81) correctly determines, Kafka's contribution to *Arkadia* was hardly noted by the critics. But the reactions by the press that Born cites can be supplemented by the fact that Dr. Theodor Reik wrote about *Arkadia* in a published review in the Viennese *Zeit* on August 10, 1913: "I especially liked *The Judgment* by Franz Kafka."

15. Wolff to Brod, unpublished letter (MBA) on Jan. 10, 1913 from "Silvaplana."

16. Toward Wolff, who was making efforts at the time to bring the editor of *Die Fackel* into his publishing house, Kraus reacted with a forceful attack against *Arkadia*; he labeled Brod's collection a "most horrible literary deformity!" (As cited in Ludwig Dietz, *Das Jahrbuch für Dichtkunst Arkadia*, op. cit., 186. Cf. also WBr123.)

17. Cf. no. 10 in the Bibliography. *Arkadia* was distributed at a price of 4.50 marks (pamphlet) and 6 marks (bound); the annual remained in stock for several years.

18. In his unpublished diaries (MBA), Max Brod sets his first meeting with Rowohlt and Wolff as the morning of June 29, 1912: "*2 bosses*, both younger than I; Rowohlt appears robust; the other, although also very strong and athletic, makes a more refined impression. Offices similar to those at Juncker." [Author's italics.]

19. As cited in ERV536 and 540. In this otherwise well-founded and informative monograph of Ernst Rowohlt Publishing the person of Kurt Wolff is idealized in a certain way, i.e., in a disproportionate relationship to the activities of Ernst Rowohlt. Thus after a conscientious evaluation of Kafka's first relationship with a publisher, Wolfram Göbel arrives at the noteworthy result: "If we look beyond the beginnings of the publishing relationship, a paradoxical picture actually results." (ibid., 541); the basis for looking at the situation, as formulated in the heading, actually did not apply to the real situation.

20. Letter from Wolff to Kippenberg on July 24, 1910 (WV560).

21. Kurt Wolff, "Porträt der Zeit im Zwiegespräch," op. cit., 2054.

22. On Sept. 1, 1912, Wolff noted in his diary: "Became a limited partner with Rowohlt with a 35,000 mark partnership investment and approx. 55,000 mark loan (previously I was a silent partner)" (Wo104).

23. Wolff's diary entry for Oct. 24, 1912 reads: "Disagreement with Rowohlt has begun." And on November 2 of the same year: "Signing of the dissolution contract with Rowohlt" (Wo105). Object of, and external reason for, the separation was Franz Werfel. This was in 1911, after Wolff, against the wish of Rowohlt, did not want to consider Werfel's initial work *Der Weltfreund* in the publishing house he had financed; however, he then changed his mind when he read Werfel's verse in print—which in the meantime had appeared as a literary success with Juncker—and became an admirer of the young Prague poet. Making the effort to win Werfel back over as an author (as Mayer writes in his monograph on Rowohlt [op. cit., 49]:) "Kurt Wolff invited the one he first shunned and then admired to dinner. He did not appear to place any importance on the presence of his associate Rowohlt; he reminded Rowohlt that he still had an appointment on this evening with Gerd von Bassewitz.

Rowohlt, who loved and admired Franz Werfel and had argued for the acceptance of *Der Weltfreund*, at a time when Kurt Wolff showed no understanding of it, was understandably deeply offended by the behavior of his partner." Kiaulehn describes the same incident (op. cit., 48f.).

24. As soon as it developed beyond a purely financial involvement, the profession of publisher was not totally regarded as a wise move in the higher circles of society. From an (unpublished) private letter by Wolff to his wife, one learns that the company was renamed only after "serious reflection and hesitation" and without any further programmatic ideas (according to an oral statement by Göbel to the author).

25. Kurt Pinthus, "Ernst Rowohlt und sein Verlag," in *Rowohlt Almanach 1908-1962*. (2nd. ed.) Reinbek bei Hamburg, 1962, 19. Hasenclever reported to Wolff from Berlin on the rather affected reaction of the departed Rowohlt: "E. R.'s speech climaxes in the 'non plus ultra' of S. Fischer Verlag. Your publishing house has no future, because you have no nose for literature (*based on the fact that when he was there you would have declined Brod, Werfel, Walser, while you now openly propagate and publish*—furthermore the case of Bassewitz, who fell on your account, etc.). This rhetoric concluded with a praising of S. F[ischer]., which was gigantic and unique and the most volksy, all-encompassing publishing house publishing mature things, no 'manure,' and which owned the future because it was bringing literature to the people." (Unpublished letter from Walter Hasenclever to Wolff on April 24, 1913 [KWA], author's italics.)

26. From a letter by Wolff to his mother-in-law Clara Merck. As cited in Göbel, "Der Kurt Wolff Verlag." Radio program of RIAS Berlin, broadcast on October 2, 1977 (Transcript, 14).

27. Tally according to Carl Christian Bry, *Buchreihen, Fortschritt oder Gefahr für den Buchhandel?*, Gotha 1917, 33 (and note 3).

28. Fischer, op. cit. 13f.

29. As cited in Mendelssohn, op. cit., 528.

30. Text of a publisher's advertisement for *Der Jüngste Tag*, nos. 19-24. On the goal of the series cf. especially WBr80.

31. Cf. Deleuze/Guattari, *Kafka. Für eine kleine Literatur*, op. cit.,

40ff.

32. During this period Kafka completely stopped writing in his diary; the formulas conjuring up his creative condition now show up in the letters to Felice.

33. The unpublished diary entry of Max Brod (MBA) for Oct. 6, 1912 states: Kafka reads "his beautiful novella"—"In Ms. part I of the novel. Very good. The Man Who Disappeared." On Oct. 20.: "Reads the first chapter of 'Der Verschollene' (*America*) to me. Marvelous! First class!" After Kafka had already read the first chapter at Baum's toward the end of October, he reads there on "Nov. 3" the second.—The fact should be noted that Brod is speaking here at this early stage about "Der Verschollene," the actual title of Kafka's novel *America*, but later, following the edition from the posthumous writings, he no longer remembers this title.

34. Cf. Canetti, op. cit., 85.

35. Unpublished letter by Arthur Seiffhart to Max Brod on Dec. 24, 1912 (MBA): "P. S. Kafka, MEDITATION has not been sent off for discussion. As soon as it receives some reaction from *Das Literarische Echo*, I will let you know."—The fact that Brod put together a list of critics for *Meditation* at the end of January is revealed in his diary entry of Jan. 23, 1913. (MBA).

36. At the time Franz Werfel was not only actively involved with expressionistic poetry at Kurt Wolff Publishing, but he was also responsible for conducting publication negotiations for Wolff with Karl Kraus. Werfel wrote to Brod in 1917: "My insistence and my convincing caused him [Wolff] in 1913 to negotiate with Kraus, up to that point . . . he knew almost nothing of him." (Unpublished field post letter by Werfel to Brod on March 1, 1917, MBA.)

37. All citations from the unpublished diaries of Max Brod (MBA). Author's italics. For a long time it was not known that Kafka had already read the complete version of *The Metamorphosis* on Dec. 15, 1912.

38. Cf. no. 9 in the Bibliography.

39. Letter from Wolff to Kafka on April 2, 1913 (WBr29). Wolff's comment could of course also refer to their first meeting in Leipzig on June 29, 1912. It is therefore not certain whether in

fact a second meeting between Wolff and Kafka actually took place in April 1913.

40. Göbel emphasizes especially the time pressure under which the first series of *Der Jüngste Tag* was put together. Thus still "on April 23 neither the sequence nor the titles to be included had been decided . . . Ferdinand Hardekopf's dialogue *Der Abend* and Carl Ehrenstein's *Klagen eines Knaben* had already been sent in during March for examination, and for a long time Wolff was indecisive about including [these titles]" (WV583). The last title of the first series, the poems of Emmy Hennings' *Die letzte Freude* ("The Last Joy") was as well put off at first as being too sparse in size; Wolff's resurrection of these titles documents the difficult situation the publisher found himself in. With the resistance of Georg Trakl a further edition of poems for *Der Jüngste Tag* that Wolff also wanted to bring out with "greatest speed" failed because he did not consult with the poet on the planned edition. (Cf. WBr80.)

41. L97. [Author's italics.]

42. Canetti, op. cit., 49; cf. F236-37.

43. Cf. no. 11 in the Bibliography. Brod also notes the appearance of *The Stoker* in his diary entry for May 25 (MBA).

44. Thus Kafka writes later to Kurt Wolff Publishing: "*The Stoker* was not handsomely bound. There was something sham about the binding which after a while produced a kind of disgust" (L113).

45. Unpublished postcard from Brod to Kafka on July 14, 1913 (MBA).

46. Cf. no. 12 in the Bibliography.

47. Kafka continues: "Just because his friendship for me, in its most human aspect, has roots far deeper that those of literature, and for this reason is effective long before literature gets a chance, he overestimates me to a degree that makes me feel embarrassed, and vain, and conceited . . ." (F194)—Max Brod's review of *Meditation*, "Das Ereignis eines Buches" (Bo24ff.).

48. Oskar Loerke, author and literary advisor of S. Fischer, noted on Nov. 1, 1913, in his diary: "I read publications by Kurt Wolff Publishing. New names, new talent, we must be careful not to box ourselves in." (As cited in Mendelssohn, op. cit., 647.)

49. Letters from Moritz Heimann to S. Fischer on April 5, 1914 and

Jan. 10, 1914, as cited in Mendelssohn, op. cit., 668 [author's italics].

50. Cf. L150. The close-knit nature of literary intervention is shown here in exemplary fashion: At the time of Kafka's request, Musil was in close contact with Blei, his discoverer and promoter, and simultaneously a discoverer and promoter of Kafka. In similar fashion there were contacts with Brod and Rowohlt; the latter had been business manager at S. Fischer Publishing since 1913. Blei and Brod were the primary promoters of Walser and alluded early on to the literary affinity of the Swiss writer to Kafka. In August 1914 Musil discussed Walser and Kafka in a joint review in *Die neue Rundschau*.

51. Since none of Kafka's publishing contracts has been preserved, it is not known whether Kafka entered option clauses. In one of Georg Trakl's contracts with Kurt Wolff Publishing from April 1913, the following clause is contained: "§7. Herr Georg Trakl obligates himself to offer initially any work he writes within the next five [!] years to Kurt Wolff Publishing and specifically that Kurt Wolff Publishing owns the right of first refusal." (As cited in Georg Trakl, *Dichtungen und Briefe*. Salzburg 1969, vol. II, 688.)

52. Binder ("Kafka und Die neue Rundschau," op. cit., 107) assumes that Kafka generally had reservations about a publication of *The Metamorphosis* and therefore "hesitated for such a long time before handing over the manuscript to Wolff." The fact is, however, that Wolff did not mention the story again after the appearance of *The Stoker*, except when he was asked directly about it, which led Kafka to assume that the publisher had no interest in the publication. Later comments (especially to René Schickele) show how much Kafka was interested in the publication.

53. As cited in a draft of a letter from Kafka to Musil. Undated (approx. July 1914). Passed on and commented on by Binder (ibid., 103f.).

54. Kafka suggested either publishing only the first part or waiting with the complete publication, "perhaps" until the next volume (ibid.).

55. Letter from René Schickele to Norbert Jacques on October 31,

1916. (As cited in Mendelssohn, op. cit., 681.)

56. From a prospectus of the publisher, undated (1913), original in DLA.

57. Cf. Kurt Tucholsky, *Ausgewählte Briefe 1913-1935*. (*Werke*, supplemental volume), Reinbek bei Hamburg 1962, 16f. and 22f.

58. Thus among others the following works were preprinted in *Die Weißen Blätter*: Max Brod: *Tycho Brahes Weg zu Gott*, Carl Sternheim: *1913*, Gottfried Benn: *Gehirne*, Kasimir Edschmid: *Jossuf*, René Schickele: *Aissé*, Carl Sternheim: *Napoleon und Schuhlin* (cf. WV660f.); in the case of Kafka a new typesetting was undertaken. Göbel states: "Above all, the works for which Wolff feared financial risk were entrusted to the millionaire friend [i.e., Schwabach]" (WV674).

59. Meyer spread these comments by Blei in a letter to Schickele on November 27, 1914 (as cited in WV685f.; cf. also WBr198).

60. Cf. Blei's comments on "contemporary literature," written around September 1915: "In all these things nothing is expressed even in a stammering way that one can call the spirit of the most recent literature; and when the stammering is over, this new spirit is only the old spirit in the last throes of death . . . And finding the new spirit in a unity that connects Heinrich Mann, Sternheim, Frank, *Kafka*, Stadler, Walser and 723 expressionist poets and sketch writers and others, means only determining this spirit once again from the old and with it . . ." (Franz Blei, *Über Wedekind, Sternheim und das Theater*. Leipzig, 1916, 124-29.) [Author's italics.]

61. Letter from Walter Hasenclever to ("The Publisher") Erik Ernst Schwabach on Oct. 1, 1914. In this letter Hasenclever referred—somewhat flatteringly—to the fact that "the journal would only become something necessary and final under your [i.e., Schwabach's] more personal direction" (as cited in *Briefe der Expressionisten*, ed. Kasimir Eschmid, op. cit., 29).

62. Letter from Kafka to Schickele, in *Expressionismus. Literatur und Kunst 1910-1923*. An exhibition of the German literary archives in the Schiller National Museum, Marbach a. N. (Exhibit Catalogue, 140). Author's italics. Kafka writes further: "I am not pressing at all for a speedier appearance of the story, but I do request news as soon as possible as to whether you are able to

even accept it. Since you want to avoid serials, I can see where accepting my story might cause difficulties."

63.   The last news that Kafka received from Kurt Wolff Publishing was in October 1913. At that time Wolff sent him an author's copy of *Das Bunte Buch* (L104). Also the fact that Meyer did not know Kafka's address when the correspondence resumed and had to address the letter to Brod is an indication that besides the letters that have been preserved no further contact had taken place.

64.   Cf. no. 14 in the Bibliography.

65.   Otto Flake writes: "I suggested establishing one [prize] for prose writers and giving it the name Fontane Prize."—Schwabach and Flake met "quickly and not only the Fontane Prize came about; already in February I concluded a contract with Schwabach to establish the publishing house *Die Weißen Blätter* and a journal of the same name, which I would edit." (Otto Flake, *Es wird Abend. Bericht aus einem langen Leben*, Gütersloh, 1960, 199.) The Fontane Prize, which along with the Kleist Prize was one of the high literary honors of the German Empire, was awarded periodically until 1922. Other recipients were: Alfred Döblin, Paul Adler, Gina Kraus, Max Brod, Albert Paris Gütersloh. It is unclear whether a definite title by Kafka was recognized, such as *The Stoker*, as Brod writes. The official notifications of December generally state that the monetary award was going "to the young Prague prose writer Franz Kafka for his novellas [sic] *Meditation, The Stoker, The Metamorphosis* (*Prager Tagblatt*, Dec. 6, 1915).

66.   *Robert Musil: Tagebücher, Aphorismen, Essays und Reden*, ed. Adolf Frisé, Hamburg 1955, 771.

67.   There are few documents on which to base an estimate of the first editions in *Der Jüngste Tag*. Werfel's *Versuchung* ("Temptation") appeared as the first volume of the series with an initial run of 2000 copies. It is unlikely that other titles by unknown authors reached even this number.

68.   A similar case shows that Meyer believed in this kind of advertising effectiveness for literary prizes; on Nov. 16, 1915, he wrote in a letter to Schickele: "Since Zweig will now receive the Kleist Prize, we can be in charge of it [!], if we publish him"

(WBr201).

69. Kasimir Edschmid, *Lebendiger Expressionismus. Auseinandersetzungen, Gestalten, Erinnerungen*, Vienna (etc.) 1961, 134.

70. L114—Meyer had of course advised Kafka to write to thank Sternheim for passing on the prize money to him. However, the publisher did not mention the actual initiator, Franz Blei, who had recommended this gesture to Sternheim. Thus Kafka also asked in his letter to Meyer: "You advised me to thank Sternheim, But don't I also have to thank Blei? And what is his address?" (L114).

71. On this matter Ottomar Starke noted years later: "None of the authors I did illustrations for, most of whom I was friendly with (Kafka I did not know personally!), had ever expressed their 'wishes' regarding an illustration." ("Kafka und die Illustration," *Neue literarische Welt*, 1953, no. 9, 3.)

72. No contract of Kafka's with Kurt Wolff Publishing for the book edition of *The Metamorphosis* has been preserved. Kafka received a one-time lump-sum royalty of "350 marks" for the "small edition" (WBr34), probably 1000 copies, according to what can be gleaned from the publisher's letters. The price of the double volume was 1.60 marks for the soft-cover volume and 2.50 marks for the hardbound volume. Cf. no. 15 in the Bibliography.

73. According to the publisher's accounting records from Jan. 13, 1917 (WBr41), 258 copies of *Meditation* were sold between July 1, 1915, and June 30, 1916. Also because of the sales lull until the end of 1915 that was caused by the war, the bulk of the copies could only be sold in 1916—after the awarding of the Fontane Prize.

Chapter IV

1. FK145—Cf. Kafka's diary entry from June 6, 1914: "Back from Berlin. Was tied hand and foot like a criminal. Had they sat me down in a corner bound in real chains, placed policemen in front of me and let me look on simply like that, it could not have been worse. And that was my engagement . . ." (DII42).

2. From an article by Werfel in the *Prager Tagblatt* from June 3, 1922, 6 (As cited in Lore B. Foltin, *Franz Werfel*. Stuttgart 1972,

24.) On the situation of German writers from Prague, cf.
especially W65-98.

3. At the end of June 1914 a short meeting between Kafka and
Wolff apparently took place in Leipzig. They met in the company
of others, so Kafka could not have spoken alone with the
publisher. When Kafka made the decision a day later "to go not
to Berlin but Leipzig," he however did not find the publisher
there. (Cf. Kafka's diary entry on June 30, 1914, DII64.)

4. Oskar Bie's essay in *Die neue Rundschau*, September 1914.

5. Robert Musil, *Tagebücher*, Hamburg 1955, 169.

6. Hans von Weber, "Krieg und Buchhandel," *Der Zwiebelfisch*,
vol. 6 (1914/15), double number 4/5, 171.

7. Meyer spread this statement by Pinthus in a letter to Werfel on
October 28, 1914 (unpublished, KWA). As cited in WV692.

8. Salzmann, op. cit., 368.

9. Bertold Hack, "Georg Heinrich Meyer," op. cit., 1201.

10. The year 1913 saw over 35,000 titles, a record to date; in 1914
there were another 29,000 new publications. Since at this time the
publishers arranged for very high volume editions, publishers'
capital tied up in warehouses was very high at the outbreak of the
war and at the immediately decreasing demand; suppliers' credits
were canceled the publishing houses had to temporarily curtail
their work because of liquidity problems. When in 1915 the
desire to buy—led by the public's need for war experiences and
writings justifying the war—increased again, the publishers could
draw again on their substantial stock. An interesting economic-
psychological cycle developed: while other warehouse products
experienced horrible rises in price, books were able to maintain
a relatively stable price since they mostly came from stock. By
virtue of this comparatively very low price purchasing books
became attractive. This manifested itself especially during the
Christmas shopping season; books experienced a renaissance as
gifts.

11. Julius Zeitler, "Kriegsbibliophilie," *Die Weißen Blätter*, vol. 2,
no. 1 (January 1915), supplement, 3.

12. Arthur Seiffhart, *Inter Folia Fructus. Aus den Erinnerungen eines
Verlegers*, Berlin 1948, 24.

13. Letter from Meyer to Werfel on Feb. 28, 1915 (KWA). As cited

in WV715.

14. Thus Meyer made deliveries in the following way: '7/6' (i.e., for six paid copies the bookseller received seven) at a 40% discount, introduced as well for *Der Jüngste Tag* a 'mixed batch'; large sale items like Meyrink's *Golem* were later offered in bonus batches of 40 copies for the price of 30 at 40% discount, which equaled at that time an unparalleled effective discount of 55%.

15. Letter from Ehrenstein to Wolff on April 26, 1916 (WBr235ff.) [author's italics]. Previously Ehrenstein had defended Wolff against Herwarth Walden, who had attacked the publishing policy of Kurt Wolff a number of times in *Der Sturm*. A letter from Ehrenstein to Walden on March 16, 1916 (Sturm Archives) reads: "By the way, you are doing an injustice . . . by repeatedly identifying Kurt Wolff Publishing with the bankrupt Herr Meyer, who . . . is directing it awfully, like a book-seller obsessed with *Golem*. Since the beginning of the war Kurt Wolff has been in the field . . . and should absolutely not be identified with *the unliterary direction of Herr Meyer!*" (as cited in WV728, author's italics).

16. As cited in a review of Wolff's almanac *Vom Jüngsten Tag* by Dr. Hans Christoph Ude (*Allgemeine Zeitung*, Munich, June 17, 1916).

17. Unpublished letter from Wolff to Rudolf Werfel, the father of Franz Werfel, on March 13, 1917 (KWA, as cited in WV753). In this letter Wolff emphasizes that he did not want to hire anyone other than Franz Werfel as editor.

18. In Hartmut Binder's and Klaus Wagenbach's notes to Kafka's letters to his sister Ottla we read: "End of July [1916]: Kafka is offered a lectorate with Kurt Wolff Publishing in Leipzig." (Ot235) Bezzel also wrote in his *Kafka-Chronik*—however, noted with a clear question mark—"End of July [1916]: Kurt Wolff Publishing offers K. a lectorate (?)" (op. cit., 115). All of these suppositions are based on a correspondence from Meyer to Kafka on July 10, 1916, which has not been preserved; Kafka answered on July 28 as follows: "For a wide variety of reasons I cannot at this moment accept your kind suggestion that I take a day off and come to Leipzig. Four years ago, three, and even two, my outer circumstances and my health might have allowed me to do so"

(L124). A few lines previously in the same letter Kafka had rejected the writing of a larger new work that Meyer wanted from him with the same reasoning. Since there was talk in 1916 of an "Urlaub" ("leave")—even for a one-day visit to Leipzig Kafka would have had to submit a request for leave—the most that can be safely assumed is that Meyer asked Kafka to come to Leipzig for a definite period of time, where—freed from the constraints of bureaucratic work—he could finish the novel. Under such direct constraint (of completing the novel under the eye of the publisher) any writing would have been impossible for Kafka. Moreover, he would have accepted a request from the publishing house only through Kurt Wolff himself.

19. Max Hermann(-Neisse) and Albert Ehrenstein seized S. Fischer's offer to be editors, and J. R. Becher became literary advisor to Anton Kippenberg. The departure of these editors from Kurt Wolff Publishing can probably be traced to reasons other than just work-related ones.

20. As cited in Kurt Wolff, "Porträt der Zeit im Zwiegespräch," op. cit., 2057.

21. In Kurt Wolff's "inclinations" in 1917 Göbel sees the foundation already of a "change from literary expressionism as the actual publishing task" (WV791). The expansion of Wolff's endeavors in 1917 can easily be demonstrated:

—"Publisher of the Writings of Karl Kraus" founded by Wolff in 1916 specifically for the works of Kraus, because the latter had rejected appearing in Kurt Wolff Publishing (until 1923).

—Publisher of *Die Weißen Bücher*, Wolff took over the publishing house founded in 1913 fully in 1917; in 1924 he ended book production.

—Tempel Publishing, a subsidiary of the Verlag der Weißen Bücher (classical literature).

—Der Neue Geist Verlag, the publisher for cultural politics and contemporary history Wolff founded together with Reinhold Schneider in 1917; Wolff departed already in 1919.

—Hyperion Verlag (Hans von Weber), in 1917 Wolff purchased the company founded in 1906; in 1927 he ceased publishing books.

—Musarion Verlag, the company founded in 1918 was

temporarily owned by Wolff.

—Pantheon Casa Editore S. A., Florence; Wolff was involved with this ambitious bibliophile and international concern between 1924 and 1930.

Moreover, in 1918 Wolff purchased a private bibliophile press (Ernst Ludwig-Presse), the Leipzig Offizin Drugulin, and was a member of the Leipzig Theater (Schauspielhaus).

22. Canetti, op. cit., 86.

23. Along with Kafka's continuing attempt to reach a breakthrough as a writer with the publication of his first major book, there are other references that speak to the fact that he had written *The Trial* with the intention of publishing it, e.g., the diary entry of December 1914 in which he speaks of his "need to make so great a display of art . . . with the reader" (DII102).

24. Unpublished letter from Meyer to Brod on July 7, 1916 (MBA).

25. Unpublished letter from Meyer to Brod on July 5, 1916 (MBA).

26. Oskar Walzel's Kafka portrait "Logik im Wunderbaren" was published in the *Berliner Tagblatt* on July 6, 1916, and reprinted in abbreviated form in *Das Literarische Echo*, Berlin, Aug. 15, 1916 (reprint in Bo143-48). Walzel's attempt to interpret *The Stoker* and *The Metamorphosis* can be viewed as the most cogent contemporary presentation of Kafka's writings up to that time. On the mark is the establishment of the "unique" fantastic element in Kafka's work, that of being catapulted into the narrative situation, which Kafka then realistically continues to work out under the "protection of the impression of reality." Interesting for the thesis presented here—that Meyer renewed contact with Kafka on the basis of the Walzel article—is a note by Walzel comparing Kafka's *Metamorphosis* with Meyrink's (Wolff best-seller) *Golem* and Paul Adler's *Elohim* and maintaining: "Kafka moves our heart more strongly than they, because he remains closest to life" (Bo148). This could have brought Meyer—who scarcely knew Kafka's texts—all the way to the idea of including Kafka along with the successful Meyrink in the series *Der Neue Roman*.

27. The commercial impetus in the activities of Meyer for Kurt Wolff Publishing are shown very clearly in the example of Kafka. On August 1, 1919, Brod wrote to Kafka: "It would be very nice if you could speak with Meyer sometime—he says repeatedly that

he wants to make a sensational success out of a novel by you."
(as cited in Max Brod, 1960, op. cit, 111.)

28. Letter by Kafka to Brod from Marienbad, about mid-July 1916
(L118-19—author's italics). In his letter to Meyer of July 28,
1916, Kafka then repeated his opinion almost literally: "In fact I
feel that the only right thing would be for me to present a new
and complete work; if I cannot do this, perhaps I should rather
keep quiet [!]" (L124). Reacting to this letter Meyer apparently
proposed bringing out *The Penal Colony* together with *The
Judgment* in a volume of *Der Jüngste Tag*, which Kafka reacted
with resignation; for a publisher with a sense of feeling that
would be a "dreadful combination," he commented, "'Metamorphosis' might still mediate between them, but without that story
you would have two alien heads knocking violently at each other"
(L126).

29. Advertisement in the *Börsenblatt* from October 20, 1916, under
the heading: "Künftig erscheinende Bücher" ("Future Publications") (no. 245, 6956.). A contract with Kafka for *The Judgment*
has not been preserved, it is (in looking back on *The Stoker*)
furthermore unclear whether one was actually concluded; thus
Kafka—as was common with *Der Jüngste Tag*—was paid in a
lump sum. The exact number of copies is not known (1000
copies?). Upon publication the retail price was .80 M for the
stitched volume and 1.50 M for the hardbound copy. Cf. no. 19
in the Bibliography.

30. According to the findings of Ludwig Dietz, the second edition of
The Stoker was run about the beginning of 1916. While the first
was printed by Poeschel & Trepte, the second bears the imprint
"Printed by E. Haberland in Leipzig-R." The dating derives from
a publisher's announcement on the back side of the softbound
copy, which shows numbers 1-25 of the *Der Jüngste Tag* as
having appeared (cf. Dietz, sy107 and no. 18 in the Bibliography). Kafka's letter of March 14, 1917, to Kurt Wolff also
shows that there was no second edition of *The Metamorphosis* at
this time; in this letter he inquired about the "statement for the
second printing of *The Stoker*," but not about *The Metamorphosis*
(L131).—Wolff called the inventive marketing and psychological
measures of his director "Georg Heinrich Meyer nonsense"

(WBr210f.).

31. Announcement of Kurt Wolff Publishing for the volumes 20-24 of *Der Jüngste Tag.* (*Börsenblatt*, no. 267, Nov. 16, 1915, 7009).

32. Brod, "Kleine Prosa," *Die neue Rundschau*, July 1913 (as cited in Bo32). This comment by Brod is also the earliest testimony for the use of the non-literary term 'expressionism' for the "New Poetry." Later (from 1916 on) Brod revised in a very forceful way his initial listing of Kafka with the literature of the expressionists.

33. Thus in his essay "Wie verhält es sich mit dem Expressionismus?" ("What is the status of Expressionism?") Schickele still stated in 1920 [!] that Franz Kafka belonged among the German expressionists (*Die Weißen Blätter*, vol. 7 [1920], no. 8, August 1920, 337-40). The fact alone that Kafka was among the authors of Kurt Wolff Publishing was reason enough for many conservative critics to include this unknown writer with the 'new literature.' Franz Herwig thus wrote about "literary expressionism" in 1916: "their manner of thinking, of feeling, of speaking is so uniform [!] that one can speak of an intellectual uniform. Schickele is a little less calm, more playful than the others, *Kafka is a little more obdurate*, Schwob simpler and more artistic, Sternheim more grotesque, and Edschmid more intoxicated—but finally they are all uneasy, obdurate, simple, artistic, grotesque and intoxicated without any one of them being the personality that one could hope could lead to the health of literature." (Franz Herwig "Vom literarischen Expressionismus," *Hochland*, Munich, May 1916. As cited in Bo69f. Author's italics.)

34. Kafka wrote to Meyer in August 1916: "Incidentally—if 'In the Penal Colony' were not to appear right off in *Der jüngste Tag*, I would be able to offer it to the *Weissen Blätter*" (L126). Kafka was of course aware of the close connection between Meyer and *Die Weißen Blätter*.

Chapter V

1. The following authors were signed up for the series of lectures: Else Lasker-Schüler, Theodor Däubler, Salomo Friedländer,

Kasimir Edschmid, Albert Ehrenstein, Johannes R. Becher, Wieland Herzfelde, Alfred Wolfenstein, and Ferdinand Hardekopf. Brod was supposed to give the fifth lecture of the "Cycle" (cf. F529). On September 19 Kafka wrote to Felice: "I may be able to go [to Munich] after all. I heard today, though, that it was Max who arranged the invitation; my inclination to go has diminished correspondingly" (F504).

2. Kafka's reading was announced several times in brief newspaper listings. On November 9, 1916, the following ad appeared in the *Münchener Neueste Nachrichten*: "Evenings for New Literature. / Franz Kafka, the writer, who was awarded the Fontane Prize last year, reads / on Friday evening, November 10 in the Kunstsalon / Goltz a previously unpublished novella; / in the second half poems by Max Brod" (as cited in Bo118). A more detailed sketch of Kafka's reading is given in Max Pulver, *Erinnerungen an eine europäische Zeit*, Zurich 1953, 50-57. See also: Bo115ff., FK157, ÜFK212, and SL186f.

3. Kafka not only followed the newspaper critics attentively, but also took them to heart—which had special significance for his later corrections to the manuscript of *In the Penal Colony*. ("In any case I have to admit that these opinions are justified, indeed almost true" [F536].)—The three reviews are reprinted in Bo120ff.

4. The development of Kafka's writing during this phase of artistic creativity should be emphasized. In contrast to the previous creative phases of 1912 and 1914 (narrative in the third person in predominantly single-minded perspective), Kafka now struggled with a new narrative style: personal, first-person perspective, parable, and parabolic narrative.

5. *Beim Bau der chinesischen Mauer* (*The Great Wall of China*), *Ein altes Blatt* (*An Old Manuscript*), *Der Schlag ans Hoftor* (*The Knock at the Manor Gate*), *Elf Söhne* (*Eleven Sons*), *Eine Kreuzung* (*A Crossbreed [A Sport]*), *Ein Bericht für eine Akademie* (*A Report to an Academy*), *Die Sorge des Hausvaters* (*The Cares of a Family Man*).

6. Malcolm Pasley, "Drei literarische Mystifikationen Kafkas" (sy21-37).

7. Cf. note V, 11.

8. As cited in Buber, *Briefwechsel aus sieben Jahrzehnten*, op. cit., vol. I, 429—author's italics, cf. also: ibid., vol. I, 462.

9. Letter from Kafka to Buber on Nov. 29, 1915. Ibid., vol. I, 409. Brod had previously written to Buber to inquire whether he would invite Kafka to collaborate.

10. Letter from Brod to Buber on June 21, 1916. (As cited in a typescript, MBA.) Brod had always emphasized to Buber Kafka's significance as a writer. Brod's reference to Buber in his letter of June 21, 1916: "It is extremely difficult to get Kafka to publish anything. One has to actually tear the manuscripts away from him" is of course also a part of Brod's attempt to encourage the printing of Kafka's prose text *A Dream*. Thus Brod continues in his letter: "I personally consider Kafka along with Gerhart Hauptmann and Hamsun the greatest living writer! Oh, if you only were familiar with his large, but unfortunately incomplete novels, that he occasionally read to me in rare moments. What I wouldn't do to make him more active! Until now I have had only modest success as his spiritual doctor, but successes that give me hope (for after the war)."

11. Letter from Kafka to Buber on April 22, 1917. Buber, op. cit., vol. I, 491f.

12. Letter from Kafka to Buber on May 12, 1917, ibid., vol. I, 494.

13. Cf. no. 24 in the Bibliography.

14. Cf. especially Hartmut Binder, "Franz Kafka und die Wochenschrift Selbstwehr," op. cit.

15. Cf. no. 21 in the Bibliography. *Die Selbstwehr* (December 15, 1916) lists the collected work as having just appeared.

16. L349—In the article "Prager Dichter von ferne gesehen" Pick writes: "But Kafka does not betray to what belief he ascribes" (Bo151f.).

17. Cf. nos. 31, 33, and 39 in the Bibliography.

18. Citations from the printed announcement of *Marsyas* (also in folio format) from May 1917, p.4 and p.10.

19. Letter from Kafka to Buber on April 22, 1917. Buber, op. cit., vol. I, 492.

20. Cf. no. 23 in the Bibliography.

21. As was already the case in the preceding years, behind this apparent readiness to publish there was already that—previously

often demonstrated—typical rhythm in Kafka's life: the will to publish is joined temporally to the ebbing of the inspirational phase. Already in February 1917 Kafka's writing bogged down, soon thereafter Kafka put together the first table of contents for the new collected volume (cf. H440); the second table of contents (H447) he then put together around the end of March or beginning of April when his writing really threatened to cease. With the total cessation of his creative power he rekindled the relationship to Felice. His efforts to publish the previously written pieces now ran parallel to his courting of Felice. This typical schematic representation of Kafka's rhythm for the period between summer 1912 and spring 1918 reached its high point at the beginning of July 1917; at that time Felice came to Prague and the second engagement took place—almost exactly to the day Kafka sent his *Country Doctor* manuscript to Wolff.

22. Along with Max Brod, Rudolf Fuchs, Paul Leppin, Frantisek Langer, Otto Pick, etc., the name Franz Kafka stood on the list of collaborators of this journal printed below the table of contents from no. 1 (July 1917) on for the first volume. *Die schöne Rarität*, ed. Adolf Harms. Selbstverlag, Kiel 1917-1919. However, no contribution by Kafka appeared in this journal.

23. *Der Orkan.* A numbered extra edition to foster new German art and culture. Ed. Rolf Conrad Cunz. vol. 1, no. 1, April 1917 (cf. RaI54). In this edition excerpts from "essential excerpts from recently published or soon-to-be works" (p.26) were published. On p. 29 an excerpt from vol. 34 of *Der Jüngste Tag*, *Das Urteil* by Franz Kafka."

24. At the end of December 1917, Kafka wrote Brod: "Please have copies made at my expense of 'The Bucket Rider' and 'An Old Manuscript' and send them to me—I need them for Kornfeld" (L184). On Jan. 16, 1918 Brod answered him: "I'm having both novellas banged out and am sending them to you. I would have really been happy if you would have added another one (this call which falls on deaf ears!) which I had especially requested from you. I was also very annoyed that you didn't send along 'The Trial,' which I had enjoyed so much." (Unpublished letter from Brod to Kafka—MBA.) On Jan. 28, 1918 Kafka wrote to Brod: "Thank you very much for the copies of the manuscripts

(although I no longer need them, at least not for Kornfeld, since I have found another solution [!] . . . (L195).

25. Emanuel Hurwitz, biographer of Otto Gross, gives the name of the journal project: "Kafka too was impressed with Otto Gross and was enthusiastic for a time about a joint journal project. He had gotten to know Otto Gross during a night train trip from Budapest to Prague. Gross then apparently tried to explain his theories to him . . . With the title proposed by Gross for the planned journal, *Blätter zur Bekämpfung des Machtwillens*, one of Kafka's own life problems resonated." (Hurwitz, *Otto Gross. Paradies-Sucher zwischen Freud und Jung*, Zurich and Frankfurt a. M., 1979, 130.) Max Brod recalls "quite a large party" in his apartment on July 23, 1917, "at which were present in addition to Kafka, Adolf Schreiber, the musician, Werfel, Otto Gross and his wife. Gross unfolded a plan for a newspaper which very much interested Kafka . . ." (FK157). In a letter to Max Brod from around the middle of November 1917, Kafka mentioned this meeting again: "If any magazine seemed tempting for me for any length of time . . . it was Dr. Gross's, perhaps because I felt the warmth of a certain personal connection glowing from it, at least for that evening. Perhaps a magazine can only be a sign that people are moving toward a common point" (L167, cf. L153).

26. From Zürau Kafka wrote to Brod on Jan. 18, 1918: ". . . the Writer's Association informs me of an unauthorized reprinting of 'Report to an Academy' in an Austrian morning newspaper and requests permission to collect on my behalf a fee of thirty M. (of which they would keep 30%). Shall I consent? The twenty marks would be very welcome to me for, say, more Kierkegaard. But this association is a dirty business, so is collecting, and the newspaper might be the Jewish *Österreichische Morgenzeitung*. So should I consent? Could you order the issue for me through Wltschek (it must be a Sunday edition, either in December or January)? (L195). Cf. nos. 26 and 27 in the Bibliography. Neither publication was authorized by Kafka, but he nevertheless wanted to see author's copies of them.

27. Br519—This citation does not appear in the English edition of the letters.

28. Pasley writes: "We maintain the following: With his story 'A

Visit to a Mine' Kafka so to speak reacts to the reception of the almanac 'Der neue Roman.' One can imagine the situation: At the beginning of 1917 he was working very intensively, in his somewhat cave-like room in the Alchimistengasse, on the stories designated for the 'Country Doctor' volume (thus for Kurt Wolff). There he receives Wolff's newest collected work; he interrupts his work and begins to page through it; there he finds the leading figures of contemporary literature collected, who as it were pay him a visit—Heinrich Mann, Hugo von Hofmannsthal, Carl Sternheim, Max Brod and others. Kafka considers himself a mere miner in comparison, while the authors named in the almanac are transformed into engineers, who climb down to him in the deepest tunnel" (Pasley, "Drei literarische Mystifikationen Kafkas," sy 21-37, cf. 32). Consequentially carrying out the metaphor, Pasley recognizes in the "chancellery servant of the directorship," who arrogantly obeys the engineers, the 'employee' of Kurt Wolff Publishing, who writes an arrogant afterword for this almanac. As she states upon remembering a comment by Kafka himself about the *Country Doctor* stories, even Dora Gerrit talks of "variations on the fruitfulness of this [writing] profession" (ÜFK370).

29. Unpublished letter from Wolff to Brod on Dec. 30, 1921 (MBA). Wolff also asked Brod for permission to reprint his "little essay 'Der Dichter Franz Kafka' from the November number of the *Rundschau* in the almanac, which is very important to me."

30. Letter from Meyer to Werfel on July 19, 1915 (as cited in WV708).

31. Cf. no. 17 in the Bibliography.

32. The reconstruction of the history of publication of Kafka's text *Der Mord* is based on a letter from Wolff to Brod on Jan. 8, 1917, which reads in part: "Having returned from my trip, I find your correspondence from December 31, 1916, with which you sent me two contributions for an almanac, a poem by you and a prose piece by Kafka" (unpublished letter—MBA).

33. Cf. no. 25 in the Bibliography.

34. Cf. no. 20 in the Bibliography.

35. On Jan. 28, 1977 Herzfelde wrote to Hartmut Binder: "I accepted the story *A Dream* in 1916 for the *Almanach der neuen Jugend*

auf das Jahr 1917 on pages 172-74, and also announced in the same volume Kafka's books *The Stoker, The Metamorphosis* and *The Judgment* on page 178. Unfortunately, I never personally met with Kafka." (Correspondence from Binder to the author.) See in this regard the memoirs of Wieland Herzfelde, "Zehn Jahre," Malik Verlag, in *Literarische Welt*, vol. 3 (1927), no. 10, 5 and Herzfelde, *Der Malik Verlag 1916-1947*. Exhibition catalogue. Berlin, Deutsche Akademie der Künste, 1966 (especially the chapter "Erste Krise").

36. Hans Reimann, *Mein blaues Wunder. Lebensmosaik eines Humoristen*. Munich 1959, 131.

37. Cf. no. 29 in the Bibliography.

38. A handwritten note by Brod on a letter from Kurt Wolff Publishing to him from Dec. 29, 1910 reads: "About Kafka: Krell" (MBA). Brod often made such margin notes in preparing his letters; thus one may assume here that he wanted to ask about Kafka and Krell in his next letter to Wolff, which at this point in time could only refer to the anthology that just appeared.—Cf. no. 36 in the Bibliography.

39. In a very personally phrased letter to Wolff on Aug. 20, 1917, Kafka outlined exactly the format for his book: "May I propose *A Country Doctor* as the title for the new book, with the subtitle *Short Tales*. For the table of contents I would suggest . . ." (cf. L135-36). Since April 1917 Kafka had changed the table of contents several times. This is indicated by other handwritten lists of titles, which document Kafka's efforts for a good composition of pieces for his collected volume (unpublished lists of titles by Kafka in MBA). The principle of composition was not the "mining practice" of his first book, *Meditation*, but more organic and very reflective; the longest text is the conclusion, each piece is "connected with one another by a special motif" (KI235).

40. In his own "layman's diagnosis" (Br242), Kafka not only alluded immediately to the exact type and seriousness of his illness (which he recognized earlier than the doctors as tuberculosis), but also referred expressly to its actual psychical origin. "So that is the status of this mental disease, tuberculosis," he wrote in August 1917 (O19). Most striking is the description (Kafka often analyzed his illness) he gave to Brod in the middle of September

1917: "In any case my attitude toward the tuberculosis today resembles that of a child clinging to the pleats of its mother's skirts. If the disease came from my mother, the image fits even better, and my mother in her infinite solicitude, which far surpasses her understanding of the matter, has done me this service also. I am constantly seeking an explanation for this disease, for I did not seek it. Sometimes it seems to me that my brain and lungs came to an agreement without my knowledge. 'Things can't go on this way,' said the brain, and after five years [!] the lungs said they were ready to help" (L138).—This interpretation (thus the association with his—now five-year-long—attempts at marriage, possibly also the association with the failed novels—he began *America* in 1912—and the failed book publications—his first book appeared in 1912) remained with Kafka; as late as 1920 he repeated the description in a letter to Milena. ("What happened was that the brain could no longer endure the burden of worry and suffering heaped upon it" [M21-23].) Cf. also: L137f., Br242, DI46F., FK157, F543f., and Dora Diamant in Hodin, op. cit., 29; also Dieter Beck, *Krankheit als Selbstheilung*, Frankfurt am Main, 1981), 14f. and Alice Miller, op. cit, 346f.

41. Although Kafka himself—somewhere between August and October 1920—selected and assembled those aphorisms, and although one can conclude from the numbering Kafka undertook that he intended them to be prepared for one publication, the writer left behind no title for the collection. The present title chosen by Brod (WP38) is therefore misleading because its interpretation is one-sidedly conceived in that it carries a religious (Jewish) implication.

42. On March 19, 1918 Brod told Kafka about the publisher's misunderstanding: "From the publishing house there was only one representative present. I asked him among other things to send you further corrections. With the success that Wolff writes me about today: 'About your wish to read the corrections to K.'s Country Doctor, I have taken note and arranged that they be forwarded to you in the next couple of days.' I am correcting the error right away—" (Unpublished letter from Brod to Kafka, MBA, author's italics.) This misunderstanding is also to be

emphasized because it illustrates how a request by the 'prominent' house author Brod was answered immediately with a positive decision by the publisher, while Kafka had to wait.

43. L201-03—This ultimatum by Kafka has not been preserved, and it is therefore not known to what extent Kafka made demands to the publisher. Also other letters in which Kafka must have been critical of the publisher have not been preserved; this is especially true for the difficult year 1919.

44. On March 29, 1918, Brod wrote to Kafka: "I wouldn't advise leaving Wolff. The disorganization, as the bookdealers say, is now pervasive with all the publishers. Not even Insel Publishing can deliver its classics (because of the paper shortage)—nor even Staackmann new editions of his most dear Bartschke! [The bookseller] André reports this with teary eyes . . . sad news." (Unpublished letter—MBA.) On the basis of this letter from Brod Kafka decided not to change publishers.

45. This plan by Wolff did not materialize. Since the emergency decree of 1917 paper in Germany was also strictly rationed; the publishers received on average up to 50% less paper. Fischer had—acting at this time of crisis more cautiously than Wolff—already reacted early on to the paper shortage by establishing a branch in Vienna (cf. Mendelssohn, op. cit., 773f.). When Wolff considered his establishment, the war was already over and the revolution had broken out in Vienna; Wolff therefore did not follow through with the branch, which he must have regretted later on during the German inflationary period.

46. A handwritten note by Meyer (?) on Kafka's letter to Wolff on Aug. 20, 1917 reads: "Something new: Der Mord," and was in the first position of the sequence of the prose pieces as Kafka listed them for the publisher (original letter: KWA). Meyer's communication that the book had not been able to be typeset because of the lack of type, must have annoyed Kafka, since Wolff himself had assured him eight months prior (!) that the type was "now free" (cf. WBr46). Wolff's letter from the end of January 1918 must have now sounded like an ironic aside to Kafka; it read: "Your wishes regarding the sequence, title, and dedication will be carefully acknowledged" (WBr47). As Kafka later found out, not even the title page was printed according to

his wishes.

47. Klaus Wagenbach, *Veröffentlichungsgeschichte*, op. cit., 61-64; cf. Bezzel, op. cit., 146, KI176, sy 114.

48. *Prager Tagblatt* from Sept. 28, 1919 (vol. 44, no. 229, morning edition, supplement II—cf. KH I 548).

49. Letter from Brod to Kafka on August 1, 1919 (cited from the original, MBA) printed in Max Brod, *Die verbotene Frau*. Stiasny Verlag: Graz and Vienna, 1960, 111.

50. *Börsenblatt des deutschen Buchhandels*, Oct. 29, 1919, no. 238, 11034 (reprinted in Bo92). The announcement reads: "Despite the major problems with materials and manufacturing, model printings in excellent format at relatively low prices will appear in the new series on high-quality paper." Regarding Kafka's book it reads: "A nerve-wrenching, gruesome event is told here with calm, manner-of-fact reserve. And precisely this report-like, linguistically simple account raises the story to an impact that is not achieved by the most uncanny of stories in world literature. Only a great artist and master of language could frame this story to a unified, pure work of art with the uniqueness of the material."—*The Penal Colony* was printed in a single edition of 1000 copies. The price per copy in October 1919 was: 6 marks (hardbound) and 12 marks (half-leather volume). Cf. no. 32 in the Bibliography.

51. Dietz, "Franz Kafka. Drucke zu seinen Lebzeiten," *Schiller Jahrbuch*, no. 7 (1963), 442f. References to the fact that Kafka had also seen corrections after those of March 1918 are an (undated) postcard from 1919 (WBr51) and the fact that Kafka removed *The Bucket Rider* from the collection—which must have taken place after Meyer's letter of Sept. 13, 1918—and later published this text separately. Also the correction of the title page must have been done much later—approximately the end of 1919 —(and here it would not be understandable if Kafka had received no other corrections from the publisher except for the title page). See also the following note.

52. In his Kafka biography Brod quotes a recollection of "Dora Gerrit" (that is, Olga Stüdl), at whose rooming house Kafka lived in Schelesen during the middle of November 1919: "At that time he [Kafka] gave her a little package of corrections, asked her to

read them and give an opinion, saying a friend had sent it to him. She read his *Country Doctor*, the variations about the fruitfulness of this occupation" (ÜFK370).

53. See M7-9. The dating of the letter to Milena at the end of April is based on the simultaneous appearance of *The Stoker* in Czech in *Kmen* on April 22, 1920—translation by Milena—and Kafka's letter to his sister Ottla on May 8, 1920 (O48-49). Kafka must have written the letter in the interim. Approximately in the first half of May Kafka received another letter from Milena with the message that Wolff had not yet sent her the *Country Doctor*. (Cf. M11-13).

54. *Börsenblatt für den deutschen Buchhandel*, Dec. 17, 1920, no. 285, 15369, heading: "Completed Books." On March 2, 1921 the publisher repeated the same announcement in the same place. The edition size of *A Country Doctor* is not known, it should not have been under a thousand, but was also not more that two thousand copies. In his memoirs Kurt Wolff writes of an edition of around one thousand copies (Wo67). The price in December 1920 was: 12 marks (softbound) and 40 marks (half-leather). Cf. no. 34 in the Bibliography.

55. These figures reflect the rise and fall of production after 1921.—(The number after the year indicates the new literary publications of the main publisher, the cumulative number of all the titles with a primarily literary content appearing in Wolff's various companies follows in parentheses:) 1913: 40 (65)—1914: 39 (57)—1915: 41 (48)—1916: 73 (83)—1917: 48 (68)—1918: 49 (91)—1919: 50 (95)—1920: 61 (135)—1921: 44 (62)—1922: 27 (41)—1923: 29 (37)—1924: 15 (30); from this point on the number of new literary editions decreases steadily to 0 in 1930. The catastrophe of 1921—the beginning of the period of inflation in Germany—can be clearly seen.

56. As Göbel describes, private motives were primarily responsible for moving the publishing house to Munich (WV792). The publisher planned to stay away from the company for a time after the end of the war (cf. WBr238). Wolff, who never much cared for the book industry metropolis of Leipzig, thought it reasonable, in light of the good, cordial relationships that he had established at the court in Darmstadt to move the publishing

house completely to Darmstadt. After the proclamation of the first German republic, however—and the abdication of the regent—Wolff altered his plan and decided—against the express opposition of several of his coworkers—to move the publishing house to Munich. Meyer and Pinthus had advised the publisher to move to Berlin. Thus Meyer was still writing to Elisabeth Wolff on November 12, 1919: "Certainly I do not fail to recognize for a moment that there is now no other and no better place for Elisabeth and Kurt Wolff [than Munich], but we want to be clear about it, that for KWV [Kurt Wolff Publishing], if it is to continue developing as is has been, actually Berlin and only Berlin could be the place, today more than ever . . . And just as a leading French publisher today is conceivable only in Paris, so too in my opinion is a leading German publisher only so in Berlin" (WV792f.). While Meyer then followed the publisher to Munich, Pinthus separated himself from Wolff in order to go to Berlin to Ernst Rowohlt, who had established a second publishing house in the city.

57.   The boom for luxury editions lasted from approximately 1917 to 1919; after that the expensive, bibliophile art volumes found no buyers. The shortage of raw materials and the general inflation after 1917 led at that time to a quick decline in book production in Germany. In 1913 there were still approximately 35,000 new publications, in 1916 it was only 22,000, in 1917 15,000, in 1918 15,000, in 1919 the figure rose again to 22,000. The difficulties in book production can be sketched with the following statistics: the prices for paper rose, starting from July 1915 in the same period: January 1916: 10%, January 1917: 20%, January 1918: 40%, January 1919: 70%, January 1920: 2000%. (Only then did inflation set in.)

58.   With his recently founded second publishing house, Rowohlt survived the period of inflation and the following economic depression only with the help of large credit loans; cf. Paul Meyer, op. cit., 107 and 76. Fischer also had periodic difficulties in paying production costs and authors' honoraria on time. Many literary publishers had to give up entirely at the time.

59.   Inflation hit the publishing company hard. On August 23, 1923, Wolff described his situation to Mardersteig: "We have limited

our production to a minimum, many ongoing projects have merely been canceled. It is an untenable situation. We have to pay paper suppliers, printers, and bookbinders in gold marks, recalculated to the exchange rate of the day in paper money and with such ridiculous amounts, while our delayed payments from retail sales are made in bad paper marks . . . Of course sales have been reduced to a microscopic minimum. And in our small operations in August three and a half billion have been paid out in salaries—I think you can hardly imagine such numbers. We can't either. But unfortunately they are for us a real condition" (WBr399).

60.   The publisher felt especially offended by an ironic poem by his highly regarded Karl Kraus with the title "Elysisches. Melancholie an Kurt Wolff," which had appeared at the end of 1916 in *Die Fackel* (no. 443/444, 26f.); the final verse reads:

> "And raise our lament to the eternal God
> that the present-day pack of writers
> find their elysium,
> for whoever only rubs words together
> is printed with Drugulin in Leipzig
> Noble Master Wolff, I complain about it."

Elisabeth Wolff thereupon sent Kraus a very ambiguous telegram, in which she vouched for the future friendship of the publisher: "It is nice that melancholy will remain and a Jüngster Tag will pass." (Passed on in a letter by Karl Kraus to Sidonie Nadherny from Nov. 23-24, 1916. In Karl Kraus, *Briefe an Sidonie Nadherny von Borutin*, vol. I, 396f.) Already at that time a disagreement arose between Werfel and Wolff. Werfel accused the publisher of defending this parodistic poem of expressionist and even of Prague literature and even of supporting the "standpoint of the author" Kraus. (This is taken from an unpublished letter by Wolff to Brod on Dec. 7, 1916—MBA.) Franz Muncker, literary historian in Munich, wrote a (scathing) commentary in April 1916 about the almanac *Vom jüngsten Tag*, for which Wolff himself had apparently asked ("Much that is in it makes an impression on me as in Jüngster Tag."). Muncker included everything except the texts of Werfel and Brod (WBr233ff.).

Brod, who had been advising Wolff for many years in literary
matters, had become an opponent of the literary expressionistic
movement after his turning to Zionism. This position did not
change; still on Jan. 19, 1921 he wrote in an (unpublished) letter
to Kafka: "Serious literature is bankrupt, people only want
sensationalism, dancing . . . swindling" (MBA).
Pinthus wrote in March 1921 to Wolff's new advisor
Mardersteig: "The drought in literature continues, and that which
is good, or at least promising, is so mired in pathological
eroticism that one cannot even print it." (As cited in WV864f.)
The candor regarding his position as a publisher in the first years
of his activity Wolff owes—almost against his actual position—to
the fact that the initially bibliophile publisher schooled in classical
literature is today called *the* publisher of literary expressionism.
Wolff himself later turned "against this label." In a "credo" he
wrote: "It was my cursed, hated fame to have been the publisher
of expressionism" (Wo23).

61. Kurt Wolff: "Porträt der Zeit im Zwiegespräch," op. cit., 2057.
62. The climate between the publisher and authors worsened during
     the period of inflation because of the unfavorable rates of
     exchange. Werfel especially reproached the publisher for not
     backing up his authors. A letter from Werfel to Brod on Feb. 9,
     1923 (MBA) states: "K. W. is behaving outrageously," he is
     acting "deceitfully" and that he has not seen one nickel for 3/4 of
     a year from his publisher despite the greatest sales successes . . .
     Remember Zsolnay." Kafka too appears not to have approved the
     inflation calculations of Kurt Wolff, for right at the end of the
     inflationary period he wrote to Brod: "In your fears about the
     future you forget that you will also be paid in stable currency by
     Wolff, who must truly have made a fantastic amount of money"
     (L394).
63. Also because of the long delay with the publication, both books
     encountered little critical response. The only noteworthy review
     is that of Kurt Tucholsky (Peter Panter) on *In the Penal Colony*
     from March 6, 1920 (cf. Bo93-103).
64. His satisfaction and joy about a published text was normally
     dismissed by Kafka as "vanity." (Cf. Kafka's comments:
     WP71f., WP91f., WP110f., F193-94, L163, L166f., L179,

L328f., L332ff., DI266.) What can actually be clearly shown in the history of publications of all of Kafka's works published during his lifetime in his unconditional wish to see corrections before any printing. He always became very upset when galley proofs were not sent and when the publishers and their reactions were "sloppy." (Cf. note I,47, note I,54, note V,45, note VI,69, and L97, L130f., L207.)

65. Kurt Wolff: "Porträt der Zeit im Zwiegespräch," op. cit., 2055.
66. Ibid., 2056.
67. Phrased this way Brod told Kafka about Werfel's comment on a postcard (unpublished postcard from Brod to Kafka on Dec. 18, 1917, MBA).
68. That even at this late point in time Wolff needed an external stimulus or push in order to contact Kafka is shown clearly in two letters by the publisher to Brod from Feb. 18, 1920 ("I am writing to Kafka right away at your suggestion" and from March 3, 1920 ("Franz Kafka: This opportunity, which you have pleaded so passionately for with me, is a priority")—both letters (unpublished, MBA) only referred to Kafka's illness and his search for a sanatorium. Wolff began his "courting letter" of November 1921: "The conversation with Ludwig Hardt motivates me to once again show you directly that I am still alive" (WBr54).
Ludwig Hardt had met Kafka in Prague shortly before (L306f.). A second impetus for the letter may have come from the major Kafka essay by Brod which had just appeared in *Die neue Rundschau*. Hartmut Binder even speaks of a "letter to Kafka perhaps instigated by Brod or Werfel" (cf. Binder, *Kafka in neuer Sicht*, op. cit., 353f.). The examples continue. Wolff wrote to Brod on Jan. 30, 1922 (after a meeting with Ludwig Hardt on Jan. 29, 1922): Kafka appears "very depressed and edgy, and I myself, who love his works so much, regret unceasingly that he cannot make up his mind to release something from the rich treasures of unpublished works" (letter from Wolff to Brod on Jan. 30, 1922, unpublished, MBA). In what manner Hardt took up Kafka's case, also privately, is shown in the recently published diaries of Thomas Mann; the date Aug. 1, 1921 contains the note: "For tea with Ludwig Hardt, who read me prose from a

Prague author, Kafka, noteworthy enough. Otherwise very boring." But Hardt persisted, and Mann noted already on Sept. 22, 1921: "I was very interested in the writings of Franz Kafka, whom the reader Hardt recommended to me" (Thomas Mann, *Tagebücher 1918-1921*. Frankfurt a. M., 1979, 542 and 547). Mann then recommended Kafka's *Trial* to his readers in 1925 as "Christmas reading" (cf. KHII603).

69. Peter Panter: "Drei Abende," *Weltbühne*, Berlin, Dec. 1, 1921. While two other critics panned *The Penal Colony* (which hurt Kafka very much), there was an enthusiasm which came from the critique of Peter Panter for Kafka's work (cf. Bo93ff.). Kafka knew who published this critique under the pseudonym Peter Panter, for on June 9, 1920 Brod wrote to Kafka: "First, two pieces of news you will be happy about: 1) Felix (not I) read in the Weltbühne a major essay by Peter Panter (Tucholski?) on *The Penal Colony*, very charming comparisons to Kleist, etc. . . ." (as cited in an unpublished original, MBA).

70. Letter from Rilke to Wolff on Feb. 17, 1922 (WBr152). A few days after receiving Rilke's letter the publisher wrote a second solicitous letter to Kafka; part of it reads: "If in connection with your cure and following the advice of your friends you occupy yourself a little with your manuscripts and work, then please think of the urgent requests that my last letters brought to you. There is a need to repeat these to you again: the number of copies per edition of books published with us have nothing to do with inner relationship to the author or the work, and the urgency with which I am soliciting you must be clearer to you than words" (WBr55). Also, just shortly before this solicitous letter Mardersteig had written to Wolff that Ludwig Kirchner was prepared to illustrate another book, and to be sure only "a modern work like one by Kafka" (WBr385).

71. About another writer Kafka expressed the opinion that he could have had no success with this "strategy" of waiting, "because real necessity hampered him. Necessity does not permit such gossamer successes to occur" (L326).

72. Kurt Wolff: "Porträt der Zeit im Zwiegespräch," op. cit., 2055f.

73. Wolff's complete answer to Eulenberg's question: "What was your worst flop?" reads: "The books of the great writer Franz

Kafka were the greatest business failures—despite marvelous reviews by leading German minds and despite Ludwig Hardt's artistic presentations." (As cited in the original of the questionnaire in the Herbert Eulenberg Archives, Düsseldorf-Kaiserwerth.) That the books of Kafka had been this "greatest failure" is questionable even in comparison with the totals that the publishing house invested at that time for another "unknown" author, Alfred Brust.

74. Kurt Wolff: "Porträt der Zeit im Zwiegespräch," op. cit., 2056.
75. Ludwig Dietz: "Kurt Wolffs Bücherei *Der jüngste Tag*," op. cit., 104. On the future editions of the texts of Kafka, cf. sy 106-120.
76. The complete citation reads: "It is a mistake to assume that the more splendid the printing that the books *A Country Doctor* and *Meditation* have had, would be reason enough that the works could not become popular. You forget that we brought out three other books by Kafka in *Der jüngste Tag* in simplest format for 80 pfennigs and that the sales figures for these little volumes were not essentially higher than those of the more expensive books." (Letter by Wolff to Brod on July 5, 1924, unpublished, MBA.) On this background that just these small volumes had an essentially higher edition, the argument of Brod that the large typeface had a basically negative influence on sales is plausible. Heinrich Scheffler, later a coworker at Kurt Wolff Publishing, shares in his memoirs the fear "that this unusual typographic form has made broad public access to the prose writings [of Kafka] difficult." (*Wölffische Lehrjahre*, Frankfurt a. M., 1975, 39).
77. As cited in Heinz Liepmann ("Ein wahrer Grandsigneur der Literatur. Erinnerung an Kurt Wolff," *Die Welt*, Oct. 24, 1963).
78. Cf. note 2 for the Preface.

Chapter VI

1. The reflex impulse to write here too during this phase forms a regular pattern of writing and publishing: the publication of one of his works spurred him on to write more. The largest part of the aphorisms came about between October 21 and 23; at just that time his story *Jackals and Arabs* appeared in the October number

of *Der Jude* (cf. KHI516f. and H71). And (at the end of October) a few days before writing the *Letter to His Father, In the Penal Colony* appeared. His writing during the winter months is worth noting as well.

2. This is simultaneously the first known translation of Kafka's work. Milena intended to translate the "collected works" into Czech; in the further course of 1920 other Czech publication of Kafka appeared—all in Milena's translations: after *The Stoker* (*Kmen*, vol. 4, no. 6), which took up the entire number of this literary journal, and about which the editor Stanislav K. Neumann wrote: "The story . . . belongs among the best modern German stories," selections from *Meditation* followed there (*Kmen*, vol. 4, July 9, 1920, 308-10).—On Sept. 26, 1920 *A Report to an Academy* appeared in *Tribuna* (1-4), where the small piece *Unhappiness* had been already printed on July 16, 1920. This piece bore the subheading: "From the prepared volume of translations of Kafka's prose"; actually Milena prepared a volume with the texts *The Judgment, The Stoker*, and *The Metamorphosis*, which was to appear in Neumann's series *Červen* (FK235). Neumann requested that Milena write a foreword to it for the Czech reading public. Milena asked Brod—insofar as he would have no reservations writing for the (communist) *Červen*—to assume this task for her. Brod wrote this preface; "I have no recollection whether the book translated by Milena was actually published, or of what became of my preface," Brod writes later (FK236). The author found a manuscript in Brod's literary estate (MBA) with the heading crossed out by Brod: "(Introduction to a Czech edition of his works)." The same text was printed unaltered in the November number of *Die neue Rundschau* (1921) under a new heading ("The Writer Franz Kafka"). Brod thus recouped his loss after the Czech volume failed to appear for financial reasons; the article instigated at Milena's prompting became the first comprehensive positive commentary of Kafka's work.

3. In his note from January 29, 1922, there were strong resemblances to the beginning of *The Castle* ("Suffered some attacks on the road through the snow in the evening . . . a senseless road, moreover, without an earthly goal [to the bridge? . . .]" [DII214]).

4. This publication was unknown for a long time. (Cf. no. 37 in the

Bibliography.) As can be seen from a corresponding note, the editors took this text with the "approval of the publisher" from *A Country Doctor*, which had already appeared. The *Prager Presse*, a republican Czech newspaper in German, had been appearing with the support of the new Czech state since Easter 1921. Otto Pick, who had already endeavored early on to translate Czech literature into German, was apparently the director of the literary section of the newspaper from the start. Kafka was first referred to this printing (and to the publication itself) by Brod in his letter of May 14, (1921); Brod also mentioned here the collaboration of Oskar Baum and Paul Adler (unpublished letter by Brod in MBA). Then Kafka wrote back to him: "So Oskar [Baum] is with the *Presse*, and not with the *Abendblatt*? Is the quality of the newspaper such that you could recommend it? . . . I have not yet seen the paper. Is Paul Adler also on it?" (L281).

5. Cf. nos. 38 and 40 in the Bibliography. For Kafka's later publications in the *Prager Presse*, a more active participation of the author can be shown. He now began to read this newspaper more actively (L281, L287f., L311, L315) and personally spoke with Otto Pick at the beginning of September 1921 (L299, L303), and later also with Paul Adler. Kafka interceded on behalf of his friend Robert Klopstock, who was looking for work, at that time with Pick and Adler; one can assume Kafka released the small prose pieces for publication to a certain extent in response to Pick's and Adler's favor (cf. L303f.).

6. Cf. no. 39 in the Bibliography.

7. Max Brod's role in the relationship between Kafka and Wolff had become less and less visible during these years. Still in 1917 Brod had been unconditionally advising an affiliation with Kurt Wolff Publishing. Also in 1918 he recommended to his friend (despite the failed printing of *A Country Doctor* and the resulting problems it caused in the relationship of Kafka to the publisher) not to leave Wolff, and now on top of it all with the directive that the disorganization in all publishing houses because of the war would be the same. At the beginning of 1920 Brod tried several times to move the publisher to write to Kafka; but at the end of 1920 he advised Kafka openly to break with Wolff and to change

publishers (on Dec. 27, 1920 he wrote to Kafka from Berlin: "Rowohlt would like very much for you to read to him in Berlin . . . He would also like very much for you to publish something with him. He thinks that Wolff is doing too little for you. That's what the vast majority of people who ask me about you think" (MBA). The impression becomes clearer and clearer that Brod confused Kafka's problems with publishers with his own (in no way unproblematic) relationship to Wolff. For in December 1920 he complained to Meyer (with reference to "friend Rowohlt") that for his own books "too little" was being done (from a letter by Meyer to Brod on Dec. 12, 1920, unpublished, MBA). Obviously impressed by the splendid solicitous letter of Wolff to Kafka in November 1921, Brod tried again immediately to intensify the contacts between his friend and Wolff and wrote to Munich again apparently in detail about Kafka. Wolff then answered Brod: "Of course I am pleased to find out from you that in the end it was health reasons that prevented Kafka from answering personally the letter I sent him, for I would have gladly had some reaction." (Letter from Wolff to Brod on Dec. 12, 1921, unpublished, MBA.) In view of Wolff's readiness, Brod advised Kafka still in September 1922 to travel to Munich to speak personally with the publisher. When Wolff then at the beginning of 1923 got behind in his payments to Brod, and could scarcely pay them because of the inflation, Brod advised Kafka again to the contrary.

8.   On May 6, 1922, Wolff wrote to Mardersteig: "Kafka has sent a small contribution with an accompanying letter that is captivatingly beautiful and that you must remind me of when you are here; for this accompanying letter deals directly with you for reasons we must discuss in person" (WBr394). On May 10 Wolff turned directly to Kafka: "Since Dr. Mardersteig is off now on a trip, I would like to thank you first of all for the cordial letter that you sent to my friend and collaborator, thank you in his name, and express our happiness to you for sending this beautiful story *First Sorrow* to *Genius*" (WBr55).
     Kafka's "accompanying letter" is not known.

9.   Ludwig Dietz traces Kafka's submission back directly to Wolff's efforts: Only after a further "correspondence of March 1, 1922 . . . does Kafka answer. In May he sends the story *First Sorrow*

. . . " (Dietz, *Franz Kafka*, op. cit. 73). The same in sy122 and Dietz, "Kafkas letzte Publikation," op. cit., 122, as well as KI253 and KHI378.

10. An unpublished letter from Wolff to Brod on July 21, 1919 (MBA) reads: "*Genius* is essentially an art journal." Göbel mentions that Meyer argued against Wolff's vote "for a mixture of art and literature, in order to reach both groups of potential customers" (WV874).

11. Mardersteig's letter to Kafka on November 18, 1921, is cited here without abbreviation. This previously unknown letter shows in exemplary fashion how Kafka had to be spoken to in these later years before he would release a text for publication. (Unpublished letter in MBA.)

"Dear Herr Kafka: I fear that you will just put my letter aside unread when you see the letterhead 'Genius.' But I am taking the liberty of turning to you again with the request to make a contribution to the next number of Genius, which will appear in the spring. We are afraid and almost sure that because of the unfavorable conditions that we will be forced to cease publication of the journal with the appearance of number 6, which is supposed to appear in spring. And we would be very sad if this journal had to shut down without having been able to publish even a small piece by you. It is no idle talk when I say that no author had been so important to me as you, and I ask you not to look upon my previous letters and assurances as empty formality. The work on a journal such as Genius, presents very extraordinary difficulties, and the joy at publication therefore remains relatively modest. But if the most important individuals whom one would like to publish in it supply no contributions, then the publication of such a journal is a sham. I would like to add that I leave it entirely up to you what length your contribution should have and tell you that I am prepared to make every concession in case you only have a lengthier work on hand. Max Brod told me occasionally in earlier years that you had several uncompleted works: Perhaps you will decide, if you are opposed to completing these works, to send us one of these fragments.
Hoping to receive agreement from you, I remain
                Sincerely yours, Dr. Mardersteig"

12. Cf. no. 41 in the Bibliography.

13. Letter from Brod to Kafka on "Tuesday" [June 26, 1922], unpublished in MBA.

14. As cited in Peter de Mendelssohn, op. cit., 818. A substantial change had also become urgently necessary for another reason: *Die neue Rundschau* lost about 4000 readers for the year 1920, i.e., the total edition (12,000) declined to 8000 copies.

15. From an unpublished letter by Brod to Hiller (MBA) on Feb. 11 [1916] we learn that Brod had a major argument with Bie and was no longer on good terms with *Merkur*. From a kind of friendly solidarity Kafka thereafter no longer published anything in these journals. Also an invitation by Pick probably failed in a similar way. On March 3, 1918, Brod wrote to Kafka: "I received an invitation from Pick for an anthology of Prague authors. I declined . . ." (unpublished letter, MBA). Kafka then wrote back: "Fortunately I have not yet heard from Pick, would probably politely refuse; it's a temptation that does not lead me astray but that really is a great one" (L200).

16. Cf. note VI, 2. Max Brod, "Der Dichter Franz Kafka," *Die neue Rundschau*, Berlin, November 1921 (reprinted in Bo153-60).

17. Cf. nos. 42 and 43 in the Bibliography.

18. Only *after* writing his novel *The Castle* did Kafka come to a new definition of his writing and to a new evaluation of it. In a letter of several pages from July 1922, that "treatise" (L336), in which he tried to discuss with Brod the essence of his existence as a writer, he still explicitly referred to himself several times as "writer." But he wrote already in a limiting way—for "writer" for him implies writing *and* publication: "Writing sustains me, but it is no more accurate to say that it sustains this kind of life? By this I don't mean, of course, that my life is better when I don't write. Rather it is much worse then and wholly unbearable and has to end in madness" (L333).

19. As cited from the original (handwritten—ink—undated, MBA). Cf. T328.

20. In his Kafka article in the *Die neue Rundschau* of November 1921 Brod writes about Kafka's "greatest work," . . . "the novel The Trial, which in my view is complete, in the view of the author obviously incomplete, uncompletable, unpublishable" (as

cited in Bo158).

21. In this letter from October 1923, Kafka refers to his plans the previous spring.

22. Brod's letter to Kafka from "Thursday" (September 1922), in Max Brod, *Die verbotene Frau*, op. cit., 118.

23. Letter from Brod to Kafka on Dec. 27, 1920, in Max Brod, *Die verbotene Frau*, op. cit., 113. In this letter Brod describes for his friend the "eternal" impact of Berlin.

24. Ibid., 118.

25. Dora Diamant, as cited in Hodin, op. cit., 27.

26. Cf. Dietz, "Kafkas letzte Publikation," op. cit.

27. Rudolf Förster, "Deutschland im Spiegel seiner Verleger. Die Schmiede AG," op. cit., 174.

28. Kurt Tucholsky, "Schmiede und Schmiedgesellen," op. cit. Under Tucholsky's pseudonym Peter Panter a title appeared with *Die Schmiede* in 1927 (*Ein Pyrenäenbuch*); Tucholsky's *Philippika* is also based on his own experience with *Die Schmiede*.

29. *Buch der Toten*. Ed. Wolf Przygode, Munich: Roland Verlag, 1919. XIII, 88 pages (First special printing of the work) —Pryzgode's quote from the "Afterword."

30. *Menschheitsdämmerung. Symphonie jüngster Dichtung*. Ed. Kurt Pinthus. Berlin: Rowohlt Verlag 1920 (appeared at the end of 1919), XVI.

31. Kasimir Edschmid, "Stand des Expressionismus" (1920). As cited in *Expressionismus. Der Kampf um eine literarische Bewegung*. Ed. Paul Raabe. Munich 1965, 174. (Paul Raabe named the chapter that deals with expressionism between 1920 and 1921 "Necrology".)

32. *Verkündigung. Anthologie junger Lyrik*. Ed. Rudolf Kayser. Munich: Roland Verlag, 1921. In his prologue Kayser proclaims the end of expressionism: "This time—it is fall 1920, and the atmosphere very tired and exhausted—is anything but progress or completion. It is decline and transition . . . final knell of a (very fruitful and creative) culture that began with the Renaissance . . . After years of youthful exuberance, inflammatory outcries, and revolutions, we must today confess: there was no fulfillment for us" (as cited in RaI147).

33.   Förster, op. cit., 173.

34.   The quote from this letter is printed in: Peter de Mendelssohn, *S. Fischer und sein Verlag*, op. cit., 930. Hans Jacob was himself active for many years as a translator for *Die Schmiede* and translated above all the works of Balzac and the two novels of Radiguet.

35.   Of Ernst Weiß's works appearing with *Die Schmiede* were: *Die Feuerprobe* (1923), *Olympia* (1923), *Daniel* (1924), and *Der Fall Vukobrankovics* (1924).

36.   This series included titles by Hermann Kasack (*Der Mensch*), Richard Huelsenbeck (*Verwandlungen*), Ivan Goll (*Der Torso*), Arnold Zweig (*Bennarône*), Rudolf Leonhard (*Beate und der große Pan*), Friedrich Burschell (*Die Einfalt des Herzens*), Kurt Heynicke (*Gottes Geigen*), Max Hermann[-Neisse] (*Die Preisgabe*), among others.

37.   The series *Kleine Rolandbücher* also encompassed a total of twenty-five titles of which eight already appeared by 1922 with *Die Schmiede*, among them: Hermann Kasack (*Die Heimsuchung*), Kurt Heynicke (*Gottes Geigen*, 2nd ed.) and Klabund (*Die Geisha O-Sen*).

38.   These two series remained the publisher's best known. The "Novels of the Twentieth Century" encompassed modern German as well as foreign literature; in it appeared titles by Francis Carco (*Der Gehetzte*, 1924, *An Straßenecken*, 1925), Karel Čapek (*Das Absolutum oder die Gottesfabrik*, 1924), Albert Daudistel (*Die lahmen Götter*, 1924, *Das Opfer*, 1925), Joseph Roth (*Die Rebellion*, 1924), Alphonse de Châteaubriant (*Schwarzes Land*, 1925), Raymond Radiguet (*Das Fest*, *Den Teufel im Leib*, 1925), Henry Barbusse (*Kraft*, 1926), as well as three of Marcel Proust's volumes that appeared with *Die Schmiede*. In the series *Aussenseiter der Gesellschaft* (Publisher's announcement: "Crimes of the Present Day—A Collection of Interesting Criminal Cases of Our Day") were above all those authors writing in the style of "grande reportage" (Kurt Kersten, Leo Lania, Karl Otten, and Egon Erwin Kisch). The series edited by Rudolf Leonhard was to be an encyclopedia of the "times and society." Leonhard himself announced the program up to volume 32 in 1925 (only fourteen titles appeared). *Die Schmiede* dropped

the series *Der unbekannte Balzac* when Rowohlt introduced his sensationally inexpensive 44-volume pocketbook edition of the works of Balzac. The *Kleine Rolandbücher* were also not continued.

39. Meyer wrote on Feb. 2, 1925 in a letter to Brod about *Die Schmiede* (unpublished, MBA): "I heard all sorts of things in Berlin: Some say *Die Schmiede* is publishing a lot, but that the books aren't being sold. Others (including one of the printers from whom I accidentally heard it) view the publishing house as already finished, because they aren't making payments. I had assumed in the fall that the new series "Aussenseiter der Gesellschaft" would have carried the whole company financially, but the volumes do not appear to have sold as well as I had thought . . . today I too personally don't have the confidence that *Die Schmiede* will succeed in developing itself further on *that* basis on which it began."

40. Proust's *Swann's Way* appeared in 1926 in two volumes in the translation of Rudolf Schottländer about which the review by Ernst Robert Curtius read: "poorly done by the German translator . . . It is approximately like having Debussy rearranged for the harmonica." (*Literarische Welt*. Ed. Willy Haas, no. 4, 4, 1926.) The publisher then assigned the translation to Walter Benjamin and Franz Hessel, whose translation of the second volume *In the Shadow of the Young Girls* was still able to appear in the same year. By E. E. Kisch, the "raging" reporter, appeared *Kriminalistisches Reisebuch*, by Klabund *Harfenjule*, by Tucholsky —under the pseudonym Peter Panter—*Ein Pyrenäenbuch*.

41. The series edited by Eduard Trautner included only the six editions appearing in the first volume; the authors were Kisch, Lania, MacOrlan, Roth, Siemsen, and Trautner.

42. From a publisher's announcement we learn that the collection edited by Walter Petry was to be continued. But the project was abandoned again after the first five titles that appeared in 1926, probably because the desired level of sales was not reached.

43. Tucholsky emphasizes this in his *Schmiede* pamphlet, adding: "And here is now the face of that salesman type . . . very evident . . . the boundless impudence of the publisher, not to react to complaints, inquiries, warnings, deliveries, written notes of any

sort." ("Schmiede und Schmiedgesellen," op. cit., 287.)

44. Unpublished postcard from Arnold Zweig to Brod on July 30, 1924. (MBA. Completely reproduced above on p. 282. See also: note VII, 16.) Tucholsky also mentions the poor payment habits of *Die Schmiede*.

45. Letter from Joseph Roth to Erich Liechtenstein on Jan. 22, 1925. In *Briefe 1911-1939*. Edited and introduced by Hermann Kesten. Cologne, Berlin, 1970, 44.

46. Roth commented in a letter to Bernard von Brentano about his book that appeared with *Die Schmiede*: "The book could have been a bigger success if it had not appeared with *Die Schmiede*" (ibid., 104). The publisher's announcement of the *Fall Hofrichter* in Arthur Holitscher, *Ravachol und die Pariser Anarchisten*, Berlin: *Die Schmiede*, 1925, 90.

47. This statement by Leonhard, who could comment not only on the delay tactics but also on the sloppiness of the publishing work at *Die Schmiede*, has been passed on by Tucholsky in his article on *Die Schmiede* (287).

48. Ibid., 288f.

49. An assertion without any basis is that of Hans Reimann, who maintains in his memoirs that he himself discovered Kafka for *Die Schmiede*. The editor of the satirical journal *Das Stachelschwein* published there under the title "Verhaftung" (12-23, no. 8, vol. 1925, May 2, 1925) the first chapter of *The Trial* with the note: "With the permission of the publisher *Die Schmiede* Berlin, I publish the beginning . . ." However, in his biography (*Mein blaues Wunder*, Munich, 1959) the version appears that Wurm, i.e., *Die Schmiede*, *on the basis of* the publication in *Das Stachelschwein* was made aware of Kafka (377). Reimann continues: "Said Wurm had somewhere or other got hold of those 'Stachelschweine,' which contained the Kafka and since then intended to publish not only Kafka but also my journal" (386). Of course, this was not the case.

50. In his memoirs Brod maintains that there was such a change in Kafka's conception of being a writer, which simultaneously became his greatest argument in not following the (previously written) testament of his friend. Also Dietz ("Kafkas letzte Publikation," op. cit.) sees in Kafka's last book a "clear will to

publish and the expression of a new orientation" (120).

51. The royalties that Kafka received for the six books that appeared
     with Wolff were quite modest. In February 1921 he wrote Ottla
     that a "small sum in marks . . . about 125 M." was supposed to
     have come (O62). Since the publisher did its books semi-
     annually, it can be assumed that this sum was for the second half
     of 1920, a small amount, when one considers that *A Country
     Doctor* and *The Penal Colony* had just recently appeared and the
     volumes in *Der Jüngste Tag* were being reissued.

52. Unpublished letter from Meyer to Brod on Sept. 15, 1923
     (MBA). Three days later Meyer wrote—probably in response to
     Brod's protest—"You see: every German writer must today with
     consequential necessity be dissatisfied with his German publisher,
     not to mention, if this writer lives in Prague. A German writer
     cannot exist from the German royalties from his books!!"
     (Unpublished letter from Meyer to Brod on Sept 18, 1923,
     MBA.) Brod certainly communicated the content of these letters
     to Kafka.

53. Dora Diamant, in Hodin, op. cit., 27.

54. Kafka wrote to one of his sisters regarding this wall calendar:
     ". . . it answers only on such odd moments in the course of the
     day . . . 'Sometimes even a blind chicken finds a grain,' it said.
     Another time I was horrified by the coal bill, whereupon it said:
     'Happiness and contentment are life's blessings,' which along
     with the irony shows an offensive stolidity . . ." (L396.) Dora
     recalls, how she once broke a glass in the kitchen: "Kafka was
     already standing in the kitchen, the calendar page in his hand, and
     read with astonished eyes: 'A moment can destroy everything.'
     Then he handed me the page." (As cited in Hodin, op. cit., 28.)

55. Ibid., 27.

56. This contract from March 7, 1924, has not been preserved.
     However, a reconstruction can be made from the extant adden-
     dum to the contract for the *Hunger Artist* from June 20, 1924
     (MBA) (with the help of the extensive correspondence that Brod
     had with *Die Schmiede* after Kafka's death): in §1 it was agreed
     that the book would contain "3 novellas," namely "*The Hunger
     Artist. First Sorrow. A Little Woman.*" "2000-3000" copies were
     set for the edition; Kafka received an advance based on an edition

of 2000 copies (which [according to §3] for the proposed royalty of 20% of the retail price of the softbound copy [2.50 marks, corrected to 2 marks] could have resulted in that 800 marks). On April 28, 1924, Kafka was paid a further advance in the amount of 300 marks; this was possible since the *Hunger Artist* finally did appear in an edition of 3000 copies. (Edition size according to the unpublished letters of *Die Schmiede* to Max Brod from Oct. 7, 1925 and Jan. 5, 1926, MBA.) Kafka certainly would not have been able to expect a sum of 800 marks from Kurt Wolff, who at this time was suffering badly from the unfavorable market conditions. At the end of 1923 Kurt Wolff Publishing had to therefore settle with a shipment of books—instead of with a modest royalty (cf. WBr57ff.).

57. As Brod reports in a letter to Buber, Kafka let "his girlfriend in the last year of his life throw about twenty thick notebooks . . . in the oven . . . He was lying in bed and watched as the manuscripts burned" (Brod to Buber, letter of Jan. 25, 1927, in Buber, *Briefwechsel* . . . op. cit., vol. II, 278). Kafka never wanted to be a burden to those around him, especially not to his parents; with the support of the royalties from the writing that alienated his parents, he returned more at ease to his home town from Berlin. The memoirs of Brod, who accompanied Kafka —seriously ill—back to Prague on March 17, 1924, confirm this impression: ". . . he himself must also endure great privations, because he stubbornly insists on managing on his tiny pension. Only in the worst case and under great pressure will he accept money and parcels of food from his family. For by doing so he feels the independence he has won with such difficulty is threatened. Hardly has he earned a few pence through his contract with the 'Schmiede' publishing house, than he thinks about paying back his 'family debts,' and expensive birthday presents . . ." (FK201).

58. Cf. Georg Kaiser, *Briefe*. (Ed. Gesa M. Valk.) Frankfurt, etc. 1980, 253-62.

59. "Since my health has gotten considerably worse since the beginning of the winter, I will now—supported by my uncle who is a doctor—go to Davos." (As cited in Klaus Hermsdorf, "Briefe des Versicherungsangestellten Franz Kafkas." [*Sinn und*

Form, 4, 1957, 649].)

60. Kafka wrote about Josefine on a conversation slip: "They have taken the story from the Rundschau because July was too late for them to have it published, but the book probably could have appeared by July." (As cited from the original in MBA.)

61. Cf. nos. 44 and 45 in the Bibliography.

62. Kafka desperately needed the money earned from the newspaper publications; a postcard of Dora's points to this when she pleaded with the *Prager Presse* for the payment due: "On behalf of Herr Dr. Franz Kafka I thank you for sending the newspaper and ask that the royalties for the contribution to the Easter edition be forwarded to the same address. Sincerely, Dora Diamant." (Postcard from May 18, 1924, as cited in Jaromir Loužil: "Ein unbekannter Zeitungsabdruck der Erzählung 'Josefine' von F. K." [ZDPh, 86, 1967, 319].)

63. Kafka once mentions (probably in connection with *Die Schmiede*—cf. L416-19) on a conversation slip: "If I don't totally decay, it will be very good to do something like that, besides: Don't you have the feeling that Leonhard has a glass of Pschorr in front of him when he is dictating?" (As cited from the original in MBA.) Brod commented further in this regard: "making a reference to some Leonhard or other which is not clear to me" (cf. FK206), from which one can conclude that Brod did not know that Kafka was corresponding with Rudolf Leonhard, the editor at *Die Schmiede*.

64. The collective designation of 'Artist Fate' can in my opinion apply without exception to all four of the stories collected in *The Hunger Artist*, even if *A Little Woman* has long been generally excluded from it. The story loses its position as an exception if one understands the "woman" described by Kafka not merely as the representation of his landlady and her relationship to her renters, but as an analogy to the art Kafka practiced, to literature in general; the description of the "woman" initially as more that of a book is something Kafka struggles with, and he uses this image in broad terms with his relationship to literature.

65. On April 28, 1924, *Die Schmiede* wrote to Brod: "after a long absence of our Herr Dr. Wurm we are only getting around today to answering your letters, insofar as there are still matters

unfinished. First of all we thank you for sending back the novella *A Little Woman* by Franz Kafka and ask you to be kind enough to send us the Easter supplement of the *Prager Tagblatt* with the reference in the main section. Meanwhile, Herr Dr. Otto Pick has also sent us the 4th novella, *Josefine the Singer*. At this point we would like to express our heartfelt thanks again for your efforts in seeing this volume come to be. / We were very distraught by the news that things are so bad with Herr Dr. Kafka. We sent him a series of books yesterday as well as another advance of 300 marks." (Unpublished letter of J. Salter and F. Wurm to Brod, MBA.)

66. Several of the "conversation pages" are printed in L416-23, L493-95, and FK205f.

67. As cited from the original in MBA, cf. also FK205f. (the first half of the sentence of this quote is contained in note VI, 59).

68. On the basis of the inexact recollection of Max Brod on this point the mistake has stubbornly persisted that Kafka had "only corrected in his own hand the first galleys of the book" (L494, cf. also FK211f) and otherwise had read no corrections. Dietz pointed already to the possibility that Kafka had previously undertaken correction of galley proofs and had read the volume thus at least one time "fully himself" in print ("Kafkas letzte Publikation," op. cit., 126).

69. The first galleys corrected in Kafka's own hand have been preserved and are stored in the MBA. The imprint of the printer reads: "Verlag: Die Schmiede / Vier Novellen *II. korr.* / Poeschel & Trepte, Leipzig," ("Four novellas, second correction"), stamped date: May 26, 1924 [author's italics].

70. Brod writes about Kafka's corrections: He gave "orders for changing the order of the stories, showed some temper with the publisher, who had not paid sufficient care to this or that instruction. Dora once said very rightly: 'Really he demanded a great deal of respect towards himself. If one met him with due respect, everything was all right, and he didn't care a thing about formalities. But if one didn't, he was very annoyed'" (FK211).

71. This last rhetorical question regarding the "opus postumum in the strictest sense of the word" was asked by Jaromir Loužil (cf. note VI, 61).

72. As cited in a handwritten note by Brod (MBA). Just how many corrections Brod himself made to the text, however, remains uncertain.

73. For a while the subtitle of *A Hunger Artist* was "Four Novellas"; finally in print it is "Four Stories." On July 1, 1924, *Die Schmiede* wrote to Brod: "A suggestion: The title *A Hunger Artist* doesn't seem very successful to us . . . Perhaps you can make another suggestion to us." On July 5, 1924, *Die Schmiede* then writes: "We have taken note of the fact that you want the title *A Hunger Artist* and are naturally in agreement with that . . . Should we omit the subdesignation '4 Novellas,' or can we make this addition?" On the edge of the sheet Brod here made the handwritten remark: "Remains"; from the next letter of *Die Schmiede* no subsequent protest by Brod is evident (on July 14, 1924): "We have changed the title and chosen '4 Stories' as the subtitle, which we like better that 'Novellas.'" (Unpublished letters from *Die Schmiede* to Brod in MBA.)

74. On August 15, 1924, *Die Schmiede* announced the appearance of *A Hunger Artist* in a letter to Brod: "The 'Hunger Artist' is finished; we will receive the first copies in the next few days and send you several right away. We will now of course advertise the volume, but with the proper propaganda after the book fair which takes place on the 31st of this month." (Unpublished letter, MBA)—Cf. no. 46 in the Bibliography. The publication price: volume in cardboard wrappers—2 marks, cloth bound—2.50 marks. Announcement in the *Börsenblatt* on Aug. 27, 1924, 11220.

Chapter VII

1. The discussion of the edition from the literary estate has been treated widely within the critical literature about Kafka. Regarding this matter, cf. among others: SL: 71, 191, 194; FK: 214, 218; ÜFK212; Beicken, op. cit., 9ff.; KHII, 11f.; Heller, op. cit., 11ff., 45f. and 55; Politzer, op. cit., 452-61; Meno Spann (*Monatshefte*, November 1955); Dietz, *Franz Kafka*, op. cit., 87-94 (among others).

2. Cf. Brod's postscript to *The Trial* (T326ff.); the "slips" that are

still today in the Max Brod Archives are totally reprinted there with the exception of first names. The exact dating of the "wills" (so named by Brod) is not in question (cf. Meno Spann, *Monatshefte*, Nov. 1955). Certainly, however, the writing of both pieces fell in Kafka's phase of total distancing from literature, that is, between 1919 and 1922.

3. In his article in *Die Weltbühne* from July 1924 Brod recalls "still precisely the answer" that he had given Kafka at the time regarding the wish to destroy his work: "In case you should seriously think I would do such a thing, I am telling you now that I cannot fulfill your request." (Brod, "Franz Kafkas Nachlaß," op. cit., 24)

4. Walter Benjamin, "Kavaliersmoral," *Literarische Welt* (October 25, 1929). (op. cit., 48) Ehm Welk had previously rebuked Brod for disloyalty and not carrying out the responsibilities of a friend after his death because he published the literary estate against Kafka's wish. Benjamin sharply criticizes Welk's argument in his article. Welk's "attack," Benjamin continues, "gives testimony to the complete lack of understanding he has for Kafka."

5. Immediately after Kafka's death Brod wrote letters to these individuals in which he requested that they send Kafka's letters and manuscripts to him, as had been Kafka's last wish. While Milena and Dora did so without further comment, he then met with opposition from Klopstock. Brod had to energetically demand letters and then the manuscript of *Josephine* that Kafka had apparently left to Klopstock at the time.

6. Brod, "Franz Kafkas Nachlaß." *Die Weltbühne*, vol. XX, no. 29, July 17, 1924, 106-09.

7. As is evident from a diary entry by Brod, he spoke with Kafka's family on June 19, 1924, about the literary estate. The definitive contract was signed on July 11, 1924. According to this contract Brod was the sole editor of Kafka's works from the literary estate, and he was to remain totally without any royalties. Point 4 of the contract addressed the division of royalties: parents 55%, Dora 45%. (Original contract in MBA.)

8. Letter from *Die Schmiede* to Brod on June 14, 1924 (unpublished, MBA).

9. Letter from Rowohlt Publishing to Brod on June 10, 1924

(unpublished, MBA).

10. Letter from Wolff to Brod on June 20, 1924 (unpublished, MBA).

11. Letter from Kayser (*Die neue Rundschau*) to Brod on July 4, 1924 (unpublished, MBA).

12. Letter from Rowohlt Publishing to Brod on July 7, 1924 (unpublished, MBA). On July 5 Wolff had written to Brod: "Regarding Rowohlt, there must be a misunderstanding . . . Rowohlt told me that despite his love for Kafka that he could in no way consider the requirements made by you . . . as a basis for discussions" (Wolff to Brod, unpublished, MBA).

13. On July 16, 1924, the "Verband der Vereine Creditreform" informed Brod that *Die Schmiede* was "a small undertaking and was suffering from an unfavorable balance of payments . . . The present means at the company's disposal are meager and for an arrangement in which open credits were involved there was at this time no real agreement." (Cited in a copy of the information, unpublished in MBA.)

14. Brod's contract with *Die Schmiede* for *The Trial* saw a printing of 3000 copies, with a total royalty of 1800 marks to be paid in monthly installments. On the legal question regarding *The Stoker*, cf. note VII, 18.

15. In the responses of *Die Weltbühne* from July 31, 1924 (vol. XX, no. 31 of July 31, 1924, 199) Tucholsky writes: "Max Brod. You inform us: 'The publisher *Die Schmiede* has acquired Franz Kafka's entire posthumous writings, which I will now gradually edit.' Good luck!"

16. Postcard from [Arnold?] Zweig to Brod on July 30, 1924, unpublished, MBA. In November 1922 the title "Sons" by *Die Schmiede* was preannounced by Arnold Zweig; however, the book did not appear with this publisher.

17. In an addendum to the overall contract Brod had added the conditions that "in case of nonpayment of an installment (§4 of the contract) Dr. Max B. [is] released from the responsibility of delivering future ms. [manuscripts]." (Cited in a handwritten draft by Brod, unpublished, MBA.) It is naturally conceivable that Brod added this condition on the basis of Arnold Zweig's correspondence. The revised contract was first concluded on Aug.

15, 1924. But already in the revised contract for the *Hunger Artist* Brod had added such an (entirely uncustomary) note: "In case of non-fulfillment—penalty of 1000 gold marks. Dr. Brod completely without royalty." (Cited in a handwritten contract draft, unpublished, MBA.)

18. Wolff had warned Brod about making a contract with *Die Schmiede* (the publisher was "too young"), but did not get involved in real discussions with Brod and remained with a very low offer ("By the way I am convinced that you will receive much more favorable offers from a whole series of German publishers," Wolff wrote to him on July 5, 1924—unpublished, MBA). Kurt Wolff Publishing took the viewpoint that as the publisher "of 6 books of the author" that it had "a primary right" to the posthumous writings. When Meyer later explained this situation to *Die Schmiede*, a fundamental point was "that we had to deny you from our point of view the use of pieces of our Kafka publications last fall, especially the piece *The Stoker*. Without this chapter (*The Stoker*), the entire novel would not be possible to publish with any publisher other than us." The hard bargaining position that Wolff took with regard to Kafka's posthumous writings rested naturally on the certainty that *America* could—because of *The Stoker* rights—only appear with him. And when *Die Schmiede* initially thought "with matters related to the novella *The Stoker* which was to be included as the first chapter in a novel from the posthumous writings, we firmly believe we will be able to come to an agreement with Kurt Wolff" (Letter from *Die Schmiede* to Brod on July 14, 1924, unpublished, MBA), they had not reckoned with Wolff. Wolff's tactics appear strange, especially in view of the fact that a contract with Kafka for *The Stoker* was never concluded, and that there was only discussion about the one-time single edition in *Der Jüngste Tag* in some correspondence (cf. WBr31).

19. On Jan. 27, 1925, Dora Diamant wrote to Brod: "And what is the case with *Die Schmiede*? Are they paying? If there is any money for me there (and the debts are paid off), I could now perhaps use it" (letter in MBA). Klopstock too lamented his dire situation in his letters to Brod; on September 13, 1924, he already asked for a share: "Would it be possible to receive

something from D [Dora's] payments? (letter in MBA).

20. Cf. note VI, 38 above.

21. Letter from Kurt Wolff Publishing (Meyer) to Brod on Feb. 2, 1925 (MBA).

22. Letter from *Die Schmiede* to Brod on April 1, 1925 (MBA).

23. Letter by Brod to *Die Schmiede* on Nov. 27, 1925 (MBA). In the letter Brod confirmed that he had transferred the rights to Kurt Wolff "after no payment was received from you for four months."

24. The contract with Kurt Wolff Publishing from April 9, 1925, dealt with the "entire literary estate." *The Trial* was to transfer to Wolff "after the first edition of 3000 copies sold out"; furthermore, Kurt Wolff Publishing obligated itself contractually to acquire the *Hunger Artist* ("by purchase") from *Die Schmiede*, if possible. In §2 of the contract the edition of the volumes was set at "ca. 3000 copies." (Contract in MBA.) Also on April 9, 1925, Meyer wrote to *Die Schmiede* that his company had taken over the rights to Kafka and added: "Should you ever find that you are not interested in publishing the two volumes appearing in your house, given the change in circumstances, you will find us to be very interested in purchasing them." (Letter in MBA.)

25. Letter from *Die Schmiede* to Brod on April 16, 1925 (MBA). *Die Schmiede* threatened further: "Since by your position you have thwarted the friendly interaction that existed in our dealings with Franz Kafka and with you regarding the posthumous writings of Franz Kafka, we are now compelled to take up a formal legal position."

26. Letter from Meyer to Brod on April 24, 1925 (MBA), Meyer's reaction to *Die Schmiede*'s letter to Brod of April 16; Meyer himself expected much "worse" than these "stupid excuses."

27. Letter from *Die Schmiede* to Brod on Jan. 5, 1926 (MBA). *Die Schmiede* argued that it was the publisher "for whom the posthumous volumes of Kafka should first be considered. Kafka handed over his last book to us before he died, and we recognize in this fact proof that it without a doubt would have been his intention that his remaining books would also appear with us." Already previously, on Oct. 7, 1925, *Die Schmiede* informed Brod that "Kurt Wolff Publishing—in any case Herr Georg

Heinrich Meyer communicated this personally to our Herr Dr. Wurm—had no interest in taking over the works that already appeared with us or those of the literary estate" (MBA).

28. Letter from *Die Schmiede* to Brod on Jan. 5, 1926 (MBA).

29. Letter from Kurt Wolff Publishing (Meyer) on May 5, 1926 (MBA).

30. Meyer wrote Brod on May 22, 1926: "Collected Works of Kafka": the deadline that we gave to Zsolnay ran out today and it doesn't seem likely to us that Zsolnay is any closer to the Kafka edition. You know what I think about *Die Schmiede* . . . Certainly the neatest arrangement would have been if Zsolnay had done the edition." (Letter in MBA.)

31. Already on Oct. 15, 1926, Meyer wrote the following letter to Brod: "Early this year *Die Schmiede* was wavering considerably, at that time it was then reorganized and afterwards placed demands in the summer which were not discussable and which no publisher in the world would have been able to negotiate on or resolve. Soon *Die Schmiede* will waver again . . ." On June 2, 1926 Meyer noted: "The difficult case of the collected edition of Kafka's work arises again." (Letters in MBA.)

32. Göbel writes: "Only in 1926 and 1927 did Wolff publish the two large novels from the literary estate despite financial reservations." ("Der Kurt Wolff Verlag," radio broadcast from Oct. 2, 1977. Rias Berlin. Broadcast script, 48.)

33. Meyer communicated to Brod on September 4: "Kafka's *Castle* is at the printers Poeschel and Trepte. The book is being set in the format of *Die Schmiede* editions." (Letter in MBA.)

34. Announcement of Kurt Wolff Publishing in *Die literarische Welt* (vol. 2 [1926], no. 51, 10).

35. Cf. Max Brod: *Die verbotene Frau*, op. cit., 111.

36. Letter from Hardt to Brod on Feb. 27, 1927 (MBA).

37. Heinrich Scheffler reports on the books of Kafka that appeared with Wolff: "Your stock made it from Munich to the warehouse on Flensburg St. and was transferred from there to Schocken Brothers." ("Wölffische Lehrjahre." Frankfurt am Main 1975, 42.)

38. Brod: letter to the "L.W." (*Die literarische Welt*," vol. 6 [1930], no. 11, 7). Brod received (indirectly) a year later at the same

place an answer to his question about the whereabouts of Kafka's books that appeared with *Die Schmiede*. In *Die literarische Welt* (vol. 7 [1931], no. 13, 5) a modern antiquariat announced having back copies of *The Trial*. While Wolff sold his stock to the Neuer Geist Verlag, which kept the books of Kafka (at least potentially) available, *Die Schmiede* sold off its remaining stock dirt cheap.

39. In a letter of Aug. 14, 1930 (MBA) to Brod, Haas inquired why Brod had "reservations" about an arrangement with Transmare Verlag, for he himself could recommend it. Dora Diamant wanted to suggest the Kafka edition to Paul Wiegler, an editor with Propyläen Verlag.

40. The publishing contract with Kiepenheuer lies unpublished in MBA. §10 reads: "The publisher will make the effort if possible to complete this three-volume edition of Kafka [agreed to in the contract] to form a complete edition . . ."

41. Heinrich Scheffler: *Wölffische Lehrjahre*, Frankfurt am Main 1975, 42.

42. Cf.: Volker Dahm: *Das jüdische Buch im Dritten Reich. Erster Teil. Die Ausschaltung der jüdischen Autoren, Verleger und Buchhändler*. Frankfurt am Main 1979, 215.

43. As cited in the unpublished diaries of Max Brod, quarto sheets begun 1935; entry from Feb. 17, 1935 (MBA).

44. The contract with Schocken from Feb. 26, 1934, for the "Edition of Collected Works" in six volumes was not voided de facto by the fake contract with Mercy Sohn. After the contract of May 23, 1936, the entire rights to Kafka's works reverted to Max Brod, who then signed them over to Mercy. (An edition of 4000 copies was agreed upon.) In the completely identical format the remaining missing two volumes of the edition appeared in "safe" Prague. On Feb. 28, 1939, the notary informed Salman Schocken that in light of the political situation the rights would be transferred to him again.

45. The further history of the publication of Kafka's posthumous works is thoroughly documented in the literature. After the immigration of the Schocken brothers to the United States, the editing of the posthumous works entered a "stable" phase. In 1946 a five volume edition of the "Collected Works" (photomechanical reprint of the "Collected Writings" of Schocken

Verlag/Berlin and Mercy/Prague with minor amendments)
appeared in the newly founded Schocken Publishing in New
York. As a "licensed edition" of Schocken Publishing, Kafka's
"Collected Works" have appeared (in individual volumes) since
1950 in Germany.

Abbreviations

AGB   *Archiv für Geschichte des Buchwesens*. ("Archives of the Book Industry") Buchhändler-Vereinigung Gmbh., Frankfurt a. M.

Bo   *Franz Kafka. Kritik und Rezeption zu seinen Lebzeiten. 1912-1924.* Ed. by Jürgen Born with H. Mühlfeit and F. Spicker, Frankfurt a. M. 1979.

DI   Franz Kafka. *The Diaries of Franz Kafka 1910-1913*, ed. by Max Brod. New York: Schocken, 1949.

DII   Franz Kafka. *The Diaries of Franz Kafka 1914-1923*, ed. by Max Brod. New York: Schocken, 1949.

DF   Franz Kafka. *Dearest Father. Stories and Other Writings.* New York: Schocken, 1954.

DLA   Deutsches Literatur Archiv, Marbach am Neckar.

DS   Franz Kafka. *Description of a Struggle and The Great Wall of China.* London: Secker and Warburg, 1960.

Dvjs   *Deutsche Vierteljahresschrift für Literaturwissenschaft und Geistesgeschichte.*

F   Franz Kafka. *Letters to Felice.* New York: Schocken, 1973.

FK   Max Brod. *Franz Kafka. A Biography.* New York: Schocken, 1947.

J   Gustav Janouch. *Conversations with Kafka.* New York: New Directions, 1971.

KI   Hartmut Binder. *Kafka-Kommentar zu sämtlichen Erzählungen.* München (2nd revised edition), 1977.

KII   Hartmut Binder. *Kafka-Kommentar zu den Romanen, Rezensionen, Aphorismen und zum Brief an den Vater.* München 1976.

KHI   *Kafka-Handbuch* (vol. I: *Der Mensch und seine Zeit.* Ed. H. Binder. Stuttgart 1979).

KHII   *Kafka-Handbuch* (vol. II: *Das Werk und seine Wirkung.* Ed. H. Binder. Stuttgart 1979).

KWA   Kurt Wolff Archives at Yale University, New Haven.

L   Franz Kafka. *Letters to Friends, Family, and Editors.* New York: Schocken, 1977.

M   Franz Kafka. *Letters to Milena.* London: Secker and Warburg, 1953.

MBA   Max Brod Archives (Ilse Ester Hoffe) in Tel Aviv. The reproduction of excerpts from unpublished manuscripts and letters from the archives came about through the cordial permission of Frau Ilse Ester Hoffe.

O   Franz Kafka. *Letters to Ottla and the Family.* New York: Schocken, 1982.

Ot   Franz Kafka. *Briefe an Ottla und die Familie.* Ed. H. Binder and K. Wagenbach. Frankfurt a. M. 1974.

PC   Franz Kafka. *The Penal Colony. Stories and Short Pieces.* New York: Schocken, 1948.

PK   Max Brod. *Der Prager Kreis.* Frankfurt a. M. 1979.

RaI   Paul Raabe. *Die Zeitschriften und Sammlungen des literarischen Expressionismus . . . 1910-1921*, Stuttgart 1964.

RaII   *Expressionismus. Aufzeichnungen und Erinnerungen der Zeitgenossen.* Ed. P. Raabe. Olten and Freiburg im Breisgau 1965.

RV   Wolfram Göbel. "Der Ernst Rowohlt Verlag 1910-1913. Seine Geschichte und seine Bedeutung für die Literatur seiner Zeit," AGB, XIV, col. 465-556, Frankfurt a. M. 1974.

S   Franz Kafka. *The Complete Stories.* New York: Schocken, 1946.

SchI   Fritz Schlawe. *Literarische Zeitschriften. Teil I. 1885-1910.* Stuttgart 1961.

SchII   Fritz Schlawe. *Literarische Zeitschriften. Teil II. 1910-1933* (2nd ed.) 1973.

SL   Max Brod. *Streitbares Leben. Autobiographie 1884-1968*, Frankfurt a. M. 1979.

sy   J. Born, L. Dietz, et. al. *Kafka Symposion*, Berlin 1965 (2nd unedited edition 1966).

T   Franz Kafka. *The Trial.* New York: Alfred A. Knopf, 1960.

ÜFK   Max Brod. *Über Franz Kafka.* Frankfurt a. M.: Fischer, 1974.

Wa   Klaus Wagenbach. *Franz Kafka. Eine Biographie seiner Jugend. 1883-1912.* Bern 1958.

WBr   *Kurt Wolff. Briefwechsel eines Verlegers 1911-1963.* Ed. Bernhard Zeller und Ellen Otten. Frankfurt a. M. 1966.

Wo   Kurt Wolff. *Autoren, Bücher, Abenteuer. Betrachtungen und Erinnerungen eines Verlegers.* Berlin (2nd ed.) 1969.

WP   Franz Kafka. *Wedding Preparations in the Country, and Other Posthumous Prose Writings.* London: Secker and Warburg, 1954.

WV   Wolfram Göbel, "Der Kurt Wolff Verlag 1913-1930. Expressionismus als verlegerische Aufgabe." Special printing in AGB, XV and XVI, col. 521-1456, Frankfurt a. M. 1976 und 1977.

Publications and Editions of the Works of Franz Kafka during His Lifetime. A Bibliography: 1908-1924

This list of Kafka's literary publications during his lifetime expands the previously most comprehensive description of "Drucke Franz Kafkas bis 1924" (Publications of Franz Kafka up to 1924) by Ludwig Dietz from 1965 (with supplements from 1966, cf. sy85-126). Also taken into account were the findings of Hartmut Binder (cf. KHII595ff.) and the comments of Peter U. Beicken (cf. op. cit., 356ff.), as well as the author's own findings, among them the communication of a previously unknown separate publication of *Auf der Galerie* ("Up in the Gallery"). Publications of translations and reviews as well as of Kafka's professional writings have not been included.

1.
Betrachtung [Collected title]
[Contents: 8 pieces without individual titles, numbered] I [Der Kaufmann] II [Zerstreutes Hinausschaun] III [Der Nachhauseweg] IV [Die Vorüberlaufenden] V [Kleider] VI [Der Fahrgast] VII [Die Abweisung] VIII [Die Bäume].
Pp. 91-94 in *Hyperion. Eine Zweimonatsschrift.* Ed. by Franz Blei and Carl Sternheim. 1st edition, vol. 1, no. 1 January-February). München: Hans von Weber 1908 [appeared March 1908 in a printing of 950 copies]. [Initial publications]
[Dietz: 1]

2.
Gespräch mit dem Beter.
Gespräch mit dem Betrunkenen.
Pp. 126-31 and pp. 131-33 in *Hyperion. Eine Zweimonatsschrift.* Ed. by Franz Blei. 2nd edition, vol. 1, no. 8 (March-April). München: Hans von Weber 1909 [appeared May 1909 in an edition of 1050 copies]. [Initial publications]
[Dietz: 4]

3.
Die Aeroplane in Brescia.

Pp. 1-3 in *Bohemia*. vol. 82, no. 269, morning edition, Prague, Wednesday, Sept. 29, 1909 [Initial publication in shortened form]. [Dietz: 5]

4.

Betrachtungen [Collected title]
[Individual titles:] Am Fenster [later: Zerstreutes Hinausschaun]. In der Nacht [later: Die Vorüberlaufenden]. Kleider. Der Fahrgast. Zum Nachdenken für Herrenreiter. [Initial publication]. P. 39 in *Bohemia*, vol. 83, no. 86, morning edition, Prague, Sunday, March 27, 1910 (Easter literary supplement). [Dietz: 8]

5.

First chapter of the book "Richard und Samuel" by Max Brod and Franz Kafka: *Die erste lange Eisenbahnfahrt* (Prague—Zürich). Pp. 15-25 in *Herder-Blätter*. Ed. by Willy Haas and Norbert Eisler, vol. 1, no. 3 May, Prague: Verlag der Herder-Vereinigung 1912 [appeared June 1912]. [Initial publication] [Dietz: 15]

6.

Großer Lärm.
P. 44 in *Herder-Blätter*. Ed. by Willy Haas and Norbert Eisler, vol. 1, no.4, October 5, Prague: Verlag der Herder-Vereinigung 1912 [Kafka's contribution under the heading:] "Anmerkungen" [Initial publication]. [Dietz: 16]

7.

Betrachtung.
Leipzig: Ernst Rowohlt 1913 [first edition, appeared end of November 1912]. 99 [paginated] pages [Impress:] This book was printed in 800 numbered copies by Offizin Poeschel & Trepte. No. [entered by hand]. Copyright 1912 by Ernst Rowohlt Verlag, Leipzig. [Dedication:] Für M. B. [Max Brod]. [Contents:] Kinder auf der Landstraße [IP]. Entlarvung eines Bauernfängers [IP]. Der plötzliche Spaziergang [IP]. Entschlüsse [IP]. Der Ausflug ins Gebirge [IP]. Das Unglück des Junggesellen [IP]. Der Kaufmann. Zerstreutes Hinausschaun. Der

Nachhauseweg. Die Vorüberlaufenden. Der Fahrgast. Kleider. Die Abweisung. Zum Nachdenken für Herrenreiter. Das Gassenfenster [IP]. Wunsch, Indianer zu werden [IP]. Die Bäume. Unglücklichsein [IP].
[IP = initial publication]
[Dietz: 17]

8.
Betrachtung [Main title]
[Reprinted text:] Kinder auf der Landstraße. P. 2 in *Bohemia*. vol. 85, no. 356. Prague, Dec. 25, 1912 [Kafka's contribution in the Christmas supplement no. 2].

9.
Aus dem wunderschönen Skizzenbuch eines neuen Dichters: [Collected title] [Contents:] Die Vorüberlaufenden. Zum Nachdenken für Herrenreiter. Das Unglück des Junggesellen. In *Deutsche Montagszeitung*, vol. 4, no. 13 (Supplement 1), Berlin, March 31, 1913.

10.
Das Urteil. Eine Geschichte von Franz Kafka.
[Dedication:] für Fräulein Felice B [Bauer]. Pp. 53-65 in *Arkadia. Ein Jahrbuch für Dichtkunst*. Ed. by Max Brod. Leipzig: Kurt Wolff 1913 [appeared end of May 1913]. [Rubric:] EPISCHES. (Prose)—[Impress:] Printed by Poeschel & Trepte in Leipzig in Spring 1913. [Initial publication—corrected by Kafka, edition of approx. 1000 copies]
[Dietz: 18]

11.
Der Heizer. Ein Fragment.
Leipzig: Kurt Wolff 1913 [First edition, appeared end of May 1913]. P 47. [Impress:] This book was printed in May 1913 as volume 3 of the Library of *Der jüngste Tag* by Poeschel & Trepte in Leipzig. [Frontispiece on art paper:] In New York harbor [actually: The Brooklyn ferry].—[Original publication, corrected by Kafka]
[Dietz: 19]

12.
Zum Nachdenken für Herrenreiter.
P. 40 in *Das bunte Buch* [Almanac]. (1st edition, 1000-10,000)
Leipzig: Kurt Wolff 1914 [appeared October 1913].—[a second edition
of 5000 was reprinted without change in 1914]
[Dietz: 20]

13.
Vor dem Gesetz.
Pp. 2f. in *Selbstwehr* (*Unabhängige jüdische Wochenschrift*), vol. 9,
no. 34 (New Year's commemorative number), Prague, Sept. 7, 1915
[Initial publication].
[Dietz: 23a]

14.
Die Verwandlung.
Pp. 1177-1230 in *Die Weißen Blätter. Eine Monatsschrift.* Ed. René
Schickele. Vol. 2, no. 10. (October). Leipzig: Verlag der Weißen
Bücher 1915 [Initial publication, errors, not corrected by Kafka].
IDietz: 21]

15.
Die Verwandlung.
Leipzig: Kurt Wolff 1915 [First edition, appeared end of November
1915] 73 pages. [Impress:] Printed by Poeschel & Trepte in Leipzig
November 1915 as volume 22/23 [Double volume] of the Library *Der
jüngste Tag* with a title picture by Ottomar Starke. [1st edition,
improved by Kafka after the first edition.]
[Dietz: 22]

16.
Betrachtung.
2nd edition. Leipzig: Kurt Wolff 1915 [only a title edition; title page
with Kurt Wolff Company—instead of Ernst Rowohlt—was newly
printed, otherwise unchanged; as no. 7. This "edition" was prepared
in October 1915; approx. 500 copies.]

17.
Vor dem Gesetz.
Pp. 126-28 in *Vom jüngsten Tag. Ein Almanach neuer Dichtung.* [With a vignette by Karl Walser]—(1st edition, 1-10,000) Leipzig: Kurt Wolff 1916 [appeared December 1915]. [A "second revised edition" appeared in November 1916; 11-20,000, Leipzig: Kurt Wolff 1917. Kafka's contribution now on pp. 124-26]
[Dietz: 24]

18.
Der Heizer. Ein Fragment.
2nd edition. Leipzig: Kurt Wolff 1916 [appeared beginning of 1916].
[Impress:] Volume 3 of the Library *Der jüngste Tag.* Printed by E. Haberland in Leipzig-R. [Minor text variations, without frontispiece.]
[Dietz: 25]

19.
Das Urteil. Eine Geschichte.
Leipzig: Kurt Wolff 1916 [first edition, appeared end of October 1916] 29 pages. [Impress:] Printed by E. Haberland in Leipzig-R. September 1916 as vol. 34 of the Library *Der jüngste Tag.* [dedication:] Für F. [1st edition, improved by Kafka compared to the first publication in *Arkadia*]
[Dietz: 26]

20.
Ein Traum.
Pp. 172-74 in *Der Almanach der Neuen Jugend auf das Jahr 1917.* Ed. Heinz Barger [actually: Wieland Herzfelde and H. B.]. (1-5,000) Berlin: Verlag Neue Jugend [appeared November or beginning of December 1916]. [Chronologically the first publication.]
[Dietz: 28]

21.
Ein Traum.
Pp. 32f. in *Das jüdische Prague. Eine Sammelschrift.* Ed. by the editing staff of *Die Selbstwehr.* Prague: Verlag der Selbstwehr (Independent Jewish weekly) 1917 [appeared on Dec. 15, 1916].

[Dietz: 27]

22.
Ein Traum.
P. 1 in *Prager Tagblatt*, vol. 42, no. 5 on Jan. 6, 1917 (Entertainment supplement no. 1).
[Dietz: 28a]

23.
Ein altes Blatt.
Der neue Advokat.
Ein Brudermord.
Pp. 80-82 in *Marsyas. Eine Zweimonatsschrift.* Ed. Theodor Tagger [Pseud.: Ferdinand Bruckner]. No. 1. (July/August) Berlin: Heinrich Hochstim 1917. [These initial publications of Kafka under the rubric:] Chronik über neue Literatur and Graphik-Anmerkungen.
[Dietz: 29]

24.
Zwei Tiergeschichten [main title]
1. *Schakale and Araber.*
2. *Ein Bericht für eine Akademie.*
Pp. 488-90 (October number) and pp. 559-65 (November number) in: *Der Jude. Eine Monatsschrift.* Ed. Martin Buber. vol. 2 (1917/18) Berlin and Vienna 1917. [Initial publications]
IDietz: 30]

25.
Ein Landarzt.
Der Mord.
Pp. 17-26 and pp. 72-76 in: *Die neue Dichtung. Ein Almanach.* With 9 pictures by Ludwig Meidner. 1-15,000, Leipzig: Kurt Wolff 1918 [appeared approx. December 1917]. [Note on pp. 26 and 76:] From a series of unpublished stories. [Initial publication of: *Ein Landarzt. Der Mord* is the early version of "Ein Brudermord" that Kafka discarded.]
[Dietz: 31]

26.
Schakale and Araber.
P. 3 in *Österreichische Morgenzeitung*, vol. 1917, no. 235 (Literature supplement), Dec. 3, 1917 [Reprinting not authorized by Kafka].

27.
Ein Bericht für eine Akademie.
P. 9f. in *Österreichische Morgenzeitung*, no. 357 (Christmas supplement), Dec. 25, 1917 [Printing not authorized by Kafka].

28.
Der Heizer. Ein Fragment.
[Dritte Auflage.] Leipzig: Kurt Wolff [ca. 1917/18] 47 S. [Impress:] Library of *Der jüngste Tag* vol. 3. Printed by Dietsch & Brückner. Weimar. [Edition not indicated, without frontispiece, with censorship stamp on the bottom right of the title page. Corrections by Kafka doubtful.]
[Dietz: 32]

29.
Schakale and Araber.
P. 233-50 in *Neue deutsche Erzähler*. Ed. by J. Sandmeier. vol. 1 (1-20,000) Berlin: Furche Verlag 1918 [appeared summer 1918]. (2nd ed. 20,000-30,000)
[Dietz: 33]

30.
Die Verwandlung.
[Second edition] Leipzig: Kurt Wolff [appeared 1918]. [Impress:] Library of *Der jüngste Tag* vol. 22/23. Printed by Dietsch & Brückner. Weimar. Copyright 1917 [numerous text changes, correction by Kafka is doubtful].
[Dietz: 34]

31.
Eine kaiserliche Botschaft.
P. 4 in: *Selbstwehr (Unabhängige jüdische Wochenschrift)*, vol. 13, no. 38/39 (New Year's Commemorative Issue) Prague, Sept. 24, 1919.

[Editor's note:] From the forthcoming book: *Ein Landarzt. Kleine Erzählungen.* [Initial publication]
[Dietz: 36]

32.
In der Strafkolonie.
Leipzig: Kurt Wolff 1919 [first edition, appeared end of October 1919]. 71 pp. [Impress:] This book was printed as volume 4 of the new series of Drugulin Printings in May 1919 for Kurt Wolff Verlag at the Offizin W. Drugulin in a single edition of 1000 copies. [Initial publication]
[Dietz: 35]

33.
Die Sorge des Hausvaters.
P. 5f. in *Selbstwehr (Unabhängige jüdische Wochenschrift)*, vol. 13, no. 51/52 (Chanukah number), Prague, Dec. 19, 1919. [Editor's note:] The story—contained in the forthcoming book: *Der Landarzt*—was graciously made available to the *Selbstwehr* by the author. [Initial publication]
[Dietz: 36a]

34.
Ein Landarzt. Kleine Erzählungen.
(München and Leipzig): Kurt Wolff [first edition, appeared in May 1920]. 189 [paginated] pages. [Impress:] Printed by Poeschel & Trepte in Leipzig. [Dedication:] To my father. [Contents:] Der neue Advokat. Ein Landarzt. Auf der Galerie [initial publication]. Ein altes Blatt. Vor dem Gesetz. Schakale and Araber. Ein Besuch im Bergwerk [initial publication]. Das nächste Dorf [initial publication]. Eine kaiserliche Botschaft. Die Sorge des Hausvaters. Elf Söhne [initial publication]. Ein Brudermord. Ein Traum. Ein Bericht für eine Akademie. [Kafka's complete corrections not verifiable.]
IDietz: 37]

35.
Das Urteil. Eine Geschichte.
[Second edition] München: Kurt Wolff [ca. 1920-1922]. 29 pp. [Impress:] *Der jüngste Tag* Series, vol. 34. Printed by E. Haberland in

Leipzig. [Dedication:] For F. [Kafka's corrections doubtful]
[Dietz: 38]

36.
Ein Brudermord.
Pp. 168-70 in *Entfaltung. Novellen an die Zeit. Mit einem
bibliographischen Anhang.* Ed. by Max Krell. Berlin: Ernst Rowohlt
1921 [appeared December, 1920]
IDietz: 39]

37.
Auf der Galerie.
P. 1 in *Prager Presse*, vol. I (1921), April 3, 1921 (Sunday
supplement). [Editor's note:] Franz Kafka titled his new work "A
Country Doctor" (Kurt Wolff Publishing, Munich), from which we
have published this sample with permission of the publisher.

38. *Entlarvung eines Bauernfängers.*
P. 11 in *Prager Presse.* vol. I (1921), Sept. 11, 1921 (Sunday
supplement).

39. *Ein altes Blatt.*
P. 5 in *Selbstwehr (Unabhängige jüdische Wochenschrift)*, vol. 15, no.
37/38 (Rosh Hashana number), Prague, Sept. 30, 1921 (Literary
supplement)
[Dietz: 40a]

40. *Der Kübelreiter.*
P. 22 in *Prager Presse.* vol. I (1921) no. 270, morning edition,
Sunday, Dec. 25, 1921 (Christmas supplement). [Initial publication]
[Dietz: 41]

41.
Erstes Leid.
S. 312f. in *Genius. Zeitschrift für werdende and alte Kunst.* Ed. by
Carl Georg Heise and Hans Mardersteig. vol. 3, second book, Munich:
Kurt Wolff 1921 [appeared in Fall 1922]. [After p. 356 the note:] The
second book of the third volume of *Genius* printed in fall 1922 W.

Drugulin . . . [Initial publication]
[Dietz: 42]

42.
Ein Hungerkünstler. Erzählung.
Pp. 983-92 in *Die neue Rundschau* (October number). vol. 33, no. 10,
Berlin and Leipzig: S. Fischer 1922 [Initial publication].
[Dietz: 43]

43.
Ein Hungerkünstler.
Pp. 4-6 in *Prager Presse*. vol. 2, no. 279, morning edition, October
11, 1922.

44.
Josefine, die Sängerin.
Pp. 4-7 in *Prager Presse*, vol. 4, no. 110 (Easter number), April 20,
1924 (Supplement Dichtung und Welt)—[Initial publication].
[Dietz: 43a]

45.
Eine kleine Frau.
P. 5 in *Prager Tagblatt*, vol. 49, no. 95, April 20, 1924, Easter
supplement—[initial publication in abbreviated form].

46.
Ein Hungerkünstler. Vier Geschichten.
[Contents:] Erstes Leid. Eine kleine Frau. Ein Hungerkünstler.
Josefine, die Sängerin oder Das Volk der Mäuse. Berlin: Die Schmiede
1924 [first edition, appeared on August 15, 1924]. 86 pp. [Series title:]
Die Romane des XX. Jahrhanderts. [Impress:] Single volume design
Georg Salter. Berlin. Printed by Poeschel & Trepte in Leipzig. [ed.
3000 copies. The complete galley corrections as well as the revision of
the first printed sheets by Kafka can be safely assumed.]
[Dietz: 44]

Selected List of Works Cited

1. Works by Franz Kafka

Gesammelte Werke (collected works in individual volumes). ed. Max Brod. Copyright Schocken Books, New York. Frankfurt am Main: S. Fischer 1950ff.

2. About Franz Kafka—General studies, interpretations, and individual studies

Babler, O. F.: "Frühe tschechische Kafka-Publikationen." In: *Franz Kafka aus Prager Sicht*. Prag 1965, 149-55.

Baum, Oskar: "Franz Kafka." In: *Der Jude*, 8, 1924, 482-83.

—"Erinnerungen an Franz Kafka." In: *Prager Presse*, 40, 1929, Literature.

Beißner, Friedrich: *Der Erzähler Franz Kafka*. Stuttgart 1952

—*Der Schacht von Babel. Zu Kafkas Tagebüchern*. Stuttgart 1963

—"Kafkas Darstellung des 'traumhaft innern Lebens.'" A lecture. (Bebenhausen, 1972)

Benjamin, Walter: *Benjamin über Kafka. Texte, Briefzeugnisse, Aufzeichnungen*. (ed. Hermann Schweppenhäuser) Frankfurt am Main 1981

Bezzel, Chris: *Kafka-Chronik*. ed., München-Wien 1975

Binder, Hartmut: "Franz Kafka und die Wochenschrift *Selbstwehr*." In: DVjs 41, 1967, 283-304.

—"Kafka und Die Neue Rundschau." With a previously unpublished letter of the author on the history of publication of *The Metamorphosis*. In: *Schiller Jb.* 12, 1968, 94-111.

—*Kafka-Kommentar zu sämtlichen Erzählungen*. München (2nd. revised edition) 1977

—*Kafka-Kommentar zu den Romanen, Rezensionen, Aphorismen und zum Brief an den Vater*. München 1976.

—*Kafka in neuer Sicht. Mimik, Gestik und Personengefüge als Darstellungsformen des Autobiographischen*. Stuttgart 1976.

—"Ein ungedrucktes Schreiben Franz Kafkas an Felix Weltsch." In: *Schiller Jb.* 20 (1976), 103-31.

—*Kafka-Handbuch* (in two volumes). Ed. Various contributors. Vol. 1: *Der Mensch und seine Zeit*. Vol. 2: *Das Werk und seine Wirkung*. Stuttgart 1979.

—"Unvergebene Schlamperei. Ein unbekannter Brief Franz Kafkas." In: *Schiller Jb.*, vol. 25, Dec. 1981.

Born, Jürgen: "Vom *Urteil* zum *Prozeß*. Zu Kafkas Leben und Schaffen in den Jahren 1912-1914." In: ZDPh 86, 1967, 186-96.

—*Franz Kafka. Kritik und Rezeption zu seinen Lebzeiten 1912-1924*. (Ed.; contributors: Mühlfeit and F. Spicker) Frankfurt am Main, 1979.

Blei, Franz: "Franz Kafka." In: (F. B.) *Zeitgenössische Bildnisse*. Amsterdam 1940, 328-39.

Brod, Max: "Kleine Prosa." (Review of *Betrachtung*) In: *Die neue Rundschau*, 7 (1913), 1043-46. (reprinted in: Born 30-32.)

—"Das Ereignis eines Buches." In: *März*, Feb 15, 1913, vol. 7, part 1, no. 7, 268-70. (reprinted in: Born 24-26.)

—"Der Dichter Franz Kafka." In: *Die neue Rundschau*, 11 (1921), 1210-16. (reprinted in: Born 153-60.)

—"Franz Kafkas Nachlaß." In: *Die Weltbühne* 29, 1924, July 17, 1924, 106-09

—"Über Franz Kafka." In: *Ein Almanach für Kunst und Dichtung aus dem Kurt Wolff Verlag*. München 1926, 103-10.

—*Franz Kafka. Eine Biographie. Erinnerungen und Dokumente*. Prague 1937. 2nd edition, New York 1946.

—*Franz Kafka als wegweisende Gestalt*. St. Gallen 1951.

—*Die verbotene Frau*. Graz and Vienna 1960. (With a small selection of the correspondence between Max Brod and Franz Kafka.)

—*Über Franz Kafka*. (*Franz Kafka. Eine Biographie. Franz Kafkas Glauben und Lehre. Verzweiflung und Erlösung im Werk Franz Kafkas*.) New, revised edition by the author, with index. Frankfurt 1966. (Fischer Bücherei, vol. 735, new edition 1974).

—*Streitbares Leben*. Autobiography (old version). München 1960. Revised and expanded new edition: *Streitbares Leben. 1884-1968*. München/Berlin/Wien 1969.

—"Afterword." In: F. K. *Beschreibung eines Kampfes* (Parallel edition). Ed. Max Brod. Frankfurt a. M. 1969 (II), 148-59.

—*Streitbares Leben* . . . Frankfurt am Main 1979.

—*Der Prager Kreis*. With an afterword by Peter Demetz. Frankfurt am Main 1979.

Canetti, Elias: *Der andere Prozeß. Kafkas Briefe an Felice*. München 1969 (5th edition, 1977).

Deleuze, Gilles; Guattari, Félix: *Kafka. Für eine kleine Literatur*. Frankfurt am Main 1976 (edition suhrkamp vol. 807).

Dietz, Ludwig: "Franz Kafka und die Zweimonatsschrift *Hyperion*. Ein Beitrag zur Biographie, Bibliographie und Datierung seiner frühen Prosa." In: DVjs 37, 1963, 463-73.

—"Drucke Franz Kafkas bis 1924. Eine Bibliographie mit Anmerkungen." In: sy (1965), 85-125. Supplemented in sy (1966), 85-126.

—"Die autorisierten Dichtungen Kafkas. Textkritische Anmerkungen." In: ZDPh vol. 86, 1967. no. 2, 301-17.

—"Das Jahrbuch für Dichtkunst *Arkadia*." In: *Philobiblon*, vol. 17 (1973), no. 1, 178-88.

—"Kafkas letzte Publikation. Probleme des Sammelbandes *Ein Hungerkünstler*. Zum 50. Todestag des Dichters am 3. Juni 1974." In: *Philobiblon*. vol. 8, no. 2, June 1974, 119-28.

—*Franz Kafka*. (Series: Realien zur Literatur) Stuttgart 1975.

Goldstücker, Eduard (ed.): *Weltfreunde. Konferenz über die Prager deutsche Literatur*. Prag (Neuwied) 1967.

—"Die Aufnahme Franz Kafkas in der Tschechoslowakei." In: *Akzente* 13, 1966, no. 4, 320-21.

Hardt, Ludwig: "Erinnerungen an Franz Kafka." In: *Berliner Tageblatt*, June 10, 1924.

—"Brief an Peter Panter." In: *Die Weltbühne* 22, 1926, no. 14, 545-46.

Heller, Erich: *Franz Kafka*. München 1976.

Hodin, Josef Paul: *Kafka und Goethe*. London/Hamburg (1972). With commentary by Fritz Feigl and Dora Diamant.

Janouch, Gustav: *Gespräche mit Kafka. Aufzeichnungen und Erinnerungen*. Frankfurt am Main 1951. (Expanded new edition,

Frankfurt am Main 1981).

Loužil, Jaromir: "Ein unbekannter Zeitungsabdruck der Erzählung *Josefine* von Franz Kafka." In: ZDPh 86, 1967, no. 2, 317-19.

Miller, Alice: "Dichtung (Das Leiden des Franz Kafka)." In: (A. M.) *Du sollst nicht merken*. Frankfurt am Main 1981, 307-87.

Pasley, Malcolm: "Drei literarische Mystifikationen Kafkas." In: sy 21-37.
—and: Wagenbach, Klaus: "Datierung sämtlicher Texte Franz Kafkas." In: sy 55-83.

Pazi, Margarita: "Franz Kafka und Ernst Weiß." In: *Modern Austrian Literature*, 1973, no. 3/4, 52-92.

Politzer, Heinz: *Franz Kafka. Der Künstler*. Frankfurt am Main 1978.

Raabe, Paul: "Franz Kafka und Franz Blei. Samt einer wiederentdeckten Buchbesprechung Kafkas." In: sy, 7-20.
—"Franz Kafka und der Expressionismus." In: ZDPh 86, 1967, no. 2, 161-75.

Sokel, Walter H.: *Franz Kafka. Tragik und Ironie. Zur Struktur seiner Kunst*. München/Wien 1964. (Paperback edition: Frankfurt am Main 1976).

Wagenbach, Klaus: *Franz Kafka. Eine Biographie seiner Jugend (1883-1912)*. Bern 1958.
—*Franz Kafka in Selbstzeugnissen und Bilddokumenten*. Ed. Klaus Wagenbach. Reinbek/Hamburg 1964, (105,000.) 1972 (Rowohlts Monographien, vol. 91).
—"Veröffentlichungsgeschichte." In: *Franz Kafka. In der Strafkolonie*. With sources, reprints, materials from the Arbeiter-Unfall-Versicherungsanstalt, chronicle and notes by Klaus Wagenbach. Berlin (15,000-17,000) 1977, 61-64.

Walser, Martin: *Beschreibung einer Form*. Frankfurt/Berlin 1972.
—"Arbeit am Beispiel. Über Franz Kafka." In: M. W. (ed.), *Er. Prosa von Franz Kafka*. Frankfurt 1963, 219-25.

3. History of Literature and of the Publishing Industry

Alker, Ernst: *Profile und Gestalten der deutschen Literatur nach 1914.* (ed. Eugen Thurnber) Stuttgart 1977.

Bachem, Franz Carl: *Die Lage des deutschen Buchverlags in der gegenwärtigen Krise des deutschen Gesamtbuchhandels.* (Diss.) Köln 1922.

Buber, Martin: *Briefwechsel aus sieben Jahrzehnten.* With a foreword by Ernst Simon and an introductory biographical sketch by Grete Schaeder. Heidelberg 1972. (with letters of Franz Kafka.)

Bramböck, Peter: "Ein früher Briefwechsel Ernst Rowohlts mit Anton Kippenberg." In: AGB XIV, col. 565-606.

Dietz, Ludwig: "Kurt Wolffs Bücherei *Der jüngste Tag.* Seine Geschichte und Bibliographie." In: *Philobiblon* 7, 1963, no. 2, 96-118.

Durzak, Manfred: "Dokumente des Expressionismus: Das Kurt-Wolff-Archiv." In: *Euphorion* 60, 1966, no. 4, 337-69.

Edschmid, Kasimir (ed.): *Briefe der Expressionisten.* Frankfurt am Main, Berlin 1964.

Fischer, Samuel: "Reden/Schriften/Gespräche." In: *In Memoriam S. Fischer.* Frankfurt am Main 1960.

Förster, Rudolf: "Deutschland im Spiegel seiner Verleger. Die Schmiede AG." In: *Neue Bücherschau*, vol. 6, no. 4 (1927), text 4, 174.

Göbel, Wolfram: "Der Ernst Rowohlt Verlag 1910-1913. Seine Geschichte und seine Bedeutung für die Literatur seiner Zeit." In: AGB, XIV, col. 465-556.

—*Der Kurt Wolff Verlag 1913-1930. Expressionismus als verlegerische Aufgabe. Mit einer Bibliographie des Kurt Wolff Verlages und der ihm angeschlossenen Unternehmen.*" Special reprint from AGB, vol. XV and XVI. Frankfurt am Main 1976 and 1977.

Göpfert, Herbert G.: "Buchhandel und Literaturwissenschaft." In:

Buchhandel und Wissenschaft. Ed. Friedrich Uhlig. Gütersloh 1965, 118-34.
—"Der expressionistische Verlag. Versuch einer Übersicht." In: *Brannenburger Vorträge 1962.* Gräfelfing b. München 1963, 41-69.
—"Wissenschaft vom Buchhandel—Wissenschaft für den Buchhandel." In: *Bertelsmann-Briefe,* no. 52, Gütersloh 1967, 3-5.
—"Vom Autor zum Leser. Beiträge zur Geschichte des Buchwesens." München 1977.
—"Die 'Bücherkrise' 1927 bis 1929. Probleme der Literaturvermittlung am Ende der zwanziger Jahre." In: *Das Buch in den zwanziger Jahren. Wolfenbütteler Schriften für Geschichte des Buchwesens.* Ed. Paul Raabe. (vol. 2) Hamburg 1978, 33-45.

Hack, Bertold: "Georg Heinrich Meyer. Versuch einer Biographie eines außergewöhnlichen Buchhändlers." In: *Hermann Broch und Daniel Brody: Briefwechsel 1930-1951.* Ed. Bertold Hack and Marietta Kleiß. AGB, XII, 1971/1972 (col. 1193-1224).
Hiller, Helmut: *Zur Sozialgeschichte von Buch und Buchhandel.* Bonn 1966.

Insel Almanach auf das Jahr 1974. Anton Kippenberg zum hundertsten Geburtstag. Ed. Friedrich Michael. Frankfurt am Main 1973.

Kiaulehn, Walther: *Mein Freund der Verleger. Ernst Rowohlt und seine Zeit.* Reinbek bei Hamburg 1967.
Kocova, Jirina: *Der Malik Verlag. Geschichte und Tendenzen.* (MA.?, n.d.) Copy at the Universitätsbibliothek Frankfurt am Main.

Mayer, Paul: *Ernst Rowohlt. In Selbstzeugnissen und Bilddokumenten.* Ed. Reinbek bei Hamburg 1968.
Mendelssohn, Peter de: *S. Fischer und sein Verlag.* Frankfurt am Main 1970.
Moufang, Wilhelm: *Die gegenwärtige Lage des deutschen Buchwesens. Eine Darstellung der Spannungen und Reformbewegungen am Büchermarkt.* München, Berlin and Leipzig 1921.

Pfennigstorff jun., Fritz: *Die wirtschaftlichen Veränderungen im Deutschen Verlagsbuchhandel. Aus Anlaß des Krieges und der*

Übergangszeit. (Diss. typed) Berlin 1921.

Raabe, Paul: *Die Zeitschriften und Sammlungen des literarischen Expressionismus. Repertorium der Zeitschriften, Jahrbücher, Anthologien, Sammelwerke, Schriftenreihen und Almanache 1910-1921*. Stuttgart 1964

—*Expressionismus. Aufzeichnungen und Erinnerungen der Zeitgenossen*. Ed. and annotated. Olten and Freiburg im Breisgau 1965.

—*Expressionismus. Der Kampf um eine literarische Bewegung*. Ed. Paul Raabe. München 1965.

—*Der späte Expressionismus 1918-1922. Bücher, Bilder, Zeitschriften, Dokumente*. Exhibition catalogue. Biberach an der Riss 1966.

—"Das Buch in den zwanziger Jahren." In: *Das Buch in den zwanziger Jahren. Vorträge des zweiten Jahrestreffens des Wolfenbütteler Arbeitskreises für Geschichte des Buchwesens. May 16-18, 1977. (Wolfenbütteler Schriften für Geschichte des Buchwesens.* [vol. 2] Ed. P. R.) Hamburg 1978, 9-32.

Rowohlt, Ernst: *Ernst Rowohlt zum Gedächtnis Dec. 1, 1961. Den Freunden Ernst Rowohlts und seines Verlages zugeeignet*. Private printing. Reinbek bei Hamburg 1962.

Salzmann, Karl H.: "Kurt Wolff, der Verleger. Ein Beitrag zur Verlags- und Literaturgeschichte." In: AGB II, 1958/60, 375-403.

Seiffhart, Arthur: *Inter folia fructus. Aus den Erinnerungen eines Verlegers*. Berlin 1948 (Memoirs about Kurt Wolff Publishing).

Steffen, Detlev: *Franz Blei (1871-1942) als Literat und Kritiker der Zeit*. Diss. (typed.) Göttingen 1966 (esp. 99-152).

Tucholsky, Kurt: "Schmiede und Schmiedegesellen." In: *Weltbühne*, no. 25 (II), 1929, 284-89.

Unseld, Siegfried: *Der Autor und sein Verleger. Lectures in Mainz und Austin*. Frankfurt am Main 1978.

Wolff, Kurt: "On Franz Kafka." In: *Twice a Year*, 1942, no. 8/9, 273-79.

—and Herbert G. Göpfert: "Porträt der Zeit im Zwiegespräch."

(Interview) In: *Börsenblatt*, Frankfurt edition, vol. 20., no. 84, October 20, 1964, 2053-67.

—*Autoren, Bücher, Abenteuer. Betrachtungen und Erinnerungen eines Verlegers*. Berlin 1965 (2nd edition 1969).

—*Briefwechsel eines Verlegers 1911-1963*. Ed. B. Zeller and E. Otten. Darmstadt 1966. (Letters by and to Kafka, 24-60).

Zeller, Bernhard: *Expressionismus. Literatur und Kunst 1910 bis 1923*. Exhibition catalogue of the Schiller-Nationalmuseum Marbach am Neckar. No. 7. Ed. B. Z.. Marbach 1960. (With an excerpt from an unpublished letter by Franz Kafka to René Schickele about the publication of *The Metamorphosis*, 140.)

Index

"We have before us a book that is to be recommended to everyone who wants to gain a nuanced picture of Kafka and the literary world he inhabited. One learns what he was like personally. . . , what kind of public he had to deal with, and why for as long as he lived he was a good bet to succeed and yet always fell short of success."

Joachim Kaiser, *Süddeutsche Zeitung*

"An unusual perspective and a rich supply of material—the happy union of these two givens is the basis for this new and successful illumination of the author Kafka."

Hartmut Binder, *Stuttgarter Zeitung*

"For Kafka, Prague represented an enormous handicap. He was isolated from the German literary and publishing world, a circumstance that was fatal for him. His publishers were not deeply concerned with this author whom they hardly knew personally. Joachim Unseld, son of a well-known German publisher, devotes a book to this problem and demonstrates that this lack of attention was the most likely reason . . . that Kafka did not complete the novels that no one demanded of him. Because if an author lacks the definite expectation of publishing his manuscript, nothing pushes him to put the final touches on it, nothing keeps him from temporarily removing it from his desk and going on to something else."

Milan Kundera, *Les testaments trahis*

"The reciprocal interplay between Kafka's professional and private lives emerges strikingly from these pages; indeed, an intimate rhythm dominates Kafka's success in writing and his happiness in love. . . It is refreshing . . . to have a work which provides us with new insights as well as new facts."

Theodore Ziolkowski, *World Literature Today*